Economics and the Real World

By
Joaquim Vergés

Economics and the Real World
By Joaquim Vergés

This book first published 2022
Ethics International Press Ltd, UK
British Library Cataloguing in Publication Data
A catalogue record for this book is available from the British Library

Print Book ISBN: 978-1-80441-056-1
eBook ISBN: 978-1-80441-057-8

CONTENTS

Introduction

Economics as a science – or viewed from the perspective of scientists in other fields

As a discipline or field of knowledge, *Economics* is clearly not an experimental science. The possibilities in this respect are extremely limited[1]. When practised with scientific rigour it is, in essence, an *observational* science: we economists are confined to observing and analysing the workings of the economic system — of this or that market economy — and thus endeavouring to build a formal description of that conceptually and schematically. A description in which a significant part refers, if not properly to 'laws', to *patterns* observed in the behaviour of individuals as 'economic agents' — citizens, companies, governments, etc. — , as well as in the key magnitudes resulting from their activities and interrelations — production of goods, employment, prices, salaries, tax collection, etc. Ideally, in addition to specifying these socially significant magnitudes and patterns in the system, this necessarily schematic formal description should encompass a conceptual formulation of the most relevant causal relationships between them; such as, for example, between **interest rate** and level of the **total demand of goods**; or between **statutory severance pay** and **employment level**.

As in any field of knowledge, or of study, the first step in an explanatory theory of the functioning of a market economy is (or was) a previous conceptual, *deductive* formulation of its basic elements, as well as some assumptions about the mentioned patterns of behaviour and

[1] Basically, to *laboratory* experiments, with small groups of individuals who are presented with designed alternative-decisions that involve receiving more or less money.

interrelations. In other words, a certain general *theoretical framework*; a *previous* interpretative model based on presuppositions or *deductive hypotheses*. That is, a conceptual outline that pre-describes, — through making some simplifications and abstractions — what is considered at the time to be the essential elements of the reality under analysis: the workings of the market, capitalist, or private-enterprise-based economic system. This would be an initial, provisional, theoretical description that should allow the formulation of verifiable hypotheses and predictions about the dynamics, behaviour, and interrelations of these essential elements of the functioning of a society.

But, of course, this is, or should be, only the first step. From this stage, it is expected that this explanatory theory based on deductive assumptions be progressively revised as a result of being put to the test; that is, confronted with empirical observations, to be gathered. And so to check whether these observations confirm or refute — in what regard and to what extent — both the general theoretical framework, axioms, and hypotheses on which the theory is based, as well as the predictions derived from it[2]. However, there are elements to affirm – as it is subsequently argued– that the *standard model* of the conventional, orthodox economics currently dominant is still largely stuck at that first step; that of purely deductivist hypotheses or assumptions; in the sense that they are kept insulated from comparisons with the overwhelming empirical evidence available.

---

[2] We might draw a parallel between the application of the scientific method to explain the workings of market or capitalist economies — the ideal foundations of *Economics* as an academic discipline — and the pair of disciplines Anatomy and Physiology; of the human species, for example. Though there is a significant difference: while in physiology we can observe certain stable regularities or 'laws' (for instance, how a particular type of fat is metabolised), economies are dynamic systems, where regularities or patterns are subject to change over time. This is, partially, because these patterns are in fact made up (or determined by) socio-political decisions regarding what are collectively deemed appropriate or not (laws, regulations, etc.); and, partly, due to 'autonomous' dynamics, such as technological and demographic changes, changes in the level of knowledge, in citizens' tastes and preferences, and in the level of collective wealth (or degree of development).

Following the scientific method, it is the accumulation of observations about the economic reality — the patterns of behaviour of people and groups as economic agents as well as of the relevant quantitative variables involved — that allows us to refine, reformulate or change the initial hypotheses. Empirical observations are fundamental to drawing inferences or inductive propositions on the regularities that define the reality under analysis. A task that allows for revising, and improving, the previous theory; so giving way to a better, useful explanatory scheme — or theoretical model — of that part of the reality: the workings of a market economy based on private firms.

From this perspective, the essential rule of the scientific method — dealing with a discipline such as Economics (or *economic analysis*)[3] — is that any given explanatory theory is or is not good insofar as it succeeds in providing a satisfactory explanation of the reality in question. If reiterated observations of that reality show that such a theory does not explain it well, or does not explain it in a significant number of cases, that explanatory theory must be revised or replaced by another that better fits with the observed reality, the empirical evidence gathered.

There is no doubt that, in terms of the scientific method, a formal explanatory scheme on how market economies work, will never be perfect. Among other things because we are dealing with a reality whose patterns, ingredients, and structures may change over time. However, there is a broad spectrum between imperfection and misrepresentation. And, certainly distorted ideas of a given social reality — whether as a result of insufficient knowledge, misapplication of knowledge, or unrealistic assumptions — can easily lead to flawed,

---

[3] '*Economic Analysis*' is a term increasingly used by contemporary theoretical economists to refer to their academic activity.

if not counterproductive, collective decisions, policies, and practices. If such ideas are imparted as *the* standard academic description in textbooks, classrooms, and through papers by the corresponding scholars, the problem grows in implications. Something that is particularly relevant in social sciences fields.

The central paradigm of the orthodox or conventional economics, that is, the *standard model* in mainstream economics (hereinafter ESM) can be introduced, in a compact format as follows:

(a) If unconstrained by interventions from public authorities, the market for each good (product or service) will *spontaneously* end up being a competitive and in-equilibrium market. That means a large number of producer/seller enterprises, perfectly efficient, none of which holds market power; all of them selling at a price equal to their marginal cost, which in turn will be equal to their average cost. That applies to any good in the economy, with only a few exceptions: situations of 'natural monopoly'.
(b) If for Labour and other production factors the situation is also that of a free market, then the overall result of this free-playing of markets forces in the whole economy constitutes a social optimum of economic well-being. A social optimum characterised by full employment of Labour and the rest of country's resources; a certain composition of the basket of goods and services made available, that maximise 'social utility'; and a fair income distribution.

Facing this modern-neoclassical background, the first objective of this text is to underline that this ESM paradigm rests upon an explanatory theory that draws mainly on conjectures, hypotheses, and deductive assumptions, which are not supported by what observations of the reality of market economies show us; either in the present day or historically. The ESM is, indeed, an explanatory theory that fails to provide a proper explanation of how a market or capitalist economic system operates in reality; or it does not explain well the workings of the economic world for the vast majority of cases, goods, sectors, or markets. Something that, moreover, I am far from being the first one to highlight.

> "Modern economics is not very successful as an explanatory endeavour. This much is accepted by most serious commentators on the discipline, including many of its most prominent (See, for example, Rubinstein 1995:12; Lipsey 2001:173; Friedman 1999:137; Coase 1999:2; Leontief 1982:104)"
> (Tony Lawson, "Modern Economics: the Problem and a Solution", in Fullbrook 2004:21)

(Note that the three last authors cited by Lawson in the above paragraph are Nobel Laureates in Economics).

That *deficiency* of the ESM has relevant implications. It is something more than a purely theoretical issue. The fact that this explanatory model of the academically mainstream economics (much dominated by *microeconomics*)[4] postulates that 'free play of markets' overall leads spontaneously to an *optimum of social utility* (as a result of a *general equilibrium* of competitive markets, GE)[5] has moreover implications beyond the economic discipline. In the political arena, neoliberalism draws on this postulate to defend its principles of no (or minimum)

[4] For most mainstream academic theorists, *microeconomics* is in fact the basic component of orthodox modern-neoclassical mathematical economics. *Micro-foundations of economics* is the standard expression to refer to that.

[5] An *optimum* that, in short, is defined in this *theory of General Equilibrium of competitive efficient markets* (GE) as a situation in which the resources available in the considered economy (a country) are fully and efficiently used to produce what is preferred by the citizens, who then pay for every product or service a price equal to the respective unit-cost. I.e., it is assumed that the private companies of a market or capitalist economy do not earn any profit (sic).

A more precise formulation of the axioms, postulates, and assumptions upon which this *General Equilibrium Theory* draws on will be seen in Appendix A to chapter 1.

intervention by governments in the economy, of no (or minimum) regulation of markets; that is, to defend what lies behind the well-known expression 'the less State the better': minimum public expenditure, minimum taxes.

And, of course, the *General Equilibrium* theory that supports the referred postulate dominates the way economics is taught, how the workings of a market economy are explained in textbooks and university classrooms: conveying to readers and students a theoretical description based upon a set of axioms and deductive reasoning which do not actually fit, regarding fundamental elements, with the economic reality of our social world. They are unnecessarily unrealistic assumptions, in the sense of not coming justified on the grounds of the usual abstractions and simplifications any formal theory entails. It is a theoretical model which rather refers to an imagined market economy (Schlefer, 2012:25). It is quite significant in this regard the use, in neoclassical mainstream economics, of certain typical concepts such as '*imperfect* information', 'economics of *imperfect* competition', or 'market *imperfections*', to refer to features that in fact are normal, central to our market economies. Scientific colleagues in other fields — including other fields of social sciences — often find it *funny* that we economists consider the economic reality to be *imperfect* because it is bent on disagreeing with the description that the standard theoretical model in economics postulates.

Nevertheless, that is the theoretical paradigm that in general the economists who advise, recommend, or decide on economic policy measures (in governments as well as international organisations) have learned — and often also teach at universities. And to the extent that such a paradigm does not match the reality of how our economies function – regarding fundamental matters, not inessential or in-detail aspects, the economic policy measures that these professional economists design or apply by taking such a paradigm as a reference framework have a high risk of being wrong, useless, or counterproductive for the collective wellbeing. In the same way that an 'anatomy & physiology' that would not describe well the functioning of a particular organism would lead to incorrect predictions or wrong diagnoses; and consequently to useless or counterproductive treatments or recommendations.

Thus, insofar the ESM is a theoretical framework that – as will be argued here – does not describe or explain well the reality of the workings of our market economies – mainly regarding the patterns of behaviour of the different economic agents (enterprises, consumers, investors, banks, employees, executives, etc.) – or that it explains such a social reality in a distorted manner, it easily leads to wrong deductions or diagnoses, or a lack of realistic predictions. Something that was dramatically highlighted by the global financial crisis unleashed in 2007-8 in the US when the finance and real estate bubbles 'burst'. A scenario that, at the time, most influential economists had not considered plausible, because simply, according to the assumptions of the models on which they were based, such a thing could not happen because 'markets self-regulate', 'investors assess risks perfectly, in their self-interest', etc.[6].

Economics, microeconomics, macroeconomics

Certainly, the 'standard model' (ESM/GE) –with the scope described in the previous paragraphs (as a construct that culminates in the paradigm of the General Equilibrium of Competitive Markets) – does

[6] Let us take into account that these models are based upon premises or assumptions, such as every market (the real estate market, the financial market, etc.) is 'by nature' efficient, it self-regulates, and spontaneously tends towards an equilibrium. In turn, this draws on the assumption that those, in the companies, who make the decisions are 'agents' who act with pure economic rationality, seeking to maximise their profits or utility in the medium and long term; and, thereby, they have incentives to be 'perfectly' informed, to 'perfectly' assess the current and future financial risks –of any operation, investment, etc.– before deciding on them; and so on.

(For most non-economist readers, the above may provide an insight regarding the 'peculiar' economic world that mainstream economics assumes as a 'base camp'.)

not encompass the whole of Economics; though it is the base. There is furthermore a set of specific autonomous theories, albeit connected to the GE paradigm. Theories not regarding the way markets function, the production world, companies' behaviour, prices, and profits, etc., but on the relationships between variables referred to the economy as a whole; they are theories mainly dealing with cause-and-effect relationships. For instance, the two opposed theories on the relationship between an increase in '**Public Deficit** financed by **Public Debt**' and the increase it induces in economic activity (**Gross Domestic Product** and, thereby, **Employment**) under a situation of economic recession. Two different theories that, in turn, give rise to formulating or defending opposite economic-policy measures: austerity, vs. expansionary policies.

To enumerate some of the most relevant of these specific economic theories on *causal relationships* – besides the above example –: The effect of (a change in) the **Rate of Interest** – applied by the banking system – on **Business investment** and on total **Saving**, (the 'IS model'); the effect of (a change in) **Money Supply** on the **Rate of Interest**, and of the latter on the **Demand for Money** (the 'LM model'); the cause-effect relationship between **Money Supply** and **Inflation Rate**, (a part of the 'theory of money'); the quantitative relationship between **(Personal) Income-Tax Level** and **(Business) Net Investment**; the causal relationship presupposed to exist between **Unemployment Rate** and **Inflation Rate**, ('Phillips curve' and 'Non-Accelerating Inflation Rate of Unemployment, NAIRU', theories). And so forth.

To conclude this merely indicative enumeration, there also are specific economic theories addressed to a previous analytical stage; for example, the *Economic Growth* theory. In this case, the issue is rather to identify the relevant explanatory variables that determine the economic-policy target variable, GDP, to thus assess to what extent each of those would-be independent variables (economic growth levers) co-determines the target variable in question. And something similar happens regarding the *Business Cycles* theory, whose development plays, in turn, a fundamental role in the formulation of economic forecasting models at the country level. Both of these theories are widely used by governments' economic departments and international economic agencies to estimate future economic trends and/or design economic programmes and policies.

As it may have resulted obvious, these types of theories on *causal relationships* are among the topics that usually make up the bulk of what a reader might find in a standard *macroeconomics* textbook (or as part II of an introductory *economics* manual) – together with the corresponding conceptual framework and definitions of the macro-variables. The formal expression of the arithmetical identities used in *national accounts* plays a key role in the latter; notably, regarding the meaning of the variables and identities in the macroeconomic central and *popular* IS-LM model.

However, these '*macroeconomics* topics' do not come within the planned scope of this text, most of whose topics would fall into the conventional reach of *economics/microeconomics* – with some exceptions. Although in this respect it should be highlighted that most academic economists do regard *microeconomics* as the core of economics/economic theory itself. In this vein, it is worth making two remarks in this introductory piece.

First, *macroeconomic* theories such as those mentioned above are at the same time – or are widely used as a basis for – arguments recommending or defending specific *economic policy measures*. Thus, these *a-priori descriptive* theories – and, thereby, normally considered and presented by the scholars devoted to them as a corpus of *positive economics* (to explain) – easily slide towards *normative economics* (to prescribe). In any case, most macroeconomic theories are in practice closely related to *Economic Policy*, something that, on the other hand, is not only perfectly understandable but that justifies in a sense the very theorising efforts in macroeconomics.

> "Economic theory obviously is concerned with explaining how economy functions. *Relevant theory equips us to improve the instrumental functioning of the economy. This in turn requires institutional change in the form of public policy.* In short, the bedrock role of the discipline is to enable us always to do the best job assuring that, given our resources and the state of technology, we are deploying both to make economic aspects of the life process for all people as adequate and rewarding as they can possibly be." (Klein, p. 368) ; (italics mine).

Second, the determinant fact of these specific, a priori 'autonomous', theories having a clear connection with the ESM itself; and especially with its core paradigm, the general equilibrium theory. This is mainly apparent regarding the methodological approaches and the premises and assumptions that macroeconomic theorising tends to rely upon. Especially regarding assumptions like 'the one-dimensional economic hyper-rationality of citizens' (i.e., the *homo economicus* paradigm) and that of 'instant and free *perfect information*'. As well as regarding the predominance, in macroeconomic topics, of the idea of *equilibrium* (for example, the IS-LM model itself), together with the peculiar graphical-mathematical language of mainstream economics/ microeconomics – which we shall critically introduce in chapter 2.

Returning to the cornerstone of mainstream economics, the ESM, – and with a view on afterwards confronting its assumptions, axioms, and propositions with the respective empirical evidence – it is appropriate to start by highlighting here a core issue: The basis of the ESM is, apparently, aseptically 'technical'. It is specifically a deductive theory as to how business establishments – firms, enterprises, companies – work and behave; how, in general, their costs for a good vary with respect to the level of production; the way the product's selling price comes determined, and, as a result, the structure for the corresponding market. This is a deductive theory (the 'modern-neoclassical theory of production') which, I will argue, is clearly and unnecessarily unrealistic. Among other things, but as a core piece, this theory assumes that in the production of any good (by any firm), economies of scale become exhausted for rather small volumes of production compared to the size of the total demand to be covered for the referred good; and that this general onset of *decreasing returns to scale* prevents companies from growing 'too much', and thus from holding market power; and, consequently, that 'without the need for any regulation from public authorities, the market of any good tends to be perfectly competitive, efficient, and in equilibrium'.

With this panorama as a backdrop, the present book builds on highlighting that the ESM – the mainstream deductive paradigm regarding how the economic world of production, enterprises, and markets works – cannot be sustained in the face of the overwhelming empirical evidence provided by observing the workings of our real market economies. The ESM does not respond to this observational evidence from real-life; this, not in terms of detail or because of excessive abstraction level but because of an as striking as unnecessary lack of realism regarding fundamental issues of economies' workings. A statement, moreover, that – as already pointed out – I am far from being the first one to underline: since the 40s of the last century, prominent economists already made similar remarks; though these have been generally neglected in mainstream economics.

To argue the above in an orderly manner, alongside the contrasting of the axioms and deductive assumptions of mainstream economics/ microeconomics with the referred empirical evidence, an alternative *explanatory conceptual outline* of this part of the socio-economic real world – as well as of economics: its 'microeconomics foundations'– is also developed here. This, by simply following the scientific method: taking into account the vast empirical evidence available — both the results of specific studies and those provided by the direct historical observations of the omnipresent realities of production, business workings, and markets' operation. All that, oriented to get inductive conclusions on the overall patterns regarding unit costs' behaviour and *economies of scale*, the usual economic behaviour of companies (prices determination and growth decisions), and the type of markets — of products and services — that really do exist or we can observe.

This is a book that I hope will be useful to *economics* students — whether or not they are pursuing a specific academic degree in this field. Though it is also written, of course, with economics professionals in mind; not only academics — albeit, in a way, the latter are the most directly appealed. Nevertheless, the text is drafted also with a view to concerned readers without specific training in *economics* but with an interest in the subject — hence the inclusion of appendixes, clarifying notes, and the simultaneous use of the standard terminology in the field along with a 'common knowledge' terminology. The standard paradigm under discussion has evident ideological implications that go far beyond economics. And some observational evidence presented here will even be familiar to a broad audience.

Chapter 1
Structure of the 'Standard Model' assumptions

To be confronted with observational evidence

> "All academic disciplines rely on assumptions, and economics is no different in this regard. But there are two kinds of assumptions: those written up explicitly and at times enshrined as axioms, and those that are built into the woodwork and thus hidden from view. While the explicit assumptions of economics have received a lot of scrutiny, those in the woodwork have largely gone unchallenged. Through force of habit many professionals have ceased to view them as assumptions, and regard them instead as immutable facts." (K. Basu, 2011, *Beyond the invisible hand*, p. 193)

To conceptually organise and better situate the referred confrontation with the wide range of empirical evidence available, it will be useful to start by making formally explicit, in a summarised way, the main assumptions and axioms that are the basis of the theoretical paradigm of the *Standard Model* in mainstream Economics (ESM). A model built around the theory of the *general equilibrium of competitive markets* and whose elements are then developed in chapter 2.

Chained premises, and oversimplifications

To start with, let us focus on the aforementioned postulate of this *economics standard model* regarding *decreasing returns*, which is used as a sort of general *law* of the economic world of production and the functioning of enterprises. A postulate that rests in fact upon premises that nevertheless are usually left implicit. Making them explicit, the summary could be as follow:

(I) A *deductive assumption*; 'deductive' in the usual methodological sense of not being presented in textbooks as derived from systematic observations of real cases (induction) but it is rather implicitly assumed like an axiom:

> in the production of any good (product or service), a comparatively small enterprise gets a lower average cost of the good as it grows in size (economies of scale). This growing path usually entails a higher degree of mechanisation and/ or automation; and, of course, to produce larger quantities per period. This possibility, however, exists up to a specific dimension associated to produce 'x' units of the good. From this point on, there appear *decreasing returns to scale*: If the firm keeps expanding in order to produce more than 'x' units, then its average cost becomes to increase. Thus, there is a given dimension, size, or structure of the firm (that associated to efficiently produce those 'x' units of the good) for which the unit cost is the minimum possible one. Consequently, all enterprises engaged in the production of the good in question tend to adopt this *optimal dimension* and to produce 'x' units of product; and, therefore, to operate with the (same) minimum average cost

And (II), an *ancillary hypothesis*; it plays an instrumental role by presupposing that:

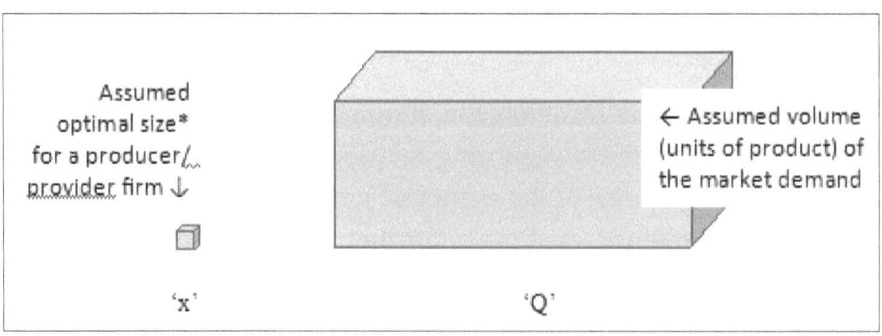

> the market demand for the good in question – when its price is close to the average cost of the producer enterprises, 'Q' units of the product or service, is – with rare exceptions (natural monopolies –) – many times greater than the 'x' units associated with the optimal scale of production for a firm.

Certainly, from the *deductive assumption* (I) about the world of unit costs of firms, and the *auxiliary hypothesis* (II) on the relative size of market demand for the concerned good – along with other more general assumptions, as that of "any (private) undertaking operates with full productive efficiency"– the theoretical proposition follows that:

> without any public intervention, the market for any good (product or service) will end up by having 'a great number' of firms supplying it; (as many as *Q*/x). All of them being as clones: the same, technology, size (that associated with producing 'x' units), and efficiency; and, therefore, they operate at the same (minimum) unit cost. A situation that gives automatically way to full competition in such a sector or industry (that is, to a 'perfectly competitive market'). And so for regarding any product or service – with some rare exceptions (natural monopoly situations)

These two core postulates underpin indeed the modern-neoclassical 'theory of production'; which, in turn, constitutes the cornerstone of mainstream economics' core model: the theory of *General Equilibrium of Competitive Markets*. A theory that can also be considered as an elegant way of formally expressing Adam Smith's metaphor of the *invisible hand* (when taking it to the letter[1]) by means of adding more assumptions and expressing it in mathematical terms. In Philip Klein's words:

---

[1] "Adam Smith's remark that individuals seeking their own self-interest in markets are led "as if by an invisible hand" to promote the good of society has received mixed reviews—beginning with Adam Smith. His most important work, *An Inquiry into the Nature and Causes of the Wealth of Nations* (1776), paints markets as powerful engines of growth but also of harm". (Schlefer, 2012:1).

> "A consensus presentation today of the central thrust of microeconomic theory, all derived from a vast elaboration of Smith's invisible hand, might run as follows. If we assume pure competition (that is, we consider many buyers and sellers, each too small to affect market price) of homogeneous products and assume as well that competition is perfect (resources are mobile, all agents have perfect knowledge of all alternatives available to them) then we can consider fairly completely the normative implications of (ESM) market adjustments." (P. Klein 2006, *Economics confront the Economy,* p. 20)

In addition to the aforementioned kernel – assumptions (I) and (II) – the ESM also rest upon other assumptions that are presented as mere simplifications. Two of these play a key role in the whole picture: the first one, that *«there is no inequality in income and wealth distribution in society»*; and the second one, that *«the labour market is also a free-market, (unregulated and without trade unions); and (thereby) there is full employment»*. Though, actually, more than methodological simplifications, these statements[2] should be regarded rather as *oversimplifications,* since they strongly reduce the realism of the model's deductions.

Other actual simplifications must be added to those assumptions and oversimplifications, such as, i) 'there are *no externalities* in the economy' (those non-monetary *costs* and *benefits* generated by economic activities but that are not reflected by markets); ii) '*a firm produces one only product/service*'; iii) these are homogenous (in terms of quality, variants, performances, etc.) and *non-differentiable* in the face of potential customers; and iv) *there is no foreign trade.*

---

[2] Together with others; like 'perfect information', 'no-entry-barriers' for anybody becoming producer of any good, and 'homo-economicus behaviour'; which are detailed in Appendix A.

A more complete overall scheme, that gathers and connects all these assumptions, axioms, and simplifications the ESM rest upon – and that therefore are sustaining its propositions, conclusions, and postulates – is presented on the following page. A more precise narrative description in this respect is summarised in Appendix A, at the end of this chapter.

Main core assumptions & axioms (and over-simplifications) in the economics standard model (general equilibrium)

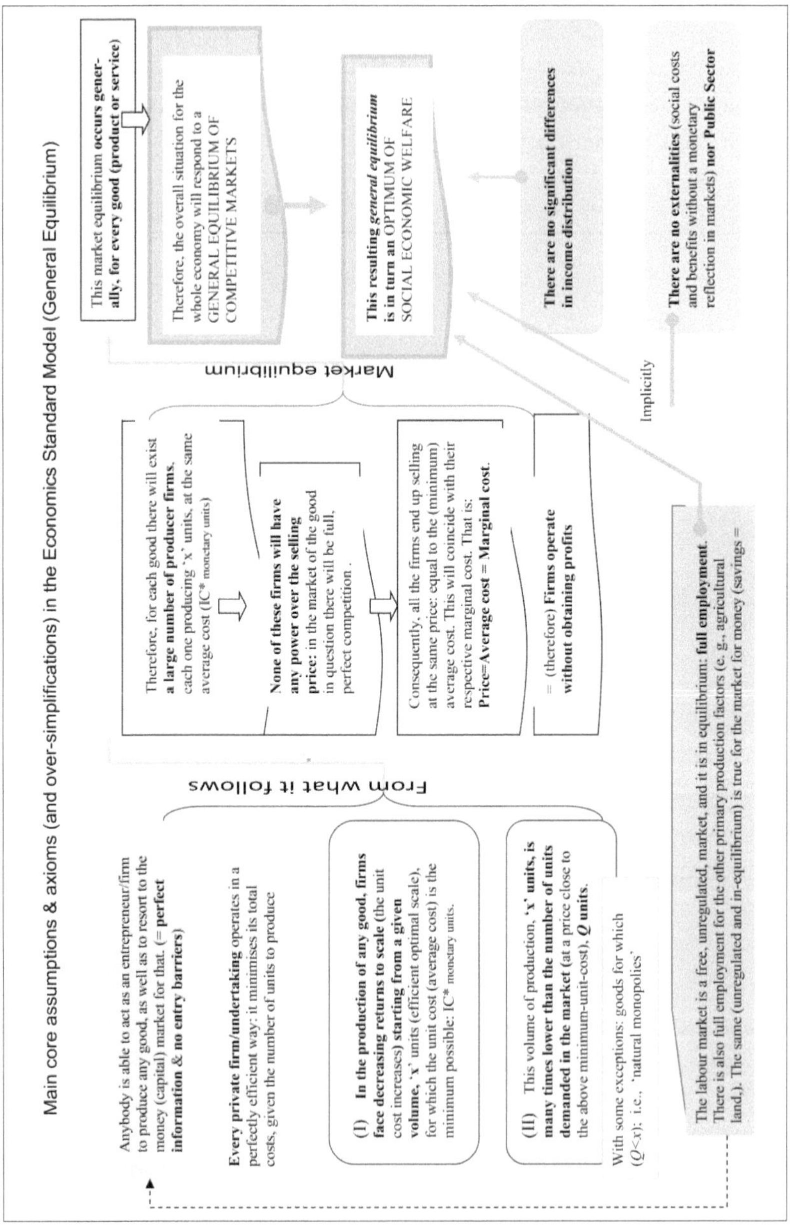

A glimpse on empirical contrasting

Having reached this point, any non-economist reader with some experience in the enterprises/business world will probably be surprised by this mainstream theory to describe/explain the workings of our market economies; especially taking into account that these are based on private – or, if preferred, capitalist – enterprises. Surprised, to start with, regarding the aforementioned deductive assumption (I), that states there is a 'natural' technical-economic ceiling to the size of any company, 'beyond which the firm is not interested in growing any further because its unit cost would soar'. To our non-economist, it will be quite obvious that this assumption does not generally correspond at all to the companies' functioning and market realities that can easily be observed (for example, simply as an employee). In fact, the dominant picture we may see in the real business world is rather the opposite: companies showing a tendency to sell as much as possible, increase their level of activity (structure, production, sales),* and ultimately grow as much as they can; precisely as a way of increasing their competitiveness (lower unit costs) and/or market share (i.e., obtaining market power) – in order so to increase or ensure their profits.

More precisely, as we will properly see in chapter 3, contrarily to what the aforementioned deductive assumption (I) postulates, there is no empirical evidence of decreasing returns to scale in the production of products or services by firms – aside from, perhaps, some exceptional cases[3]. There is no evidence that there exists an 'optimal volume or size' for the enterprises devoted to the production of this or that good; i.e. a supposed firm's size or productive dimension beyond which the firm will not be interested in growing because this would be antieconomical. Consequently, the mentioned theoretical

---

[3] As it could be the case for some rare minerals. We shall deal with this further on.

assumption (I) –which is a purely *deductive* assertion, since it has not been historically presented in mainstream neoclassical economics textbooks as a hypothesis inferred from the observation of real cases of firms or products – does not explain the economic reality well; or does not do so for the vast majority of final goods and commodities, whether material products or services.

In other words, the statement «decreasing returns always turn up, thereby, in any 'industry' there is always a given optimal size for the producer firms: that that minimises their average cost» relies on an assumption that cannot be sustained in the face of the reality that business and production activities show us. Thereby, the auxiliary hypothesis (II), «the relative size of the market demand for a (any) product or service will generally be much larger than the supposed *optimal* productive dimension for a firm in that sector: (whereby the resulting market structure will necessarily be one with many firms competing)» is meaningless. Therefore, the theoretical proposition deduced from assumptions (I) and (II), «the automatic, 'natural', trend toward perfectly competitive markets as a general rule in an unregulated capitalist market economy» is not sustainable.

Approach and book organisation

These previous assertions may sound somewhat categorical or unjustified for some readers; especially among academic economists. In fact, the proper argumentation of these statements put forward here, the references to the extensive empirical evidence they echo, occupies most of the following pages, especially from chapter 3 onward.

However, before moving on to this, it seems appropriate to begin (chapter 2) by properly developing the whole standard picture and specifying the essential of that mainstream theoretical explanation, currently *the standard model* in Economics, so far referred to only in broad terms. This will consist of setting out in an orderly manner the basis of the present standard, 'modern neoclassical', economic theory – that mainly refer to the world of production, companies, and markets. Thus, the following chapter 2 is devoted to dissecting its key statements and getting familiar with its peculiar graphic language; to start with: how and with which concepts the ESM presents the theoretical assumption (I) and the auxiliary hypothesis (II) as well as its deductions from them. Although it must be underlined in this respect – as already pointed out – that, in the ESM, these concepts, assumptions, and hypotheses are not normally presented in such terms but rather - and implicitly - as simplifications of immutable facts, or 'stylised facts'. These topics about the world of production and firms' behaviour regarding the resulting markets' conditions use to be developed in most reference manuals within the sections devoted to *Theory of costs (or Production), Theory of the Firm, Market Equilibrium Point,* and *Theory of the Competitive General Equilibrium.*

Once this conceptual framework of the standard paradigm has thus been summarised in chapter 2, the text steps to argue and present, comparably, the counterpoint we obtain when attending to the overwhelming empirical evidence about the same concepts. This means to induce – from observational empirical evidence – patterns of behaviour regarding economic variables, business undertakings, and other key elements of the world of production, enterprises, and markets (chapters 3, 4, and 5).

As the reader will have probably already guessed, in what follows some technicalities are going to be inevitable since the abovementioned explanatory paradigm of the ESM to be confronted with empirical evidence is based on concepts such as *marginal cost, average cost, size of a company, economies of scale, and market prices determination.* More specifically, it is based on a certain generic theoretical description of how the unit costs – of a (any) company that produces a certain good – are supposed to behave in relation to the volume of units of the good such a firm produces in a given period. The standard paradigm also deals with the behaviour of enterprises in this respect – by relying upon 'technical' assumptions about–; mainly regarding their decisions on the volume of production (or sales), selling prices, and their productive structure and technology; and therefore on its dimension or size as a firm. All the latter is what in the economics/microeconomics manuals can specifically be found under the abovementioned denominations of the *theory of costs* and/or *theory of the firm*.

It may come as a surprise for non-economists the fact that all that ('variable/fixed costs, marginal costs, average costs, the scale of production, ...') constitutes a set of quite 'technical' and at the same time very elementary concepts as to serve as a basis for a theoretical paradigm – that of the ESM – that concludes with such a general and transcendent proposition as that of 'the overall tendency to spontaneous equilibria of competitive markets'. Let us remind in this respect that this ESM's proposition, expressed less schematically, in terms of 'stylised facts', tells us that:

> (private) enterprises, since they tend to function efficiently (minimising their unit cost), if there are no institutional obstacles for them (intervention of public powers in the economy, prices regulation by governments, etc.), they as a whole generate, automatically, spontaneously, markets (for each good) that necessarily tend to be efficient and competitive (many companies competing by offering an identical product). Whereby, given this perfect efficiency and competition, each company ends up selling its product at a price equal to its marginal cost, which in turn will be equal to its average cost (the same for any producer firm in the market); i.e., that firms will not obtain any profit (sic)[4].

[4] For non-professional readers, a more systematic formulation of this set of pre-suppositions, assumptions and arguments of the mainstream economics' theoretical model is provided in Appendix A to this chapter.

Surprising or not, the fact is that the basis on which the construction of such a proposition (the general competitive equilibrium – and qualifying it as an optimum of social wellbeing–) rests is a deductive theory on the overall, generic behaviour of firms' unit costs. The relevant question in this respect is that – using the terminology of the scientific method– this theory does not explain such an economic reality well, as will be argued further on. Its descriptions and predictions do not correspond to the empirical observation regarding the more obvious aspects of the workings of firms and the overall behaviour of their unit costs. Moreover, this 'flaw' of being at odds with what the real economic world shows us do not refer to technical or of-detail aspects, but to key, basic points. Discrepancies with respect to empirical evidence on fundamental points are overwhelming, as we will see later.

Thus, lets us go step by step. Thinking also of readers not necessarily trained in economics – or who need to refresh their knowledge in this respect–, first, as already indicated, in Chapter 2 this standard 'modern neoclassical' *theory of costs, of the firm* – or *of production* –, and of the workings of markets is succinctly set out. That is, that part of the mainstream economic theory that leads in fact to the above-mentioned theoretical proposition on the 'spontaneity towards competitive markets', which, in turn, would flow out into 'an optimal social-economic well-being'. This summary will also serve to become familiar with (or recall) the aforementioned technical terms on unit costs and economies of scale.

In chapter 3, these core propositions of the ESM previously summarised are confronted systematically with the extensive empirical evidence available in this regard. Thus, firstly the purely theoretical assumptions, axioms, and hypotheses that underpin the ESM are put to the test by confronting them with the respective observational pieces of evidence available. This starts by confronting its cornerstone assumption – that of 'decreasing returns to scale as something general, universal in a market economy' with direct evidence from the real world of production and firms. A crucial step since the conceptual pillar of the 'general equilibrium of competitive markets' rests upon such an assumption.

In parallel, and using the referred empirical evidence, an alternative formal description of the workings of firms, their unit-costs, and of the market's equilibrium point is presented. This empirical inductive approach relies thus on the historically and extensively observable empirical shreds of evidence about such economic-business reality. In other words, a theoretical-conceptual description, that explains reasonably well (in terms of the scientific method) the referred topics, is presented. That means to schematically explain the observable reality regarding: **i)** the general pattern of behaviour of enterprises' unit-costs, in relation to the total units produced (the topic of returns to scale), and consequently, **ii)** the overall pattern of behaviour and decision making of companies (of their managers) concerning the company[5] size, production scale, or dimension that is adopted, decided, or pursued.

Next, in chapters 4 and 5 the assumptions and axioms of the ESM that complete the sequence of its arguments (the standard explanation it gives on how prices, and therefore business profits, are determined, as well as on the resulting type of markets in the competition/monopoly axis) are confronted with the also overwhelming empirical evidence that the observation of business and markets reality offers to us in this respect. As a result of this confrontation, a remarkably different explanatory picture emerges of how that central part of a market economy based on private enterprises works.

---

[5] In this text the terms 'firm', 'enterprise', 'undertaking' and 'company' are used indistinctly.

Simultaneously, throughout these chapters, the essential features and core elements of such an alternative, new formal explanatory scheme are summarised. This, mainly by outlining the empirical inductive conclusions on the *general patterns of behaviour* of companies as regards: **iii)** how the prices they apply/require in the market are actually determined; and which the companies' *attitude* or typical *strategies* regarding their product's market are. This, in turn, leads us to pay attention to the relevance, regarding firms' behaviour and markets' running, of concepts such as 'market share', as well as of so generalised policies or practices like: 'growth orientation', 'product differentiation', 'diversification', 'market segmentation', or (searching for a) 'niche market'; together with the more traditional practices of marketing & advertising, taking-over other firms, etc.. And, as an overall outcome of all that, **iv)** an assessment about which market-structures – in the competition/monopoly axis – are most frequently observed in real economies is carried out.

The development of the above does not intend to theorise a new overall paradigm but simply to formulate a general theoretical explanatory *package* that be coherent with the omnipresent empirical evidence on the matter – some of which, on the other hand, is so obvious that it constitutes common knowledge. The choice has been just to specify a formal set of specific explanatory models that results simply from not being impermeable to evidence, that is, from covering the inductive phase of the scientific method.

Finally, in chapters 6 and 7, the different topics separately worked out throughout the prior chapters are connected by developing the main overall conclusions and findings, and discussing their implications beyond economics itself. These overall conclusions are organised and presented around an axis or argument: that of the outcome derived from the systematic confrontation of the core theoretical framework of the ESM (chapter 2) with the reality of the economic world, as carried out and schematised in chapters 3, 4 and 5.

This outcome could be roughly synthesised with the conclusion that the ESM core proposition on "the automatism towards a general equilibrium of competitive free markets, which in turn constitutes an optimum of social wellbeing", can not be sustained in front of the observable reality of our market economies. But that, nevertheless, such an ESM core proposition keeps being the dominant paradigm. And its overreaching use of the popular Adam Smith's rhetoric image of the *invisible hand* has consequences that go beyond the academic debate on the (unnecessary) lack of realism of mainstream economics manuals (Schlefer 2012:2-8).

> "This metaphor (invisible hand) underlay the misguided thinking that helped to cause the 2008 financial crisis, (...). Until invisible-hand thinking changes, we can not devise workable ideas to solve a range of problems."(p. 4).

It also has consequences in the day-to-day economic life of our societies, as exemplified by the lingering mythification that comes been observed about (a given idea of) *competition*: as a supreme axiomatic principle in economic policy – this, in the sense of the real example-cases that are discussed at the end of chapter 7. We will review there this socio-economic discourse that, going itself beyond the obvious instrumental virtues of competition as for the workings of a decentralised/market economy, mythifies *Competition* by taking it as an end in itself – instead of a useful mean or mechanism – regardless of the consequences of that on social life. A mythification that appears associated with a certain ideology: underlying neoliberalism. Sometimes it consists of political decisions or positions that seem to neglect the existence of economic inequalities or of collective preferences expressed throughout democratic institutions – like to fight, 'because *unfair* or *démodé*', this or that regulation on economic activities–; mythification that in some cases translates into public decisions leading to absurd social results, even in economic terms.

Appendix A

Appendix A: Summary of the assumptions, axioms, and postulates of the Economics Standard Model

*'market economy with perfect competition' and 'general equilibrium of competitive markets'

Assumptions that are, in principle, presented as methodological simplifications

- A static market economy: with no demographic or technological changes or changes in consumers' preferences.
- A closed economy, without foreign trade
- There is no public powers' economic activity: there is not a system of tax-and-public- expenditure affecting business undertakings or consumers as such. (sic).
- Each undertaking (enterprise, firm, company) produces only one good (product or service), which does not accept differentiation in the face of potential customers/users.

Premises and deductivist assumptions about the workings of the economy

The 'homo economicus' paradigm

1. Individuals, whether as consumers, producers/entrepreneurs, employees, savers, or investors, behave (make their decisions) trying to maximise their utility; which is equivalent to maximising the income they receive. In this regard, ...

   "Human beings, in the formulations of modern economists, are regularly endowed with perfect foresight, rational expectations, omniscience, amazing powers of calculation or 'rationality', rendered homogeneous, placed in scenarios where just two commodities exist etc., etc." (Lawson, 2017, p.26).

Production and firms

2. There is perfect information: Markets of products and factors operate with full transparency. Information on prices, technical features of this or that good, and possible production technologies for it, as well as how to foresee its respective production cost, are totally and immediately available, free of charge, to any person. (Thus, the *homo economicus* is also assumed to be omniscient).

3. There are no entry barriers to markets. Any person can become a producer (firm) of this or that good (by, if necessary, requesting a loan in the capital market; which is also perfectly transparent, and with the attributes as in '(2)').

4. All companies/ firms behave in a perfectly efficient manner (minimising total cost, for a given production). Furthermore, for any market or industry (product) there is an optimal firm size (production volume), for which the product's average cost is the minimum possible. If the firm exceeds this optimal size, it will face decreasing returns: its average cost will increase. Whereby, all firms in the industry tend to adopt this optimal size or production structure; and consequently, they operate with the (same) minimum average cost – which will then be equal to the corresponding marginal cost.

5. For any good (product or service) the market demand (units), for a price close to the abovementioned average cost, is many times greater than the volume of units associated with the above indicated optimal size of a firm, for that good.

Markets: perfectly efficient, and in equilibrium

6. Consequently, [(4) & (5) given], each product or service is produced by many companies, all of them with the same size/productive

structure, thus obtaining the same minimum average cost, and competing with each other. They take the selling price as external data from the market. Whereby, they end up selling at a (same) price, equal to marginal cost, which in turn is equal to their common average cost. Thus, they operate without obtaining profits. (*sic*).

7. Thereby [and (2) and (3) given], every market tends towards equilibrium: the aggregate supply of any good (whether product, service, or factor) adjusts systematically to demand. There is therefore neither unemployment nor any other under-utilisation of the economy's resources.

Additional assumptions that are required by the ESM to postulate that the above* general equilibrium of efficient and competitive markets (6 & 7) *can be considered as a social optimum.

Explicitly

- The differences in income and wealth between the individuals that make up society (citizens of the economy under consideration) are not appreciable (sic). Thus, the marginal utility of money is identical for each person. Consequently, their individual utilities can be added, forming the total 'Social Utility' to be maximised (in the model). This aggregate (taking into account (1)) is equivalent to the sum of the incomes received by all persons: individuals (employees) and households, firms' owners, and land (and other natural resources) owners.

Implicitly (realities simply omitted in the standard model)

- There is not Public Sector. That is, public powers' economic activity is absent in the model.
- There are not externalities*, whether positives or negatives. In other words, the production and/or use or consumption of any good does not generate external or indirect effects; whether positive (*indirect social benefits*) or negatives (*indirect social costs*).

Non-monetary 'costs' and 'benefits' which are not, therefore, 'registered' by markets: they affect other people different from the producing/ supplying undertaking and its customers/consumers.

- Consequently, since every person acts maximising their income and there is full employment of resources, the social utility will be maximum, given the economy's existing resources. Therefore, the overall outcome will be a 'social optimum' (in terms of economic wellbeing).

Chapter 2
The mainstream economics taught in classrooms and textbooks

A theory of the firm (or of production) and markets

> "Perhaps the real trouble is our age-old belief, going back to Ricardo, that economics is essentially a deductive science, in which we infer economic behaviour on the basis of some assumptions about motivations and some stylized facts about prevailing institutions, suppressing even the temptation to ask whether these are descriptively realistic assumptions and accurately chosen facts."
> (Mark Blaug, 1998, p. 30)

> "Newton took the environment – the real environment – as basic to his theory. (For an economic micro-theorist to base theory on real environment would be a real departure. Instead conventional micro-theorists customarily begin with an effort deliberately to imagine a simple play world, to begin with a set of 'givens' –i.e., the necessary assumptions to create the play world and then to set about explaining that world.)"
> (Philip A. Klein, 2006, p. 47)

This chapter focuses on the core basic subjects of conventional economics introduced in the previous chapter: the theoretical explanatory model of mainstream or standard economics (ESM) about the workings of the economic world of production, prices, and markets; which in turn underpins the ESM's theory of the *general equilibrium of competitive markets* (GE). That is, a corpus of theory about: business undertakings' functioning, their unit costs' behaviour regarding economies of scale and firm's size, and the translation of all this at the sector or 'industry' level (*neoclassical theory of production*), as well as about the types of market –as for the axis 'competition' / 'monopoly'– resulting from all the former (*theory of prices and markets, market equilibrium, and, finally, general competitive equilibrium*).

Thus, what follows is intended to offer a synthetic review of how the fundamental basis of mainstream economics/microeconomics is usually presented in reference manuals and textbooks most used over recent years –or rather decades–. This objective includes introducing their most common standard terminology and notation, as well as their typical graphical language –which is decisive since it is used in the ESM, in part, also as a way of implicitly introducing assumptions and axioms.

As noted in the Introduction, the theoretical models of cause/ effect relationships between aggregates at the whole economy level, which make up the macroeconomics parcel, are not dealt with here.

Throughout this chapter, it would be convenient to have in mind that the *methodological simplifications* and *assumptions* of the ESM stated in the former Appendix are implicit along the standard arguments schematised below; especially those of a static and closed economy, no public powers activity, and no externalities; as well as the premises of *homo economicus* and *perfect information* for everybody.

2.1 The standard theory of unit-cost in the short-run, or static analysis: a firm in operation, with a given production structure or size

The starting point regarding the *theory of costs* (or *theory of the firm*) in manuals is systematically one not less simplification: that any firm considered produces a single product or service, and that such a good cannot be subject to differentiation in the market (either via different models or by level of quality), as could be the case, for example, of '98º surgical alcohol'. From this perspective, the central concept is then the *average cost* of the good, the usual definition of which is:

$$AC = \frac{\text{Total costs (for consume or used factors) during periods "t"}}{\text{Units of production obtained during period "t"}} \equiv \frac{C}{q}$$

When moving on to specifying the numerator, what is most common in manuals – of economics or microeconomics – is to assume (a second over-simplification) that there are just two *factors* (sic): Labour factor costs, and Capital factor costs. The latter referred to machines, equipment, building facilities, etc. Only in some manuals is the over-simplification somewhat minor: when the specification of the numerator includes (costs of) 'raw materials' and 'intermediate components'; or, although less frequently, by extending the specification to other factors, such as 'external services' and 'energy' – factors which are so common and relevant in practice. But let us admit this, for the moment, as a methodological simplification. We could assume that the ESM implicitly refers to the costs of all the factors required to produce and deliver the good, product or service in question.

The next step in the *theory of costs* of the ESM is the introduction of an additional simplifying assumption – again, not a minor one: that the costs of a given factor are either fixed or variable –in relation to the number of units of product produced/sold; or that a given part of the costs of this or that factor is clearly fixed and the rest variable. This then allows the model to reason in terms that Total Costs (the numerator) can be unambiguously broken down into two parts: Fixed Total Costs and Variable Total Costs, C=FC+VC. Whence, the quotient C/q, the average cost, can be decomposed as the sum of two quotients: Variable Average Cost, VC/q = v, and Fixed Average Cost, FC/q = f.

average cost = variable average cost + fixed average cost; $AC = v + f$

Following this thread, a new concept of unit cost is then added in the manuals: that of *marginal cost* (*mc*). It is defined as the increase in *total costs* (the numerator) when the number of units produced in the period, *q*, is increased by one unit. This increase in costs can only come, given the previous assumptions, in the form of *variable costs*.

Finally, the ESM makes key specific assumptions about the behaviour of those three concepts of unit costs, *v*, *f* and *mc*, in relation to the volume of production, *q*. These assumptions are, again, deductive hypotheses or, at least, they are never presented as inferences or inductions derived from real cases or studies. Moreover, in most reference manuals, these hypotheses are expressed not in narrative form, explicitly argued, but simply via graphic language. They are implicit in the way each of the unit cost concepts (*AC, v, f, mc*) is drawn or represented in a diagram with axis 'unit costs' and 'units of product', *q*, (for a given – unspecified – period). This mathematics-suggesting representation invariably consists of drawing *v(q)*, *f(q)*, *mc(q)* and *AC(q)* as continuous functions, specifically in the form of perfect parabolas. (This induces in readers the idea that the reality the textbook is schematically describing responds to perfectly-derivable second-order mathematical functions (differential calculus). What can convey to students the idea that they are learning a topic, economics, which reminds them of what they saw in Physics in high school, for example).

In short, the theoretical explanatory model of the behaviour of the unit costs (i.e., how they change in relation to the volume of units produced, per period), and therefore the underlying assumptions and axioms that are being assumed, are basically expressed in graphic language. This specifically consists of drawing shapes visually associated with mathematical functions, although in an abstract way (not specifying them in mathematical terms), mainly as vertical parabolas. The standard representation (the most popular diagram) in this respect is as follows:

Figure 1: *Unit costs of a single-product firm, in the short run*[1] *(according to the standard non-linear model)*

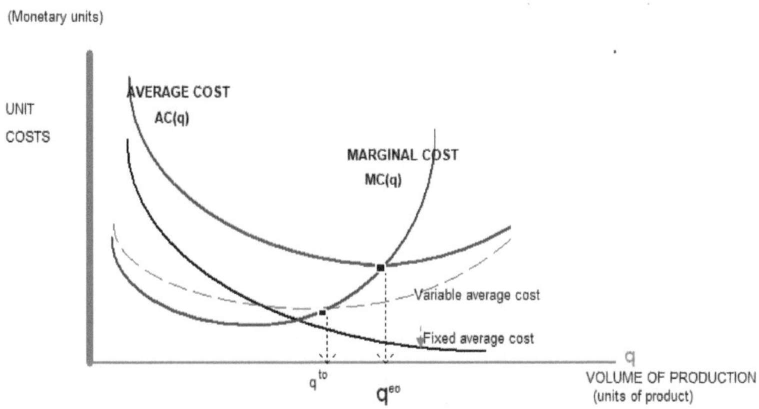

Where,

q = Units produced in a given period (month, quarter, year, ...) the concerned firm takes for its successive accounting statements.

qto = Volume of units 'technically optimal' for such a time-period. It is the number of units for which the variable average cost, v(q), is the minimum one – given the firm's size, production structure, or capacity at the time (=¶).

qeo = volume of units *'economically optimal'*: It is the number of units for which the average cost, *AC(q)*, is the minimum one –given the firm's size, production structure, or capacity at the time (¶= qeo).

This diagram, which is used as graphical-conceptual language, responds in fact to certain hypotheses on the general behaviour of companies' costs. However, as already pointed out, these hypotheses are normally left *implicit* in the textbooks. They are simply embedded in the way the above curves are drawn. If we make them explicit, these hypotheses are:

[1] 'in the short run' (or static analysis), with the meaning of: without the concerned firm changing the productive structure or size (production capacity, ¶,) it has at the time.

- 1st hypothesis: Fixed total costs (FC) are exactly constant, whatever the volume of units produced, whereby the *fixed average cost* (f=FC/q) is geometrically a downward function, asymptotic to the units-of-product axis.

- 2nd hypothesis: Starting from a very low production/occupation level, the *variable average cost* (v=VC/q) is at first decreasing as the volume of units produced increases. This would be so (*2nd .1*) mainly because as the quantities of materials (or energy, external services, etc.) purchased become higher, lower purchasing prices may be negotiated. But, from a given volume of units to be produced, q^{to}, just the opposite occurs: the *variable average cost becomes ever increasing*.

  In turn, this latter statement implies the assumption (*2nd.2*) that such a production level, q^{to} units, is *the specific volume* that, the structure / facilities / size of the firm allows *in normal conditions* (that is to say, the possibility of, for example, more than one work-shift is tacitly ruled out), and that producing above this volume of units is possible but this – on having to force the installed capacity – will entail an increase in variable costs proportionally greater than the increase in units of product.

  Furthermore, the statement also implies assuming (*2nd .3*), that, as the volume of units to be produced increases, the latter effect (*2nd.2*) soon predominates over the former, (*2nd .1*). Whereby, the variable average cost for a good, v, moves from being decreasing to be increasing (dashed line in Figure 1).]

- 3rd hypothesis: This trend of v increasing for volumes of output beyond q^{to} units, ends up overcoming the simultaneous decreasing trend of the *fixed average cost*, *f*; whereby, starting from a certain volume of units to produce, q^{to} – for which the *total average cost*, ***AC***, reaches its minimum, the latter (AC) also becomes then increasing.

- As for the *marginal cost, mc,* a behaviour, *mc(q),* is simply assumed (drawn) that is consistent with the graphic translation of the above underlying hypotheses regarding variable costs (figure 1).

These are the standard-model's main implicit hypotheses and assumptions about how the *unit costs* of business undertakings for producing any specific good behave in general – in relation to the volume of units produced per period, *in the short run,* i.e., the undertaking having a given installed capacity. These theoretical assumptions on the general behaviour of costs and returns are in fact implicit through the peculiar graphical language used in textbooks: these behaviours are represented concretely by perfect parabolas (figure 1); i.e., as continuous second-order functions. What finally allows an elegant mathematical demonstration of what can be visualised in the popular diagram in figure 1: that the *marginal cost* will necessarily coincide with the corresponding *variable average cost* when it reaches its minimum (production volume of q^{to} units), and that *marginal cost* will also coincide with the total *average cost* when this in turn reaches its minimum (production volume of q^{eo} units).

It should be underlined, as a background matter, that this standard approach pre-assumes *that the abstract enterprise whose unit-costs' behaviour is being represented in the figure operates with full management efficiency.* In this context, this expression means that in each 'accounting' period the enterprise's total costs are the minimum strictly necessary – given its productive structure at the time – for the actual volume of units produced/sold in such a period. Usually, this background hypothesis is also not explicit in the economics/ microeconomics manuals when presenting the diagram of figure 1. The explanation for this is that such a hypothesis works more like an axiom: throughout the chapters (of this or that reference manual) prior to those devoted to these topics (theory of costs, theory of the firm), the idea floats – as if it were fairly obvious – that every private firm, as such, will necessarily operate with full productive efficiency.

In turn, this axiom stems from assuming that its managers are perfectly competent to do so and that they have perfect information as to technology's possibilities and on the factors' markets[2]. In other words, it is taken for granted that business undertakings are managed in a perfectly efficient manner, systematically minimising their total costs given the specific volume of units to produce/provide in each period.

Regarding the theoretical description expressed by the diagram of Figure 1, empirical observation – especially via business cost accounting – shows, however, that the most common situation for a going undertaking i.e., with a certain productive structure or size at the time – is that the *average cost* for a product / service tends to be constant for a considerable interval of output units (Mansfield 1994:242). This is basically because it is observed that variable costs per unit of product (v), contrarily to the abovementioned 2nd standard hypothesis, tend to remain constant rather than to increase, mainly because a company can work with more than one shift, outsource part of the productive process to other companies, or make use of other flexibility options. However, we will leave this – the empirical evidence on these issues – for chapter 3.

Thus, let us continue with the mainstream economics standard model on firms' costs, and its hypotheses. According to its axiom that 'the enterprise (any enterprise) behaves in a perfectly efficient way', if a firm wants to produce and sell a volume of units higher than its optimal quantity at the time (i.e., q^{eo} units; for which its *average cost* is the minimum, given its productive structure at the time), because market conditions allow this move and it is convenient for the enterprise in terms of profits, its managers will have no interest in forcing its productive capacity (since that would increase the *average*

[2] A more complete statement on this and other assumptions about 'perfection' that sustain the *perfect competition standard model* can be seen in Appendix A.

cost) but rather in expanding it, scaling up its installed capacity, moving to a bigger enterprise's size[3]. This will likely also allow the firm to use a more mechanised/ automated technology (which tends to mean proportionally more equipment and fewer personnel) and, as a result, to achieve an *average cost* not only equal to but even lower than the minimum one with its current structure/size.

This perspective, which incorporates the dimensions 'time' and 'technology' when talking about the workings of companies, is the one that leads to the general and more relevant question: How do the unit costs of a firm vary when it changes its scale of production (firm's size), in the sense of growing? More specifically, what is or how is it usually defined the minimum average cost for a given good in this dynamic context? This is what in economics is commonly labelled (the theory of) the unit costs of a good *in the long run*, or 'in equilibrium' (or, also, the theory of *industry's average cost*). Where 'in the *long-run*' means giving time for the company in question to change its size or productive structure and *technology* – the latter understood in a broad sense, including the different ways of carrying out and organising the enterprise's activities; and where 'industry' stands for the set of enterprises producing the good in question (as in common expressions like "the cement industry"); i.e., as synonym for 'sector'.

2.2 The standard theory of units costs in the long run, or dynamic analysis: firms' size is a decisional variable, it changes over time

As we have seen, the graphic 'model' in figure 1 is intended as a theoretical description of the general relationship between the *unit costs* of a good and the *number of units* produced per period by *an*

[3] As it will have been noted, in the test the terms 'firm', 'enterprise', business 'undertaking' and 'company' are used indistinctly, with the same meaning.

operating firm at a given time; i.e., *in the short run*. Such a figure may be understood as a still photo of an existing enterprise with a given size, productive structure, and technology. This size/structure is associated with the volume of q^{eo} units of product in figure 1. But the size or productive structure of an enterprise is a strategic decisional variable for its managers. They can decide to resize the company in the medium/long run, to scale it up (or down). Which will give rise to a different production structure, and therefore to a different 'figure 1', a new 'unit-costs diagram in-the-short-run'.

Thus, let us suppose that the enterprise managers' decision is to grow, and that the starting situation is of a relatively small size. To change to a bigger structure/size will likely mean moving to use a more advanced, mechanised, automated, technology, and/or a higher division of labour. The enterprise will legally remain the same, but technically speaking it will be 'another (bigger) enterprise'. It will therefore have another 'still photo' as diagram of unit-costs. It will probably have proportionally more equipment costs and less personnel costs. Furthermore, if thanks to this new *technology*, an average cost even lower than the minimum of the previous situation can be achieved, then we talk about '***economies of scale***'.

The following figure 2 would illustrate such a kind of move, by means of overlaying the two still photographs. [For the sake of clarity, in this figure only total average costs *AC* and marginal costs *MC* are represented; i.e., the components of the first, *variable* average cost (v), and fixed *average costs*, (f), are omitted].

Despite the debatable ESM assumptions about the behaviour of variable costs pointed out in 2.1, this classic diagram offers an elegant and useful general description of what is meant by *economies of scale*, or *increasing returns to scale* as a result of a company moving from one scale (size/ structure/ technology) to a larger one: total costs increase less than proportionally to the increase in production, thanks to the use of a more cost-effective 'technology'; which translates into a lower *minimum average cost* (in the above numerical example it moves from €80 to €60).

Figure 2: *Economies of scale (or 'increasing returns')*

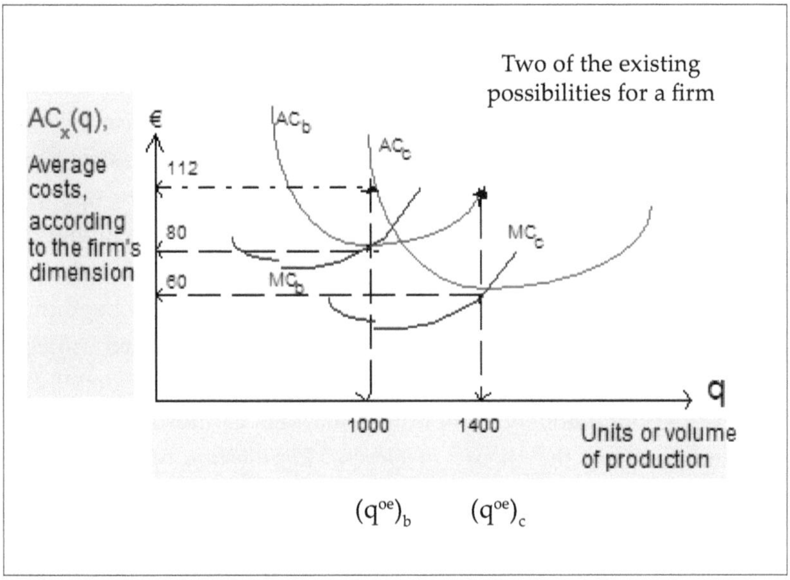

This simple conceptual diagram is also useful more in general – regardless of the limitations and arguable deductive assumptions pointed out before: it easily shows that a size-and-technology which is in principle 'superior', in the sense of more economical, (such as 'c' in the diagram) may not necessarily be preferable for a given company at a given time. It will depend on the volume of units per period (each month, for example) that the company estimates it will produce and sell on a stable basis. Using the example in the chart, if such a volume is, for instance, 1000 units per month, the cheapest size/technology for the firm will be 'b' (the average cost will then be €80), since to produce 'only' 1000 units with the upper size/technology 'c' would result in a higher average cost, €112 – due to the weight of the (higher) fixed costs such a 'c' size/structure entails.

2.2.1 The crucial 'U' shaped (decreasing returns) hypothesis of mainstream (micro)economics

Generalising what is expressed by figure 2 above, it is normally accepted that in an *industry*[4], i.e., for a certain good, there will not be only one option of 'most-cost-effective' size/technology for a company, but several, indefinite, options, each one opening up the possibility of producing more cheaply. And it is precisely at this step that the standard model of the *theory of costs* adds the key assumption of "up to a certain limit" – q^{os} units of product, in the classical chart of figure 3 below, from which the ESM assumes that just the opposite occurs: "the bigger the firm size/production structure, the higher the minimum average-cost" (sic). This is the deductive assumption on *decreasing returns to scale* that has been discussed at the beginning as a cornerstone in the modern neoclassical standard (micro) economics[5] without which, as we shall see here more in detail, the model of spontaneously competitive markets cannot be sustained; nor therefore can the theory of *General Equilibrium* of competitive markets.

The graphical expression of this crucial assumption of 'decreasing returns' consists of representing (drawing) the ***long run (or industry's)*** *minimum* ***average cost*** for a good – in relation to the number of units to produce per period: LRAC(q) or IC(q), also as 'U' shaped (like in the case of the short-run-average-cost, figure 1). This determinant orthodox diagram follows:

[4] 'Industry' meaning, here, 'sector'; like, e.g., when we talk about the 'glass industry' or the 'road transport industry'.

[5] The kind of arguments that we find in mainstream textbooks to justify this key deductive assumption are made precise and specifically discussed further in section 2.3.

Figure 3: *Minimum average cost of a Good in the long run (or industry's average cost) in the mainstream standard model*

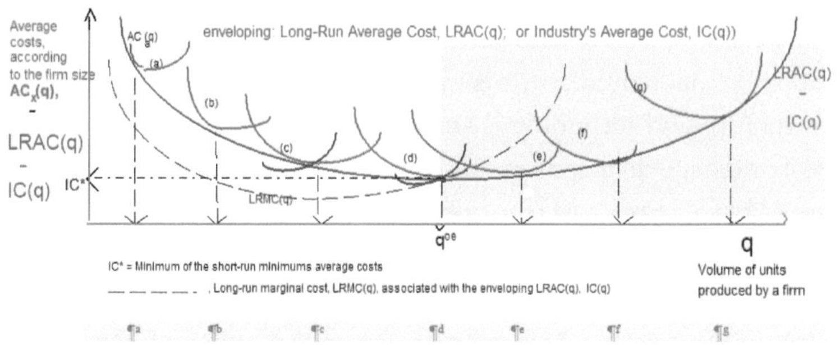

Where,

- The set of 'small' curves (in red) represent the short-run average cost of a firm, as a function of the units it produces per period, according to its dimension/technology *(a, b, c, d, …, x):* $AC_x(q)$.

- The 'big' curve (green line) drawn as enveloping the small ones is defined as representing our protagonist: The minimum ***long-run average cost*** for a firm according to the number of units to produce per period on a stable basis; (also, ***Industry's average cost***). This concept reflects that a firm (any firm) makes decisions over time about the dimension (size/ production structure/ technology) to adopt as more convenient according to its possibilities and strategy in the market of the good in question.

- ¶x stands for firm size (or production structure/capacity/ technology) 'x', expressed it in units of product at which a firm so dimensioned reaches its minimum average cost. Thus, it corresponds to the concept q^{eo} in Figure 1, associated with dimension/technology 'x'. The specific dimension/size to adopt (a, b, ...f, g, ..) is a decisional, strategic, variable for a firm operating in the industry.

- As a back-drop assumption on the meaning of the short-run (red) cost functions: 'any active enterprise in the industry operates with perfect efficiency (minimising its total costs), given its dimension technology at the moment and the specific volume of units produced in a period'.

In leading modern-neoclassical economics/microeconomics manuals, this graphic-postulate plays a determinant role insofar as it is the main carrier of the deductive assumption of decreasing returns in-the-long-run; which in turn is a key issue for the theory of General Equilibrium. Indeed, the assumption is expressed in standard texts more through this graphical language than in narrative language. In any case, the idea this crucial diagram transmits to readers is, as can be seen, that

> 'the economies of scale a company enjoys by moving from a relatively small dimension/structure, such as 'a', to a larger one, such as 'b', etc., become exhausted beyond a certain dimension/ structure' (the 'd' in the above diagram). Thus, in the standard model, 'that would be the company's optimal size or productive structure-and-technology, since by adopting it the company can manage to produce the good in question at the lowest possible average cost (the minimum of the different minimums associated with every other possible sizes), IC* monetary units, by producing a certain number of units of product' (q^{os}, in the graph). 'This specific volume of units defines, thus, the firm's efficient or optimal scale –for the corresponding good's industry. 'However, –continuing with the assumption embedded in the diagram– starting from that company's size, for a larger productive dimension (shaded rectangle), the opposite occurs the minimum attainable average cost becomes higher, increasingly higher (company sizes 'e', 'f', 'g', ...), due to the emergence of decreasing returns (diseconomies of scale), because those are "too big" enterprise's sizes'.

The reasoning within the standard economic theory on why that is supposed to happen relies, in turn, on second-level assumptions. But this deserves a separate section, (in section 2.3 below).

In short, the standard diagram for the minimum long-run average cost, *LRAC(q)*, is drawn in most manuals also as 'U' shaped; and, more specifically, represented as a perfect vertical parabola: one (large) 'U' that wraps the (small) 'Us' representing the short-run

---

[6] Among the most popular: Varian (1987: 414-418), (1992: 84) and (2014: 411-416); Browning & Browning (1989: 192-220); McCormick (1993: 309); Sloman (1996: 215-217); Schotter (2006: 219); Mankiw et al. (2006: 287-289; and successive editions); Gravelle & Rees (2006: 133-4); Monchón (2009: 129-133); Samuelson & Nordhaus (2010), though in these last editions they do not include the traditional 'U shape' enveloping function of Figure 3; Jehle & Reny (2011: 143); Estrin et al. (2012: 176-183); Pindyck (2013: 277); Krugman & Wells (2013: 336).

average cost for different (x) company sizes, $ACx(q)$. In other words, this 'U-shaped hypothesis' – or hypothesis of '*decreasing returns in-the-long-run*, as companies become too big' – is the usual one in most popular economics/ microeconomics textbooks[6], with some exceptions, as we will see further on (in 2.5).

The thesis: 'There is always a natural limit to the size of firms'

This *decreasing returns* assumption is certainly crucial, since it is the piece that allows the ESM the theoretical deduction that 'every company producing the good in question will be interested in reaching or adopting this dimension/ structure (*efficient* or *optimal scale*, 'd') and producing precisely the corresponding $\boldsymbol{q^{os}}$ units of product per period, because so it will be able to work with the minimum possible average cost, IC*; hence, it will never be interested in growing above that size, because then its average cost would be higher'.

More precisely, what figure 3 expresses is that the 'minimum-of-the-minimums' average cost, $[AC_d(q^{oe})=LRAC(q^{oe})=\boldsymbol{IC^*}]$, will necessarily (arithmetically) coincide with the corresponding *marginal cost* $[MC(q^{oe})=LRMC(q^{os})]$. This is just what point (q^{oe}, IC^*) in the graphs in Figure 3 is telling us; (for the sake of clarity, only the marginal cost curves for firm's dimensions 'c' and 'd' – 'small' curves in blue – have been represented).

The academic use of this traditional Figure 3, however, goes further: such lowest-possible average cost (IC^* monetary units) is supposed to be the same for every enterprise operating in that *industry*, producing the good in question – since the ESM assumes that such (any) enterprises operate in a perfectly efficient way, and therefore they will end up by adopting the same dimension/ technology 'd', and producing the same volume of units per period, q^{oe}, thereby to achieve the absolute-minimum average cost, IC^* monetary units. Therefore – the standard model continues – the condition

Average Cost *(AC)* = ***Marginal Cost*** *(MC)* = ***IC**** will be fulfilled for all the industry/market's enterprises. It is relevant to mention this 'technical' detail here because, from this basic 'graphical statement' (figure 3) on, in the ESM development preference is then given to speak of *Marginal Cost* – rather than of Average Cost. I will return on this apparently unimportant curiosity further on

The thesis: 'There will be many competing efficient firms in a sector, and will get zero profits'

Once stated the above conceptual basis, the standard approach then introduces the auxiliary hypothesis II mentioned at the beginning, in chapter 1. Or, rather, such a hypothesis is implicitly assumed, as something that would not need to be argued that:

> 'total market demand for a (any) good, –for a price close to its minimum average cost, ***Q*** units of the good, is many times greater than the volume of units associated with the *efficiency's optimal size/scale* for a company producing such a good: q^{os} units (with a few extreme exceptions: goods under *natural monopoly* situations). Whereby – the standard theoretical argument continues – in equilibrium, in the long run, in the market of such a good there will necessarily be a *large number* of producer/supplier companies (as many as Q/q^{os}) to cover the total demand; all of them having the same size/ production-structure-and-technology –that of the *efficient/optimal scale* (q^{os}) – and producing such a volume of units, q^{os}, at the minimum average cost of the industry, *IC** monetary units. Consequently, being so many supplier companies (a number equal to Q/q^{os}), each one will be too small to be able to have any influence over the selling price in the market. Thereby, due to the resulting strong competition, the market price will be equal to the average cost of the good for all the companies (*Price=IC**); therefore, these will operate without making profits'.

Thus, in short, in the *ESM* it is assumed that, for all undertakings operating (competing) in the market of a certain product or service, the situation is such that they will apply a price equal to its average cost, without therefore obtaining profits (sic); schematically, ***[P=AC=****MC****=IC*]***, for any firm in this market. This statement may be striking in a theory that supposedly intends to describe/explain the economic world of production and markets in our economies based on private enterprises. But the fact is that when the ESM deals with costs and the workings of companies it supposes (states indeed) that the above is true for all goods/*industries/markets* 'with some few exceptions', (which we will pay attention to further), and that thereby all markets tend to be perfectly competitive and efficient; which entails that all enterprises in it operate with full efficiency and end up selling at cost price, without any profit. Thus, to cite from a well-known manual

> "… If all firms, active and potential, take prices as unaffected by their own actions, this implies that active firms must earn exactly zero profits in any long-run equilibrium; .." (Mas-Colell et. al, 1995, p. 335).

In some standard manuals this is qualified by elaborating that, when the text speaks of *total costs*, it should be understood that these include a certain business profit, 'the *normal* or minimum per-unit profit that an entrepreneur in a specific *industry* requires to continue as such'. That is, that when it is talk about average cost, this is understood (in the standard textbook) to include a certain amount of '*normal* unit-profit'.

In those mainstream texts where this specific assumption is somehow made explicit, the concept of *firm's 'normal profit'* is usually understood as 'the cost of the firm's (financial) capital factor'; meaning by that 'the opportunity cost of the investment made by the firm's owners'. That opportunity cost would consist of a certain rate of interest (*i*) on such financial capital invested, *FCI*, (which would be equivalent to the 'Equity' amount on a balance sheet of a firm); thereby, *i x FCI*. Therefore, when this assumption/definition is made in this or that text or manual, whether explicitly or tacitly, the authors are understanding by 'average cost' the usual concept itself plus a 'normal' unit profit equal to $(i \times FCI)/q$. Within this standard theoretical context, the abovementioned interest rate (*i*) is supposed to be 'that of equilibrium in the capital market', which, in turn, in the ESM is also assumed to be perfect ('any person who wants to become an entrepreneur in a certain industry has access to borrow the necessary capital, at the market interest rate').

Certainly, such an interest rate (*i*) is just a theoretical variable, not observable in practice, among other things because the required assumptions that imply to postulate 'a *perfect capital market*' do not fit in with what we can observe in the reality of a market economy – which is what the theory is supposed to describe. That is not, however, the only relevant remark to make in this respect. We will complete this discussion in Chapter 4.

What has been reviewed and summarised so far, in this and the previous section, configures a map of assumptions, axioms, and deductive hypotheses (in the sense of not defended based on empirical observations). This map draws the set of conditions, the scenario, of what in standard economics/ economic theory is understood as the 'perfect competition' model. This theoretical description of the workings of a market economic system leaves out, as noted before, just what the ESM considers to be 'exceptional cases': products or services for which the market demand size, *Q* units of product/service, is clearly lower than the units corresponding to the *optimal scale* for an enterprise producing such product/service: q^{os} units. This means that, for this kind of goods/situations, competition is not only technically impossible but also that it is more economical (in terms of unit cost) for a single enterprise to produce and cover the total demand. That is what is technically known as *natural monopoly* situations. We will pay special attention to these ESM exceptions in section 4.2 – mainly because they do not seem actually to be so exceptional.

2.3 What underpins the ESM's conventional assumption of "*decreasing returns* when firms grow beyond a given point"

As we have seen, the theoretical assumption of '*decreasing returns*' (i.e., *increasing* long-run average cost), in the production of any good, starting from a certain comparatively small volume of units compared to the market demand size for such a good, is the key to later postulating automatism towards competitive markets in general. For illustrative purposes:

> ".. in the case of decreasing cost industries [also phrased as *non-convexities*' situations], no long run competitive equilibrium can exist …", (Mas-Colell et al., 1995, p. 336); ".. if the efficient scale of operation is large relative to the size of market demand, it could well turn out that the equilibrium number of active firms is small. In these cases, we may reasonably question the appropriateness of the price taking assumption..." (p. 338)

It will probably come as not too much of a surprise that the non-fulfilment of such a traditional assumption of '*decreasing returns*' had been already pointed out by leading economists. Moreover, this remark has usually been done by them underlining precisely the opposite situation, *increasing returns*, as a relevant reality observed in the economic world; either as an evident general reality, or as a possibility more or less relevant as for its scope (first quotation above?). Something, in any case, that should be taken into account when dealing with the standard model. The former stance (increasing returns as a general reality) would be the case, for example, of Blaug (1968, p. 465; 1985, pp 456-7); and perhaps of Arrow himself – who together with Debreu (also Nobel laureate in Economics, 1983) brought the mathematical rigour of the model of General Competitive Equilibrium, and of the specific assumptions required by it, to the maximum– when he stated:

> " .. (to) deplore the failure of David Ricardo and his mainline successors to grasp this important aspect of Smith's thought. (..). *David Ricardo completely ignores the presence of increasing returns*, and it is Ricardo more than any other single individual who has set the tone of modern economics."

> "It was Cournot (1838) who first explicitly classified the laws of return. He was primarily interested in the effects of returns on pricing and output, the theory of value as we may say. One hundred and sixty years later, not a great deal has been added to Cournot's work, which, along with Mill's, was the main source for Alfred Marshall's synthesis. There are many individual observations of great importance in Marshall's work, many more than in Cournot or Mill, but the *increasing returns passages remain isolated from Marshall's central core of competitive equilibrium theory*. Arrow, 2000, p. 172;

Nevertheless, it is the traditional, 'Ricardian' model of decreasing returns (i.e., the 'law' of increasing long-run average cost) that continues to dominate the academic/professional landscape in Economics. It is therefore worth examining the basis of this traditional assumption more closely.

What are the specific arguments of today's standard economics/ economic theory for, nevertheless, continuing to postulate, maintaining such an unreal as determinant assumption as «when a firm continues to grow beyond a certain *'optimal size'*, *decreasing returns* appear»? When these deep-rooted arguments are made explicit in this or that manual – since most often they are given simply as something obvious, already established by previous authors – again they consist, as we will see, of deductive assumptions; i.e., they come not as inferred from real situations or cases but referring to imagined examples. These underpinning deductive assumptions are basically one of the two following or both (it depends on the manual we take):

i. The assumption that, from a certain size, the company is less efficient because it becomes 'too big, unmanageable'.

ii. The assumption that for the production of any good 'there always is a 'limiting (fixed) factor of production'.

Here it follows a briefing of both:

i. The assumption that "*the company becomes too big*" is the most popular in standard economics/microeconomics textbooks. Its more usual line of argument is of the following type: «For a given good/industry/sector, there is an *efficient/optimal scale* for a producer firm: q^{os} units of product-per-period. If the company grows beyond this size then it becomes 'a too complex organisation', and as a consequence *diseconomies of scale* start to arise in the form of more-than-proportional increases in *management costs* (costs of organising, supervising, controlling and coordinating the productive and commercial activities of the company) as well as of bureaucratic dysfunctions. By way of example:

"Diseconomies of scale can arise because of *coordination* problems that are inherent in any large organization. The more cars Ford produces, the more stretched the management team becomes, and the less effective managers become at keeping costs down" (Mankiw et al. 2006: 289).

For many readers it will come out as fairly obvious that the above theoretical proposition – emergence of diseconomies of scale in management/controlling costs when the firm becomes 'too big' – is in contradiction with any close observation of business reality[7]. What we can observe overall is rather the opposite: that companies tend toward growth as much as their sales possibilities allow them; and, as profit-driven undertakings, if they do so it will be for reasons of economic advantages (profits)*.

* ***Remark:*** *The very existence of large industrial and services companies, as well as giant commercial chains, provide us direct evidence of the above. Though, they are not exceptional cases in this respect. The same trend toward indefinite growth as a source of economic advantages is widely observed as the usual pattern of enterprises' behaviour and decision making in general. In any case, large corporations, with their complex organisation, are representatives of the fact that the costs of organising, managing and controlling (in short,* ***management costs****) do not tend to grow more than proportionally to the corporation's volume of activity; or that, if this actually happens to some extent regarding some of these costs, this is more than offset by economies in other types of costs (because of buying production factors on a larger scale, or having reached market power, for example). In fact, mergers would come to show that, in general, the opposite is rather true: by the resulting company becoming a larger organisation, management costs tend then to be proportionally lower; partially because the resulting corporation does not need to maintain (duplicate) some prior management positions as well as certain related internal services.*

ii. As for the other standard argument – the assumption that there is always *'a fixed factor of production,* necessary to produce the

[7] It is significant, for example, that Mankiw does not support the above statement, which he illustrates by making reference to the Ford Company, with no empirical reference to/from Ford itself, or to any other company. It must therefore be deduced that he simply imagines(ed) that this is how things happen in Ford; that is, in the world of (large) companies. Thus, the apparent empirical/observational character of his example is not such; it is actually an imagined, invented, example.

good in question, *that is available, to any producer firm, in a limited quantity*, this is indeed the most traditional (old) argumentation in economics and microeconomics manuals to sustain the deductive hypothesis of *decreasing returns* as something general.

Since David Ricardo[8], and later on Alfred Marshall (who generalised it by formalising his mathematical model of competitive equilibrium), such deductive reasoning is illustrated by an abstract, imagined, example referring to some agricultural production. The typical purpose-built example, and the deductive reasoning underpinning it, use to go commonly as follows: ' … if a coffee plantation goes increasing its production, at a certain point it would be driven to use those parts of its land less suitable for coffee farming; and therefore it will run into decreasing returns (rising average cost). So, if coffee plantations compete in the coffee market, each would expand until it runs into the referred limitations in the form of rising costs and thus diminishing profits. Consequently, the coffee market will end by being shared by many plantations, all with the same unit cost, ...[9]'.

Nevertheless, this more traditional deductive assumption is not corroborated by observable experience either. In fact, in no economics/microeconomics manual will we find, as an illustration/ basis of the argument, an example referring to a real case. Nor are they found in Ricardo's texts, or Marshall's, for example (as we will see later, in 3.5). To start with, such an assumption is based on the axiom that each 'plantation' competes with the others; which lacks realism regarding the agricultural business market. It

---

[8] Ricardo formulated his deductive theory of 'decreasing returns because of a limiting factor' by making reference to wheat farming in the Great Britain of his time; i.e., first half of the 19th century. Wheat, and other cereal grain cropping, had got special relevance in England on the occasion of the parliamentary debates on the 'Corn Laws'; see, e.g., Blaug (1957, p. 12). We will return on this historical root, especially in 3.5(2).

[9] I have summarised the usual abstract example, as discussed by Brian Arthur in his critical work on the topic: Arthur (1996, p. 101).

is self-evident that it is not 'plantations', or farms, (a certain area of land, in a certain location, with a certain dedication of human and material resources) that act (compete) in the market, but their owners (agricultural enterprises). Thus, an enterprise /entrepreneur owning a coffee plantation that wants to increase its production beyond what 'its' present availability of suitable land allows can buy another plantation, or rent it, or buy a firm owning another plantation; or, more generally – as is easily observed – to buy or rent other equally suitable lands; since the axiom itself that the existing type of suitable land is limited (with respect to what demand for the product? the domestic one?) is also not generally observed.[10]

Remark: *The same above counter-argument is applicable in the case the imagined example in a standard textbook – for 'a limiting fixed factor'– refers to the other major primary sector: extractive activities, such as the oil or coal industries. Certainly, a specific coal pit or mine, for example, has certain quantitative possibilities regarding tons of commercially-standard ore to extract, say, per quarter; and this over a certain number of years. However, if the firm (person) that owns that pit wants to place a greater quantity in the market, it is not observed that the firm try to force the exploitation of this single pit to produce more and more tons of standard-quality coal at a unit-cost becoming more and more expensive. What is rather observed is that the firm resorts to exploiting or opening other pits; either on its own land or other rented. Or it buys other coal pits, or other firms owning pits, etc. To ignore this evidence amounts to assuming that the people owning a pit behave – as entrepreneurs – in a stupid way (forcing the exploitation of 'the pit').*

[10] By way of example, Guatemala produced 204 million kg of coffee in the 2015/16 campaign, while its internal consumption was 7 times lower. More generally, overall observation of the sector shows that coffee is basically an export product for producer countries. Moreover, it has long been traded by big companies; especially over recent decades when a few trademarks/companies have become to control most of the coffee market on an international level.

> *In any case, neither in the coal nor the iron nor the oil sector is it observed that the technical features typical of extractive industries have led to a situation of 'many small mining/extracting firms, each owning a single mine, pit or well, constituting together a mass of suppliers of similar size in the market'. The opposite is rather true: in most countries, these primary sectors are dominated by large companies (more on this in section 3.5(2).*

In conclusion, it is not 'plantations', farms, mines, pits, or wells that act in (and configure the structure of) the market, but the people or companies that own (usually numerous) plantations, wells, pits. etc.. Nowadays and in Ricardo's and Marshall's times. More in general, this traditional deductive assumption of 'a limiting fixed factor of production' amounts to systematically presupposing that the availability of land with the required characteristics to rise an agricultural product traditionally produced in the country is less than that necessary to cover domestic demand; as well as to assuming that there is no possibility of importing the product in question. This set of assumptions is as unrealistic at present as it was in the 19th century (more on this in section 3.5). In any case –and maintaining the focus, for the sake of tradition, on the farming sector– a business behaviour of "moving to making use of less and less suitable land" is something simply not historically observed in practice. In the same way, and for the same reason, that we do not observe agricultural undertakings producing coffee or mangoes in, for example, The Netherlands or Bulgaria. Certainly, one could theorise about how the unit-costs of mangoes produced by an enterprise in Bulgaria would behave, in the imaginary case that these enterprises existed (one could imagine the use of sophisticated greenhouses). Though it is difficult to see how useful this theorisation would be.

To sum up, the 'U' hypothesis of mainstream economics, 'in the production of any good, *decreasing returns* (long-run average-cost rising progressively) appear, starting from a certain volume of units or size of the producer enterprise', relies upon assumptions (diseconomies due to the firm becoming 'too large an organisation' and/or due to a 'limiting fixed production factor' always existing) that are clearly unrealistic.

> "Most economics students are not required to study psychology, philosophy, history, or politics. They are spoon-fed models of the economy, based on unreal assumptions, and tested on their competence in solving mathematical equations. They are never given the mental tools to grasp the whole picture."
> (Robert Skidelsky, "Economics versus the Economy", Project Syndicate, Dec 23, 2016.

(I must apologise for having partially entered here –last paragraphs, and especially the two 'remarks'– into empirical contrasting, breaking so the afore stated discursive plan for this text. The aim of this chapter, as pointed out at the beginning, is just to summarise how mainstream economics/ESM explains the functioning of the world of production, companies, and markets; not actually to discuss those explanations at this stage. That will be in the next chapters. However, regarding the specific topic dealt with in this section, the simple observations of the real economic world are so direct and general that it seemed 'obliged' to make reference here to the most obvious aspects of the contradiction of the standard assumption regarding the real world).

Let us close this incursion into the more obvious findings that result from contrasting the standard axiom of 'decreasing returns' with observations of the real economic world, and return to the overview of the explanatory model of mainstream economics/ economic-theory.

2.4 The 'production function', a math device to also speak of 'returns to scale'

The conventional assumption of 'decreasing returns' is also related to another independent core piece of the standard model: the *production function*. The standard argument behind the drawings in figures 1 and 3 connects with how the concept of 'production function' is formally defined and used in mainstream economics; or the reverse: the production function somehow connects with such diagrams.

"Since the 1870s economics has been bedevilled by the idea that it should give itself the appearance of resemble Newtonian physics ...", (Fullbrook, 2007, p. 2). The standard 'Cobb-Douglas' *production function* is likely the better example (the second one could be the 'utility function') about that neoclassical founders' tenet of re-building economics (economic theory) according to an epistemology resembling physics'. Such a *production function* is indeed an ambitious economics mathematical construct that does seem inspired by physics formulae. Rather than referring to monetary values, it is intended to describe, in abstract terms, nothing less than the technical quantitative relationship between the units of inputs (production factors) employed and the units of output (a given product) obtained as a result; and this for any good in the economy! In economics texts the most common in this regard is to simplify by implicitly talking about 'production' in the specific sense of 'manufacturing'; i.e., that the good in consideration is a material or manufactured product, for example, 'steel' or 'cars'.

To start by the classical formulation, the standard Cobb-Douglas (C-D) *production function* entails the simplification/assumption that the good in question is produced out of just two inputs, Capital and Labour, together with the assumption of a specific mathematical expression –a multiplicative-exponential function – that would link the units of output with the units of inputs. This expression specifically entails that inputs 'Capital' and 'Labour' – so considered, in abstract terms– may be combined in whatever proportion to produce a given volume of the good in question: something less of one input may be compensated with something more of the other. What is usually termed as 'the firm moving along indefinite technological options'. Such a conventional C-D (two inputs) math expression is

$$Y = a \cdot K^{\alpha} \cdot L^{\beta}$$

where ***Y*** stands for the units of the product obtained (e.g., tons of steel) by a firm, ***K*** symbolises the units of input 'Capital' the firm has installed (machinery, equipment, production facilities, etc., though considered in abstract or monetary units), ***L*** stands for the units of input Labour employed by the firm (also in aggregate terms: for example, the number of workers hours). And $\boldsymbol{a}$, $\boldsymbol{\alpha}$ and $\boldsymbol{\beta}$ are parameters, associated with the good in question. Parameter '$\boldsymbol{a}$' is understood to reflect the technological development level at the time (regarding the production of such a good); while parameters $\boldsymbol{\alpha}$ and $\boldsymbol{\beta}$ are assumed to be positive, below 1 – since, according to the math expression, they may be interpreted as the *elasticity* of the volume of output with regard to increases in one or the other input: thus, $\beta = 0.6$ would mean than, say, 10% increase in the units of Labour – keeping constant the units of Capital – will result in 6% increase of the units of output produced[11].

As it might have been noticed, the standard C-D mathematical expression does not result from neoclassical economists having observed some given patterns through studies on the production of this or that good. The expression is just the result of the abovementioned deductive, theoretical, assumptions. Moreover, inputs so normally present in most production activities, as different types of energy, materials (raw materials, intermediate goods, parts, ..), and industrial services, are absent from this standard function. Or it is assumed that they are someway subsumed within the abstract

[11] Formally expressed: ΔL; -> $a \cdot K^{\alpha} \cdot (L + \Delta L)^{\beta} = Y + \Delta Y$; $\rightarrow (Y + \Delta Y)/Y \equiv (L + \Delta L)^{\beta} / L^{\beta} \equiv [(L + \Delta L)/L]^{\beta}$, $\rightarrow$ $\rightarrow ln[(Y + \Delta Y)/Y] = \beta \cdot ln[(L + \Delta L)/L]$; $\rightarrow$ (rate of increase in *output*) $= \beta \cdot$ (rate of increase in *Labour*)

aggregates of either 'Capital' or of 'Labour'; or, simply, that the function is just an oversimplification[12]. Nevertheless, in mainstream economics, the above elegant formulation allows to speak precisely of the sign of the *returns to scale* (decreasing, constant, or increasing) in the production of a good. The reasoning for this consists of pure mathematical deductions from the above expression.

A first deduction builds on the fact that the partial derivative of the function with respect to variable L may be interpreted as an expression of the *marginal physical productivity of Labour*. That is, the increase in the output (ΔY) when one of the inputs, Labour, is increased in one unit –the other input, Capital, maintained constant. This partial derivative is $a \cdot \beta \cdot (K^{\alpha} / L^{1-\beta})$, which, as can be seen[13], will have a lower value, the higher the units of Labour. In plain language, the volume of Capital installed by the producer firm taken as fixed, the *marginal physical productivity of Labour* (in units of product) will always be – according to the C-D function – decreasing; which entails that for successively obtaining one more unit of product, the required increase in the units of Labour will be higher and higher. And, thereby, the average cost of the product will go increasing.

A second math deduction from the C-D function that also speaks of returns to scale takes as starting point the sum of parameters α and β. This deduction requires, however, supposing that the proportion between both inputs is kept constant. That is, that a given relative

[12] This initial expression was afterwards extended to more than two inputs –as we will see further on; but the main analytical results in this regard can be illustrated with the classical Cobb-Douglas formulation.

[13] $Y = a \cdot K^{\alpha} \cdot L^{\beta}$; $\frac{\delta Y}{\delta L} = a \cdot K^{\alpha} \cdot \beta \cdot L^{\beta-1} \equiv a \cdot K^{\alpha} \cdot \beta \cdot \frac{1}{L^{1-\beta}}$; as a partial derivative, it implies that the units of the other factor, *K*, are kept constant; as well as the rest of terms; thereby, the greater *L* the lower $\delta Y/\delta L$ (since $\beta<1$). In other terms, the second partial derivative of the function with respect to Labour is always negative: $\frac{\delta^2 Y}{\delta L^2} = a \cdot K^{\alpha} \cdot \beta \cdot (\beta - 1) \cdot \frac{1}{L^{2-\beta}} < 0$
Symmetrically, all the above can equally be asserted regarding input Capital considered as the variable input. That is, when the units of Labour are taken as fixed and the units of Capital as successively increased.

increase in the units of Labour comes necessarily accompanied by an increase of the same proportion in the units of Capital. Under such a condition of a given, fixed, proportion between the units of Capital and Labour, it can be deduced from the math C-D expression that[14]: when $\alpha+\beta=1$, a given proportional increase of the units of both inputs (independent variables, K and L) generates an increase of the same proportion in the output (dependent variable, Y). What means a situation of *constant returns* to scale. Alternatively, if $\alpha+\beta<1$, the increase in Y will be less than proportional; thereby describing a situation of *decreasing returns*. And when $\alpha+\beta>1$, the increase in Y will be more than proportional (*increasing returns* to scale).

Without such a condition of a fixed proportion between the inputs i.e., if we return to the C-D initial definition entailing that any proportion between the inputs is possible to efficiently produce the output– then the above mathematical deductions about the sum of parameters α and β as an indicator of the sign of the returns to scale simply do not apply.

As the previous paragraphs may have suggested, there is a sort of ambiguity or contradiction between the above two formal postulates derived from the traditional *production function*, and the function itself. The first postulate talks about *returns to scale* when one of the factors is fixed; specifically, the stock of Capital; which entails indeed different proportions between the units of Capital and Labour, but in a restrictive way; not properly in line with the function's basic assumption of 'perfect substitutability of inputs' ('any proportion

[14] Proportion between inputs: $p=\frac{K}{L}$; → $K=p\cdot L$; → $\equiv \frac{\delta Y}{\delta L}=a\cdot\beta\cdot p^{\alpha}\cdot\frac{L^{\alpha}}{L^{1-\beta}}$ $\frac{\delta Y}{\delta L}=(a\cdot\beta\cdot p^{\alpha})\cdot L^{\alpha+\beta-1}$

Therefore, under such a condition of a fixed proportion of inputs: the increase in output when, for example, Labour is increased in one worker, is constant when $\alpha+\beta=1$, whatever the volume of inputs (L, K) be. The growth in Y is less than proportional when $\alpha+\beta<1$ (since exponent for variable L is then negative), and progressively so the greater the volume of inputs be. And, when $\alpha+\beta>1$, the growth in Y is more than proportional, and progressively so the greater the volume of inputs be.

of inputs is technically possible'). Nevertheless, this postulate gives way to the key lemma in mainstream economics of 'marginal physical productivity of Labour is decreasing'. As for the second postulate – about the sum of parameters α and β as an indicator for the sign of returns to scale – is based on assuming that the proportion between the units of inputs Capital and Labour is constant; i.e., that there is not any kind of inputs substitutability in play, contrarily to what is implied in the basic C-D definition.

Those apparent ambiguities or contradictions raise the question of whether the production function itself, and these two postulates, must be understood as referring to the short-run of a producer firm, the long-run, or both. For example, would the first postulate specifically refer to the short-run, that is, to an *operating company*, at a given time?

The postulate on *'marginal physical productivity of labour'*

Regarding the first postulate – where it is assumed that one of the inputs, Capital stock, is fixed and the units of the other, Labour, are variable, it suggests a *short-run* scenario. That is, a static analysis; the one of figure 1: at a given time a firm is producing with a given technology. That means it has set up a series of equipment and production facilities, within some premises (*Capital* endowment, K); which will entail a given production capacity. Consequently, the firm will have hired a certain number of workers to run such equipment. (More precisely, it will have hired a certain number of employees with different backgrounds, tasks, and wages. But let us continue with the standard simplification of referring to an abstract aggregate of 'workers'/'labour', for the sake of comparability).

This reading of the C-D production function somehow matches the standard explanatory scheme on the unit costs *in-the-short-run* in Figure 1, since there the stock of Capital (the installed equipment, facilities, etc.) is also considered as given (constant). However, this correspondence is only partial. As we have seen, the standard argument behind Figure 1 is, in short, that, when a producer company, e.g. a carmaker, is operating below its full occupancy level, by successively adding a certain number of worker-hours (i.e., a given increase in variable costs) to operate the existing stock of capital, the company gets more-than-proportional successive increases in the number of cars produced (average variable cost per car diminishes). But this to a certain point, where the successive increases in the number of cars produced become lower and lower (average variable cost of a car becomes increasing: 'diminishing marginal returns'). Such a *point* (q^{to} in figure 1) is related to the full normal occupancy level of the installed Capital stock. It would be just from this volume of production onward that the standard argument on the behaviour of unit-costs *in the short run* correlates with the first postulate of the C-D production function. That is, just from such a volume of production beyond which marginal cost becomes to grow.

This pointing out here the relationship between the math construct of the standard 'production function' and that of the unit-costs 'functions' (drawings in figure 1) in the standard model does not respond to a simple technical note. Such connection is indeed the reasoning underpinning the so-called, in mainstream economics, 'law of diminishing marginal product of Labour'; which, as we have seen above, is just a label for the 'first partial derivative of the *production function* with respect to input Labour'. This purely mathematical deduction has indeed a central role in the ESM's theory on employment and salaries. Such a theoretical concept of *(diminishing) marginal physical productivity of labour* is formally used in modern neoclassical economics (within the topic: 'salary-and-employment-of-equilibrium') as the value that would /should determine nothing less than 'the fair salary for an industry's workers': 'the market value of the marginal product of Labour'. In short, this C-D math definition form plays anyway a key role in the ESM.

> 'The production function is arguably the heart of neoclassical theory because only it can "disentangle" the distinct product of labour from that of capital[15] (...) (but, in the real world of production) specific workers use specific equipment to carry out production. The contribution of capital cannot then be separated from that of labor.' (Schlefer: 106).

(We will return on this determinant normative topic of mainstream economics in section 3.3).

Nevertheless, from a more general outlook, interpreting the standard C-D production function as referred or applicable to the short-run scenario entails a contradiction. Firstly regarding the basic premise of the mathematical expression itself, 'a firm producing a (any) given good is able to operate adapting its production process, moving along a continuum of changing proportions of the factors, *capital* and *labour*, according to a greater or lower volume of units of good to produce in each period'. Or we should conclude that the above basic premise is simply unrealistic if the production function is interpreted as referred to the short-run.

> 'The notion of the production function and the possibility of substituting one factor for another seem to be a kind of academic lore passed down sotto voce from one classroom to the next' (Schlefer, 112).

Otherwise, such a 'substitutability' would imply to assume that, say, from month to month a firm may change its technology like when it changes its fuel provider.

---

[15] Formally, the first partial derivative of Y with respect to L; and the equivalent regarding K: $Y = a \cdot K^{\alpha} \cdot L^{\beta}; \rightarrow \frac{\delta Y}{\delta L} = a \cdot K^{\alpha} \cdot \beta \cdot L^{\beta-1} \equiv a \cdot K^{\alpha} \beta \cdot \frac{1}{L^{1-\beta}}$ and, in parallel: $\frac{\delta Y}{\delta K} = a \cdot L^{\beta} \cdot \alpha \cdot \frac{1}{K^{1-\alpha}}$

The postulate regarding *returns to scale*

An alternative reading of the standard C-D production function would consist of taking it as an extreme over-simplified mathematical model referring to the *long-run* scenario for a producer firm. This could 'a priori' make sense insofar as the function assumes that there is always a continuum of different possibilities (technologies) to produce a good; which entails different proportions between the metaphorical aggregates capital and labour. From this dynamic analysis' perspective, within the context of modern neoclassical economics, it is implicitly understood that a simple, low-scale technology would proportionally require more *'labour'* and less *'capital'* than a complex, mechanised-automated, high-scale, one – the term technology here understood in its usual engineering meaning.

The first problem regarding this reading of the standard C-D production function is that in the real world there is not a continuum of indefinite technologies available to produce a given good. What can actually be observed in general are situations where there exist just several, some given, cost-efficient technological options available at a time to produce a certain good; options mainly differing in the degree of automation/ robotising of processes, as well as in the production capacity each option allows for. Nevertheless, to continue exploring this alternative reading of the standard mathematical function, it could be taken as a highly abstract model to symbolise (rather than to describe) the world of production; a model that, moreover, by theorists adding to it some variables representing inputs' prices, gives way in mainstream mathematical economics to, equally highly-abstract and assumptions-depending, costs functions.

In this 'in-the-long-run' interpretation of the standard C-D function, there is not, however, much place for talking about decreasing returns to scale when $\alpha + \beta < 1$, etc., since the deductive postulate regarding the sum of exponents relies on assuming that the proportion between Capital and Labour remains constant as the firm moves along strategic decisions of either expanding or downsizing its volume of production. Or the reverse: since the production function would then be understood as reflecting several, 'indefinite' technological options for a firm at the time, then parameters α and β would logically be different for each of these 'technologies', i.e., for different points in the function; which is just contradictory with the postulate regarding the sum of exponents as an indicator about returns to scale (see note 14).

A more up-to-date and something less abstract C-D type production function, encompassing more than two inputs, as the also standard $Y = a\cdot (K^{\alpha 1}\cdot L^{\alpha 2}\cdot E^{\alpha 3}\cdot M^{\alpha 4}\cdot S^{\alpha 5})$ –where E, M, and S stand for the units of new aggregates: 'Energy', 'Materials', and 'Services'– does not substantially change the above remarks: parameters αi would be different when considering points of the function corresponding to different technologies, and, thereby, to different proportions among the five factors in the function. In short, in a dynamic analysis, into an in-the-long-run interpretation of the neoclassical production function, its *parameters* would actually not be such but rather *variables* in the function. This means, among other implications, that the sum of them will a priori have no specific meaning regarding the issue of 'returns to scale'.

In short, the standard production function's premise of inputs exchangeability – which entails that the proportion between inputs may be arbitrarily changed – is in full contradiction with interpreting and using the function to mathematically side-support the axiom of the 'decreasing returns to scale in the long run' that the classical figure 3 depicts. To sum up, the basic idea behind the C-D production function – that any mix of inputs is possible for a firm to produce some given units of a good; or, in other words, that there is always a series of indefinite *alternative technologies* to produce a good – does rather remit, even if metaphorically, to the *long-run* scenario for a firm. But then to use the function to talk about decreasing returns *in the long-run* 'in the case $\alpha + \beta < 1$', etc., (were it actually possible to determine such exponents in a real case) entails a formal contradiction. The sum of such parameters might have a meaning in that sense, but provided we assume just the opposite scenario: that the proportion between inputs is kept constant; which equals to say that just one only technology is feasible to apply. Something that, when a firm moves towards greater volumes of production, growing in size and adopting a higher automated – and cheaper – technology, simply does not happen.

The Leontief's alternative production function

The so called 'Leontief production function' was retrieved by the author in 1953 from former works on the topic, and more formally stated, as a rejection to the above orthodox neoclassical economics' C-D function. It builds mainly on the idea that the pattern in the world of production is that of fixed proportions between the different inputs required to produce a given commodity by a firm; in a similar manner as for a chemical reaction:

$$Y = \min\,[(1/a_1)\cdot X_1,\ (1/a_2)\cdot X_2,\ \ldots.,\ (1/a_n)\cdot X_n]$$

where $\mathbf{X}_i$ stand for the units of each of the different, n, inputs actually used or consumed, in a given period, to produce Y units of the good in question; and $\boldsymbol{a}_i$. are parameters. More precisely, a_1, a_2, ... a_n are *technical coefficients*; this concept so familiar within the industrial world: the units of each input that are strictly necessary to produce one unit of output. The form '*min(...)*' stands here for expressing just an efficiency condition: that the units of each factor really utilised or consumed, X_i , is such that the difference X_i - $a_i x Y$ be minimum.. The relationship with the Leontief's famous previous (1930's) contribution, the 'input-output tables' are quite evident in this formulation.

As can be seen, the above function is properly not an operational mathematical expression but just a definition of efficiency in production activities, expressed in mathematical language. A definition that implies fixed proportions among the units of the required inputs; that is, fixed input/output proportions; with an exception: at least one of these X_i units, capital stock's, is assumed to be fixed. Therefore, Leontief expression should be understood as rather referred to *the short-run*; i.e., a producer undertaking which is operating with a given technology.

The fact that the function above is basically a definition that fixes quantitative conditions rather than a general math expression is compatible with it being right applicable to efficiency measuring in real cases. Put schematically:

Period: ... ; Units of OUTPUT: Q					
INPUT	Technical coefficient	Units used/ consumed	Efficiency target	Efficiency deviation (-)	Rate of occupancy
1	a_1	X_1	$a_1 \times Y$	$X_1 - (a_1 \times Y)$	
2	a_2	X_2	$a_2 \times Y$	$X_2 - (a_2 \times Y)$	
3	a_3	X_3	$a_3 \times Y$	$X_3 - (a_3 \times Y)$	
:	:	:	:	:	
Capital stock	a_k	X_k (fixed)			$(a_k \times Y)/ X_k$

Nevertheless, most of the later developments of this Leontief production function in the economics literature (economic theory/ economic analysis)[16] consist of transforming its formulation into an operational mathematical expression through introducing deductive

[16] An outlook on this may be found in Ferran Sancho (2019) "An Armington-Leontief model", *Journal of Economic Structures*, 8, 25 (2019). https://doi.org/10.1186/s40008-019-0158-y; and/ or in the survey by Mustafin and Kantarbayeva (2018), "Opening the Leontief's black box", Heiyon, 4(5), 1-28. https://doi.org/10.1016/j.heliyon.2018.e00626 .

assumptions and simplified situations; among the latter, for example, that of assuming just two inputs, like with the previous C-D function.

An interpretation or reading of the function as referred to a dynamic scenario – in the *middle to long-run* – implies to consider that the producer firm goes changing the technology it is operating with; or, simply, that the firm is incorporating innovations in processes and/or regarding the type of inputs. Either way, that entails that the set of technical coefficients ai will change, as well as that the set of specific inputs themselves can also be different – like it usually rather happens, because of the conjunction of technological progress and firms' growth policies.

2.5 The 'Supply Curve' and the standard formulation of 'market equilibrium' in the ESM

Let us continue with the summary of the ESM, its axioms, and assumptions. The large 'U-shaped' enveloping curve in Figure 3 – an abstract representation of the *'long-run' average cost function* for a firm that produces a given good, *LRAC(q)* – interpreted as the *'industry's average cost function', IC(Q),* is in turn the connection of all of the above with the market of the good in question – where *Q* represents the sum of the units produced by all the firms in the *sector* or *industry*. Let us remark that in this stage the abstract term 'industry' (of good 'x') becomes interpreted as the 'sector': the set or enterprises that produce the good in question. This concept-diagram plays such a role by deriving from it a new theoretical-graphic concept: the *supply curve,* or *supply function's* representation, for the good under consideration.

2.5.1 The standard *supply function*

The concept of supply curve/function refers to the total number of units of product that the set of active firms in the industry will/would offer, as a whole, (Q_s) at a given market-price (P_s). That is, the sum of the quantities of the good offered to supply by every sector's firm, as a function of the market selling price: $Q_s(P_s)$. Or, to put it the other way round – which is the most common in economics texts, the market selling price for which the sum of quantities produced/offered by the sector's firms will be a given total quantity; i.e.: the offering price of the firms as a whole, as a function of the total quantity to be produced and supplied to the market, $P_s(Q_s)$. This latter version is the one normally taken in economics texts as industry's *supply curve/function* for a good. It is specifically defined in the theoretical context of mainstream economics as just equal to a part of the long-run (or Industry's) *marginal cost* curve *(LRMC(q),* represented by the blue dashed curve in former figure 3) for the good in question. More specifically, equal to its 'right-side' stretch: from the volume of units of the corresponding efficient/optimal scale, q^{os}, on; i.e., that stretch of units associated to *'decreasing returns'* (shaded area in the diagram in figure 3).

Let us look at the reasoning behind such a definition, 'industry's *Supply curve* ≡ Long-run *Marginal Cost* (growing stretch)'. As we have seen, in the standard approach it is assumed –mainly via graphic language– that the 'enveloping curve', the long-run *average cost, LRAC(q),* for any good, behaves according to a function in the form of a perfect parabola of vertical axis (the 'U-shaped' hypothesis). Whereby, by generic mathematical deduction, its associated *marginal cost, LRMC(q),* will also be a vertical parabola. And that is the way it is represented in the standard model (dashed blue curve, in figure 3). This parabola (mathematical deduction tells us) goes below the former, for volumes of units lower than q^{os} units; and then above, for higher production volumes; i.e., marginal cost curve, *LRMC(q),* will cross (coincide with) average cost curve, *LRAC(q)*, for $q=q^{os}$ units; the point where the latter (*LRAC*) reaches precisely its minimum (see diagram in next figure 4).

Why to define, in the ESM, the *supply* curve (function) for a good precisely as equal to (a part of) the long-run *marginal cost* curve (function)? Let us remind ourselves that one core axiom of the standard model is that 'every firm –and therefore all those in a given industry/sector– operates with full efficiency (Appendix 1); which entails, as we have seen in section 2.2: in the short-run they operate minimizing its total costs, and in the long-run they adopt the economically optimal productive dimension for the concerned good' (point 2.2.2). According to this, every firm in the sector will end up having the same size/dimension, producing the same volume of units (q^{os}), and operating with the same, minimum, average cost; which, mathematically, will coincide with the corresponding marginal cost. None of them will be interested in producing more units, because their marginal cost, *which is increasing,* would make their average cost also to increase to some extent. And (the standard approach continues) that is what the growing *Long-run* (interpreted as *Industry's*) *marginal cost* represents: the unit cost for each firm increasing in one unit the volume of production. Hence the ESM deduction: 'such *marginal cost* will be the *selling price* required by producer firms for higher production volumes'.

As to why to take (as supply price *curve*) just the stretch of the marginal cost curve from the optimal scale (q^{os} units) on, this has to do with another of the axioms of the general equilibrium model we have reviewed in the previous chapter: that of 'for any good, with few exceptions, its market demand (for a price close to the minimum average cost), Q_d units of product, is (much) higher than the volume of units of the corresponding *efficient/optimal scale,* q^{os} units'. Thereby, to define the supply curve, the relevant stretch of the marginal cost curve is that corresponding to production volumes higher than q^{os} units; i.e., production volumes for which *decreasing returns to scale* are assumed in the ESM.

[At the risk of repeating myself: these ESM's axioms are usually not made explicit as such in most modern neoclassical textbooks. When the supply curve concept is introduced, mainly via graphical language, such axioms are simply taken for granted.]

The above is, in summary, the basis of the ESM's theoretical proposition that 'the ***supply*** *price* ***curve*** of a product in the market, $[P_s(Q_s)]$, comes given by the growing stretch of the long-run (interpreted as industry's) marginal cost, to the right of the optimal scale . I will allow myself to use the standard graphic language to summarise the above theoretical approach in this respect:

Figure 4: *Diagram of the ESM's deduction for the 'supply function'*

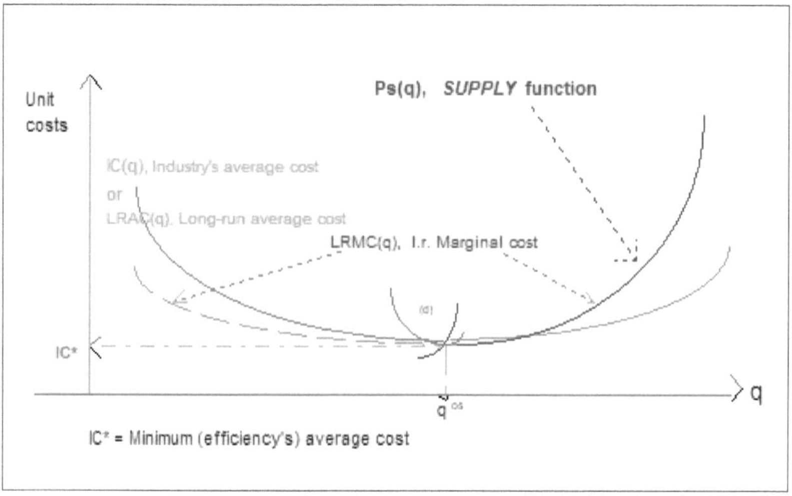

Translated from the graphical language, this definition means 'that, starting from q^{os} units, to offer a greater quantity of product in the market, the set of producing companies require, as a whole, a higher and higher price'. That is ultimately the meaning of the standard model assumption when representing (drawing) the *supply* price *function/curve* like a growing bent arch (encircled area).

[The reader might have detected inconsistency abut notation in the above diagram (as well as in the following one): '*q*' instead of '*Qs*', for meaning the total-sector units offered? This has precisely to do with the above remark 'interpreted-as', and the discussion in point 2.5.3]

2.5.2 The 'market's equilibrium point'

Returning to the ESM usual diagrams, finally, such a supply *curve/* function is then graphically confronted with a descending line representing the *demand function* for the good in question, $P_d(q)$[17]; thus giving rise in the standard model to the paradigmatic and popular diagram of the ***quantity and price of equilibrium***, as a representation of the *competitive market's equilibrium point* for a good:

Figure 4a: Usual diagram/formulation of the *Market Equilibrium point* in the ESM for a given product (Sector/Industry)

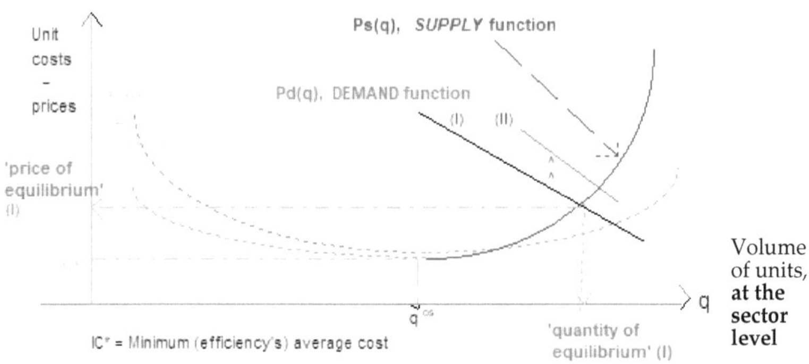

$P_s(q)$ Supply function: Price for which the sum of the quantities which each firm in the sector is willing to offer is equal to a certain volume of units of the product, *q*.

$P_d(q)$ Demand function: Price at which the sum of quantities demanded by all customers equals a given volume, q, of units of product. (Two alternative *demand functions* are represented in the diagram, I and II. They can be interpreted as corresponding to either two different possibilities or two different points in time.)

[17] Or, more precisely, the '*inverse* demand function'. The orthodox definition for the *demand function* itself refers to the quantity demanded as a function of the price, $q_d(P)$. They are thus two ways of looking to the same relationship; in graphical terms, the representation for $q_d(P)$ is the same than for Pd(q), simply exchanging the axis.

Regarding *demand functions, Pd(q),* they are usually represented in modern neoclassical textbooks by –and, therefore, defined as – either *linear* (as above), or convex (in the sense of the southwest arch of a circle) decreasing lines (functions). The linear option/definition implies the assumption that, for the good considered, the price-elasticity of demand[18] decreases as price goes down; That is, starting, f. e., from a comparatively high price, a given percentage of reduction in price generates a lower percentage of increase in the demanded quantity; the lower as we move along price reductions. As for the option/definition of a *convex* decreasing line, it is associated or compatible with assuming that price-elasticity of demand for the good in question is constant (e.g., equal to 1) whatever the market's price and quantity demanded.[19]

Returning to the *supply function*, as can be seen, this part of the standard model entails the assumption that, for the companies that produce a given good to increase the total volume of units offered into the market, they, as a whole, require a progressively higher selling price. Or, see it from the customer/buyer perspective, if the total demand for the good scale-up whichever the price – because of a change in customers preferences: they pass to more 'appreciating' the good in question – (case illustrated by demand function *II* in the above diagram 4a), the referred assumption implies that the unit-cost of the good will become higher for producers (sic), and thereby the product more expensive for customers.

2.5.3 Internal inconsistency

It must be pointed out here, however, that the above orthodox definition of the *supply curve/function* implies an internal inconsistency

[18] Price elasticity of demand, between two points $(P_0, q_0), (P_1, q_1)$, $\varepsilon = (\Delta q/q_0) / (\Delta P/P_0)$; where either the variation in price will be negative or the variation in quantity do; in any case, the absolute value of ε will thus have a negative sign. In a theoretical reasoning, we may assume both points to be infinitely close, and so expressing price elasticity in a given point of the function as $\varepsilon = (dq/dP) / (P \, . \, q)$

[19] Conversely, a *concave* line option – either for the whole demand function or for a stretch of it – would, be associated with assuming that the price-elasticity for the good concerned decreases as price goes dawn, though proportionally faster than in a linear option.

within the standard model itself. The concept so defined – and its use in the above standard diagram to represent market equilibrium – contradicts two central assumptions in the standard model, which at this point will already come out as familiar to us:

The first one, the assumption that 'in equilibrium, in the long-run, firms active in a given industry (product) will not be interested in having a productive dimension larger than the one that allows them to minimise the average cost (industry's *efficient/optimal scale* – firm's size or dimension 'd' in the graphical example of figures 3 and 4, associated with producing q^{os} units)'. Whereby, 'all the firms in the industry will end up by adopting such a size, and therefore operating with the same (minimum) average cost: *LRAC*, or *IC**, monetary units; which in turn will coincide with the respective marginal cost'. And the second one, the assumption that: 'there are no entry barriers for new firms (entrepreneurs) wanting to enter into such an industry' (see Appendix A).

From these two assumptions, it follows that the number of producer firms in the market (all of them operating at the same, minimum, average cost, *IC**) will be higher the higher market demand be – for a price equal or close to such an average cost. That is, these two core assumptions of the standard model logically lead to the (inner) deduction that in any industry 'there will be many offering enterprises, all of them with the *optimal scale* of production ('d', in diagrams 3 and 4), and, thereby, all of them operating with the minimum average cost in the industry'. So many offering enterprises as the demand size at the time allow for. Consequently, since the industry's supply function is arithmetically defined as the aggregate of the volume of units offered by every of the industry's enterprises at a given price, such a supply function, for total volumes of units higher than the corresponding q^{os} units, will be given by,

Total Supply (=total number of units offered, at industry level),

$$Q_s = (\textit{number of firms}) \times q^{oe};$$

Following this logical deduction from the two ESM's above assumptions, this aggregate volume of units would be offered by the *industry's* active enterprises as a whole at *a constant price* (IC* monetary units = industry's minimum average cost), rather than at a progressively increasing price. What comes to draw, as supply function, $P_s(Q_s)$, a flat, horizontal line, rather than an upward-bending curve. That is ultimately the internal inconsistency or formal contradiction.

Looking to the inconsistency in another way: to assume an upward supply curve ('the greater the volume of units to be offered by the *industry* as a whole, the higher the selling price required') implies that the 'equilibrium price' in the market be higher than the average cost of each for the enterprises that make up the industry, *IC** monetary units – as it can be visualised in figure 4a. Obviously, this would mean that all these industry's enterprises would be obtaining substantial profits: *P-IC** monetary units per unit of product ('extraordinary profits' in the ESM terminology). And this is in direct contradiction with the (other) basic assumption/proposition of the general equilibrium model: that, 'in equilibrium, for any good/product, it happens that the producer firms sell it at cost price: (market) *price (P) =average cost (IC*)=marginal cost*'.

In other terms, the fact of postulating – through graphical language in figure 3 – that the long-run average cost for a good/product, *LRAC(q)*, will increase if the firm's size grows beyond a certain point (the corresponding optimal scale) formally entails that the corresponding marginal cost will also increase (even more). But, to then deduce from this that the market *supply function* for the product, $P_s(q)$, will precisely be such a *marginal cost, LRMC(q)* for volumes of units beyond the optimal scale (q> q^{os} units) entails to implicitly assume a stupid behaviour by producer firms. In other words, it *is contradictory with the two aforementioned core assumptions of the standard model itself*. Or, the *upward* supply price function entails *confusing the concept of unit-cost in the long run* (*LRAC*: an enterprise adjusts its size over time by pursuing the most economic productive dimension) *with that of industry's unit-cost* (IC: average of the unit costs of the enterprises that make up the industry or sector): precisely under the assumption of 'decreasing returns' (increasing 'long-run average cost, figures 3 and 4), both concepts (*LRAC* and *IC*) are no longer quantitatively equivalent –according to the standard model itself.

I must hasten to clarify that I am not discovering anything new by pointing out the above. Such internal inconsistency in the standard model, as regards the paradigmatic concept-postulate of the *supply* price *curve* as growing, has long been pointed out by renowned academics. This, formally under the label of 'the aggregation problem' i.e., the aggregation of the individual supply functions of the different companies actives in the concerned industry. This was already discussed by Sraffa (1926: 540-541), and then by Morgenstern (1972: 1176) and Keen (2011: 128, 136), among others. Though, certainly, these remarks have had little success in terms of its reflection in popular mainstream manuals; except, though in an implicitly way, in that of Samuelson & Nordhaus (2010: 156). We will return to this curious topic-situation later (sections 3.4 and 7.2).

2.6 The minority assumption in manuals: constant returns ('lying-down L' hypothesis)

Nor is it an originality or novelty in economics to acknowledge what has been shown in section 2.3: the unrealistic nature of the traditional arguments used in the ESM to support the thesis that firms growth is limited by the unavoidable appearance of diminishing returns to scale: Some authors have echoed the obvious empirical evidence to this respect, that shows us that the reality of business is systematically very different: that the long-run average cost of this or that good (for a producer enterprise) tend, as an overall pattern, to be rather constant – or even decreasing – as the volume of units produced/

sold by the enterprise increases indefinitely; in other words, as the producer enterprise grows in size.

Thus, we do can find in certain economics/microeconomics manuals that this observational evidence of *non-decreasing returns* as firms grow is assumed[20].

Consequently, in these cases the hypothesis made by the authors regarding the typical behaviour of the *long-run average cost* for a product, LRAC(q), is that in general it tends to remain constant for production volumes or enterprise's sizes beyond the corresponding *optimal scale.* This leads then authors to a graphical representation of the long-run average cost in the form of a diagram as in figure 3a below; which gives rise to speak regarding this cases of the '(lying down) L' hypothesis.

The empirical verification of the above is certainly easy, as we will see in the following chapter. Although so is the acknowledgement of the logical-deductive plausibility of constant returns for production volumes several times higher than the corresponding optimal scale ('L' hypothesis). The reasoning is rather direct: the obvious fact that it is possible for a firm to duplicate, triplicate, ..., indefinitely *replicate* the production unit, line, or production plant associated with the *optimal scale* for the product or service in question. Thus, if a company that is producing a given good and is dimensioned for the corresponding optimal scale – and so producing q^{os} units – wants to double, triple, multiply by 20, ... etc. this production volume, it is

---

[20] This is the case, for example, of Varian (1992:85, diagram for long-run average cost); Lancaster (1974:206-208); Zamagni (1987: 280); Hague (1074: 176-179); Koutsoyiannis (1977: 126, where he discusses the 'canonical' '*U*-hypothesis' he himself has previously assumed, in pp. 112-114); Mansfield (1994: 242; and in other works by him that are mentioned in section 3.3). There are also authors that present both possibilities ('*U*' and '*L*' hypotheses). And others, such as Quirk (1980: 197-206), who eclectically considers that in the long-run the three possibilities may occur: constant, decreasing, and increasing returns to scale. This is also the case in Eaton & Eaton (1996: 292-298), Frank (2007: 319-323), Morgan et al. (2009: 317-320, and figure 9.17), and Samuelson W.F & Marks, S. (2012:243-251).

sufficient for the company to set up 2, 3, 20, ... etc. identical production units in parallel (understanding as production units: production lines, plants, factories in other locations, etc.). Each of them with the same productive structure: the one of the corresponding *optimal scale*. And therefore all of them operating with the same minimum average cost[21]. Consequently, the long-run average cost for the company, for production volumes several times higher than q^{os} units, will not be increasing but rather approximately constant[22]. Logically, the same will also be true for all the companies of the industry (good) in question. Thus, in the standard graphic language:

Figure 3a: *Long-run (or industry's) average cost, [LRAC(q), IC(q)], 'lying-down L' hypothesis*

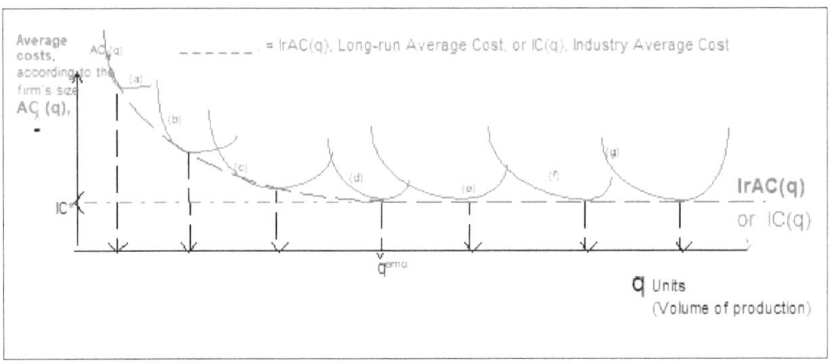

This conceptual diagram – alternative to that in figure 3 – seems to better explain what empirical observation shows us: companies that

[21] The argument (acknowledgement, in fact) of the replicability is neither something new, of course. By way of example,

> "... The assumption of constant returns to scale, which simply implies that if we can produce a ton of product in a given way we can double the productive process and produce two tons with double the productive factors, is both theoretically acceptable and compatible with empirical data in many cases ..." (Lancaster, 1981: 200).

[22] Or rather it will be decreasing to some extent, since an apparently indefinite extension of economies of scale (lower average costs for very large production volumes) is in many cases evident; especially in manufacturing industries, from those of photovoltaic panels, or USB memories to producers of sliced bread.

grow by adding parallel production lines, or setting up different production plants, chains of clone establishments, or branches; or they grow by purchasing competitor firms, etc. In any case, we have not available any empirical evidence on enterprises producing goods that face a frontier of volume of activity beyond which they are not interested in growing any more because they would hypothetically have a higher unit cost. Rather the opposite is easy to observe: the notorious tendency of numerous large industrial multinational companies to produce on a very large scale precisely in order to reduce their unit costs (Intel, Samsung, Volkswagen, ...), as well as the 'chains' with tens, hundreds, or thousands of stores (such as Walmart or Zara), comes also to illustrate this.

On the other hand – and going back to the theory, let us note that the pattern of behaviour of the long-run/ industry's *average cost* of a good that the above diagram describes is also compatible with an ESM's competitive-market-type scenario: There may be many producer/ supplier enterprises in the sector, each one dimensioned to produce around q^{os} units (size/curve 'd') at the minimum average cost, IC^* monetary units. However, the above diagram 3a – different from that in fig. 3 – is also compatible with a scenario where the market for the product in question is dominated by a few firms of a much larger size, though operating with an average cost not higher than IC*. Furthermore, either in this second scenario (some few companies, with a relevant market share) or in the former (many similar 'small' companies competing), the aggregated supply *function* of the set of all producing firms, $P_s(q_s)$, will logically be a constant price, P_s, (since industry's *marginal cost* and *average cost* will coincide from the corresponding production volume of q^{os} units on)[23]. Therefore, the diagram for the *supply function* would be not an upward curve but a flat line: a parallel conclusion to that argued in point 2.4.1.

---

[23] This constant would be $P_s = IC^*$ *+average unit-profit of firms*, where in the case of the first theoretical scenario such unit-profit would be zero.

Despite all this, it is nevertheless the 'U hypothesis that is dominant in academic textbooks. Or, in any case, it is the one taken in the standard economic theory (microeconomics) when it comes to formalising on costs and enterprises behaviour within the model of the 'general equilibrium of competitive markets', as pointed out before. Why? Such a '*U*' hypothesis – or *decreasing returns* hypothesis – is precisely necessary in the standard model to later postulate that 'a totally free market economy will necessarily lead to many efficient firms competing, for supplying each product, whereby such an economy will reach a spontaneous and socially optimal equilibrium'. Such hypothesis is necessary to the ESM in the same way that the assumption (mostly implicit) of 'the optimal scale's volume of production for a good, q^{os} units, is normally many times lower than the total units demanded at the market – for a price close to such a good's minimum average cost' is also simultaneously necessary to the model.

By way of self-test

Let us recap using a specific *industry* as an example:

What has been reviewed and partially discussed so far in this chapter, is understood and used in mainstream economics/ microeconomics as an explanatory theory (compacted in a graphical language in diagrams in figures 3 and 4) of how a country's market economy works; specifically regarding that part related to the enterprises' behaviour and decision making, the relationship between the volume of production and the cost of any good, as well as to market prices determination. What this explanatory theory is telling us regarding any specific good –among other things; and apart from the 'dissident', partially heterodox, textbooks mentioned in section 2.5 – is, by way of example, that:

> If car-making companies produced only one type of car (let's say, a Megane/ Focus/ Ibiza/ Golf/ ... type), basically with the same characteristics, performance and quality, and assuming that these attributes, and the production technologies, are not subject to change, ..

(so far, the kind of acceptable simplifications, and abstractions of certain aspects of reality, usual in any theory)

> .. it will happen that, as more and more units of cars are produced by companies year after year so to cover growing market demand, the cost per car will progressively increase year after year for those companies.

According to this *explanatory theory*, the following logical prediction might be derived from it:

> 'since statistic data show that year after year carmakers have been increasing the number of units they produce, we should expect/observe that their cost-per-car will have been progressively higher. And that, as a *consequence, the selling price these companies will have demanded – in order they to accept to offer such a steady-growing volume of car units* (of the Megane/Focus/Golf/Ibiza/.. type) per year *in the market – will have been increasingly higher; growing year after year (as the '(upward) supply curve' of the ESM teaches us).*

I leave to the reader to consider the degree to which such a theoretical prediction about a secular price increase for cars holds in the real world (or real cars-market, to be more precise) since for that matter any of us could be in a position to make a valid appraisal. In any case, it is not necessary to be an expert in the cars sector to deem the plausibility of this explanatory theory, or of the prediction that follows on from it, since if it were met in the real world, simply as citizens-consumers, we should have observed an appreciable increase, year by year, in the market price – for any specific type of car. Furthermore, I presume that if, by chance, the reader has some close or professional knowledge of the sector – or, for that matter, of industrial companies in general – s/he will likely conclude that not only such a prediction is not fulfilled in the real world, but rather the opposite is precisely true.

Certainly, the above 'case'/remark is something like to anticipate the announced empirical contrasting of the standard model's theories; and, moreover, in a not very rigorous way. A properly comprehensive, observational-based, analysis sustained upon broad observational evidence is the overall subject addressed in the following chapters.

Chapter 3
The workings of the economy, according to empirical evidence

The production sphere, and firms' dynamics

> "Since the 1870s economics has been bedevilled by the idea that it should give itself the appearance of resemble Newtonian physics (...) Whereas empirical research had identified the fundamental properties of the physical universe that Newton and others modelled, the founders of neoclassical economics merely defined a set of concepts that lent themselves to being combined in a model with the same formal properties as Newton's model (equilibria). In doing so they disconnected theory generation from empirical observation, thereby turning it into a purely formalist operation"
> (E. Fullbrook, *Real World Economics*, 2007: 2-3)

> "Observations of managers' behavior as they play their roles in their actual businesses will surely be necessary to the construction of a realistic science describing the functioning of the economy. (p. 2) [...] A knowledge of business behavior based on observation rather than mere conjecture could revolutionize the formulation of public policy and the managing of the business cycle."
> (Barbara R. Bergman, "Needed: A New Empiricism"; *Economists Voice*, March 2007)

In this and the two subsequent chapters, the core propositions of the economics' standard model (ESM) summarised in the previous chapter are confronted in a systematic way with the extensive empirical evidence available in this regard. The deductive assumptions, axioms, and hypotheses that underpin the ESM are thus put to the test. This contrasting is carried out following the same topics' sequence as in the

ESM; that is, as in the previous chapter. The method adopted has been to simultaneously present a formal-schematic empirical-inductive alternative explanation, according to the patterns an observation-based analysis provides. As well as to use, in a selective way, the traditional 'diagram' language, to facilitate the comparison with the respective ESM explanations.

This task starts in this chapter, by reviewing what the ample empirical evidence tells us about the general pattern of behaviour observed regarding the unit costs of goods – for their respective producer firms, general firms' behaviour in the production sphere, and prices –and profits – determination. This especially entails contrasting the ESM's cornerstone assumption of the 'decreasing returns to scale' against observations of the real economic world in this regard, and the conclusions are then extended to reinterpret the classical concepts of 'supply (price) function' and 'market equilibrium'.

This confronting the ESM's axioms and hypotheses with the empirical evidence – and the parallel formulation of an alternative empirical-inductive explanatory scheme – continue in chapters 4 and 5.

Taking the extensive evidence available, some of it already pointed out in the previous chapter, let us start by discussing what would be a more realistic formal explanation regarding the general pattern of behaviour of the unit costs for a firm, in relation to its volume of production; that is, the key topic regarding 'economies of scale'. This will mean empirically testing the axioms and deductive assumptions of the ESM's explanatory theory in this regard, and discussing it, as well as simultaneously formulating an alternative 'theoretical' description of that part of the economic reality.

Since this reality is so varied and casuistic, some simplifications will be not only convenient but also necessary. However, the intention in what follows is to avoid those usual over-simplifications that fatally lead to a detachment from reality; as well as to discuss those standard simplifications that, instead of a schematic description of reality – or stylised facts, are rather a schematic simplification of a *belief*. In that respect, it must be underlined that the conventional, traditional or mainstream explanatory theory, in addition to the assumptions and hypotheses identified in the previous chapter, begins by making a *hard* simplification of the world of production. It is a double simplification to be more precise: 1) to consider a 'firm' as an entity that produces only one good, product or service, which, moreover, is assumed to be a final good for consumers, users, or customers[1]; and 2) to consider that such a good cannot be subject – by the producer enterprise – to differentiation (as regards quality, for example) in the market, in the face of potential buyers.

Is this double simplification methodologically too excessive to be kept for our analysis below? In our case, might it condition the relevance of the resulting alternative explanatory theory, especially regarding the key issue of the pattern of behaviour for unit-cost vs. producer firm's size? Let us start by looking at this issue.

3.1 A realistic scheme for the 'production' context: the network of firms - products - costs

The most usual case is for a firm to produce or provide several goods (products or services). Their production is usually partially according to a *sequential* schedule (equipment is now devoted to one product, then to another, etc.), partially as joint production (most production processes are common to several products), and partially

[1] This simplification is necessary to the ESM to formulate the mathematical model of the General Equilibrium (conditioned optimisation in a system of equations), since this requires, on one side, the consumers' utility functions, and on the other side, (indirectly) the firms' unit-cost functions, for every specific good. Or, in other terms, on one side the demand function for each final product – with their associated concepts, as the 'consumer's surplus'– and on the other side the supply (price) function for each product – which is supposed to be determined by their respective long-run marginal cost.

under a given mix of both these practices. This 'on-the-workshop' reality makes it complex for any firm to calculate the unit cost for each of its products. This is the case to such an extent that there is a specific academic discipline devoted to it: *Cost* (or *Analytical*) *Accounting*. One of the core issues of which is – as it is easy to deduce – to describe and analyse the different alternatives or criteria to distribute the total costs among the different products.

On the other hand, not all the business undertakings in an economy produce or provide final consumption goods, not even the majority of them (→). The landscape picture that offers us a direct observation of the economic reality in this respect could be summarised as follows: There are undertakings/firms that produce/provide final consumer goods[2]; others that produce/provide goods to other firms[3], and others that sell both to other firms and to final consumers[4]. The picture becomes even more complicated because most of the final consumer goods (a washing machine, for example) do not reach us, citizens, from 'the producer' firm but from marketing companies ('stores')[5].

However, as we have seen, the standard methodology in mainstream Economics/ Microeconomics textbooks starts by simplifying this rich and complex landscape <*firms ↔ goods*> in the sense of considering that a (any) firm produces only one product or service; that it may not be subject to differentiation in the market; and that it is for final consumption.

---

[2] For example, firms producing/providing food products, cars, home appliances, furniture, pharmaceuticals, public transport services, clothes, etc.

[3] F. e., metallic raw materials, mining, chemicals, parts or components for other manufacturers, industrial machine tools (including robots), consulting firms, etc.

[4] F. e., power plants'; agricultural, livestock, and fishery undertakings; fuel companies; insurance companies, etc.

[5] F. e., there are agricultural and livestock undertakings that sell to both final consumers (through food shops) and hotels and restaurants; cars manufacturers sell mainly to individuals (through dealers' shops) but also to other companies (car rental undertakings, 'corporate fleets'); etc. was to companies included in the same sector; thus, only 3% of this (statistical) sector's commercial flows would therefore correspond to final products transactions.

(→) Social 'division of *production*'
The instrument we have in Economics that most closely approximates a description of the above complex reality is the *input-output table*, initially developed by Vassily Leontief (1930's). Although, of course, in its most detailed application, it does not go as far as computing by each product or enterprise but at the level of production sectors; i. e. it, unavoidably, (also) simplifies the reality since works with (monetary) sectoral aggregates. This is understandable since it is sectoral data, regarding a country's economic activities, which is regularly collected by official statistics bodies: at a *sectoral* level of aggregation (wide productive sectors, in fact)[6]

Thereby, the relevant question is: Since the point here also is to develop an alternative formal explanatory framework taking into account the historically accumulated empirical evidence (i.e., applying the *inductive* path), will the above 'standard' simplifications turn out to be methodologically excessive? This is in the sense that what results from such a stylisation of reality may be scarcely useful – even if it is only intended to provide a generic, broadly, explanation of that part of the economic reality.

The main problem in that sense is that with such a simplified conceptual-theoretical framework, it is certainly difficult to 'fill' it

[6] By way of example, for the preparation of the *input-output tables* at the European level (*Eurostat* model), the annual economic activity of a country is detailed at the level of 65 sectors. Thereby, the Table for a given year gathers all monetary transactions among them (65 x 65), in addition to those transactions related to final buyers. To mention one specific case: Sector 12th. (CPA-C21//NACE-C21) is 'Pharmaceuticals'; so stated, in these general terms; obviously, it encompasses a lot of different products or production activities. By way of example, for this specific sector, the Table corresponding to 2009, for the Spanish economy, shows that 97% of the total invoiced by the undertakings included in this statistical sector was to companies included in the same sector; thus, only 3% of this (statistical) sector's commercial flows would therefore correspond to final products transactions.

with empirical evidence from observations about, for example, the overall pattern of behaviour of firms' unit-costs, as reality deviates substantially from such a simplified scheme. There is also the problem that the empirical evidence that can be used would only be referred to 'in general, roughly': that is, *indirect* or *generic* evidence that would reasonably allow general inferences to be formulated.

Accepting the latter – in order to be able to confront our alternative formal description/explanation with the ESM's standard one (summarised in the previous chapter) – the standard simplification that "one (any) firm produce only one good, product or service; and that this is of given quality and features, i. e., that there is no possibility of playing *product differentiation* in the market, will be assumed in this and the following (4) chapter". However, we will not presuppose that the product in question is specifically a final consumer good.

Later, in chapter 5, we will see what changes – in prior preliminary conclusions – on eliminating the above (great) simplification. There, we shall go on to consider realities like the fact that firms are generally *multi-product*, and that *product differentiation* in the market is not a lateral but fundamental characteristic – from the side of firms – in any market economy.

A framework closer to reality, for 'factors of production' and 'costs'

Thus, provisionally maintaining here the above simplification (one firm = one product; non-differentiable), to calculate its *average cost* – for a given period t (month, quarter, ... etc.), for the firm that is producing it, is quite elementary (as in chapter 2):

$$AC = \frac{\text{Total costs (from the different factors) during period "t"}}{\text{Units of product obtained during the period "t"}} \equiv \frac{C}{q}$$

In the case of an industrial undertaking (producing a physical good; for example, a specific type of refrigerator) the 'Total costs' in the numerator stands for the sum of all the costs that the firm has had during the calculation-period 't' in order to produce and put in the hands of its clients the q units of product. This includes not only the strictly 'manufacturing' costs but also the commercial costs, administration costs, overall firm's costs, etc.

Dismissing the traditional over-simplification of talking about 'two' factors, 'work' and 'capital', the most general scheme in the business world regarding *factors & costs* would be as follows:

Factors	**Costs**
Work(s): Different types and qualifications; with different salaries. From workshop workers to executives	Amount of salaries and other job compensations, plus enterprise's social security contributions.
Equipment ('capital goods'). Different types; with different duration or service–life: Machines, automated/ robotised lines, installations, computing hardware, buildings premises and facilities, ...	i) Amortisation / depreciation: Proportional part of the Equipment initial cost (investment), to compensate the normal wear and tear during the period. Or ii) rent paid for the Equipment. Plus maintenance and repairing expenses.
Materials (purchase of): Different materials, components, pieces, intermediate products, ...	Amount of purchased items consumed in the production process during the period: quantities of each item, valued at the purchasing price (as from providers' invoices).

Services provided by other firms: Outsourcing of production activities A, B, C, …,. Professionals' Services type a, b, c, …, ..etc.	Sum of the invoices' amount for the different external services contracted.
Energy Power and fuels	Power and piping gas: Amount of the invoices for the kWh consumed over the period. Other fuel: amount of the units of fuel consumed during the period, at purchasing price.

In the case of services-providing companies – rarely referred to, by the way, in the standard textbooks – 'Materials' costs do not tend to be significant (some small material consumption – by an advertising firm, for example); and likewise regarding 'Equipment' costs: their proportion is likely to be comparatively low (they are not enterprises requiring significant investment in equipment – except in the case of the 'industrial services' such as telecommunications or electricity supply).

In any case, it is easy to conclude that, in general, the number of different factors (different types of 'work', of 'materials', etc., each with a different cost price) tends in practice to be notable for any business undertaking.

3.2 Empirical evidence on the general pattern of costs, in relation to the activity level of an enterprise

Thus, provisionally adopting the simplification of 'one enterprise=one product', what is the empirical evidence regarding the unit costs' behaviour in relation to the activity level of the enterprise? In principle, it is not easy to have direct empirical evidence available in this regard. This should consist of historical data on *unit cost* and *volume of production* for one or more companies producing the same good. Such information is usually generated, of course, and is well-known and used by the respective business managers to make decisions. However, it is normally not observable to outside analysts or researchers: companies consider their unit cost data to be strictly confidential, and therefore rarely provide them to outsiders.

We thus have to rely on completing the relatively few direct empirical studies available with generic empirical findings, 'broad-brush' evidence, or indirect observations that may lead to robust inferences. The main source of this *generic* or indirect evidence is that from those professionals with experience as economic, financial, or accounting managers of companies, when they convey their experience in this regard – for example, on the issue of economies of scale and company growth decisions – to public audiences; or when being surveyed on the occasion of an academic study on the pattern of behaviour of costs in their company: to talk about the *behaviour* of unit costs in one's company does not entail to provide confidential data (costs' figures) to the surveyor.

Let us start with this indirect evidence:

Generic evidence's inductive statement 1: The distinction between total *fixed* and *variable costs* (relative to the volume of production of a company) is conceptually useful, but it entails inevitable ambiguities and problems in making it quantitatively precise in practice, having specific enterprises in mind. The concept of 'fixed costs' – meaning, in the *short run* – is traditionally associated with the costs of equipment, premises, installations, and some personnel. Roughly speaking, those costs associated with the production *structure* or *size* of a company.

However, empirical observation of how companies operate shows us that to qualify a specific cost as 'fixed' or 'variable' inevitably stumbles upon ambiguities of the type: "it depends ...", "partly fixed and partly variable"; or "it depends on the time-interval we consider"; or "fixed, with jumps (discrete variability)"; or "variable for increases in activity level, but practically fixed for reductions"[7]

> Consider, for example, the costs of Personnel ('Labour factor'). For a company in a market economy, whether these are fixed costs, partially fixed and partly variable, or variable costs, depends on the specific local legal system, the labour laws of the country, as well as the company's own strategy given the options offered by this labour-contracts regulation (indefinite/temporary, full/part-time contracts, etc.).
>
> Or let us focus on the costs of equipment, installations, etc. In the case (most generally) of being assets owned by the company, the corresponding costs (amortisation or depreciation) are basically fixed. However, in the case of leased equipment, the cost will be variable. Etc.

Nevertheless – and within the limitations suggested by the above– if we consider the enterprise's operating costs as a whole, the observation of the business management practices shows that, in the short run, a certain part of the *total costs* (monthly, quarterly, ..) of an undertaking can be considered as 'practically fixed' in relation to the volume of activity (monthly, quarterly, ..); understanding here by 'short-run', 'without making substantial changes to the structure or size of the company'.

As regards the rest of the total costs, the *variable costs*, mostly relate to materials, energy, other purchases or contracts (of other elements and services from outside), plus a part of those of staff (personnel). Indirect, professional, evidence provided by *cost accounting* practice

---

[7] We have a technical label for this case of cost behaviour: 'hysteresis of costs'.

in companies shows, moreover, that *variable costs* are generally the quantitatively dominant costs within firms. Generic evidence also points in that direction. For example, taking data from the Banco de España's annual report *Central de Balances*, it can be deduced that the variable costs of companies in this database accounted for more than 75% of the total costs of such companies, on average[8]. This can be considered as reasonably representative at the international level since the forms of production tend to be similar in companies overall within industrialised countries.

Generic evidence's inductive statement 2: Observational evidence from professional business practice – especially from cost accounting – shows that, for a company with a given structure, size, or productive capacity, *variable costs are approximately proportional to the volume of activity*, except for extreme levels of it: very low occupancy rate, or, at the other extreme, over-occupancy. That is, the variable cost per unit of product (v) tends to be approximately constant – for the relevant range in which a company's volume of production tends to oscillate in the short-run.

Direct evidence to this respect (case studies) is relatively scarce, though the available case studies along these lines confirm the above pattern. Thus:

---

[8] The annual report reviewed (2016 data) covers a total of 379,000 companies. Focusing on the sections devoted to the consolidated *Income Accounts* of the whole sample, the following figures are deduced: *Costs of purchased Materials*, 33.4%; *Other purchases of goods and services*, 30%; *Other Operating Expenses (outsourcing)*, 16.4%; *Staff costs*, 16.1%; *Amortisation costs (from Equipment, and other fixed assets)*, 4.1%.

(Compiled by the author, from: Banco de España, 2017: "Central de Balances. Resultados de las empresas no financieras, 2016", p. 85).

The first two blocks of costs can be considered as clearly *variable*, and the last one as *fixed*. The third ('Other Operating Expenses') is mostly variable; and the fourth (Staff) mostly fixed. Making the estimate that 2/3 of the third block are variable; and that three quarters of the Staff Costs are fixed for the companies included in the report, the result is: Variable costs, 78.3%; Fixed costs, 21.7%. On replicating the above calculation for the 2012 data, the results obtained are similar: 77.6% and 22.4%.

- Eiteman & Guthrie (1952: 87) surveyed 366 company managers, asking them which of 8 diagrams (curves) intended to represent the *unit cost in relation to the number of units produced* was best suited to their company's experience. Of the 344 answers, 316 selected a curve associated with a constant average variable cost until reaching the maximum production capacity (203 responses), or constant until close to that maximum capacity and thereafter increasing slightly (113 responses). Only 4 answers chose curves like the usual diagrams in neoclassical economics (i.e., as in Fig. 1 in the previous Chapter).

- "...(an) interesting conclusion of the empirical studies is that marginal cost in the short run tends to be constant in the relevant output range ..". Mansfield (1994, p. 242).

- Blinder et al. (1998, pp. 103-105), surveyed 200 large American companies, asking about the short-run *marginal cost* (actually, the *variable unit cost*, in the replies). The results were: 48% of the replies indicated that they (the companies' officers) believed (sic) that it was constant; 41%, declining, and 11% growing.

(for some reason, regarding the researcher's ecosystem in mainstream economics, there is a striking lack of more-recent empirical studies in this line. I shall retake this thread further on.)

When a company operates outside its above-mentioned 'normal' range of activity – that is, if it operates temporarily at a very low occupancy rate or, at the other extreme, forcing its productive capacity at the time – it is observed that the *variable unit-cost* tends to be somewhat higher. Albeit the upward differences for both extremes are in general proportionally small – in addition to being unrepresentative since companies only exceptionally operate at those extreme levels of activity in relation to their installed capacity.

For the lower end – very low levels of occupation of the production capacity, the cause of a somewhat higher variable unit-cost is basically the some-higher cost price for certain materials and other items purchased abroad:

> It is frequently observed in business – in fact, it is sort of common knowledge – that when purchasing/hiring comparatively small quantities of materials, parts, fuel, certain services, etc., the purchase/hire prices are somewhat higher than when larger quantities are purchased/contracted.

As for the other extreme, for activity levels close to the maximum capacity of the facility (e.g., the enterprise moving from two work shifts to three; or to operating 7 days a week; or subcontracting part of the production process, or certain activities, with other companies), *variable unit-cost* may increase. The quantitative reason is generally the company's having to resort to using more variable factors (e.g., services from other companies) so to force the limitation from its fixed elements at the time (production structure, equipment, middle management staff, etc.):

> For example, personnel overtime – or work on non-working days – is more expensive than normal working hours. Also, by outsourcing certain productive activities, they may result more expensive than when carried out internally. Moreover, equipment maintenance and repair costs can increase more than proportionally if the rate of use of the equipment is above-the-normal.

Thus, to sum up, the following can be accepted as a good description of business reality, regarding the pattern of behaviour of the *variable average cost* of a product for the producing company: 1) variable average cost tends to be constant for a wide interval of units; that within which the level of production oscillates most of the accounting periods (months, quarters, ... etc.). In the case of a manufacturing company, for example, such a stretch of units used to be associated with the company operating at a level between one and something over two work shifts. This 'normal' range of activity/production volume (units) will depend on the specific structure/size that the company has at that time. 2) Outside that interval, for very low or, at the other extreme, very high occupancy levels (forcing the installed capacity), the average variable cost tends to be somewhat higher.

To sketch that in graph-drawing language: In the short run (the company's structure/size being given) the most general pattern of behaviour of the *average variable cost* of a good, in relation to the number of units produced, could be plotted by an approximately horizontal line framed by two small segments; the one on the left decreasing, the one on the right, increasing.

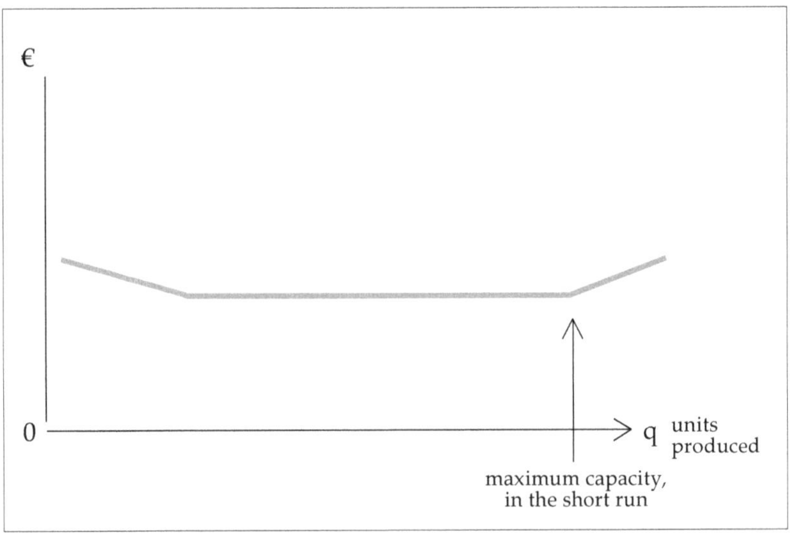

That is, a 'cost function', v(q) in the form of, say, 'tray-profile' rather than the traditional U-shaped ('bowl profile') representation in standard economic theory (Chapter 2, Fig. 1, dashed curve).

Generic evidence's inductive statement 3: In accordance with the above, it is not observed that the concept of 'optimal volume (of units produced)' – represented by q^{ot} in fig. 1, in the preceding chapter – has a significant presence in the business undertakings practice. Or, more precisely, such a concept does not consist of a specific number of units, but rather of a wide interval of units, as illustrated by the flat line in the diagram above.

Conversely, the concept of '*maximum production volume or capacity,* in the short-run' does show up to be relevant in practice: It is the higher volume of production/units that a company may reach – with the structure and dimension that it has at the time – resorting to elements of capacity-flexibility, such as overtime, an additional shift of work, adding small improvements to the existing equipment, working on non-working days, or outsourcing part of the production process.

3.3 The pattern of unit-costs, according to empirical evidence: (i) In the short-run, or static analysis: a firm with a given structure/dimension)

Inferences from the previous 'statements'

When we consider all the costs of a company, in the short run, the *average fixed cost* is logically decreasing regarding the volume of units produced; and the *average variable cost* is generally constant, with the nuance commented above regarding extreme operating levels. Therefore, the typical pattern that results for the sum of both, the *total* ***average cost*** is:

> Starting from very low occupancy rates (of an enterprise's installed capacity) *total average cost* (henceforth simply *average* cost) decreases when passing to higher volumes of production; progressively to a lesser extent; till becoming approximately constant all along the central interval of the enterprise's 'normal' activity level. For production volumes close to its maximum

capacity, the *average cost* may show a certain increase, as far as the average-variable-cost component increases (due to the enterprise's forcing the installed capacity) more than what the average-fixed-cost component comes decreasing.

To express the former in graphical-conceptual terms, a quantitative simulation has been carried out. The specific parameters assumed for that were as follows: 1) *average variable costs* (**v**) remain constant for the interval of production volume between 27% and 96 % of the installed, normal, capacity; (since situations outside this range are rarely observed); 2) The proportion of *variable costs* is 78% of *total costs*[9] for an occupancy level of 85% of the installed capacity[10].The result of this simulation (see appendix B) is outlined in the following diagram, as a graphical-conceptual representation of the most general pattern of behaviour of the *unit-costs* in relation to the *volume of activity* of an undertaking in operation.

Figure 5: *General pattern observed for the Average cost of a good, in the short-run* (*: for a firm in operation, with a given size / structure/ production capacity)*

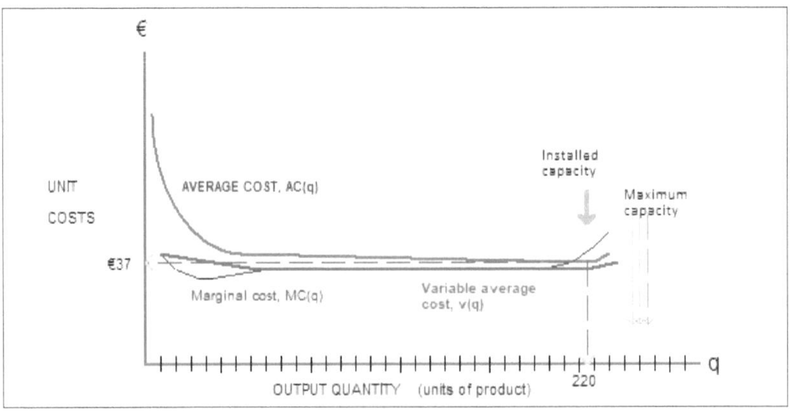

[9] Parameter deduced from the report of the '*Central de Balances del Banco de España*' mentioned above.

[10] This is the average percentage of occupancy of the companies included in the report mentioned above.

This inductive inference goes in line with generic evidence from the field of cost accounting. It is moreover easily identified in the business world: it is normally observed that, for a company producing a given good or service, its average cost – in the short run – tends to remain approximately constant, or slightly decreasing, for a relatively large interval of units or activity level: a central range of units, or 'normal' range of activity. The usual possibility of more than one work shift is a key element in this respect, together with resorting to partial outsourcing.

> Let us consider, for example, the case of a manufactured product; an industrial firm. Simply by switching from 1 work shift to 1.5 (i.e., resorting to employees' overtime, and/or part-time additional employees) or to 2 shifts, the production volume may even double, while the average cost remains approximately the same[11]. And there is also the fact that its own installed capacity is to some extent 'flexible', insofar certain phases of the production process may be, partially or fully, outsourced to specialised companies, at a cost not always greater than if carried out internally.

In short, the general pattern observable points to an approximately constant *average cost* for the company producing a good, for a wide interval of its production level. The possible exceptions are when the company operates at a very low occupancy rate, or the opposite, when it operates forcing its production capacity to the limit; that is, producing the maximum volume of units that it can achieve – given its current structure/size – by straining the flexibility elements of its installed capacity; i.e. eventually resorting to working more than two shifts, and/or 365 days a year, and/or to outsourcing parts of their production process to other companies[12].

---

[11] Or, more likely, decreases somewhat since Fixed Costs are divided into more and more units.

[12] Thus, in the graphic-numerical example of fig. 5, the average cost of the product reaches its minimum value (about €37) when the company produces between 200 and 240 units per period.

Having reached this point, I must underline that, since the preceding paragraph-summary on the general pattern-of-behaviour of the average-cost of a good, in the short-run, (and its graphic expression: in fig. 5) is derived from empirical evidence observable in business practice across time, it is neither an original statement on my part nor a new one – something that some reader may probably have already guessed. The above assertion is indeed in line with available empirical studies; e.g., those already cited by Eiteman & Guthrie, Mansfield, and Blinder et al.[13]; as well as Cohen's (1983:218); by way of summary of such contributions:

> " ... (an) interesting conclusion of the empirical studies is that marginal cost in the short run tends to be constant in the relevant output range (for a firm) . This result seems to be at variance with the theory presented earlier ..., which says that marginal cost curves should be U-shaped ... Although marginal costs may well be relatively constant over a wide range, (...) they .. eventually increase with increases in output (in the short run). ..."
> (Mansfield, 1994: 242)

Our (economists') problem is that this long-acknowledged evidence continues, however, to be ignored by mainstream economic theory – and derived manuals; what, in some way, has a certain relation with the dominance of *marginalism* in it.

[13] In the already cited broad empirical study, researchers underline that, in the vast majority of the answers they received, the companies surveyed consider their *marginal cost to be constant or decreasing* in the short run. Although researchers add that they reached to the conclusion that the respondent companies' officers were rather thinking of the variable average cost when giving their answers. "*While there are reasons to wonder whether respondents interpreted these questions about (marginal) costs correctly, their answers paint an image of the cost structure (in the short run) of the typical firm that is very different from the one immortalized in the textbooks*" (Blinder et al., 1998; pg. 105).

A look to marginalism

As far as the *marginal cost* is concerned, it is an exclusively theoretical concept, normally without use or reflection in the business reality (*); mainly because rarely a firm varies its production volume from one period to another by '1 unit' of product. Variations are normally of a certain number of units[14]. The calculable concept in practice closest to the idea of marginal cost is that of *differential cost* per-unit; which is defined as (Δ Total Costs) / Δ Units of Product). And this is precisely what has been calculated as 'marginal cost' in the simulation of Appendix 2, and represented as such in figure 5[15].

* *This is also the case with the theoretical concept '**marginal physical productivity of** a given factor (normally, **Labour**)', commented before in section 2.4., so central in most economics textbooks. In modern neoclassical economics, it is defined as 'the increase in the units produced by a firm, when the quantity of a specific factor is increased by 1 unit'. This theoretical abstraction lacks, however, significant reflection in the real production world: it is usually impossible to increase the units produced of a good by only increasing one of the production factors required for its production. It is not possible, for example, to increase the units of tyres produced by increasing only the factor 'labour', or only the factor 'rubber',*

---

[14] Drawing parallels with physics -as early economists with a scientific vocation liked to do- the economic reality here analysed does not vary in a continuous but discreet way, in 'packages', in 'quanta'. Economics should therefore be 'quantum economics', if I may be so 'bold'. Though 'packages', in economics, would be not constant but randomly sized –to make it more difficult for us, economists.

[15] As can be seen from the diagram in Appendix B, the *marginal cost* values are graphically overlapping (roughly coincide) with the *variable average cost* along the entire central interval [70-210 units]. As for the *maximum production capacity*, in the simulation-example it would be around 250-260 units.

or only the factor 'energy', etc.[16] *And so on for a loaf of bread, a medicine, a bike, one hour of a concert, etc. Again, this claim about the unrealism of such a deductive concept – and by extension about the production function it derives from (see box **) – is nothing new at all; see, for instance, Leontief's 1982 statement quoted some paragraphs below.*

Students of economics come across this neoclassical economics' concept of '(diminishing) *marginal physical product* (*of Labour*)' – introduced in the chapters regarding 'theory of the firm', or 'of production' – in advanced chapters or readings. Normally, when the concept/model of the *production function*** is developed, and then put in connection with the section devoted to 'markets equilibrium'; and this specifically regarding the '*Labour market* and the *salary of equilibrium*' – for an industry or a given producer firm. This is an ESM concept, 'salary of equilibrium', which is defined as the 'market value of the physical marginal product of Labour' in such an industry or enterprise; (an empirical-based discussion about can be seen in Komlos, 2019:109-110). The ideological implications of this crude consideration of *Labour as merchandise* will be dealt with later, in chapter 7.

---

[16] At most, the concept ('marginal product of Labour' / 'marginal physical productivity') may have a certain metaphorical sense or use, such as when talking about the additional metres of valid, unflawed, fabric produced as a result of having established (or increased) an economic-incentive-per-production to the workers involved. However, this is precisely not the meaning the standard concept 'marginal physical product of Labour' has in standard texts.

[17] As we have seen in section 2.4, parameters α and β may be mathematically interpreted as the *elasticity output-input*, for each input; that is, the result of a quotient where the denominator is the rate input Labour has increased, and the numerator is the rate the output, Y, has increased as a consequence; and the parallel for input Capital (and each of the rest); thereby, each parameter is assumed to be below 1. And parameter '**a**' stands for a measure of the state of the art **regarding technological** development in the economy, as for the production of the good under consideration; consequently, it is assumed to be subject to an increasing trend over time (technological progress).

More specifically, in the case that $\alpha+\beta=1$, parameter '**a**' is also used in mainstream economics as a given definition of the *joint productivity* of both factors, Capital and Labour: namely, *total factor productivity* in the production of the good in question; –this, according to the standard reasoning summarised in section 2.4.

** *The **production function** is, as we have seen in section 2.4, a core concept in mainstream economics/ microeconomics. The neoclassical Cobb-Douglas two-inputs Production Function, its mathematical expression, is a widely used concept in mainstream economics texts and manuals; and the one that graduates in economics usually will know:*

$$Y = a \cdot K^{\alpha} \cdot L^{\beta}$$

*where **K** stands for the units of (aggregate) Capital stock used; **L** stands for the units of (aggregate) Labour employed; and **a**, **α** and **β** are parameters*[17]*. This exponential function – as well as its subsequent generalisation to more than two inputs: $Q = a \cdot F_1^{x1} \cdot F_2^{x2} \cdot (\ldots) \cdot F_n^{xn}$ – is simply a deductive definition, an abstract formulation, not induced from cases-observation. It is an instrumental assumption that responds to the notion that to produce a given quantity of a good, any proportion of factors is possible (sic); i.e., that inputs are perfectly substitutable with each other since the function is considered differentiable. Thereby, mainstream textbooks talk about 'elasticity of substitution' among inputs, as well as of '**marginal physical product of Labour**' in the production of a good: namely, the partial derivative of the **mathematical expression** with respect to such an input: $\delta Y/\delta L$ – which, thereby, implies to assume that the units of the other/s input/s remain constant. This partial derivative –a pure deduction from the math definition – is a decreasing value, for successive increases in the units of Labour (see 2.4); it is, however, the base of the mainstream postulate of 'the marginal physical product(ivity) of Labour is always decreasing'; which, later on in a standard textbook leads to the orthodox-economics lemma: 'the **salary of equilibrium** for a firm/industry is the **market value** of its **Labour physical marginal product**'.*

As has been argued about this topic in the previous chapter, the definition (properties) of parameters (α and β in the standard Cobb-Douglas production function), as well as the mathematical form of the function itself, do not respond to their proponents having detected indicative patterns in this respect from observing specific production activities. Simply the function comes defined in such a way that math deductions from it meet conventional theoretical preconceptions regarding how the production world works. Preconceptions such as that Capital, Labour, and the rest of the inputs are freely substitutable with each other in the production of a (any) good. More precisely, that 'a firm that produces a given good changes freely and constantly the proportion of the required production factors – inputs Capital, Labour, etc. as the market prices of these go changing, to so get its good's unit cost to be the minimum possible.

As for the referred standard postulate regarding that '*physical marginal product of Labour*', ($\delta Y/\delta L$), is a decreasing quantity, lower the greater the total units of Labour', it comes from assuming – in the standard C-D production function – that the units of Capital stock are fixed. Which is consistent with, or suggests, understanding the production function as referred to a firm in operation, that is, to a *short-run scenario*. As can be deduced, such a postulate implies that the unit cost of the product, for the producer firm, will be growing – since successive equal increases of output would require growing additional Labour-units. Thus, the conventional assumption, in the standard Theory of Unit Costs, regarding diminishing returns (parabolas-shape curves in Figure 1) is this way linked to the (Cobb-Douglas) production function. Or the other way round: the formulation of the latter responds to the implicit presuppositions such mainstream economics curves reflect. Moreover, in the standard model this core premise of the (decreasing) *marginal product*, or *marginal physical productivity* (of Labour), comes as a convenient elegant assumption, in the sense of symmetric to that of 'decreasing marginal utility (of consumers) in the Demand field.

> "The assumption about diminishing marginal returns, whether in consumption or in production, is so central to neoclassical theory that the theory is sometimes called "marginalist economics".

> The story of demand requires diminishing marginal utility (...). Likewise, the story of production requires diminishing marginal productivity". (Schlefer, pp. 103-104). "I find assumptions about marginal productivity a peculiar way to visualize how firms actually produce goods. I doubt that economists spontaneously conceived of them as a plausible way to describe production and then proceed to build a model. Rather, they saw a theoretical necessity for the assumptions about production to complement the theory of utility." (pp. 106-7).

On the other hand, the other popular marginalist postulate derived from the standard C-D production function – regarding the sum of the exponents as an indicator of the sign of the returns to scale in the production of the good in question[18] – comes out from assuming that the proportion between the inputs is constant; which is sort of contradictory with the definition of the production function itself, as far as such a definition entails perfect substitutability among the production factors. Contrarily, such a situation of constant proportions between the production factors would in fact suggest the specific case of a firm in the short run that is operating just at 100% occupancy level.

The above lines on the standard concept of *production function* go beyond just a technical note: One of the theoretical propositions of the ESM is, precisely, that the 'natural' (equilibrium's) level of salary for an employee (or group of employees, professional profile, etc.) is 'the market value of its *marginal physical product*'; a theoretical normative assertion of obvious relevant socio-economic implications.

---

[18] To summarise this most applied mathematical deduction from the standard production function, here summarised before in 2.4: When it is assumed that the proportion between the units of both inputs, K and L is kept constant, then: if $\alpha+\beta<1$, the resulting function exhibits decreasing returns; if $\alpha+\beta=1$, this would signal constant returns; and if $\alpha+\beta>1$, increasing returns.

Taking into account all the above regarding 'marginalism', the provocative recommendation by Emmanuelle Benicourt, professor at the EHSS, can be well understood:

> "... ask the teacher to give just one example of a production function describing, even approximately, a real-life firm. You can also request a concrete example of (instantaneously) substitutable inputs. If the teacher cannot offer any examples, ask him: 'then, what is the use of all the mathematics'?".
> (Benicourt, "Five Pieces of Advice for Students Studying Microeconomics", en Fullbrook 2004: 88).

More than two decades earlier a similar observation was already made by Wassily Leontief. In a short text (1982's) he discussed 'the irresistible predilection (of theoretical economists) for deductive reasoning (..) to avoid or cut short the use of concrete factual information'. As an illustration of his argument, he cites 'a typical example of a theoretical "production function"', developed by renowned specialists, which considers four inputs. A function, he remarks, that is intended to describe the relationship between output and inputs for any good; and, thereby, between, for example, the amount of steel produced by a firm and the quantities of the main different inputs required to produce it. And he concludes,

> 'To ask a manager of a steel plant or a metallurgical expert for information on the magnitude of the six parameters appearing in these (...) equations would make no sense. Hence, while the labels attached to symbolic variables and parameters of the theoretical equations tend to suggest that they could be identified with those directly observable in the real world, any attempt to do so is bound to fail: the problem of "identification" of aggregative equations after they have been reduced – that is, transformed, as they often are – for purposes of the curve-fitting

process, was raised many years ago but still has not found a satisfactory solution.' (Leontief, 1982, p. 104).

Decades later, it appears that the problem he underlined remains yet the same. We might ask where the ESM's hypothesis of a 'U'-shaped 'average cost function' (in-the-short-run; fig. 1) stems from –since it does not respond, and never seems it did, to the overall pattern observed in the real world of Production? As we have seen before (2.1) it derives from the theoretical assumption that, in general, the *total variable costs* of a firm increase more than proportionally to the volume of production, starting from a specific volume of units quite below its maximum production capacity. Why such a clearly unrealistic assumption? Likely because it fits with a mathematical deduction from the standard *production function*; that of 'decreasing marginal product' of Labour, it considered as 'the' variable costs. Or simply because it allows to represent the unit costs in an elegant mathematical-language: as perfect parabolas in a diagram; as if the economic reality to be explained would just respond to perfectly differentiable second-order equations, and as if this reality would admit such an easy mathematical expression. (The possible mathematical expressions that would fit in with the discontinuity of the 'functions' depicted for the unit costs in the 'empirical' fig. 5, would certainly be considerably more complex).

There does not seem to be other explanations for maintaining across decades and manuals authors (and editions) an assumption that clearly does not respond – and has never historically responded– to the empirical observation of the production/business world. Though there may also be as an explanation, regarding specific texts, the fact that an author simply adopts (reproduce) the classical graphic-conceptual definition because this is what she/he learned within a previous textbook by a prestigious author; and even that this forms part of an academic chain over time.

3.4 The pattern of unit-costs, according to empirical evidence: (ii) In the long-run, (or dynamic analysis: the structure/size of a firm varies over time)

Let us finally move to the whole picture, starting from the short-run situation depicted in the previous numerical-and-graphical example (fig. 5). If the concerned company estimates that it can place on the market, not temporarily but in a stable situation, well over 210 units of product (say, 250-500) at the same selling price, it has no incentive to force its current productive capacity –since its average cost would then increase rapidly above €37. The company will rather have an interest in growing in size. It will come out economically more convenient (cheaper) for the company to follow an expanding strategy; to switch to a larger production structure/ dimension, so that its average cost remains approximately the same (around €37); or even lower if that larger productive structure allows the company to apply a cheaper way to produce (a different, more efficient, 'technology').

3.4.1 Firm's growth and economies of scale

Typically, this *growth path* means the company to increase – via information technologies resources and greater use of equipment – the mechanisation or automation of certain activities of the production and delivery process, as well as to adopt a greater division of work, specialisation, etc. This allows the firm to produce more economically, and thereby to obtain successive reductions in its average cost. That is in essence the definition of *economies of scale*. In the economics jargon, we then talk about the company has moved to apply a *more efficient*, cheaper, 'technology' (giving here to the word a wide meaning). Figure 2 in the previous chapter may yet be useful for illustrating in a broad sense such dynamics: a company's leap to a larger dimension/ size, associated with achieving a reduction in its unit cost.

Obviously, over time a company can make successive leaps in size/ structure, so increasing its volume of activity by means of growing, moving to an upper scale. This sequence of moving to a 'superior' dimension and 'technology', thus achieving a successively lower average cost, has been outlined in the following diagram in figure 6 below. It depicts the graphical-conceptual description of the overall pattern observed for the long-run *average cost* of a product; a diagram 'alternative' or parallel to that of the *traditional* 'U-shaped' of mainstream economics (figure 3, in chapter 2).

In Figure 6, the successive curved-straight lines represent the *short-run average cost* (applying the general pattern depicted in Figure 5) according to different size (structure/ dimension/ technology) alternatives for a company, when it follows a growth path. The graphic sequence begins with the size/dimension alternative 'a', then 'b', 'c', etc.

This possibility of taking advantage of the *economies of scale* and thus to produce ever more and cheaper has in general a certain limit: when the productive dimension/scale already allows the company to use the *optimal technology available* at that time; this, in the sense of the most cost-effective, the cheapest in terms of average cost for the product in question (€14 in the numerical example) given the current costs prices for the production factors required. This is the case represented in the above diagram by productive dimension 'e'. This productive dimension or firm's size would be the so-called '*minimum* optimal (or efficient) scale' (***mos***) for the product in question – at that time. Albeit expressed it in terms of specific units of product, such a ***mos*** would actually be a certain range of units (central interval of production in short-run average-cost mixed line 'e') starting at q^{mos} (750 units, in the corresponding graphical example) for which the average cost remains the same (€14 in the example).

Figure 6: *General pattern observed for the long-run* average cost of a good, LRAC(q), or industry's average cost, IC(q)*
(*): Any Producer firm decide /adjust their size (structure & technology / production capacity, ¶ˣ) over time

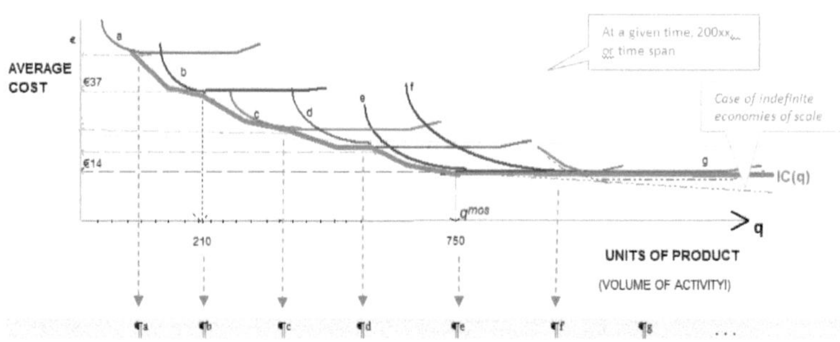

Where:
Each of the 'small curve-straight line' represents the short-run average cost (in relation to the units of output produced by the firm in a given period) corresponding to a given alternative as far as the firm's size (structure & technology, or productive dimension): a, b, c, d, ... , x. These mixed lines represent therefore the concept of short-run average cost, denoted before by ACx(q).

Consequently, the enveloping broken grey line represents the long-run average cost attainable by a firm, LRAC(q), or also Industry's average cost, IC(q) –for the product or service concerned.

¶ˣ stands for the units of good for which the short-run average cost –for a firm with dimension 'x'– reaches its minimum value #.

(#): It is assumed that the firm in question (any producer firm) tends to operate efficiently, in the sense of minimizing its total costs given the volume of output to be produced per period.

Once a firm has adopted or reached this dimension 'e' and is therefore producing a volume of units within the said interval (between 750 and, by way of example, around 1200 units in the above diagram), whether it wants/plans to produce far more units than that, following the path of growth, it can move to a larger structure/dimension (a larger production capacity), like 'f', 'g', ..., in the diagram, while the average cost will remain the same because the technology to apply will, in fact, be the same: the 'superior' one at the time. And so, for even larger production volumes; what thus defines a scenario of *constant returns*. Though, in some cases, we may even observe that the average cost keeps decreasing indefinitely, to a certain degree, for ever-larger firm's dimensions. This is the case for certain *mass production* enterprises; e.g., manufacturing of cars, photovoltaic modules, or flat TV screens. There exist, therefore, cases *of indefinite economies of scale*; a scenario, thus, of *increasing returns*. The tilted-down dashed line below the solid IC(q) line in the former diagram stands for representing one of these cases.

As can be seen, the resulting graphic-conceptual outline for the LRAC, IC, (enveloping line in grey) converges basically – for the more usual situation of *constant returns* beyond the respective ***mos*** with the 'lying L-shaped' hypothesis, for the long-run average-cost of a good, we have seen before, in section 2.5 (figure 3a); traditionally a minority hypothesis among the more used economics/ microeconomics manuals, and practically ignored in the specialised literature within mainstream economic theory.

The key point in this regard is to take or not into account something that is implicit in the above arguments: the *replicability* in production activities.

3.4.2 Replicability of the '*minimum* optimal scale'

Let us thus complete the above argument: if the company concerned has already a structure/dimension such as 'e', is producing around 750-1200 units, and can and wants to place on the market double the units (or three, six, thirty, ... times more), the most cost-effective, cheapest, way of doing it (to keep operating with the minimum average cost; €14 in the example) is to move to install two (three, six, thirty, ...) production lines, workshops, or plants, each with a dimension/technology such as 'e' (or, for the matter, 'f', ... etc.). That is, the company to follow the strategy of resorting to replicating several times the corresponding '***mos***' plant or production line.

Indeed, this is exactly what we can see generally in the real economic world. To refer to well obvious examples: manufacturing companies with multiple, parallel, production lines in large industrial facilities, and/or with several similar production plants in different locations – as is usually the case with automobile or household-appliance firms, for instance. There are also parallel situations regarding services companies, such as airlines (several daily flights London-Frankfurt), power generation companies (several identical turbines within a given power plant), and a very long *etc.*

From these statements, it can be concluded that there is generally not '*an* optimal scale' of production or 'an optimal size of the company' for a given good. What we actually find in the real world is that there is generally a given '*minimum* optimal scale (or firm-size)'. In the numerical example in Figure 6, that *minimum* optimal scale – which allows an enterprise to get the minimum possible *average cost* at that time, would be 750 units. More precisely: it would be the 'e' productive structure/size, associated with a defined *interval* of volumes of production *starting at* 750 units, < – – >, along which the average cost is approximately the same, constant, as well as the *minimum* one technically and economically possible at the time considered[19].

Thus, we can more generally say, by zooming in on the above diagram, that the 'optimal scale' would actually be an *indefinite interval*, starting

[19] As can be seen, again we come across this sort of economy's 'quantum' reality: the cost-effective ***minimum*** *optimal scale* for a certain good does not appear in the observable reality as a specific number of units of output but rather as a given interval ('package') of units. The only difference is that, like almost everything in the workings of our economies, the size of the package (number of units) –for a given good– is subject to changes over time, due to technical progress. This is an epistemological problem that I would say does not occur in physics –luckily for physicists.

from those 750 units on, (<– – · · ·). This is because of the obvious reason of the overall *replicability* of the cheapest technology/ scale at the time ('e', in the diagram). Something that, on the other hand, comes out as clearly evident from empirical observations.

Let us underline that this statement –which, to simplify, avoids the cases of mass production (*increasing returns*) is ultimately equivalent to describing what is meant by *constant returns to scale* in the production of a good: starting from the corresponding volume of q^{mos} units (750 units, in the example).

Again, I must point out that this obvious fact – that the technically-economically minimal optimal production scale for a product or service can be replicated several, indefinite, times by any producer company – has obviously not gone historically unnoticed in academic economics. Though, indeed, it has been rather ignored by the mainstream economics approach. Thus, Piero Sraffa argued as early as 1929 that business managers would consider the standard neoclassical model in reference manuals to be absurd, since it stems from the assumption that the average cost (in the long-run) of a good, for a given firm, always becomes increasing beyond a certain volume of production, thus limiting the expansion of any producer firm (Sraffa, 1929: 543). Along the same lines, more explicitly referring to the obvious fact or possibility of replicability of the 'optimum-size plant', we find the arguments of Lancaster (1977)[20], as well as Blaug (1968: 465-6; 1985: 457), and especially Beckenstein (1975), in his more specific work on the evidence of replicability – to which he refers using the term of 'multi-plant firm'.

---

[20] "… The assumption of constant returns to scale, which simply implies that if we can produce a ton of product in a given way we can double the productive process and produce two tons with double the productive factors, is both theoretically acceptable and compatible with empirical data in many cases …" (Lancaster, 1977, p. 200).

3.4.3 Summary of the overall pattern observed for the unit cost of a good, in the long-run

To sum up, looking at the above graphical-conceptual scheme as a whole (Figure 6), the grey broken line is the envelope of the 'family' of short-run average cost 'functions'; i.e., it results from uniting the points of each of them where their average-cost is minimum. That is, the points (volume of units to produce) of minimum average cost for each of the possible alternative as far as firm's size or dimension (*a, b, c, d, e* and *f*), for producing the good in question. It thus represents a schematic description of *the general pattern observed* on how the minimum *average cost* of a good varies *in the long-run*, as a production company moves adopting an increasing size/structure: *LRAC(q)*. This concept (broken grey line) is often also referred to in the textbooks -as we have already seen - as the *Industry's* minimum *average cost*[21], *IC(q)*. The following figure 6a is simply a generalisation of the descriptive diagram in figure 6, using the same numerical example. It, thus, summarises the behaviour observed as empirically more general of the *long-run average cost, LRAC(q)*, of a good, enterprise or 'industry'. (For the sake of clarity, I have dispensed with representing in 6a the different short-run average cost; moreover, the graph has been horizontally 'zoomed out', in order to provide a broader and more representative perspective of the most general case).

This figure also allows us to highlight a crucial dynamic issue, also generally relegated in the economics' standard model (ESM): that what this scheme describes – illustrated by the numerical values that appear by way of example – would be the reflection of a given situation as regards the state of technology, and the cost prices of the production factors. This situation will correspond to a specific time – for example,

[21] With the sense for 'industry' like when we talk, for instance, about the 'sugar industry'.

the current one, year 20xx. That is, the above schematic descriptions will be the result of a given set of *technology options available,* and a given *cost price for each factor,* at the time taken as reference. Therefore, the relationship depicted in Figure 6a between minimum ('efficient') average cost, *IC,* and volume of units produced, *q*, [*IC(q)*], describes a technical-economic situation subject to changes over time. Within this dynamic perspective, technological changes would play the dominant role. These changes tend historically to displace the (minimum) average cost in the industry, IC(q), downward, in the sense of the double arrows in the diagram.

Figure 6a: *General pattern observed for the minimum average cost of a good (or for an 'only-one-product-firm'), in the long-run*, LRAC(q), or industry's average cost, IC(q)*

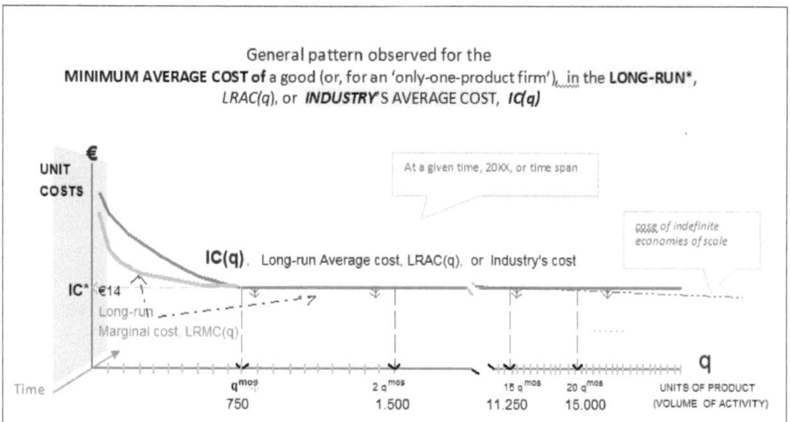

In any case, the empirical evidence on *non-decreasing* returns to scale as an overall pattern is both overwhelmingly obvious and reinforced by those technology changes.

***Generic evidence's inductive statement* 4.** From the systematic observation of the overall business panorama of any of our market economies (countries), it is easy to identify clear generic patterns, as the followings ones:

- Large-scale production by large companies - both industrial and services – allows them to operate at constant, or even decreasing, unit costs (seemingly indefinite economies of scale).
- The merger, absorption, or purchase of companies from the same sector of activity by a leading firm is usually explained and defended by the top executives involved in these operations as a source of synergies, of costs savings. These transactions are generally associated with the aim of producing or operating at a larger scale (at least, the sum of those of the merged companies'); as well as with obtaining savings in overhead, structural's costs, (costs of 'administration', 'management', logistics, internal services, etc.). Also, the purchasing of other companies respond sometimes to the strategic aim of the leader firm of absorbing current or future competitors (e.g., entering into a new market/ territory by buying companies that are already selling there). All of this corroborates the fact that becoming a big(ger) company (we then tend to talk about *corporation*) is associated with savings in, precisely, overhead costs per unit of output (not the opposite, as the ESM assumes, and we will discuss more in detail in the next section) for the enterprise leading the merger or purchase.

In short, what the empirical observation of the business economic world shows us regarding the unit costs of a product or service for a given producer enterprise is that:

> For volumes of production higher than the corresponding ***minimum*** *optimal (efficient) scale (**mos**)*, the *average cost* tends to be constant, or keeps decreasing to some degree. That is, in general *returns to scale are non-decreasing*: the overall observed pattern is ***constant returns***[22], or *increasing returns* for certain

[22] If any reader - a colleague by profession or not - knows of any real case of a good/company/ industry for which decreasing returns are observed (as the company size grows, and thus the volume of units produced/delivered, the average cost is higher) I would sincerely thank s/he for let me know about. It will be a curious thing for me, for in my professional life I have not ever detected or read of any real case at all.

large-scale-produced goods, for which economies of scale are not entirely, or not at all, exhausted for a company's volumes-of-production/sizes beyond the corresponding ***mos***.

In more formal terms, the *long-run average cost* of a good, *LRAC(q)*, – or *industry's average cost, IC(q) – generally tends to be constant* indefinitely from a given volume of units on (the corresponding q^{mos} for the good in question), or declining (remnant economies of scale)[23], (Figures 6 and 6a). Also, therefore, the corresponding *long-run marginal cost, LRMC(q)*, will tend (by mathematical definition) to be equal to the average cost, i.e., also constant (or slightly decreasing) in relation to the volume of units, q.

Furthermore, certain agricultural and livestock products – the type of usual fictional examples that are common in standard economics texts for arguing the opposite – do not actually show up as an exception in this regard: when the minimum climatic-geographical conditions for certain crops do not occur or the appropriate land is not well available in a given country, the concerned example-products simply are not produced in that economy. The same is overall applicable to mining industries, another source of imagined examples about these topics in mainstream economics. (This issue deserves a more systematic discussion and arguments: we will have the opportunity for this in point 3.5, 2).

---

[23] This is the case for certain goods, for which, as already noted, the seemingly indefinite scope of *increasing returns or economies of scale* (increase in total costs somewhat less than proportionally to the increase in the volume of units produced/delivered) is something in the public domain, 'common knowledge'. This is particularly evident for certain manufacturing companies: from those producing photovoltaic panels, TV sets, or USB sticks, to those producing loaves of bread, or ready-made food, for example as well as in some software-services type companies.

3.4.4 Empirical contrasting of the standard models of the *supply* (price) *function*, and the *market equilibrium point*

A remarkable consequence of the above observations is the conclusion that the economic reality does not show evidence of upward *supply curves*; i. e., it does not support the ESM's assumption that, for any good or service, the more total units to be offered in the market by the producer-supplier enterprises as a whole, the higher the offer price they 'come obliged' to require. This classic postulate about the *supply function* for a good (offer-price, as a function of the sum of the quantities offered by all undertakings in the sector), which in graphic language translates into an upward curve, cannot be sustained empirically –as several authors have already pointed out[24]. However, such axiom plays a core role in mainstream economics/ microeconomics textbooks, especially for building and defining the ESM's sub-model of the *market equilibrium* for a good.

Moreover, that classic postulate implies a contradiction internal to the ESM itself, as we have seen before in 2.5.3. Let us review the argument here, now with more empirical insights from the *production* world: The *supply price's function* for a good means the total number of units of product/service that the producer/supplier undertakings *as a whole* are willing to offer at a given price. This function, is defined in the ESM as equal to the *long-run marginal cost, LRMC(q)*, for a number of units greater than the corresponding ***mos***. And, at the same time (and here the contradiction starts) in the ESM this *LRMC* is supposed to be higher the greater the number of units produced beyond the corresponding q^{mos} units (hence the classical '*upward* supply curve', we have seen in figure 4). However, this ESM's definition of the *supply function* is contradictory with other of its basic assumptions: that of

---

[24] Sraffa (1926: 540-541), Morgenstern (1972: 1176) , and Keen (2011: 128, 136), among others.

"There are no entry barriers in the industry, and all of the firms in it behave with perfect efficiency, in the short and long run; therefore, all of them have the same (optimal) size or production scale (q^{mos} units) and operate at the same average cost (the minimum possible one, IC* monetary units; which for each firm will 'mathematically' be equal to its marginal cost)"[25]. According to the latter – and, thus, following the logics of the ESM itself – the sum of the quantities offered in the market would be: (q^{mos} units) x (*number of active firms*) ≡ Q; and thereby the price required by firms always the same, IC* monetary units; i.e., a constant, not increasing, offer price. So, the adjusting variable, to meet the market demand, would be the *number of active firms* in the market. Therefore, within the standard model itself the supply function for a good should be represented by a flat line – as already argued, for example, by the authors cited in the prior footnote 24.

Figure 7: *Overall pattern of the supply function for a good, according to empirical inductive conclusions, and the related market equilibrium point*

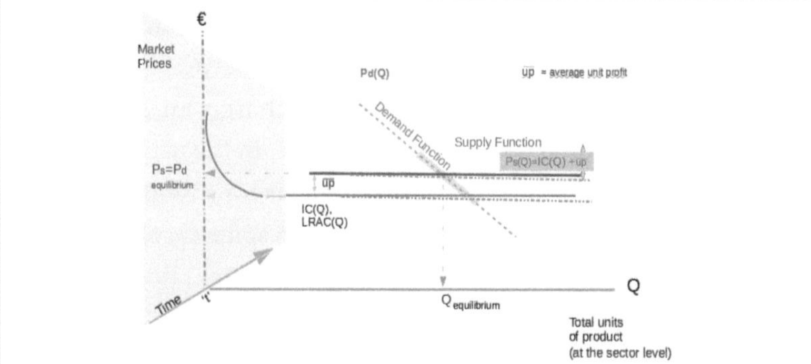

[25] Why then the usual reference in the ESM to 'marginal cost' – and not to 'average cost'? because the ESM, 1) assumes that all the enterprises producing and supplying the good in question are perfectly efficient, and thus the average cost for each of them *is the minimum possible one and therefore equal to the corresponding marginal cost*; and 2) as has been commented in 3.3., one of the ESM's tenets is 'marginalism'; so when marginal cost is quantitatively equal to *average cost*, reference is systematically made to the former instead of to the latter.

(Exploiting the advantages of the standard graphical language): The shadowed segment partially overlapping the dashed line representing the demand function *Pd(Q)* stands for emphasising the unavoidable constrains for estimating the demand for a given good: the pairs of values *Pd, Q* valid to approximate the demand function at a given time, t, come usually limited to those values observed over recent periods[26]. Indeed, just the shadowed segment should be used for representing the demand function itself, for period *t*. To consider points (Pd, Q) beyond the two ends of the segment – as is the usual – implies to make counterfactual estimates of the type: "which would the quantity demanded be if the price was significantly higher, or lower, than that recently observed?"), which, certainly, entails a low degree of likelihood for the resulting pairs (*Pd, Q*).

In any case, even if we accept the ESM's classical generic definition for the 'supply function', "*Ps(Q)*, equal to *LRMC(q)*, from q^{mos} units on", according to observational evidence (outlined in figure 6a above) such a function would not generally turn out to be an upward-slope curve (which would mean that for the active enterprises to increase their total supply they would require to charge an increasingly higher price), but rather a flat, horizontal, line, in the usual graphical language (price, P_s, in the vertical axis, and sector's total units, Q, in the horizontal axis). Moreover, such flat (or, in some cases, somewhat downward, thanks to indefinite economies of scale[27]) line would not actually indicate the supply price but merely the *lower supply price limit* on the part of producers, since in the real economic world they

[26] Older historical observations (for example, a time series of past years' data) use not to be valid for the above because the *ceteris paribus* condition is rarely fulfilled along time for such issues: the determinants of Demand – customers preferences, available substitutable goods, per capita income, overall economic situation, regulations, etc.– are ordinarily changing over time.

[27] Dashed line in figures 6a and 7; especially in the case of many mass-production manufactured products (footnote 23).

normally operate with a given profit margin over cost (this basic observation – market prices are normally higher than the respective unit costs – is empirically dealt with further, in point 4.1). The supply price that will actually prevail in each case depends basically on the minimum *industry average cost* at the time (IC* monetary units) for the good in question, and on the *average unit profit* in the sector (which in turn will depend on the supply-side market structure: how many active companies, with which strategies, market shares, etc.). While the total traded quantity (*Q* of equilibrium) will basically be determined by the demand function at that time, $P_d(Q)$.

The former assertion about the 'market equilibrium point' has also an important consequence for comparisons with the *general equilibrium theory* in this point: that it cannot be said that there is a single point of equilibrium for this or that good; i.e., a specific pair price-and-quantity of equilibrium where – as the ESM states (see figure 4a) – a timeless downward demand curve intersects an also timeless upward supply curve (the higher the total quantity, the higher the price). On the contrary – since both, demand function and average unit profit, are subject to short run changes, the only prediction suggested by the above scheme derived from empirical inductive patterns is that – using the numerical example in Figures 6, 6a– the price that will tend to prevail in the market for the concerned good ($P_s = P_d$) will be around IC* (€14) plus a certain *average unit profit*; but that the quantity (Q, total traded units) comes not mainly defined by the supply side. It will rather depend on the size of demand for the good in question – besides on the abovementioned average unit profit, at the time. This unit profit will depend, in turn, on the existing market structure and situation regarding the competition/monopoly axis; (these issues regarding market structure and profit rates prevailing in our markets economies are those that are dealt with in Chapter 4).

3.5 The 'decreasing returns' axiom cannot be sustained

The assumptions on which the axiom is grounded are not supported by empirical evidence.

Given the relevance of this assertion, let us review more precisely the already advanced arguments. We have now presumably more elements to focus more narrowly on them. Figure 6a is a graphical-conceptual representation of what the observation of the business-economic world shows us as the general pattern regarding the key relationship, *unit cost* vs. *company size* or production capacity: that the *average cost* of a good tends to be constant (or somewhat decreasing) indefinitely starting from a certain volume of units or production dimension (***minimum** optimal scale*). This mos depends on the type of good, the technological possibilities available, and the prices of the factors at the time. In other words, what reality most commonly shows us is the situation of constant (or increasing) returns to scale for larger and larger volumes of production/size of the firm, not decreasing returns. On the other hand, the logical ('theoretical') explanation for this observed evidence is, certainly, elemental: replicability of the *minimal* optimal scale.

However, as we saw in chapter 2, in most 'reference' manuals as well as mainstream economics literature the theoretical hypothesis of 'decreasing returns to scale' remains as the 'normal' pattern, as a cornerstone of the standard model. So, in mainstream textbooks the general behaviour of the *long-run average cost* of any good, relative to the volume of units produced by an undertaking, is usually still represented by a 'U-shaped' curve; i.e., graphically asserting that the average cost rises progressively when the respective volume of q^{mos} units for the good in question is surpassed by a producer firm. This is formally a deductive hypothesis; which, as we have seen, simply does not correspond with economic-business reality; but that is necessary in the ESM for later to conclude with the universality of efficient competitive markets. In any case, the persistence of this 'U-shaped' hypothesis as dominant in most economics/ microeconomics textbooks is certainly a surprising phenomenon; one for the sociology of science indeed.

It is, therefore, worth devoting closer attention to it, going back to the two second-level arguments that, as we have seen before, are often invoked to justify in this or that textbook why such a hypothesis; (this, provided that the authors say or argue something about it since the more frequent is to merely suggest in an implicit way that 'it is well known to be so').

These two, alternative or simultaneous, arguments – pointed out earlier in 2.3 are: that if a company grows beyond the corresponding q^{mos} volume of units, such a company, 1) "***becomes 'too big'***, *in the sense of uneconomical: its average cost increases, because the bigger the company, the more complex it is; which causes management and control costs to increase more than proportionately, and/or that bureaucratic dysfunctions in the company are generated.* All of this will drive up the average cost (= decreasing returns to scale)". And/or, 2) "*it always occurs that it is not possible to further increase one of the necessary (fixed) factors of production (= the assumption of* '***the limitative fixed factor***'). Therefore, if the company wants to scale up production, it will face decreasing returns." We can find also a certain mixture of (1) and (2) as a general argument; it depends on the textbook or specialised article that we examine.

However, as has been pointed out in 2.3, such assumptions simply do not hold at all in business reality. The evidence about this is obvious. Let us zoom in on them for a closer discussion, now using the additional empirical findings described so far in this chapter:

3.5.1 Refutation of *'diseconomies when a firm grows and becomes too big'*

Regarding this first deductive assumption (that management costs will rise more than proportionally as the company grows, or that the company will be so complex that it will operate with less efficiency) the empirical evidence against it is overwhelming, as already pointed out earlier. In general, what we can see as generic evidence –indeed, as characteristic of our market economies– is rather the opposite: companies tend to grow as much as their sales possibilities allow them; to such a point that annual growth is frequently presented by large companies as one of their strategic objectives. Also, as 'capitalist' companies, if they do, it will be for reasons of economic advantage (profits).

Large industrial and service companies and large commercial chains offer striking examples of this; although they are not exceptional cases in this regard. The same tendency to indefinite growth as a source of economic advantage is widely observed as a general pattern in business behaviour. In any case, large corporations, with their complex organisation, are representative of the fact that the costs of controlling, organising, and running the firm (in short: *management costs*) do not tend to grow more than proportionally to its volume of business. In the case this might occur to some extent for any of these costs, we should deduce that this comes over-compensated by savings in other costs (because purchasing at a larger scale, for example).

Mergers, as well as the acquisition of a company by a bigger one from the same sector, are another source of indirect empirical evidence in this regard[28]. These operations often tend to respond to the idea of

[28] We may think in the cars sector, for example; but also in so varied ones as insurances, beer, telecommunication services, rice, flat-rolled aluminium, banking , ...

achieving greater competitiveness, lower costs, by becoming a bigger company! A merger, or absorption, means in the first instance to produce/ provide services at a larger scale – at least the sum of the turnover of the merging companies, and to do that with the same average cost, or cheaper. This uses to be got either by exploiting remnant economies of scale or by obtaining savings – precisely in 'management' costs! (see Jones, 2004:386): when a merger is carried out, there is no need to duplicate certain internal services or to maintain certain management positions in the new organisational structure. The resulting company doesn't need to continue to hire the people in some of the 'inherited' managerial positions as well as the staff of certain internal services previously employed by the merging companies. If you are fond of economic news in the press, you will surely have some case in mind in this respect; likely, for example, from the banking sector.

On the other hand, if we think about it, the absence of a topic about 'not to grow too much' as a teaching unit on MBA courses, constitutes also a piece of indirect evidence in this respect. A circumstantial evidence, but significant of what the business world shows us about the topic: If you have attended an MBA, or simply review the contents of prestigious MBAs – and, more in general, business schools' programmes – you will find nothing about the idea that for each good/ industry/ sector there is a maximum volume of units, an optimal *company* size, which no industry/sector company should be interested in exceeding.

As is generally accepted, MBA programmes offer high professional training for business management. The bulk of their topics is addressed to conveying knowledge on business management and on 'best practices' that the accumulation of personal and corporate experiences has shown to be successful; an on which there is some professional/academic consensus. Thus, professionals with extensive experience in management, generally still at office, play a relevant role in the cadre of teachers. This tends to be composed more of experts or business management specialists than of academics. The use of real cases ('case method') and simulations about taking current business decisions (business game) play a leading role in the teaching methodology. All this is intended to train the attendants in decision-making, oriented at eventually improving business profits.

All of this is precisely what the persons who enrol in them, and are willing to pay their high fees (MBAs and the like, with some prestige, are often quite expensive) expect to get: to learn from experienced people the 'best practices' to run an enterprise, to manage a company, or a functional area of a corporation, with professional success.

This is why subjects such as ('best practices' on) selling prices policy, growth strategies, niche market search, product differentiation, market segmentation, cost accounting, strategic decision-making, advertising decisions, managers' motivation, mergers and takeovers, financial strategy, ... etc. are commonly found on the courses listing. We will not, however, find any topic about "optimal size of the company", anything remotely similar to "experience shows us that in each case you have to look for the right size of the company: not too small, not too big"; neither anything about "not to grow beyond a certain volume because it is uneconomical'. On the contrary, the topic 'Enterprise's growth strategy and policy', which goes around the idea of ensuring or improving the company's competitiveness – and ultimately, its profitability, is repeatedly and transversely present within MBA subjects.

3.5.2 Refutation of 'lower average costs end by increasing because of a *fixed, limiting factor*'

About this second deductive assumption of the ESM, again it is a situation that simply is not observed in the real economic world, except for some anecdotal cases, as already pointed out in 2.3. The examples that often accompany this deductive assumption in the standard economics textbooks are in fact abstract, imagined examples, specifically relating to certain instances of agricultural production (such as the coffee plantation, mentioned earlier). [Currently mainstream neo-classical economics is still indebted, on issues like these, to the prevalence of farming for classical, pioneering, economists.] The examples usually referred to are moreover unrealistic, and illogical in a market economy with companies that behave in pursuit of a profit. None of the textbooks or manuals referred to earlier (2.2, footnote 6) provides any real case as a demonstrative illustration.

In these imagined examples and their argumentation – which is almost literally that of a classic, David Ricardo[29] – the starting point is the implicit axiom that each farm or plantation competes with the others; which is clearly unrealistic regarding the agricultural/ business market. Obviously, it is not 'plantations' (farm/plantation: a certain area of land, in a certain location, with a certain dedication of human and material resources) that operate (compete) in the market. It is the owners of the same (i.e., agricultural undertakings). Thus,

[29] David Ricardo stated his theoretical deduction about *decreasing returns* 'because the availability of suitable agricultural land is limited' by referring specifically to wheat farming in England, in the first half of the nineteenth century. That was the time of debates in the British Parliament on the 'Corn Law'. However, as it was demonstrated shortly after, even the empirical evidence at the time on wheat production and prices in England did not support Ricardo's theoretical assumption (Blaug, 1957, p. 182).

Decades later, another father of classical economics, Alfred Marshall, not only embraced Ricardo's *decreasing-returns-due-to-a-limiting-production-factor* theory, but also generalised it to all goods, by formalising mathematically/graphically the idea of 'spontaneous equilibrium of markets' formulated in the previous century by Adam Smith and summarised in his attractive semantic image of 'the invisible hand.'

In any case, Ricardo's initial argument, "(land-owners) coming forced to use land that is less and less suitable" (or its possible equivalent for industrial and service sectors), presupposes a kind of business behaviour that is simply not observed historically in practice as relevant. In the same way, and probably for the same reason, there is no indication of farming enterprises producing bananas in Germany, for example.

if an undertaking or company that owns a coffee plantation wants to increase its production beyond what 'its' existing availability of adequate land allows, it can buy another plantation, rent it, or buy another company that owns other plantations. More generally, as is easily observable, it can buy or rent other equally suitable lands, because the very axiom that the appropriate type of land existing (in which territory? in the whole country?) is limited for every company that produces the good in question is at odds with what we can observe in the real world.

Similar reasoning applies to the other large primary sectors: extractive activities, from oil to mining. As argued before (2.3-ii), it is not observed that the specific characteristics of these productive activities – be they iron, coal, copper or cobalt mining, or oil extraction – have led to a market situation where 'many' small mining/drilling companies (each of them owning only one mine/well of a similar size) make up a mass of supplier companies jointly covering the respective market[30]. It is rather the opposite that we can observe: in most cases, they are primary sectors dominated by large or very large companies.

Could, nevertheless, the mining of gold, platinum, and other precious metals and/or that of 'rare earths' be examples of decreasing returns because of a limiting fixed factor?

---

[30] One could think that the closest to the idea of decreasing returns 'by a limiting fixed factor' that can be observed in practice is, for example, when the international price of oil rises – and it is perceived in the sector as a relatively stable rise, some oil companies put into activity wells that were inactive because they were somewhat more costly to exploit. However, it should be noted that in such a case the cause-effect relationship is the opposite: the market price rises (cause), and this makes this or that company in the sector decide to increase its production even if it means exploiting its 'expensive' wells (effect).

On the other hand, a representative counter-example can be seen in ***Appendix C***: the general relationship observed between total oil production in the USA and the price is the opposite of what would be expected according to the theory of 'decreasing returns'. Production fell steadily from 1985, while the price was generally rising. And the opposite is true from 2008 onwards: production shot up, while the price stayed the same or went down.

The point here is that no empirical data on production costs in relation to variations in Tn of metal obtained (with the usual degree of commercially standard purity) is actually available for researchers. There are not even any generic data on this: the comparatively few involved companies do not disclose this kind of information. We simply know generalities about what these special productive activities – concentrated in rather few countries – involve: exploiting the ores of a certain set of pits or mines, each one with varying pure-metal percentages; separating, concentrating the metal, etc. And we may also obtain a global overview of the market for these metals and 'rare earths'; for example, on the gold market, which is a typically worldwide market – as is also the case with the other examples. But we cannot know much more regarding these sectors, due to obvious information difficulties.

Thus, given the absence of a minimum of observational data, the deductive assumption/prediction that "if the producer companies (of gold, for example), having observed a stable increase in demand, increase the number of Tn produced quarterly, this will increase their average cost per Tn (on having to exploit deposits of poorer metal)" could not be ruled out. But it is obviously hard – if not impossible in practice– to verify such deductive assumption.

However, this 'research problem' would not actually be the essential one on the issue. These mining industries (gold, coltan, diamonds, ...) are not in fact relevant to our present discussion because their respective market *is not a domestic one* (the country where these products are obtained) – which is the reference framework of the standard model – but a worldwide market. A market, moreover, with relatively few buyers, by the way; (for example, a significant share of the world's gold purchases are made by central banks, to be kept in their safes).

Therefore these goods (precious metals/'rare earths') are not significant as examples when speaking, in economics, of the 'limiting-fixed-factor issue', or of an upward supply price function that confronts the corresponding consumer demand function, *within a given economy* (country). They are goods whose production-and-trade conditions do not respond to those assumed in the frame of reference of mainstream economic theory; i.e., that of producers on the one hand (with their respective marginal costs), consumers on the other (with their respective marginal utility), perfect competition in the market, general markets equilibrium, etc., within a given economy (a country/state); which, moreover, in such a standard explanatory model is supposed to be a closed economy, without foreign trade.

To extend this discussion of the axiom of the 'limitative fixed factor' to industrial and service productions would result in even more obvious conclusions – because in general, those business activities are closer to most of us. In these cases –the prevalent ones in our market economies – it would even be difficult to build an 'imagined example'. What would this supposed 'limitative fixed factor' be, which would prevent an industrial undertaking from growing –because it would imply an increase in the average cost of the product? Perhaps the company not being able to buy or rent more machines like the ones it uses at the time? Or not being available in the market more factory buildings to buy or rent? Or that the possibility of recruiting more staff with certain qualifications does not exist in the medium-long run? ... It would be between absurd and unreal.

In short: it is 'companies' that produce in their different plantations, farms, or production plants, have a certain average cost, and operate in the market. It is not each farm, plantation, production line, manufacturing plant, well, or mine. This is so both today and in the days of Ricardo and Marshall.

Moreover, no company is known that, to grow in production volume, was bent on having a single coffee plantation – or a single modest production plant, or being constrained to a single mine, etc. while absurdly trying to produce more and more units in it, even though its unit cost rocketed. From a business perspective, this would be stupid behaviour. What is rather observed overall is that when companies perceive possibilities of selling – in a stable way (middle-long term) – considerably more than their present structure allows them – and of doing that with some improvement in their profits, they take the path of growth. They move to buy or hire more 'fixed factors' (land, machines, industrial facilities, new production plants, more workers, technicians, etc.). That is, they make a significant leap in their production and selling capacity – in their size, in a word, while maintaining or even reducing their average cost.

Looking at the matter from another side: to use the traditional deductive assumption of the 'limitative fixed-factor' –historically based on agriculture– amounts to pre-supposing the unreal situation that a plantation or farm belongs to a company (or entrepreneur/s, or owner/s), which cannot own another farm/plantation (!). Furthermore, it entails that, for some unspecified reason, the different 'plantations' existing in the economy (country) have a similar extension; that that allows to apply the same (a given) 'technology'/ degree of mechanisation –since the ESM implicitly assumes in this regard that all 'plantations' achieve the same minimum average cost. (In the above argument we may substitute 'plantation' with production plant, farm, factory, etc.). This set of assumptions is as unreal now as it was in the nineteenth century.

The fact that, in spite of all the above, this 'limitative fixed-factor' argument is still being used in many current economics/ microeconomics textbooks – as a base to postulate the 'decreasing returns' paradigm, should give food for thought. However, we cannot rule out that in some cases (textbooks) the explanation for maintaining such an assumption of the 'limitative fixed-factor' may be the fact that the author is inadvertently confusing in some way the *long-run* average cost (Figures 3; or 6 and 6a) with the *short-*

run average cost (Figures 1 and 5). As we have seen, in this latter scenario we are looking at an enterprise with a given size, structure or installed production capacity, which, if forced up, will certainly make the firm's average cost progressively to increase. But, of course, this current productive structure of the firm can be enlarged; throughout a process that will logically take *a certain time*; and this time span is precisely what makes us use the expression (in the) *short-run*. A time perspective that then brings us to the *long-run* average cost scenario, the relevant one here, in which – in a nutshell, to avoid further repetition – the explanatory framework and unit-cost's general patterns are different (fig. 6, 6a, vs. fig. 3).

The point is that, despite all that, this 'limitative fixed factor argument is still being used in many current economics/microeconomics textbooks to describe the world of production and firms – and as a base to postulate the 'decreasing returns' paradigm. In this regard, we cannot rule out that in some cases (textbooks) the explanation for maintaining such an assumption of the 'limitative fixed factor' may be that the author is inadvertently confusing in some way the *long-run* average cost (Figures 3; or 6 and 6a) with the *short-run* average cost (Figures 1 and 5). In this latter scenario, let us remind, we would be considering an enterprise with a given size, structure, or installed production capacity, which, if the firm forces up, will certainly make the firm's average cost progressively increase. This current productive structure of the firm can, of course, be enlarged; but throughout a process that will logically take a certain time and require a given investment; which leads us to analytically get out of the 'short-run' scenario. And is precisely this dynamic perspective that brings us to the long-run average cost scenario, which is the relevant one for our present topic; a scenario in which – in a nutshell, to avoid further repetition – the explanatory framework and unit cost's general patterns are different: average cost constant or something decreasing.

In this respect, the following summary of the overall patterns induced from observing the world of production regarding companies' dynamics will result useful.

3.5.3 The dynamic perspective: technologies and firms' occupancy level

Overall pattern of the sequence short-middle-long run

In the world of production, and especially in industrial sectors, there do is normally more than one way or technology to produce a given good (product or service) – using the term *technology* with the usual engineering meaning. A starting-up firm may thus decide among the different options available at the time. A decision that will depend on the technological state-of-the-art for the good in question and on the volume of production-per-period the starting firm is planning for.

Once in operation (i.e., *in the short run*), a given firm has one of those available technologies installed; which means it has set up a specific production plant or unit, endowed with a given *equipment set*: machines, production chains, fixed installations and facilities, etc. This specific set will be associated with a given *production capacity* in terms of volume of units, which will also depend on whether there is the possibility that the equipment set may be run for more than one *work shift*. Whatever the case, the firm will also have hired a given team of workers to run such equipment, to produce the planned number of units per period. And will regularly purchase specific inputs – energy, materials, services, etc. that will also come determined, as for their features and proportions, by the installed technology itself. In short, a given technology to produce a given good entails a certain quantitative and qualitative mix of inputs, a certain 'formula' or 'recipe'. In other words, a fixed proportion among inputs; except regarding the equipment set when the firm is operating below its full occupancy level. Otherwise, i.e., if it is operating at full capacity, the leeway regarding the proportions of inputs uses to be irrelevant.

If the referred firm decides to expand to producing beyond its current installed capacity, it may decide: (a) add some additional machine, robotic unit, or assembly chain to the existing ones, within the same production facilities and premises, as well as hire the required additional workers to run the additional equipment; or – to continue within this, say, some-weeks *middle-run* scenario, the firm may decide to establish a second shift; and eventually up to a third shift. Or (b) the firm may decide – here the *long-run* scenario – to carry out a technological leap in the sense of moving to an, if available, 'superior', technology. This, usually in the double sense of a more automated/ robotic/ digitalised technology that entails, both, a larger production capacity (scale) while allowing operating at a something lower average cost (economies of scale). This moving across technologies entails a firm's strategic decision, whose implementation requires a certain time and normally a significant investment. It is, thus, an issue that refers to the long-run scenario. This option of carrying out a technological leap may, however, not exist for a firm; either because there is just one 'technology' for efficiently producing the good in question at the time, or because the company is already operating with the 'top' and cheaper available technology.

Alternatively, regarding (b), or in the case the firm already is in this latter situation– such a firm may decide simply to duplicate (triplicate, etc.) the set of equipment and workers it has currently in operation, so as to be able to produce two, three, ... times more units than it is producing at the time. Such expanding path means setting up parallel *lines of production* using the same technology, or, directly, new clone *production plants* (Schlefer: 107). Along this expansionary path, the firm grows in size, uses *the same technology*, produces at a larger scale, and with a not-higher unit cost. That is, it operates under *constant* or even *increasing* returns to scale; the latter possibility in so far that for some fixed inputs (some management positions, overall services, ...) it is not necessary they be duplicated (triplicated, etc.).

The above arguments and sequence, markedly referring to an industrial type sector or firm, are also applicable to services and commercial activities, just by modifying the references to the components of the *equipment set*.

To sum up

The deductive hypothesis of the *Economics Standard Model*, ESM, of 'for each good, there is an optimal volume of units of product, a certain size for a producer enterprise –relatively small compared to market demand, for which the average cost is the minimum possible, and that for larger production dimensions of the firm its average cost is progressively higher ('law' of *decreasing returns*)' is not supported at all by empirical evidence.

What is actually observed as a general pattern in the world of firms and production is that for each good (product or service) there is a ***minimum*** *optimal scale* of production or firm's dimension, at a certain point in time. 'Optimal' means here that it corresponds to producing a given quantity of output (q^{mos} units) with the cheapest-possible technology; i.e., at the *lowest possible average cost* at that time. Companies in such industry that are able or want to sell more or much more units than that, simply *replicate* internally this ***minimum*** *optimal unit of production* 2, 10, 40, ... times; be it through expanding to a larger production plant with parallel production units or lines, and/or setting up separate production plants, etc. This, for a specific company, to the extent its possibilities of selling in the market – with a given rate of profits – make it advisable for its managers.

Based on the arguments put forward in this section, it can therefore be said that the so-called 'law' of *decreasing returns to scale* is more a persistent belief than an unfortunate simplification of reality in mainstream economics/microeconomics texts. Or it is rather a schematic simplification of a belief. From the beginnings of the classical approach, when in textbooks the 'law' is accompanied by examples, these are in fact, as has been argued in this section, descriptions of invented, non-real, business situations.

3.6 What specific studies tell us about economies of scale

The problem of *direct* measuring of firms' *economies of scale* in practice

The empirical evidence commented so far on economies of scale – which strongly points to constant or indefinite economies of scale (non-decreasing returns; i.e., constant or decreasing long-run average costs) – has been on the one hand basically generic, indirect, and on the other hand, direct, in the sense of studies on unit costs' behaviour, based on business surveys. This observational evidence have allowed us to develop overall assertions on the economic real-world as that companies generally behave tending to grow as much as they can (and so increase their 'market share'), that is not infrequent to observe large companies operating as leaders in a given market – in which case it is difficult to smaller companies to compete, that large companies or corporations do not show to have proportionately higher management/control/ administration costs, but rather the opposite, and that there are no recorded significant cases where the progressive increase in the scale of production of a good i.e., in the size of the producer enterprise – is limited (in economic terms) by the existence of a *limitative* production factor (no possibilities of it being increased).

Yet, somebody familiar with the economies-of-scale subject might well ask: but what about the *specific* research on *economies of scale*, a field on which there is such abundant literature? Let us now consider that: The ideal scheme of such case-specific research, the way to obtain specific direct empirical evidence on scale economies for specific goods, would be to measure the correlation between *average cost* and *volume of units produced/sold,* for enterprises of different size, producing the same good, 'g'. This would, therefore, require having available data on *unit costs* of firms with different sizes that are or have recently been in business producing this good 'g'. But the problem (for researchers) to conduct such research is that in practice it is impossible to obtain the mentioned required data. Companies are generally unwilling to disclose data on their *unit costs,* production capacity, technologies, etc. to people from outside (researchers) because firms consider them to be strategic, highly confidential data. If these data were disclosed, it would be valuable information for other companies, especially their suppliers, customers and, of course, competing – present or future – companies.

On the other hand, the most common situation is that any company that is producing a given good or service also produces numerous others, which share some of the productive factors[31]. This situation makes the calculation of the unit cost for each of its products unavoidably subjective. (Each company applies a certain criterion of allocating the common costs among its different products – including the criterion of not distributing those common costs. This is the big issue in *cost accounting*). In other words, in the hypothetical event that the researcher obtained the data on unit costs of the different companies, these would not be either conceptually homogeneous or reliable enough.

All of the above explains that, despite the abundant literature on 'economies of scale'/ returns to scale/ increasing returns', it is not

[31] The consequences of this determinant feature of the business world for the realistic economics are developed further, in section 5.1

easy to find in it *specific* empirical research itself: at the level of specific products or services, which is the conceptual level the ESM postulate at on *increasing/decreasing returns*.

This statement will probably create raised eyebrows among some colleagues specialized in this field and/or with relevant contributions to such literature on *economies of scale*. So, let me develop the argument and scope of the above statement.

The academic literature on *economies of scale*

Most of the *empirical* articles on *economies of scale* refer nominally to such academic concept of the production world, discussed here, but it applied not to data on such or such a product or service but to more general data: sectoral data, which means statistical aggregates. This is not because of a preference of researchers but of factual lack (for them) of individualised data at the level of products and enterprises. These 'field's limitations' lead to research works that, for example, compare the size or volume of *activity* of a given *statistical sector* (the activity measured in monetary units) with its respective productivity indicators, for various countries. All the calculations are, therefore, made using aggregated figures corresponding to that statistical sector[32]. The main problem this entails is that data from a *statistical sector* (for any country) are unavoidably aggregate figures from (companies that produce/supply) products and services that are actually different, heterogeneous; i.e., outputs of a different nature, to which the Administration has assigned the same statistical code or 'label' – for example 'electronic components'.

---

[32] By way of example: "Differences in Increasing Returns between Technological Sectors: A Panel Data Investigation Using the EU KLEMS Database", Romero, Joao P; McCombie, John S L. *Journal of Economic Studies* 43.5 (0, 2016): 863-878.

Let us take into account that (1) those enterprises included, for statistical purposes, in a given sector or sub-sector are generally multi-product firms. Therefore, the data that each of them provides to their country's statistical Agency (a figure for 'quarter production', a figure for 'total costs', etc.) are already heterogeneous statistical figures. On the other side, (2) any statistical classification of business activities ('sector'), of any public institution and country[33], inevitably groups data from business undertakings of a wide variety of activities and products under the same label or activity code. By way of example in this respect: 'Pharmaceutical Industry' (code NACE-2100); 'Rubber and plastic materials' (code 2200)[34].

Some empirical work can be found that apparently refers to the concept of *economies of scale* itself, as it is defined in the standard economics/ microeconomics textbooks: at the level of specific products and firms.

In other words, the concept associated with the behaviour of the *long-run average cost* of this or that good. From this perspective, the research would ideally address to ascertain whether this average cost is observed to be constant, decreasing or increasing, in relation to the *volume of units* produced by companies of different sizes. This approach is also a traditionally discussed topic in the field of industrial economics.

---

[33] The ONS in the United Kingdom, INSEE in France, DESTATIS in Germany, INE in Spain, BEA in the United States, ... etc

[34] NACE is the statistical classification of economic activities used by EUROSTAT for the EU countries (Standard Industrial Classification, SIC, in the UK). It does not differ substantially from that in USA and other OECD countries. To give an idea of the heterogeneity referred above, here it follows a sample regarding the level of aggregation of the more-detailed data researchers may have available: (in brackets, the corresponding NACE/SIC code, at 4-digit level): "Growing of pome fruits and stone fruits" (code 0124), which therefore groups undertakings producing, oranges, peaches, grape, apples, ...); "Production of meat and poultry meat products" (1013); "Weaving of textiles" (1312): "Manufacture of electric domestic appliances" (2751); "Wholesale of meat and meat products" (4632); Book publishing" (5811); "Wired telecommunication activities"" (6110); "Other monetary intermediation (banking)" (6419); "Management consultancy activities" (7020).

However, invariably these papers actually consist of research works based again on data from an economic sector, in the statistical sense of this expression[35]. Thus, the empirical quantitative data of the research are in fact statistical data, from which 'proxy' variables are constructed by introducing some assumptions. These proxies are then used in the place of those variables that would formally be necessary in order to measure or obtain a certain approximation to the sense and degree of the economies of scale that, on average, prevail in enterprises of that economic sector. Consequently, the quantitative results obtained in such works are difficult to interpret. Mainly because – in addition to having introduced assumptions (given the lack of sufficient or proper data) and using proxy variables – to the fact that sectoral statistics consist (excuse repetition) of highly aggregate, inevitably heterogeneous, data: not referring to a specific good or service.(The title of the above cited article could illustrate this).

Because of all this, despite the abundant and sophisticated academic literature accumulated on the topic of '*economies of scale'/returns to scale*, even the fraction of it that consists of empirical – non-methodological or model-building – studies do not provide indeed precise evidence on the behaviour of *economies of scale* for specific goods (which is the level at which standard economic theory, the ESM, argues). Only empirical evidence on certain 'proxy' algorithms associated with the concept of economies of scale is actually provided. Though, as been said, these proxy variables are calculated based on statistical data for this or that *economic sector*; and thereby for a heterogeneous set of companies, each of them in turn multi-product (e.g., "*Rubber and plastic materials* companies").

---

[35] By way of example: "Does Microelectronics Reduce Economies of Scale? A Case Study in the Turkish Chemical Industry", Karaomerlioglu, Dilek Cetindamar. Review of Industrial Organization 14.3 (May 1999): 219-238.

So heterogeneous are, in general, statistical groupings of economic activities.

3.7 Non-decreasing returns: empirical evidence repeatedly exposed though curiously ignored

The evidence regarding the non-existence in general of a specific *optimal firm's size* for producing/providing a given product or service (a supposed volume of units from which average cost would be increasing) has certainly long been pointed out by prominent economists, who stressed that what is observed in the production and firms sphere points to constant (or increasing) economies of scale, i.e., to *constant or decreasing average cost*. However, these calls to take into account the evidence have surprisingly been mostly 'unattended' by the academic world adhering to mainstream economics. Although he was not the first to underline the above, Piero Sraffa already highlighted the unrealism of the deductive assumption of the presence of decreasing returns when surpassing a certain (comparatively small) volume of production/size of a company:

> "Everyday experience shows that a very large number of undertakings and the majority of those which produce manufactured consumers' goods work under conditions of individual diminishing costs. Almost any producer of such goods, if he could rely upon the market in which he sells his products being prepared to take any quantity of them from him at the current price, without any trouble on his part except that of producing them, would extend his business enormously." (Sraffa, 1926: 543)

And some paragraphs later, (when he refers to the neoclassical theory's assumption of a 'U'-shaped behaviour for the long-run average cost function), he adds,

> "Business men, (…) would consider absurd the assertion that the limit to their production is to be found in the internal conditions of production in their firm"

In the same vein we have, for example, Lancaster (1977: 200), when – as we have seen in section 3.4 he points to the obvious possibility for at least constant returns for any firm producing a given good; a possibility derived from the general fact of the *replicability* of the corresponding *minimal* optimal scale.

Cohen is another academic who continued with Sraffa's *claim*, insisting on the overwhelming evidence on the matter, and in particular asking himself why such evidence was still not considered by the authors and academics of mainstream economic theory. His answer: because admitting such evidence would invalidate the model of *perfect competition* and *general equilibrium* held by such modern neoclassical economic theory:

> "These *auxiliary assumptions* (of *diminishing marginal returns in the short run and decreasing returns to scale in the long run*) provide (to the neoclassical theory) a basis for questioning and discounting empirical evidence of non-increasing costs and thereby retaining the theory.' (...) The theory of the cost conditions of the firms was derived from the conditions necessary for equilibrium in a perfectly competitive industry rather than being derived from historical observation of firms. It is this procedure that accounts for both the empirical inconsistency of the theory and why it cannot be sacrificed without sacrificing the more general theoretical framework of equilibrium economics." (Cohen, 1983: 218)

The title of Cohen's subsequent work on the subject is illustrative in this respect: "Why haven't introductory textbooks resolved Sraffa's 1926 complaints?" (Cohen, 1996). In it he insists on the evidence of *non-decreasing returns to scale*, as the general situation for firms; i.e., that of constant or decreasing average costs. And, consequently, he also insists on the non-sustainability of the *perfect competition* paradigm of the *general equilibrium of competitive markets* – as far as it requires assuming that overall there are decreasing returns to scale in the production of any good.

Other authors should be added to the above critics, even if they do not explicitly challenge the standard model itself. It is the case of those authors (referred to in section 2.5) that represent the exception, regarding reference manuals, in the sense that they effectively take on this obvious and old empirical evidence that provides the real-world observation regarding firms' management and workings. And consequently, in their texts, they present as the general situation one where, starting from a certain volume of units (*minimum* optimal scale), constant returns to scale is the pattern. In other words, they use as an explanatory diagram one in the line of Figure 3a: the representation of the long-run average cost by a lying-down 'L-shape' plot – instead of the orthodox vertical parabola ('U-shape hypothesis'). Thus, for example, one of these authors, Mansfield, summarises the ESM's inconsistency with empirical evidence as follows:

> "(an) interesting conclusion of the empirical studies is that marginal cost *in the short run* tends to be constant in the relevant output range (of a firm) . This result seems to be at variance with the theory presented earlier ..., which says that marginal cost curves should be U-shaped ... Although marginal costs may well be relatively constant over a wide range, (...) they .. eventually increase with increases in output (in the short run). ... *(in) the long-run* average cost function in most industries seems to be L-shaped ... not U-shaped. That is, there is *no evidence* that it turns upward, rather than remaining horizontal, at high output levels (in the range of observed data)' (1994: 242)"

Likewise, the authors of the popular textbook on industrial economics, *Economics of Industrial Organisation*, William Shepherd and Joanna Shepherd, note in their text –when analysing the empirical observations available– the non-evidence on decreasing returns to scale for firms. And they also underline what they consider to be the surprising, repeated, and old ignorance of this reality in the ESM field; in economics in general and in most microeconomics texts in particular (Shepherd & Shepherd, 2004, 5th Ed.; 162-6). Philip Klein argues in the same vein in his 2006 work (Klein, 2006: 27-9).

In short, that obvious reiterated observational evidence has been – and for some reason is still – ignored in mainstream economic theory, which holds itself to the assumption of 'decreasing returns to scale' as a universal pattern. A deductive assumption that is certainly untenable when weighted against the overwhelming evidence on the issue. However and this is the likely explanation for its persistency in spite of everything (as Cohen points out in the above quoted paragraph), it is an assumption that is necessary for the ESM to postulate the automatism toward competitive markets. That is, it is a key piece within the chain of assumptions/axioms presented in chapter 1 and analysed in detail in Chapter 2 – as well as contrasted and discussed in the present one–. A chain or sequence which – as a reminder – states that, in general,

> «In the production of any good, 'g', decreasing returns to scale (average cost grows) appear from a given volume of production by a firm (qos units); this volume defines, thus, the optimal size for any undertaking producing such good. An optimal size in the sense it is the one that allows a firm to operate, at full efficiency, i.e., with the minimum long-run average cost. This firm size, expressed in volume of production, is small compared to market demand. Thereby, demand ends by being covered by many firms (suppliers, sellers), all of them of such optimal, size, the same efficiency, and thereby the same average cost (which is the minimum possible; and thereby equal to the respective

marginal cost). This leads to a situation of strong competition in such a market; none of the sector's firms has power over the price and other elements of the market of 'g'. Therefore, these companies will sell the product at a price equal to their (identical) average cost, which in turn equals the marginal cost. This means that, for the good in question, a perfectly competitive and in-equilibrium market will automatically result, characterised by: Price=Average cost=Marginal cost; thereby, zero profits. This applies to every good (product, service, or 'industry'), what ultimately will spontaneously lead to a general equilibrium of competitive markets in the economy.»

Or, to put it in more formal terms, it is the chain-sequence of the theoretical paradigm that draws upon the deductive assumption that in general the long-run average cost for a (any) good behaves – in relation to the volume of units produced by a firm – following a 'U-shaped' diagram ('law' of decreasing returns to scale). A paradigm that has as its correlative deduction that the *supply* price *function* for the (any) good comes depicted by an upward-slopping curve; which means to graphically postulate that the higher the sum of units jointly offered in the market by the supplier firms, the higher the price they will require. Such paradigm, with its correlative *supply price curve,* is kept in most textbooks in spite of its obvious unrealism because it comes out necessary for still maintaining – in an inertial manner, by each generation of authors – the theoretical model of the General Equilibrium of Competitive Markets (GE), with its qualification of 'an economic social optimum', that pervades mainstream economics/ microeconomics (ESM)[36].

[36] Or it is necessary for them to maintain it as an overall descriptive framework, while laterally admitting the existence of non-decreasing returns situations but as exceptional situations (see the following point).

Something similar can be said, of course, of other ESM elements. To start with, its instrumental assumption of "there exists an equal distribution of income among citizens", which is implicitly maintained in most manuals despite its obvious unreality. As it is also the case with the no-consideration of externalities – or their relegation to side chapters or specialised texts. Both analytical 'exclusions' are also necessary to formulate the General Equilibrium model. Specifically, to consider the market price of each good as the value of the 'marginal-social-utility' of one unit of the good, and so to claim that such a GE will amount to an optimum of social-economic well-being. In this case, these are two instrumental assumptions used – or implicitly presented through the development of the standard paradigm – as simplifications in mainstream economics textbooks. However, insofar both of them entail to make abstraction, not to take into account, decisive elements of the social reality, they are indeed notorious examples of over-simplifications; something that is at odds with the emphasis of modern neoclassical economists on using the ESM paradigm as a valid explanatory framework of economic reality – not only in textbooks.

Recap

The overwhelming empirical evidence shows that in the real world *decreasing returns to scale* (='increasing long-run average cost') in the production of goods (products or services) are not observed. Thus, the standard paradigm summarised (or rather, repeated; apologies) above in chapters 1 and 2, which concludes with the theoretical outcome of the GE model of competitive markets, cannot be sustained: *without the decreasing-returns condition as something general, there is no room for a spontaneous trend ('invisible hand') toward a 'General Equilibrium of competitive markets'*. Thus, GE/ESM is not a valid theoretical model to explain how our market economies work. In other words, reality does not support that theoretical model.

Again, I am not original with this statement. Even recognised exponents of the economic theory of the GE have expressed this, albeit from a slightly but significantly different discursive logic: that of 'how reality should be like, for it to fit in with the theoretical model'. Thus,

> "...(if) constant returns to scale, (...) Note, however, that J* (the number of firms) and q* (the efficient scale/firm-size) are indeterminate .." (Mas-Colell et. al., 1995: 336). (So) "... to generate the existence of an equilibrium (in the industry) with a determinate (high enough) number of firms, (...) there must exist a strictly positive output level (qmos) at which a firm's average cost of production are minimized (i.e., for output levels higher than that, firms' average cost move to be increasing)..." (p. 337). (italics mine)

The 'dragging force' of the mathematical-formal-neoclassic model

The 1972 Nobel laureate in economics Kennet J. Arrow, together with the also economist Gerard Debreu, completed the thorough formalisation in mathematical language of the 'general competitive equilibrium' model, pioneered in 1884-87 by Léon Walras and developed by John Hicks and Paul Samuelson between 1939 and 1947. However, Arrow was at the same time well aware of the economic reality regarding not only *constant* but *increasing* returns to scale –as has been pointed out earlier (2.3). He even draws attention to this fact, insofar as it entails a non-fulfilment of one of the key assumptions/hypotheses on which the ('his') mathematical model of the general competitive equilibrium rests.

> "Thus, the only non-convexities that are important for the present purpose (the existence of competitive equilibrium) are increasing returns over a range large relative to the

> economy (to the size of the market demand for a good). In those circumstances, a competitive equilibrium cannot exist." (Arrow, 1985: 112)

> " A well-operating market system leads to efficiency only under the assumption of perfect competition, but the propensity to monopolize is an intrinsic feature of the profit system and inhibits efficiency. The full set of conditions for a competitive equilibrium is, of course, never met in the real world. (1985: 113).

The perspective from which he tackles there this issue is, however, 'internal' to the theoretical model itself: he talks in terms of mathematical conditions that may or may not be met in the real world. Implicitly assuming, or suggesting, that the issue dealt with (the reality of non-decreasing returns) is not a general situation, but that, insofar there are cases of constant or increasing returns, it means that the *necessary* assumption of decreasing returns is *not always* fulfilled. Or, in other words, that the mathematically necessary conditions are not met for some, or many, cases (goods/ industries).

> "The fact that many industrial processes show increasing returns must be regarded by now as so well known that no one can be thought of as discovering it." (Arrow, 2000: 174).

It follows from these writings that Arrow takes into account the reality of the *increasing* returns to scale, although not as the overall situation in an economy but rather, implicitly, as specific cases – perhaps 'quite a few' – within a general context of decreasing returns' situations. He does, nevertheless, stress that 'non-decreasing returns' are a reality which means that (the requirements of his mathematical model are not fully met and thus) the general equilibrium of competitive markets cannot be properly – or not fully – sustained. Whereby he concludes that this reality would require further development of the ('his') mathematical model of competitive equilibrium, in order to refine it, reformulate some of its theorems or include new ones, or to apply (even) more complex mathematics, etc.

That is, Arrow adopts a perspective that can be interpreted as similar to that he applied to the externalities' topic: to consider it as a *specific* situation where another of the assumptions required for his theoretical model to be valid is not met. Although in that case – that of externalities – we might agree that these are realities associated with certain goods, industries or economic activities; not with all or a majority of them.
On the basis of the above notes, I would dare to suggest that it could be said of Arrow something similar to what he himself said about Alfred Marshall regarding, precisely, the same issue:

> "There are many individual observations (regarding no-decreasing returns) of great importance in Marshall's work, many more than in Cournot or Mill, *but the increasing returns passages remain isolated from Marshall's central core of (his) competitive equilibrium theory*" (p. 172)

> "Marshall certainly understood the key importance of increasing returns and had long discussions of downward-slopping supply curves, *even if he never integrated them well with the central competitive core of his theory*". (Arrow, 2000: 174).

Or to what he indicates regarding John S. Mill,

> "... David Ricardo completely ignores the presence of increasing returns (...). Mill (1848), (was) too intelligent not to recognize the difficulties that Ricardo skated over and, (but) *too bound to the main tradition for a major reconsideration* .." (p. 172).

In this context, it is significant to underline that in this latter work Arrow speaks of *increasing* returns to scale as an obvious and relevant reality. Although at the same time highlights the '*inconsistency* of the theory of increasing returns' (sic), in the face of the (internal) '*coherence* of the theory of competitive equilibrium',

> "... [though the latter] offers immediate answers (often not in line with observations, of course)", (Arrow, 2000: 173).

Thus, in a sense he is apparently prioritising – at least expositively, in his discourse/epistemology – whether a theory is internally coherent when formulated in mathematical language, over whether it fits in with or explains reality reasonably well.

Appendix B

Quantitative simulation for the short-run* unit costs

(*): An operating undertaking, which, thus, have a given size, production capacity, or dimension)

Parameters of the simulation (Estimates):

- *Variable unit-cost* (v) remains stable over the range of 27% - 96% occupancy level of the installed capacity[37].
- Proportion of *Total Variable Costs* on the *Total Costs*, for a period, 78%[38], for an occupancy level of 85% of the *installed production capacity*[39].
- Fixed Costs: 1.520 monetary units.

[37] Estimate based on the *generic evidence's inductive statement 2*, in section 3.2

[38] Estimate based on data from the report: *Banco de España*, 2017: "Central de Balances. Resultados de las empresas no financieras, 2016", p. 85): see note 8.

[39] This is the overall occupancy level for the companies included in the abovementioned report.

		Monetary Units				
Occupancy Level	**Units produced**	**Total Variable Costs**	**Average Variable Cost**	**Average Fixed Cost**	**(TOTAL) AVERAGE COST**	**Marginal Cost**
	10	400	40	152,0	192,0	40
	20	720	36	76,0	112,0	32
	30	990	33	50,7	83,7	27
	40	1260	31,5	38,0	69,5	27
	50	1525	30,5	30,4	60,9	26,5
27,3 %	60	1800	30	25,3	55,3	27,5
	70	2100	30	21,7	51,7	30
	80	2400	30	19,0	49,0	30
	90	2700	30	16,9	46,9	30
	100	3000	30	15,2	45,2	30
50 %	110	3300	30	13,8	43,8	30
	120	3600	30	12,7	42,7	30
	130	3900	30	11,7	41,7	30
		Monetary Units				
Occupancy Level	**Units produced**	**Total Variable Costs**	**Average Variable Cost**	**Average Fixed Cost**	**(TOTAL) AVERAGE COST**	**Marginal Cost**
	140	4200	30	10,9	40,9	30
	150	4500	30	10,1	40,1	30
	160	4800	30	9,5	39,5	30
	170	5100	30	8,9	38,9	30
82 %	180	5400	30	8,4	38,4	30
	190	5700	30	8,0	38,0	30
	200	6000	30	7,6	37,6	30
96 %	210	6300	30	7,2	37,2	30
100 %	Installed Capacity → 220	6644	30,2	6,9	37,1	34,4
	230	7038	30,6	6,6	37,2	39,4
	240	7512	31,3	6,3	37,6	47,4
	250	8100	32,4	6,1	38,5	58,8

Appendix B: Diagram (plotting) of the unit-costs figures in the above table

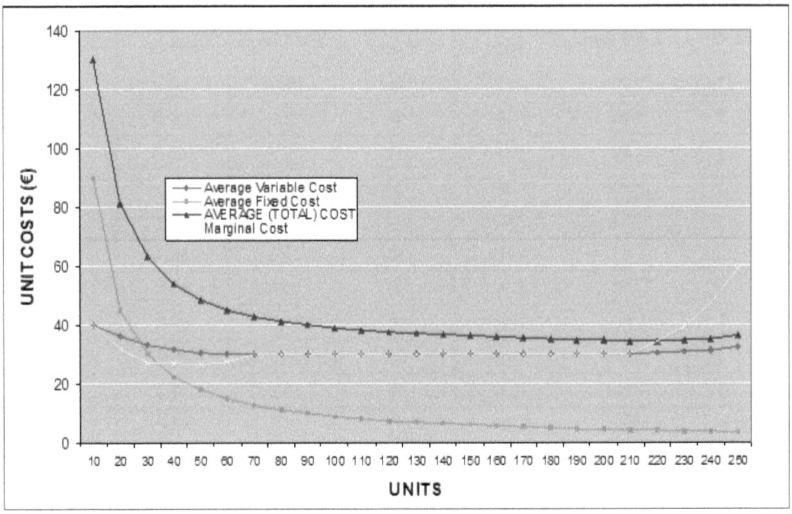

Appendix C

The oil market in the USA; production units vs price

Production - (Monthly level of U.S. crude oil production back to 1983 from the US Energy Information Administration (EIA). Values shown are in thousands of barrels produced per day).

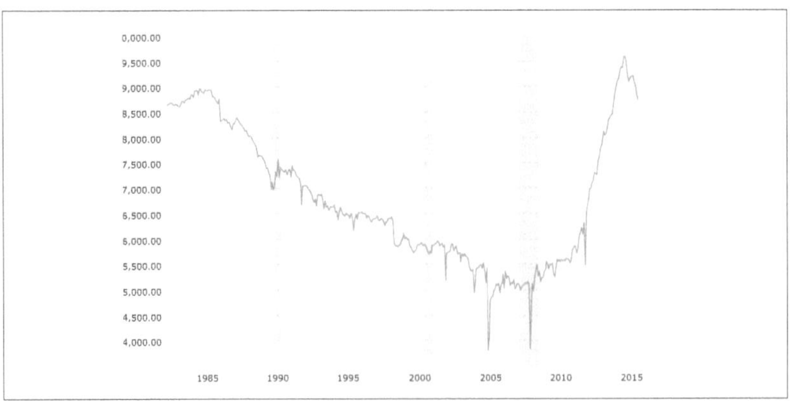

Source: <a href='http://www.macrotrends.net/2562/us-crude-oil-production-historical-chart'>Source</a>

Prices

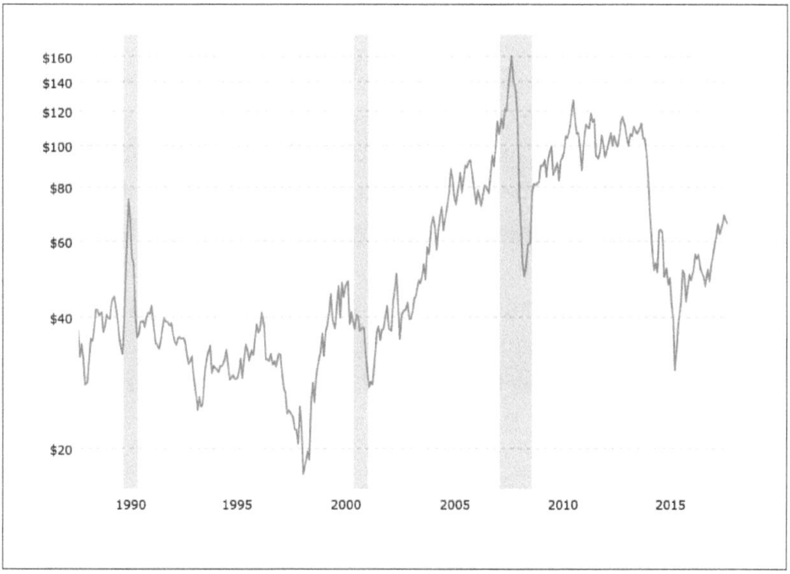

Source: <a href='http://www.macrotrends.net/1369/crude-oil-price-history-chart'>Source</a>

Chapter 4
Prices, market situations, and business behaviour, according to empirical observations

".. 'competition': the common sense meaning is one of struggle with others, of fight, of attempting to go ahead, or at least to hold one's place (...). In current equilibrium theory there is nothing of this true kind of competition; there are only individuals, firms, or consumers, facing *given* prices, *fixed* conditions, each firm or consumer for convenience insignificantly small and having no influence whatsoever upon the exiting conditions of the market (…) and therefore solely concerned with maximizing *sure* utility or profit – the latter then being exactly zero. The contrast with reality is streaking."
(Oskar Morgenstern, 1972: 1164)

"The rap of economist, only somewhat exaggerated, is that they are overconfident, unrealistic, and political. They claim a precision that neither raw material nor their skill warrants. Too many assume that people behave like the mythical homo economicus, who is hyperrational and omniscient. And they take sides in quarrels that freeze the progress of research. Those few who defy the conventional wisdom are ignored."
(Peter Coy, Economics Editor - *Bloomberg Businessweek* – 2009-04-15)

As we have seen in the first two chapters, a main idea that the standard explanatory theory of general equilibrium conveys to us regarding the workings of the economic world is that the 'free market' rule yields, as a result, that 'for each product, good or service there will end to be a multitude of companies, virtually identical (size, unit cost, product qualities), fiercely competing on equal terms, and selling at a price equal to their average cost (identical for all of them –and equal to the corresponding marginal cost), that is, without any of them making a profit' *. Thus, for example:

> "... If all firms, active and potential, take prices as unaffected by their own actions, this implies that active firms must earn exactly zero profits in any long-run equilibrium,; .." (Mas-Colell et. al, 1995, p. 335).

In contrast with this core paradigm on prices and profits –offered to us by the economics standard model (ESM) as a description of a private-firms-based (i.e., capitalist) market economy, what does an empirical observation of our real market economies tell us about? More specifically: which are the general patterns that observational evidence shows us regarding how the market prices of products and services are actually determined (i.e., regarding enterprises' overall behaviour and decision making in this regard)? What about the empirical reflection of the mainstream-economics' central topic of 'supply-demand equilibrium point' for any good? What about the relative importance of actual business profits (margin rates as from statistical data on companies' accounts as well as research works on the topic)? And, lastly, the encompassing scenario for all of that: what do the data on market-concentration indexes tell us about the type of markets (in the competition-monopoly axis) that predominate in our real economies?

The present chapter is devoted to answering the above questions.

> *(*) As a less compressed reminder of the standard paradigm regarding these points:*
>
> *«The free market rule allows that, in equilibrium (in the long run), in the market for any good, there will end up being many producer-supplier enterprises meeting the demand. Each of them of the same size*

and efficiency, i.e., dimensioned for the optimum production scale for the good in question. Therefore, each of them produces a given volume of units, qos, thus operating at the minimum average cost (which in turn will be equal to the marginal cost). As a result, since there are so many companies offering the same, none of them has market power: each one is too small to be able to influence the selling price. Thus, they all take the price as something set by the market. This price, moreover, due to the resulting strong competition, is equal to the unit-cost of production, so that all the enterprises will operate without any profit. All of which results in a market equilibrium point, Demand=Supply (in units of the good), characterized by: Price = Average cost = marginal cost. And all of this applies for all goods in the economy –with a few exceptions: (basically natural monopoly situations)».

4.1 Selling prices and firms' behaviour: observational evidence

Generic evidence's inductive statement 5: Enterprises generally do not sell at cost price

Let us start by this so self-evident empirical assertion: in a market economy, capitalist in the sense of being based on private business, enterprises do not normally sell at cost price, as the standard model in mainstream economics assumes[1], but normally obtaining profits; some enterprises proportionally more than others. They generally make their business decisions under the criteria of profit maximisation in the medium-long term.

We can observe, indeed, that sometimes, for short periods, and because of an unexpected drop in demand, a company sells at cost

[1] In some standard texts this comes with a nuance-remark, as we have seen in point 2.2: When the author points out that she/he considers, as a component of the *average cost* concept, a theoretical '*normal unit-profit*'. We will discuss this later on, at the end of this section.

price, or even below, with losses; but this as something exceptional, as a temporary situation. It is obvious that overall, in the long run, firms operate with profits. To be more precise, they try to maximise profits in the medium-long term when making decisions (on product range, activity level, firm size, workers' hiring and types of contracts for that, technology options, etc., and, of course, the selling prices to ask customers). All this is being developed within the cadre of the possibilities of each particular firm and, of course, the existing framework of legal rules and constraints.

This easily observed general pattern has even a standard expression in corporations' language in reports and their top executives' public talks or statements: "the company's guiding objective is to create value for its shareholders". Concerning this, for any attentive observer of – or participant in- business life, it is a matter of fact that companies tend to grow, to produce as much as they foresee being able to sell, as long as this increases – or allows them to ensure – their total profits. One general business strategy in this line is precisely to try to 'gain market share'; as well as to extend the market territory to be 'worked' –entering into new areas, either within the country or in other countries.

In short, it is easily observable that, in our market economies, selling prices are normally higher than the respective average cost of the product for the producer/seller enterprises. This is the case even in the case of reasonably competitive markets.

> [Understanding by that, at this stage, simply a situation where there are a certain number of enterprises in the sector; most of them with a production structure or size close to or larger than the corresponding minimal optimal scale, and operating with a similar efficiency degree. Thereby, the average cost for any of them, enterprise 'e', ACe, is approximately equal to the sector's average. To expressing this in formal terms: ACe ≈ Industry's average cost, IC.]

In fact, the ordinary business practice of applying a given percentage of profit-over-cost, M, so to determine the selling price to set/offer to potential customers, has even a traditional name: *mark-up*. This is usually expressed in terms of rate, M/100= *m; margin rate*. Thus, the most commonly observed practice in companies' behaviour, as for determining/setting their respective selling/offer prices for each of their products/ services, is of the type:

Price = *Average cost* x (1 + *net margin rate*); $P = AC \cdot (1+m)$

It is also fairly common knowledge that such a margin rate, *m*, tends to be higher – and consequently so does the price – when a firm has some market power or operates under oligopoly conditions for the concerned product. Obviously, this is even more the case when the firm holds a close-to-monopoly position over it. A 'higher margin rate' means here: in relation to the average rate that tends to prevail for companies – in a specific economy – when the situation for the product concerned is of a *reasonably competitive market*; for example, about 10 or more companies offering exactly the same good, and each of them with relatively similar characteristics and degree of access to communication channels with potential buyers.

To look at the matter from another perspective: if we want to use the standard concept of 'supply ***price*** function' regarding a specific good/ industry – in such a way that the concept is in line with the generic evidence available – then such supply function would be of the type: $Ps(q)=IC(q)\cdot[1+\bar{m}]$; where $\bar{m}$ stands for the average net margin rate over cost applied by the enterprises producing/offering such a good. And IC(q) 'industry's average cost, is the mean of the average costs of these enterprises, taking into account the sum of the units they, as a whole, offer in the market (q). As we have seen in the previous chapter (figure 6a), *industry-average-cost* for a good is observed to tend to be constant – or somewhat decreasing. And, obviously, this scenario leads us to a flat, *horizontal* – or somewhat decreasing – supply *price* function (figure

7). In other words, the *supply price* tends, in general, to be basically constant (or perhaps smoothly decreasing) with respect to the total units jointly offered (sold) in the market. As for its profit-component, the *net margin rate* observable at a given time, $\bar{m}$, will mainly depend on the specific market situation in the axis competition/monopoly at that time, among other variables – as we will see in point 4.2.1.

In those specific cases of a market situation of 'reasonable or strong competition' it is observed that the net-margin-rate (profit)-over-cost does actually tend to converge among the different firms operating in that market; and, therefore, so do their respective selling/offer prices. This is simply an empirical acknowledgement. We might interpret that picture as, for example, that there is – at such a time, and under a given regulatory and legal framework (the one of the country considered) – a certain minimum margin rate below which the owners of this or that enterprise in that 'industry' are not interested in remaining in that business in the medium-long term. Although, elaborating a deductive theoretical explanation about such behaviour (the 'why' question) would not alter the observed reality (the 'what' and 'how' questions). Certainly, it could be theorised that this *minimum margin rate* is due to enterprises' owners requiring a certain remuneration for the financial capital invested; or that such margin rate is rather related to the economic risks they assume as entrepreneurs (customer payment defaults, for example). [I will come back to this further in this section (in point 'A biased definition, with ideological implications')]. Though, in any case, such a theoretical explanation will not affect the description of reality that has been made above: that even in reasonably competitive markets, companies usually operate with a certain rate of profits; a rate which depends –among other things, like the relative size of industry's firms – on the country's economic scenario and the overall legal and regulatory framework.

In any case, for an empirical approach – on the overall patterns regarding prices (and, therefore, profits) – the relevant question would be: on average, what is the order of magnitude of *mark-up*, of net margin rate, *m*, that companies tend to apply in our economies?

Empirical evidence on the percentage of mark-up

The ubiquity of *mark-up* as a business practice of firms to decide their selling/offering prices is common knowledge; especially among people involved in enterprises' commercial and administrative activities. Though, on the other hand, it is difficult for someone 'from outside' to quantify rates of margin for a particular company or set of companies: the prices they have applied for each of its products – for a given time frame – may obviously be of public knowledge. But the unit costs for each of them are, for also obvious reasons, highly confidential internal information for the referred enterprise; a business-professional secret not only to customers but to competing firms.

Nevertheless, this fact can somehow be partially overcome by researchers. If we have access to a company's accounts statements for a given period[2], it is possible to deduct the *average* rate-of-margin-over-cost (mark-up) that was applied by such firm to its different products, over such a period, regardless of the specific option adopted by the company on the concept of *average cost* to use as calculation-base; i.e., that on which a given percentage of surcharge is applied as mark-up*. Let us suppose, for example, that the company option was to apply a certain overhead percentage on the '*direct* average cost' (*dAC*; i.e., without having allocated the common and overall costs) for each of its products/services. 'A posteriori', having available its *Income Statement* for the period, it is fairly easy to calculate from it the implicit average margin-rate applied on *the* (total) *average costs (AC)* of each product. That is, we can obtain the average net margin rate simply as, *m = (Revenue from sales/Operating expenses) – 1.* And, certainly, when the aim is just to measure the relative importance of enterprises' rates of net-profit-over-cost in an economy, as is our case here, there is no doubt that this 'de facto' average percentage of margin over *total unit (average) costs* i.e., the above introduced *net margin rate, m* is the most relevant indicator.

(*) Mark-up practices: *The most common business situation is that of an enterprise producing/supplying several or many different products (see section 5.2 further on). Direct observation of cost accounting's predominant practices shows that enterprises differ as regards the 'accounting version' of average cost they choose as the basis on which to apply a mark-up percentage –to establish the price to offer/apply to customers for each of its products. In some companies what is taken as a calculation basis is the industrial average cost, iAC, of each product (which means that commercial, administration, and overall costs have not been allocated among the different products). In other cases, it is the direct average cost, dAC, that is used (so, costs of any type that are common to several products, have not been allocated). In another cases it is the variable average cost, v; etc. And, certainly, in others it is the total average cost that is actually taken as calculation-basis; i.e., our familiar average cost, AC.*

Nevertheless, these different practices do not tend to substantially affect the final outcome in terms of prices: Given a specific firm's target regarding its total profits for a coming period, if its option for the average cost to be taken as calculation basis were the industrial average cost of each of its products/services, iAC, the mark-up percentage the firm will apply would obviously be higher than the one it would apply –to reach the same total-profits target– if its option were instead to take as a calculation basis the total average costs, AC.

---

[2] This is actually easy: in some countries annual accounts of companies are made public on a regular basis. For example, in the case of Spain, any company (SA or SL) has the obligation to deposit their annual accounts - Balance sheet and Income statement in the provincial *Registro Mercantil* by using a compulsory standard template.

As a brief on the subject, let us consider, by way of example, the simplest case as far as carrying out a direct measurement for *m*: that of an enterprise that produces/sells a single good – which is precisely the usual simplifying assumption in standard economics texts. In such a case, starting from *Price = (average cost) x (1+m)*, by multiplying both sides of the equality by the number of units of product sold the result is: *Sales = (Total Costs) x (1+m)*. And therefore the net margin rate over costs the firm has applied over a given period can be deduced ex-post with the simple calculation: ***m*** *= (Sales/ Total Costs) x 1*. Which, expressed in the usual accounting terminology of Income Statements (or 'profit-and-loss accounts') companies periodically prepare and present, would be: ***m*** *= ('Sales Revenue'/'Operating expenses'*[3]) x 1; or in a more compact way: ***m*** *= (SR-OE)-1*. Consequently, if we have available the Income Statement of such a firm for a given period, the determination of the net margin rate, ***m***, the enterprise has implicitly applied in the referred period would therefore be very simple.

However, rarely will we find such a simple real case: that of a single-product firm. The overwhelmingly common situation is that of enterprises producing/selling several or many products/services, each with its own average cost and price (see section 5.2 further on). But, again, if we have available an *income statement* of a given enterprise, the former calculation of the net-margin-rate-over-cost, *(SR-OE) - 1 =* ***m***, is equally possible and easy. The only difference is that the value we obtain for m will then mean, to be precise, the *average* of the different net-margin rates applied by the enterprise to determine the prices of its different products/services.

This is precisely the situation, and calculation procedure, most common in surveys, studies, or academic empirical research about *mark-up*. The novelty is that the ground data are, in these cases, aggregates of the Income statements of large sets of companies: those in a certain sector of activity, or from a certain area/country – for a certain year. But the quantitative determination of the implicit mark-up rates is basically of the same type described above. The only difference is that researchers work with aggregate figures (basically for *sales revenues, SR,* and *operating expenses, OE*) for a large number of firms: $(\Sigma SR / \Sigma OE) \times 1 = \bar{m}$. Thus, the resulting value, $\bar{m}$, represents in this case an average across the respective average-net-margin-rates of the numerous companies in the database used by the researchers.

Thus, by way of example, the Central de Balances of the Spanish central bank (Banco de España) regularly publishes aggregates of annual Income statements for a very large number of companies. Carrying out the above calculation, $(\Sigma SR / \Sigma OE) - 1 = \bar{m}$, for all the companies included in this database for the year 2017, (484,395 companies)[4], the outcome is $\bar{m} = 0.09$; that is, a net profit over total costs (operating expenses) of 9%, on average, for that important proportion of Spanish firms.

Here is another example; in this case from a research article strictly speaking and with much more coverage[5]. The database the author works with contains the annual accounts submitted to the stock exchange commission by all publicly traded companies in the US and covers several years. The article summarises the author's measurements for the average mark-up rates for each statistical sector (in the database used) for each of the years from 1959 to 2012. However, the results presented in the paper come just in more aggregate terms: the average rates of margin for the whole set of companies (i.e., taken all statistical sectors together), for each year. The following final results, for some

---

[3] The accounting concept *Operating Expenses* means, in short: those total costs –including depreciation & amortisation costs– necessary to produce and provide the products to customers; thereby OE include industrial, commercial, administrative, management and overall costs of the firm. The only exceptions are costs on loans (interests), costs generated from outside enterprise's normal activity, and extraordinary costs.

[4] Own elaboration, by using aggregates from *Central de Balances – Resultados anuales de las empresas no financieras, 2017*, Banco de España, Madrid (2018). pp. 85 ff.

[5] Traina, James (2018). The database used is Compustat (USA), excluding banks and other financial companies as well as public utilities.

specific years, are representative of those measurements in the time series: 1965, $\bar{m}$ ≈15%; 1980, $\bar{m}$ ≈9%; 2012, $\bar{m}$ ≈16%[6].

A much wider study by the OCDE, encompassing 14 countries, and using data for years 1970-1992, shows results in the same line[7]: in this case, the authors apply an indirect approach based on sector aggregates from national accounts and *input-output* tables of the respective countries; and, as the former paper, mark-up values are estimated in terms of 1 + $\bar{m}$; (pp. 9-10). Its quantitative results are presented as averages for every period, for each of 36 economic sectors of each country. If we calculate country-level averages for all the 36 sectors for some of the countries (period 1980-1992), the results for $\bar{m}$ are: the US, 17.5%; Japan, 25%; Germany, 20.5%; France, 18.1 %; Italy, 18.4%; the UK, 17.4%.

It is worth underlining that in this type of empirical research works – as is the case of the articles cited above – again we face the fact of authors making formally reference to *marginal cost* as the main

---

[6] Traina (2018), pp. 5-8. It should be noted that the author's calculations –and therefore the figures he presents– are expressed in terms of the equivalent to (*Revenues from Sales*)/(*Operating Expenses*). That is, they are expressed not in terms of ***m*** but of (***1+m***). He, however, uses an unnecessarily indirect approximation to determine that. It consists of the calculation formula below, which he takes from De Loecker and Eeckhout (2017):

$\mu = \theta^{V} \cdot \frac{P^{Q} \cdot Q}{P^{V} \cdot V}$; for each statistical sector (i), and for each year (t);

Putting this expression in a more standard language:

$\mu = \theta^{V} \cdot$ *[(Revenues from Sales)/(Total Cost of 'a (sic) variable input')]*

where θ^{V} is defined by the authors cited as "the elasticity of total output (Sales) to a (unspecified) variable factor". This unusual concept, θV, is in turn quantified by the referred authors, for each statistical sector of the corresponding database, by way of making assumptions and estimates grounded in the theoretical setting of the abstract Cobb-Douglas production function; (see footnote 11 of chapter 2).

However, when applying this methodology, as curious as it is indirect and sophisticated, Traina takes simply as "*Total Cost of a variable input*" the figures for *Operating Expenses* from the Income statements in the database. Therefore, the concept of mark-up he is measuring is precisely the same we come referring to here: *net margin rate over costs, **m**.*

[7] OECD, Economic Department Working Papers, No. 162; Paris 1996: "Mark-up Ratios in Manufacturing Industries. Estimates for 14 OECD Countries"; by Joaquim Oliveira, Stefano Scarpetta, and Dirk Pilat.; quantitative results, in pp. 18-25.

protagonist, instead of to *average cost*. This may come out as shocking, since, obviously, there can not be drawn data on marginal costs from companies' Income statements. It is also usual in this academic literature on measurements of *mark-up* percentages that, in the section of the article or report devoted to setting out the theoretical framework (on which the methodology and mathematical expression to be applied for calculation are justified), the term/concept '*marginal cost*' plays the leading role: in fact, authors talk rather about evaluating "the difference between price and *marginal cost*" (rather than to *average cost*). As it is the case regarding the papers cited above. This is surprising indeed since, in empirical research that uses companies' annual Income *statements* as the source of data, such a conceptual/ terminology twist is not only irrelevant (see box) but also makes the papers' reading unnecessarily cryptic to common readers.

'Marginal cost' vs. 'Average cost' in empirical research

Insofar as a company operates minimising its total costs –in the simple case of a single-product enterprise, minimising its *average cost*– the *marginal cost* for any of its products (if calculated) would be, by definition, equal to the corresponding average cost (see for example fig. 3 or 6). These are just two labels to refer to the same figure, in standard economics, and to denote that the company is 'costs efficient', this meaning that it is minimising its unit cost/s.

Therefore, as far as an author (implicitly) assumes that the companies whose *Income statements* contain the database (which s/he is going to work on, to measure average mark-up rates) have operated by tending to minimise their costs (an assumption with a broad consensus of being reasonably realistic) then it is quantitatively indifferent to speak of '*marginal cost*' than of '*average cost*' since the data to be used for calculations are the ones in those Income statements.

As can be deduced from the development of this mainstream economics' tenet in 3.3 ('A look to Marginalism') and 3.4 ('Summary of the overall pattern'), '*Marginal cost*' is a theoretical concept that simply cannot be calculated from a company's profit-and-loss account. The reason why authors formally refer generally, in this kind of study, to marginal cost instead of average cost – or simply to *Sales Revenue and Operating Expenses*, which are in fact the variables they actually take for their calculations, belongs to academic life dynamics and inertias. Something that could be explained because these articles or reports, as usual in academic articles in economics, are elaborated from within the mathematical language and referential framework of mainstream, modern-neoclassical, economic theory. And in this theoretical framework, marginal cost is – as we have already seen – a key concept (formally: 'first derivative of the total costs, for a given good, regarding the units produced') around which the postulate of market equilibrium pivots; and, therefore, so the model of general equilibrium of competitive markets; which, in turn, is the core paradigm of mainstream economic theory[8].

On the other side, *marginal cost* is not a concept or variable that appears in business accounting (i.e., periodical accounts, analytical accounting, internal economic reports, etc., for the firm's managers). And not because of ignorance of the concept by the professionals of the activity, discipline, or science – however, we'd prefer to call it – of Accounting. Nor because the marginal cost of each product/service of a company would be more o less unfeasible/difficult to calculate in practice. Simply, it does not make part of the data that modern accounting periodically records, compiles, and provides – using the term *accounting* in the broader sense of an 'information system

[8] Last but not least, let us take into account that if the authors would proceed otherwise (i.e., if in the methodological section of their research article they talk about *average cost*, or, 'even worse' because it sounds to accountants', about *Operating Expenses*, instead of *marginal cost*) this could likely raise suspicions in the future referees of the article on that the author/s do not properly master (standard, mainstream) economic theory.

(basically) for firm's management': *Management Information System*, MIS. In short, the concept of *marginal cost* is not part of the companies' regular MIS reports because simply it is not a useful variable for companies' decision making (with occasional exceptions such as whether or not to accept a possible order under abnormal conditions for the enterprise).

These assertions do not refer to the business' information and reporting practices in a specific country. The kind of information needed for (improving) decision making by the managers of a company is, in general, very similar in any context, in any country. Mainly because, the decisions to be taken by private firms in market economies are essentially of the same nature: they basically pursue the same objective – to maximise profits, or surplus, in the medium-long term; and under not-very-different legal rules and conditions.

Again, with the above statements, I am not uncovering anything that is not already obvious to many people. If you are not among them, I would suggest browsing the library you have at hand, for a manual on business management, management control, MIS, or marketing, for example. Or, as a rough approximation to that, you could even comment on the above with a relative or acquaintance who works in the administrative, accounting, or financial department of a company.

A biased definition, with ideological implications: When average cost is defined (in the standard model) by including a 'normal unit profit'

As pointed out earlier, in section 2.2, when in orthodox textbooks in economics/ microeconomics it is stated that "in equilibrium, firms sell at a price equal to their average cost, i.e. without making a profit", in some cases the authors add in some point, more or less implicitly, a nuance: that the concept of average cost they are referring to includes, in addition to the average-cost itself, AC (the one that firms' cost-accounting registers), a certain amount as *'normal' profit per unit*. This theoretical concept, *normal unit-profit, (nup)*, when explicitly defined in this or that textbook, uses to be referred to as 'the opportunity cost of the financial capital invested by the owners of the firm'. What entails considering such financial investment as a *production factor*. Those textbooks' authors are, therefore, talking about a different concept of average cost, $AC^{\#}$, equal to $AC+nup$. It is, in other words, a value higher than the average cost strictly speaking.

Should we follow such a definition, then when we observe a specific real case, *Price* = *AC* + *(unit profit)*, we should, to be coherent, express it as *Price* = *AC* + [*nup* + *(extraordinary unit profit)*]; or, shorter, *Price* = $AC^{\#}$ + *(extraordinary unit profit)*. Therefore, within this theoretical context we should understand that what the ESM presupposes is that 'with some rare exceptions (non-regulated natural monopolies), in equilibrium, the extraordinary unit profit for each good/enterprise will be zero'.

Certainly, if we take this semantic resource into account, the postulate of the orthodox model that in a free, competitive market, in equilibrium, in the long run, firms obtain zero profits (a postulate intended to describe a capitalist market economy!), turns out less shocking. We should understand, then, that what the authors meant by that is, '(in equilibrium) $P=AC^{\#}=AC+nup$'.

Is this theoretical resource useful when the aim is to explain the workings of our market economies based on private undertakings? Does it make sense, in an economic theory, to define the *average cost* of a firm's product by adding, as one of its components, a portion of the profit margin? Or, looking at the matter from another viewpoint, does it make sense to define business profits as something restricted to the above-mentioned theoretical concept of 'extraordinary profits', and to simultaneously postulate that its value will 'generally be null' for any good/firm? In essence, is it ethically neutral to talk about business profits with a meaning other than the usual one, not only in the business world (enterprises' annual accounts) but also in tax rules (corporate income tax) and the field of National Accounts as well as, of course, in common language?

In any case, to talk of *average cost* by resorting to such creative assumptions – usually implicit – is at least a source of misleading confusion for students and readers of economics books. This is even more so when in those texts the assumption that "normally the residual component, the 'extraordinary unit-profit', is zero" is added – generally also implicitly. On the other hand, the 'normal unit-profit' (*nup*) is a purely theoretical concept, in the sense that is not possible to measure/quantify it in a real case, since such a concept rests upon the standard ESM assumptions of overall equilibrium, perfect information, perfect competition, etc., etc.

Moreover, such a theoretical-semantic resource ("average cost" with the meaning of *AC* + *nup*) is like, consciously or unconsciously, presenting an idyllic (or *naive*) picture of the workings of a market economy basically made up of private and, therefore, profit-seeking enterprises. That idyllic picture comes in fact summarised by the orthodox model's motto, "(in equilibrium) companies do not obtain (extraordinary) profits"; where, moreover, the contents of the parentheses are (also) usually implicit.

In conclusion, all that does not seem to be something scientifically-academically neutral. This is a theoretical resource that would seem as intending to generate a certain idea that the capitalist market system is by nature something morally fair. It suggests something like "companies normally earn 'just what is fair' if markets are given full freedom to operate". The contrast of that with what the observation of economic and business reality shows is not worth highlighting again here.

4.2 Market structures most generally observed in real economies

Generic evidence's inductive statement 6: The situations of firms holding market power are not a minority

For any direct observer of the workings of our business-economic world the following statement will likely result self-evident: Not only the situation of a 'perfectly competitive market', but even that of *reasonably-competitive-market* where 'the unit profit of the sector's enterprises is just that that makes them keep being interested in remaining in such business in the medium/long run – does not appear to be precisely the dominant one in reality.

The direct observation of the relationship *'enterprises ⇔ market'* in our economies shows us that there seem to be as many cases of markets ('industries', sectors, products) with few producer-supplier companies (oligopolistic situations), as cases of markets with several or many competing companies (reasonable, significant, or strong competition), as well as equally numerous cases of 'de facto' monopoly situations. (Had these assertions pushed you to raise your eyebrows, please wait for a few pages further on: point 4.2.2).

With regard to this obvious diversity that the observable panorama shows, it seems useful to ask: what elements determine that the market structure for a given good (and thus the *margin rate* over cost in such industry) is tilted towards one or other of the three type-situations? Is it possible to make a theoretical prediction as to what type of market structure will tend to prevail for a given good – given the relevant parameters for this good, that we have seen in chapter 3: q^{os}, IC^*, and Q (the size of the demand for a price close to IC*)? And, changing the perspective, what does the observation of, and studies on, the real economic world tell us about the more common type of markets (along the competition/monopoly axis) and the degree of market power actually existing in our market economies?

We shall begin, in the next point, with the first two abovementioned questions, which (unlike the other points in these chapters 3 to 6) are of the type 'theoretical deductions out of an explanatory model'. We shall address the third question – so returning to the path of surveying empirical evidence, in point 4.2.2.

4.2.1 Why the market situation for a specific good could end up being of one or another type: a deductive approach

Let us take as a base the explanatory framework developed in Chapter 3 (sections 3.4 to 3.7; Figures 6 and 6a) on the overall pattern of behaviour of the unit costs, for an 'industry' (a given product or service): what will determine that a given company in that 'industry' decides to adopt a certain, more or less large, production structure/size, beyond the corresponding q^{os}? What will determine whether such a company becomes dominant in the market of the good concerned (reaching an oligopolistic or monopolistic position), or, on the contrary, whether it ends up as just one among several, or among many firms competing in that market?

In the first place, this will depend on a simple technical-economic issue: how large the volume of total demand for that product (Q units) be, compared to the volume of units of the corresponding minimum optima scale, q^{mos} units. But, ultimately, and especially, it will depend on the interaction of strategic decisions of the different companies operating in that market. The same generic answer would apply to the alternative question: considering the technology/cost situation outlined in Figure 6a, what can we expect to be the prevailing market price for that good or service? Or, can we really predict which it will tend to be? And, finally, regarding the total volume of units of the product traded in the corresponding market, what will it depend on?

In order to follow this deductive line, let us start by looking more closely at the premises or conceptual frame of reference. The elements to be taken into account for a theoretical prediction would basically be, as we have seen: 1) the relative size of the demand for the product in relation to the interval of units associated with the *minimal optimal scale* (alternative situations I, II, III, and IV, in the diagram of the following figure 8), and 2) the policies and strategies 'before the market' pursued by the different producer/ supplier companies. To what the possible existence of regulatory rules on the industry or product in question should be added.

Let us first focus on element '1)', taking as starting point the conceptual diagram in figure 8 below. This diagram is the result of overlaying four possible sizes of total demand (*I, II, III, and IV*) on the diagram for the *industry's average cost, IC(q),* in figure 6a; which in turn is the conceptual base for the *supply function,* [$P_s(q) = IC(q) \cdot (1+m)$], in figure 7[9]. In other words, in figure 8 we consider four possible alternative sizes of the total demand (volume of units) at a given price, by customers/users of the good in question.

[As usual in economics textbooks – and for the sake of facilitating comparisons, these *demand functions* are represented the other way round: price (vertical axis), as a function of the total units purchased by the buyers: Pd(q). In technical terms, 'inverse demand function'. And these 'functions' are drawn also under the usual (and generally realistic) assumption of 'the lower the market price, the more units demanded'; as well as under the simplification that such a relationship between price and quantity is simply linear.]

[9] In the most common case – where minimum average cost is constant for volumes of units beyond the corresponding q^{os} units– this function would simply be $P_s(q) = IC^* \cdot (1+m)$. As can be seen, the quantitative illustration in figure 7 [minimum average cost, €14, and sale price, or supply price, equal to €17] implies a net margin rate over costs of $\boldsymbol{m}$ = 0,214, (21,4%).

Figure 8: *Quantitative determinants of the market situation for a given product or service*

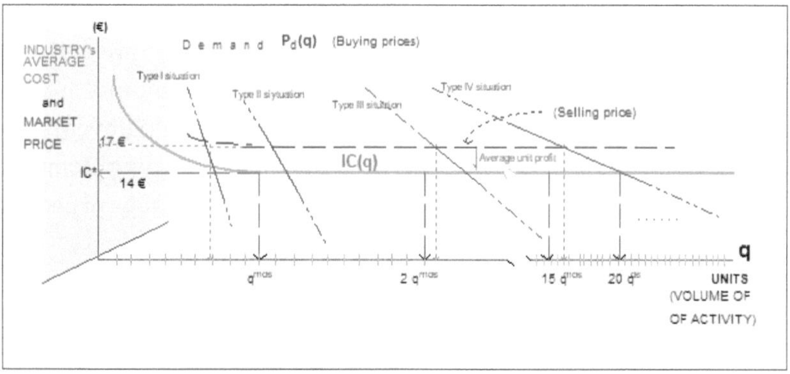

The size of the demand – let us say, the total units demanded at a given price somewhat above the average cost; for example, €17 in the above diagram-example – can be comparatively small (case *I*), large (type IV), very large, ... etc. 'Comparatively' means, with respect to the range of units associated with the *minimum optimal scale* for the product concerned, at that time. Thus, for instance, if the demand for the product in question is like '*I*' in figure 8, for any price equal to or higher than the minimum average cost, the units demanded will be lower than the minimum optimal scale, q^{mos} units. While if the size of demand is like '*III*', at a price of, for example, €17 the quantity demanded by the set of customers would be slightly more than double the q^{mos} units. And if the market situation was like '*IV*', the quantity demanded at that same price would be about 16 times q^{mos} units.

In other words, if in each of the cases the *average unit-profit* of the supplier firms were €3, and therefore the supply price is €17, in the case of a demand like '*III*' the ***market equilibrium point*** at that time would be: Price = €17, quantity = something more than $2q^{mos}$ units. And if the demand was like '*IV*', then the market equilibrium point would be: Price = €17, quantity = something more than $15q^{os}$ units.

If the market is basically domestic, internal, and we are specifically considering a *final product,* whether its volume of demand is comparatively small or large is a socio-economic issue. It depends mainly on elements such as consumers' spending preferences, consumption habits, and the level of income of the community as well as its distribution. All of which is, certainly, also changing over time. Let us explore the most significant possibilities regarding demand size in relation to the type of market structure that might be expected to appear.

When the demand is comparatively large (type IV situation)

This would be the case where the volume of market demand for the good in question (for a price close-above the minimum average cost) is much larger than the corresponding *minimal optimal scale.* In such a case, the conditions for a *reasonably competitive market* for that product are clearly present. Thus, in the specific case-example *IV* in the diagram, up to 16 firms, each one sized for producing efficiently (at the minimum average cost) a volume of about q^{mos} units, could operate and jointly cover the market demand. In this case, they would compete with each other on price (let us recall: we are still under the simplification of a single quality standard for the good; i.e., quality attributes are fixed, not subject to changes by producer/supplier firms), since in theory average cost could be perfectly the same for all of them.

This market structure is, indeed, possible to occur. *But there is no certainty that this will be the resulting scenario*: in a type-IV case the conditions for that exist certainly, but there is no guarantee that the situation will end up being so: that of a reasonably competitive market. It may well end up happening that, e.g., that three companies, with 4 or 6 optimal-scale productive divisions each, cover all the demand, thus holding market shares of 20-40% each company; an oligopoly situation, therefore. And it is equally possible that a single company with a size of about 16 of these 'efficient' production divisions could end up taking over the entire market. In this case such a company would hold a monopoly position (*de facto* monopoly); and, of course, then its selling price can be expected to be significantly higher (and thereby so its unit profit) than if there were some degree of competition in that market –for example if it were covered by 8-10 companies of similar size.

Thus, the three market structures – reasonable competition, oligopoly, and monopoly – may, therefore, end up happening in one type-*IV* technology/cost/demand situation. And there are no elements – at this deductive, 'broad', level, typical of the economic theory – to predict which market structure will prevail. The relevant issue to note here is that since companies do not experience decreasing returns as they gain market share, nothing prevents some of them from growing until having significant market power. And it should be added – not only power over the price but also over the volume of demand itself through advertising and other marketing tools.

When the demand is comparatively small (type I situation)

This would be the opposite case, those products/services for which the unit-cost/demand situation is like '*I*' in figure 8: whatever the price, the total units demanded is below the corresponding optimal scale, q^{os} units. In such a situation the cheapest (efficient) way to cover customers' demand is for a single enterprise to do so. Otherwise, if this comparatively low volume of units were divided between two or more supplier enterprises, each would inevitably produce at a higher average cost; which would be socially irrational (waste of resources). Hence the label of '*natural* monopoly' for such situations, since historical experience shows that if there are two or more enterprises 'competing' in this type of situation the market outcome tends to be that one of them, applying a leader's strategy (e.g., a temporary downward price) ends up taking over the entire market. (We might, thereby, substitute 'natural' with 'inevitable').

Contrary to the standard assumption regarding this, these situations are in fact quite more frequent, and relevant, than what may seem *a priori*. So, they deserve to be dealt with in a specific section (4.3).

When the demand is of an 'intermediate' size,(type II or III situations)

Let us finally consider the intermediate possibilities in terms of the relative size of demand for a certain good. If the demand situation is type '*II*', it could easily end up also in a monopoly, or perhaps a duopoly. And if it is a type *'III' situation,* in principle there is a possibility that it could evolve toward a certain market competition – albeit limited: oligopolistic competition–. Though with a greater probability that the marketing strategies of two or three firms in the sector, through predatory pricing policies and/or by purchasing competitors (mergers, takeovers), lead to a situation of oligopoly or even monopoly.

It can therefore be concluded that it is not possible to make a deductive prediction on the type of market structure that will prevail for a given good/industry, despite having reliable information on its basic economic parameters: $IC(q)$, IC^*, q^{mos}, and the size of total demand for the good in question, Q. Except regarding type *I* situations (to which section 4.3 is devoted), and some cases of type *II*.

4.2.2 Market structures, according to the empirical observation

Let us now return to the 'empirical' observation path: Which situations, types, or structures of markets, are observed to be predominant in our economies? We can begin simply by noting, as underlined before, that generic empirical observation of the business world – in which most people in our economies earn their living – shows that the three market-type structures – reasonably competitive market, different degrees of oligopoly, and monopoly – as well as several mixtures of them[10] occur with significant frequency. As the empirical data presented below corroborates, it can be anticipated that there are in fact as many cases of markets ('industries', sectors, products) with few producer-supplier companies (oligopolistic situations), as cases of markets with several or many competing companies (reasonable, significant, or strong competition), and equally numerous cases of monopoly situations. In other words, *market power* positions (oligopoly or monopoly situations) by one or a few companies are actually considerably more frequent than is usually assumed in mainstream economics/microeconomics textbooks (Komlos, 2019:102). Not only or mainly because of demand situations type I or II, but of type III and IV technical-economic situations, or even quite larger demand sizes.

The generic evidence of this is especially visible to those persons involved in the commercial areas of companies' activities. Notably in purchasing departments –where it is easy to witness the usual situation that there are in fact few options as far as suppliers for this or that product; though also in the case of sales departments, which are as 'natural' observatories for companies' usual internal practice of setting market-share targets to themselves for a given product or products range.

Moreover, we have available, of course, specific empirical evidence in the form of official statistics, professional empirical studies, research reports, etc. In this respect, the degree of monopoly-oligopoly in a specific market (good, industry, sector) has traditionally been measured in economics by a *market concentration ratio*, **C**. It measures

---

[10] By way of example, there are many undertakings producing kiwifruits in Spain, but one of them, *Kiwi Atlántico*, accounts for 60% of total national production (2018's data). Would we describe this situation as a 'competitive market' – because of the high number of enterprises in it– or rather a 'quasi-monopoly' because of the market dominance by one of them?

what proportion of the total sales in a market is covered by the top three, four, or five companies (*C3*, or *C4*, or *C5*, ..., ratios). Thus, if in a specific market (industry) the top four companies in terms of sales sum up 85% of total sales – an oligopolistic type of situation, therefore, then we talk about a market concentration ratio of $C4 = 85$.

Thus, for example, in the classic manual of Industrial Economics by Roger Clarke (1989), we can see market concentration ratios, measured at the level of the top 5 companies (C5), for different types of goods (in fact, statistical grouping of economic-activities, i.e., 'sectors' or 'industries') in the United Kingdom[11]. In his tables, 'industries' such as sugar, cables, cars, breakfast cereals, coffee, batteries, cement, and others, appear with C5 figures of above 90%; and for some of them (such as sugar, tobacco and hydrocarbons and their derivatives) the C5 ratio was 100%. What indicates oligopoly or monopoly situations.

Also, the detailed study by Sutton on market concentration ratios (1998) is historically noteworthy. In this case, it presents indicators, for the United States, referring to the sum of the market shares for the top four companies' (C4), for each of the 197 types of goods or 'industries' (industrial sub-sectors, according to the statistical classification of economic activities at the 5-digit level in the USA system). And percentages around 60%, 70%, and 90% appear also with a significant frequency[12].

In both cases, these are ratios obtained (or calculated) from sectoral statistics published by the official agencies of the respective country. In that context, a sector, sub-sector, or 'industry' –for example, 'Pharmaceuticals', or 'Cables' – actually includes several or many different products. Thus, their corresponding indicators

---

[11] Clarke (1989), tables 2.2. and 2.3., on p. 22- The statistics database used by Clarke to determine these C5 ratios corresponds to the years 1977-78.

[12] Sutton (1998), Appendix 4.3, tables 4.3.1 and 4.3.2, pp. 550-557.

(e.g., 'Pharmaceuticals', C5=75%) represent actually the average of the market concentration ratios of the different specific goods/ markets encompassed by the corresponding statistical grouping (classification's code level). That means that the C ratios calculated out of these statistical data give, inevitably, low-*resolution* information about markets' concentration degree.

It deserves to remark in this regard that a public statistics agency might, obviously, calculate also concentration ratios taking the market share of the leading, top, firm in an industry, or the sum of the top two – and so to obtain *C1*, or *C2* level ratios. This would give indeed more accurate information about monopolistic situations. However, we will not find data at that level (nor at the *C3* level) in statistics agencies' reports – and therefore not in academic studies either. This is because the confidentiality clauses guaranteed by the public agencies that publish these statistical data prevent that (on the grounds that otherwise specific companies' data could be easily identifiable). That explains why the most common in these statistical releases are *C4* and/or *C5* indicators.

Another significant example of empirical data is the one below, resulting from a broad study which uses statistical databases corresponding to 10 years later than the ones used by Clarke in his above-cited work. In this study, *C4* market concentration ratios are calculated for the whole set of industrial sectors of several countries, and then average values for each country are presented by the authors[13]:

	C4 (average)	(s.d.)
Germany	35.9	20.8
France	34.9	23.5
Italy	31.6	22.2
United Kingdom	39.5	22.3
US	31.4	16.4

[13] Lyons, Matraves and Moffatt, (2001), table 1, p. 12

More recent data (2004), for the UK, released by the *Office of National Statistics (ONS)*[14] shows that the situation regarding market concentration was at the time quite similar to the one three decades before, as per the above-cited work by Clarke. On the other side, a 2018's report by the OECD[15] on market concentration ratios for several relevant industries in the UK shows concentration ratios also in line with the former measures, as can be seen in their chart below. Thus, sectors such as Groceries, Broadband, Telephony, Electricity, Gas, Banks' personal current accounts, present figures for C4 of around 90-70%; of about 60% for Mortgages; and 50-40% for Cars:

C4 Market concentration ratios for several relevant sectors in the UK

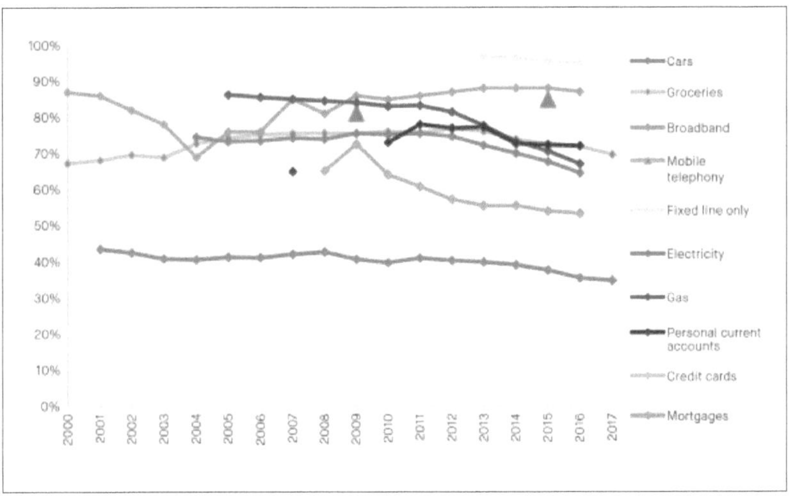

On the other hand, since the end of the 80's, simultaneously with the use of C ratios, preference has been given by researchers and public agencies to an alternative measure of market concentration: the Herfindahl-Hirschman ratio (*H*). This indicator is calculated as the

[14] Mahajan (2006); appendix 1, pp. 42-44

[15] OECD, (2018) (p. 9).

sum of the square of the market share of *every firm* in a specific market; i.e., it is taken, for calculation, not only the market share of the 4 or 5 top firms but those of all the firms operating (included) in the statistical sector/industry concerned. Thus, the possible values of this ratio go from $H = 10000$ for a pure monopoly situation (the square of 100%), to values close to zero for a situation of 'almost perfect competition'. This ratio has the advantage of allowing for good discrimination between different degrees of monopoly-oligopoly (see situations 1 to 6 in the simulation-example below). However, it has also the disadvantage of giving values that – unlike the 'traditional' C ratios– are of non-intuitive interpretation, since they do not vary in proportion to what is commonly understood by *degree of market concentration, or of firms' market power* – as can be seen in the following table:

Simulation for the Herfindahl-Hirschman market concentration ratio (H)

Different possible type-situation, for a specific market/product/sector:	Market shares for the top firms active in the market					Rest of the firms active in the market		H ratio	C5 ratio	C4 ratio
	1st	2nd	3rd	4th	5th	share	firms			
1. Pure monopoly	100 %	0	0	0	0	-	-	10.000	100	100
2. De facto Monopoly	90 %	0	0	0	0	0,25 %	40	8.103	90	90
3. Oligopoly/monopolistic (a)	60 %	10 %	10 %	10 %	0	0,25 %	40	3903	90	90
4. Oligopoly/monopolistic (a)	40 %	15 %	15 %	15 %	15 %	-	-	2500	100	85
5. 'Balanced ' Oligopoly	20 %	20 %	20 %	20 %	20 %	-	-	2000	100	80
6. De facto Oligopoly	20 %	20 %	20 %	20 %	5 %	0,50 %	30	1633	85	80
6 > (in-between) > 7	15 %	12 %	10 %	8 %	5 %	2 %	25	658	50	45
7. Reasonable competition (20 similar firms)	5 %	5 %	5 %	5 %	5 %	5 %	15	500	25	20
8. Strong competition (80 similar firms) Atomised ('almost perfect')	1,25 %	1,25	1,25	1,25	1,25	1,25 %	75	125	6,25	5
9. competition (200 similar firms)	0,5 %	0,5 %	0,5 %	0,5 %	0,5 %	0,5 %	195	50	2,5	2

By way of example, in the aforementioned work by Sutton (1998), besides the already commented *C4* market concentration ratios, we also find data for H measures for each of the sectors. And, in line with what was pointed out before on the basis of his *C4* measures, values higher than 2000 for the H ratio appear for most of the sectors in his tables cited before. Let us look, however, at more recent data using this indicator; firstly referring to the UK[16]. Working on the more recent detailed data published by the public agency *BIS*, the following summary can be produced:

Degree of market concentration (UK, 2015), Herfindahl ratio

1. Oligopoly & Monopoly situations: 1.1) 8000 < H, (10 sectors) 1.2) 4000 < H < 8000, (22 sectors) 1.3) 1600 < H < 4000, (105 sectors)	1600 < H : 137 sectors
2. Relative competition situations:	500 < H < 1600 : 129 sectors
3. Situations of reasonable or strong competition:	H < 500 : 114 sectors
Own elaboration on the basis of (see footnote 16) "BIS Analysis of key sectors (by SIC2007)/Table 5: The Herfindahl-Hirschman Index for each 5-digit SIC2007 code". BIS release 03/05/2016.	

Finally, here follows a summary of the most recent empirical measures on markets concentration available for the US:

Every five years the US Census Bureau publishes highly detailed databases (classification of economic activities at the 6-digits level) with market concentration ratios, C4 as well as H, for the different sectors

[16] The UK is probably the country for which there is more available information about market concentration indicators: In addition to the C5-ratios data regularly released by the above-mentioned *ONS*, the *Department for Business Innovation & Skills (BIS)* also publishes market concentration data; in this case using the Herfindahl index; and that in an even more detailed, less aggregated, statistical level: according to the 5-digit classification code of economic activities (392 'sectors', or statistical groupings).

included[17]. Among these sectors, the macro-sector encompassing all industrial activities[18] stands out – as for the prominence that the public agency gives to it. Focusing on these economic activities, and using the most recent data available (corresponding to 2007), at the 5-digit aggregation level there are 183 'industries' or types of manufactured goods. By first analysing the data corresponding to C4 ratios, the outcome* can be summarised as follows:

> For 38 of those 183 goods/industries/manufactures, the C4 ratio is higher than 50%. For 23 of them, it is higher than 60%. Among the latter, the most outstanding ones, in terms of sales volume and degree of market concentration, are Tobacco, Breweries, Petrochemical manufacturing, Computer and peripheral equipment, Telephone apparatus manufacturing, and Appliance manufacturing.

And by using the other market concentration measure offered by the report, the H ratio, the summary would be:

Manufacturing sectors for which,

H > 1000: 32, of which 12 with H higher than 2000 (situations of oligopoly/monopoly)

H < 500: 94, of which 24 with H lower than 125; a border-value that could be associated with highly competitive situations (see simulation table).

(*) Own elaboration, based on the database mentioned (as of December 2019).

---

[17] https://factfinder.census.gov/faces/affhelp/jsf/pages/metadata.xhtml?lang=en&type=dataset&id=dataset.en.ECN_2007_US

[18] (Manufacturing: NAICS 310000-339999); US Census Bureau, *Concentration Ratios: 2007, Economic Census; Manufacturing (EC077315R12)*.

In conclusion, the empirical measures about market concentration reviewed so far allow us to maintain the overall assertion suggested by generic evidence, as stated at the beginning of this section: the three typologies of market structure competition, oligopoly, and monopoly– (each of them encompassing different variants, as illustrated in the simulation table, first column) are present with similar frequency in real market economies.

Thus, direct empirical evidence about the degree of markets' concentration indicates that situations of greater or lesser market power, regarding specific goods by a few companies, are not exceptional situations in a market economy, but, on the contrary, are systemic. As usual, here we understand market dominance as a situation in which a few companies have a significant share of a given market; i.e., a certain control over an industry. So, a 'strong' dominance would be, of course, that associated with companies in an oligopolistic – or directly monopolistic position. Positions which obviously are what in turn allow for the involved firms to get higher profit margin rates.

The sequence of empirical findings and assertions throughout the present section will likely come as little surprise to most readers, since ultimately we are talking about, and trying to schematically describe, real market economies, basically made up of private enterprises logically guided in their decision making by the profit criterion.

Finally, it is important to highlight that *monopolistic* positions are observed both in the form of *de facto* monopolies as well as in the form of *natural monopoly*. In the first case, the relative size of demand, compared with the *minimum optimal scale* of production, is type III, IV depicted in figure 8, or larger, but in fact a single company practically dominates the market. In the second case, that of natural monopoly, it is associated with technical-economic situations like *I* (or *II*) in figure 8.

And since the latter has traditionally received special and in-depth attention in mainstream economics/microeconomics – insofar as it would be the so-called 'exceptional case', in the sense that it would break the overall fulfilment of the conditions the *general equilibrium* paradigm requires, it is both justified and interesting to explore it more in detail here, in the next point – where it is also argued how is it actually a much more frequent market situation than is assumed in standard modern-neoclassical economic theory.

Partial summary on firms' overall patterns of behaviour and decision-making regarding *prices & profits* (4.1), and on observed *market structure* – in the competition-monopoly axis (4.2)

Contrary to the predictions of the *general equilibrium* model of mainstream economic theory, the observation of real market economies shows that:

i. Firms generally make profits (selling prices are normally higher than the respective average unit cost); and in the case of many large firms, proportionally high or very high profits.

ii. There is an overall tendency of firms to grow in size as much as they are able to, thereby trying to gain market share (as a way of ensuring/improving their profits).

iii. The existence of firms with market-power positions (i.e., price is not taken by companies as a market data but rather as a decisional variable; and 'pricing policy' is a key element in companies' management) is not exceptional but rather something common, relatively frequent, in our market economies.

iv. It would be naïve to think that this leafy, systemic, reality can be substantially modified through a regulatory body such as a *competition-enforcing commission*[19] – beyond their usual regulation and control of the traditional public utilities and some cases of *natural monopoly*; and even in these specific cases, with well known limitations.

"... competition is a type of behaviour by businessmen and not a market structure like 'perfect competition' " (Blaug, 1998: 15)

4.3 Cases of natural monopoly: the restrictive approach of the Standard Model, faced with empirical evidence

There are cases of products or services for which the volume of demand of customers or users (Q units) is, whatever the price, lower than the volume of units associated with the corresponding *minimum optimal scale* (i.e., that production structure or enterprise's size that allows to minimise the average cost), q^{mos} units. This is the technology-costs-demand situation '*I*' sketched in figure 8; which is labelled in economics as 'natural monopoly'.

In such a case, the more economical, cheapest, way to produce the concerned good is obviously for a single enterprise to do it; which means that it would operate under a monopoly position, and, therefore, it might *control* the selling price. If it is a private – and therefore, profit-oriented – enterprise, it can apply a comparatively high margin rate over cost. As high as *rigid* the demand for the good in question is; i.e., the less reactive Q is to changes in the price; in graphical language: the more the demand function (line I in diagram

---

[19] The European Union competition authorities (ECN) come taking H values of around 2000 as reference in order to decide whether or not they give its green light to the merger of two companies from the same sector. In the case of the USA (*antitrust rules*) the reference level is being (end of 2019) somewhat higher: H=2500.

in figure 8) approaches verticality. In any case, should two or more enterprises share the supply to the market, then, since each of them will produce half or less of the total units to be provided, their respective average costs will be higher than if the whole production was carried out by just one of them. In such eventuality (two or more producers) economic history tells us that (if the market for that good is not regulated), one of the operating enterprises will end up, in a 'natural' way, being the single one: it will produce at a lower average cost than before and will control the whole market; all simply due to a matter of economies of scale.

In the case of certain public services ('public utilities'), this situation of natural monopoly occurs – besides of the above – by a pure question of socio-economic rationality: In a given city or urban area, the supply of, for example, gas requires a network of pipes that arrives at each particular consumer home or building. It would be not only an economic irrationality but a source of coordination problems for the supply to be carried out by two or more companies, each one having built and maintained its own parallel network of pipes. And it is easy to deduce that if that were the case, then gas would be more expensive for customers; as well as that, probably, over time one of the companies – that which implements a more aggressive long-term strategy – would end up being the only one in the market (its total costs would then be less than the sum of the total cost when two or three firms were providing the service).

From this overview, the role of this section is twofold: Firstly, to show that the attention paid by mainstream economic theory to the natural monopoly situation has historically been partial, restrictive; in the sense that it considers only certain cases of *natural monopoly*; to which, nevertheless, orthodox approaches dedicate surprisingly great attention. The latter is because *natural monopoly* situations break precisely the internal mathematical coherence of the *general equilibrium* model itself. And secondly, the aim here is to highlight that in the real world of our market economies natural monopoly situations as such are much more frequent than what is assumed in the ESM.

4.3.1 The topic of 'natural monopoly' as addressed in the ESM, contrasted with the real-world economies

(a) Marginal Cost Pricing, a mainstream economics' tenet

Marginal Cost Pricing (MCP) is an answer to a theoretical 'inconvenience'. Modern-neoclassical economic theory (especially in its so-called 'microeconomics foundations') assumes that type I market situations (fig. 8) – which lead 'naturally' (inevitably) to a monopoly – are rare, exceptional. Let us bear in mind that these are cases that would break the postulate of «free from the public powers intervention, the market *for any good* tends spontaneously to a situation of perfect competitive (efficient) equilibrium». And that, as a consequence of this 'breach', the *general equilibrium* paradigm associated with the core theoretical model of mainstream economics/ microeconomics would not be met properly, due to the 'distortion' that such natural monopoly cases entail.

As a response to this theoretical 'inconvenience', the mainstream approach *prescribes* and *defends*[20] that 'only in these exceptional cases (natural monopoly) should public powers intervene in the economy (regulation)', by obliging that a single enterprise produces the product or service in question, and setting to this enterprise the price it must apply; more specifically, setting to this single producer 'a price equal to the corresponding *marginal cost*'. Why the *marginal*

[20] When such types of verbs with the meaning of 'it should be' appear in an argument or text, economists then we speak of *normative economics*, or *economic policy* recommendations, rather than of *economic theory*. Though we, as a profession, are not always coherent in this regard.

cost? For as we have seen through former pages is something the ESM paradigm assumes 'should be met for any good to so guaranteeing a socially-optimum general equilibrium as it is so the case in general, for the *normal* goods of the economy'.

This MCP prescription entails, nevertheless, a notorious –and well-known problem. As we have seen in section 3.4 and it is easy to visualise in diagrams 3, 6 and 6a; as well as in the traditional ESM diagram in the box below, precisely in type 'I' situations (i.e., when the total units demanded by customers, whatever the price, are below the production volume of the optimal scale) the *average cost* of the (single) producer firm will necessarily be higher than the corresponding marginal cost. Therefore, if such a condition of '*price = marginal cost*' is imposed on the firm, it will be forced to operate at a loss, as it will have to apply a price below its average cost, (i.e., it will not cover all its total costs). Logically, this proposition 'Price = marginal cost, because that is what the *general equilibrium's social-optimum* requires' implies (and hence in textbooks it comes normally accompanied by) the proposition of 'the producer enterprise be it public or private will have to be subsidised by public powers, for an amount equal to its losses in every period (*allocative subsidy*; in graphical language: the area of the shadowed rectangle in the diagram below)'.

This 'allocative subsidy' is supposed to be covered out of public budgets for example, through tax revenue; which, in turn, would entail a given *social welfare loss*. A loss that, in any case, should be

---

[21] Why the general proposition of '**Price = Marginal cost**', and not '**Price = Average cost**', in the General Equilibrium model, when in this it is assumed that full efficiency in the production o all goods in the economy makes that **Marginal cost = Average cost**? Simply because the mathematical framework of the General Equilibrium is formulated in *marginalist* terms. Hence *marginal cost* is its central concept, as far as unit costs are concerned as we have seen in sections 3.3 and 4.1.

compared with the theoretical gain in terms of the 'consumers surplus'[22] associated with applying *mcp* instead of, simply, 'price = average cost'.

Marginal Cost Pricing: the classical re/presentation

When in mainstream economic theory the concept of *natural monopoly* is presented, in graphical language, an additional assumption (which could also be interpreted as a strong simplification) is made: that 'natural monopoly' refers just to cases (goods) for which there is only one possible technology/productive dimension/size-of-the-firm for volumes of production between ***0*** and q^{mos} units. (This is a restrictive simplification regarding the standard model itself, as far as firms' size & short-run average cost possibilities represented in the 'classical' diagram in figure 3). Or, expressing such simplification/assumption in other terms: it implies that the decreasing stretch of the *long-run* average cost is simply (coincides with) the decreasing stretch of the *short-run* average cost for the optimal scale/size-of-the firm.

In academic textbooks, this simplification is normally done in an implicit way, just via graphical language: simply by representing the *natural monopoly* situation using the ESM's standard diagram for the short-run average cost, as follows.

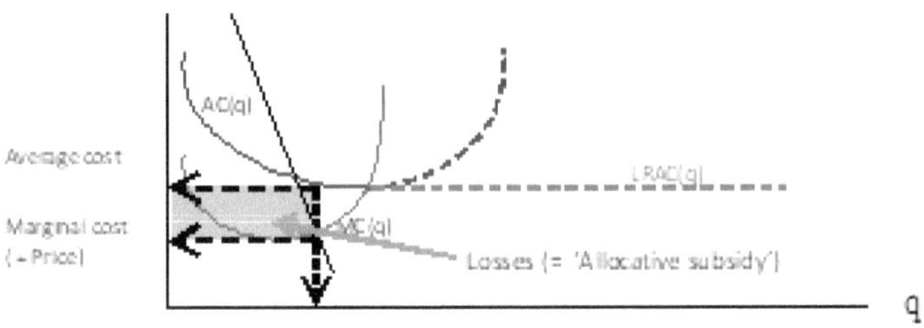

By way of example, reading the graphical case in the diagram: the *subsidy* amount (shaded rectangle) would be similar to the theoretical gain in *consumer surplus*. Notwithstanding, it is relevant to take into account that the citizens who benefit from the theoretical 'gain' (consumers of the good in question) are not necessarily the same than those that experience the 'loss' (taxpayers).

[22] The monetary value of the 'consumer surplus' is defined in standard economics as the area above the horizontal line of the price paid by consumers, encompassed by the demand line (at its left).

It should be noted that such a normative proposition of the standard economic theory (*'**marginal cost pricing**'*; and, consequently, to ***subsidise*** with public funds through the producer enterprise the buyers/customers of the good in question) is formulated simply as such, as a purely 'technical' issue: simply because the demand/unit-costs situation for the good in question is of type 'I'. That is, regardless of the nature of the good; not because it is a special kind of good for which subsidising would be socially justified either because it is a socially sensitive good (income distribution policy) or because it is a strategic good for the country. The standard theory simply prescribes/defends 'marginal cost pricing', and the consequent 'allocative subsidy, on the grounds of purely 'technical' reasoning: in terms of 'unit cost functions' vs. 'demand function (relative size-of-demand)'.

(b) 'natural monopoly' ↔ 'publicly owned enterprise': a traditional academic linkage

Furthermore, it is important to add that this 'marginalist proposition' comes also accompanied, in the standard manuals and specialised literature, by a more o less underlying axiom or assumption (as if it were something consubstantial and obvious): That 'the (scarce) situations of *natural monopoly* typically occur for *public-utilities* type goods' (such as the abovementioned case-example regarding gas distribution). And/or in some cases, the reverse assumption: *public utilities* are always *natural monopoly's* situations'. A consequence of this equalisation *natural monopoly* <=> *public services* is that the inconsistency highlighted in the previous paragraph (regarding to subsidise, whatever the social nature of the good) is left somehow partially disguised. Whereby, in a way, the argumentative line of the *marginalist criterion* is closed. Which reinforces the role of *marginal cost pricing* (MCP) as a theoretical support of the ESM's thesis that «the only type of public-powers interventions in the economy (market regulation) justified or desirable: just in the case of natural monopoly situations». In short, the implicit idea that comes out from reading the standard approach on the topic is: «natural monopoly situations = public utilities => the only cases in which the intervention of public powers in the economy is justified»[23]

Following with the standard marginal-cost-pricing approach, this market regulation can be implemented by governments by assigning the production/supply of the good in question either to a *publicly owned enterprise* (and ordering its manager to apply the criterion of MCP) or to a private company, subject to *regulation*. In this latter case regulation is understood to entail ordering to this concessionaire – either through a contract ('public procurement') or by law: i) the price it must apply (to be determined by public powers in accordance – it is supposed – with the 'marginalist criterion')[24], eventually accompanied by fixing quality parameters; and, of course, ii) the corresponding subsidy to be periodically paid to such concessionaire, in order to it may operate with a certain, agreed, rate of profit.

In short, under the MCP paradigm, whether the regulatory option is one or the other, such an economic policy proposition would entail establishing a regular subsidy to the producer company, be it publicly or privately owned, since the revenues from customers/users would not cover the total costs. Or to be more precise, it implies indirectly <u>subsidising customers/users</u> of the good in question

[23] A more complete explanation and formal discussion of this relevant part of mainstream economic theory (marginal cost pricing, allocative subsidy) may be seen, for example, in Vergés (2010:88-96)

[24] This setting of the price implies – following mainstream theory – for the government (or the public regulatory body) to carry out an estimate of the *marginal cost* of the good in question. What, obviously, entails (besides the practical handicaps discussed at the end of 4.1.1) the regulatory body to ask and obtain information in this respect from the concessionaire company itself. Which leads us to a well-known problem in Business economics: that of *asymmetric information* and *agency costs*.

The curious traditional triptych:
«Natural monopoly = Public utilities/services = Publicly-owned enterprises»

Finally, there is a certain tradition, in mainstream economics' manuals and literature, to make implicitly the above double association. As if every situation of *natural monopoly* happened for *public services/utilities* type of goods, and, besides, that all of them were provided by *publicly-owned enterprises*. As if these three expressions referred to the same economic reality. Thus, it is usual that in a given textbook, the section dedicated to "Public Enterprise Economics" deals basically with the marginalist criterion. Or the reverse. Or that in a section titled "Natural monopoly" the text essentially turns around the topic of '(marginalist) management criteria for publicly owned enterprises'.

with public funds (taxes), since they will pay a price below the average cost of the good. Furthermore, it should be noted that this publicly subsidising the consumption/use of a good derived from a theoretical argument that speaks precisely of 'achieving a social optimum'– is not, however, based on the fact that the concerned good is either essential, especially for low-income people, or that it has *positive externalities* associated with, or certain socially strategic connotations, that could justify it to be subsidised out of taxpayers' money. The marginalist prescription/ recommendation is simply based, as we have already seen, on a purely 'technical' matter, unrelated to the nature or social connotations of the good: merely that the market demand (for a price around-above the corresponding minimum average cost) is lower than the volume of units associated with that *minimum optimal scale* that allows for such minimum average cost for that good.

The incongruousness all of this entails will surely result striking for readers not familiar with this part of mainstream economics.

(c) Second-Best Pricing: a normative proposition to face the political reluctance to the 'allocative subsidy'

Thanks to the growing attention enjoyed by mathematical neoclassical economists at the beginning of the 20th century, their proposition of 'marginal cost pricing' and, therefore, of setting public prices below cost – reached the table of political decision makers; especially in the UK. Though such an economic policy proposal also soon met with, first, a logical perplexity from politicians, and then with a decided opposition regarding the idea of dedicating public budgets resources to subsidise certain goods on the grounds of complex reasons of the new economic theory: Public powers (we can focus on the UK and France of the time) were logically reluctant to fund the losses of the enterprise producing a given good, on the basis of technical considerations on 'marginal cost', 'consumers surplus', 'allocative efficiency', … etc., which in any case were unrelated to social-type considerations about the good in question.

Faced with this (understandable) rejection of the 'allocative (efficiency) subsidy' – that is, of applying the MCP proposal – the answer from theorist was a new theoretical proposition; namely, the *second-best*: «since the *first-best* (the MCP) is not accepted by public powers because of its 'allocative subsidy', let's define an alternative that, while avoiding subsidising, minimise the loss of allocative efficiency associated with deviating from the theoretical optimum»; hence '*second-best* pricing', (*sbp*).

The starting approach of the *sbp* is, in short: for a good which inevitably is produced under *natural monopoly conditions*, [marginal cost < average cost, assuming that the (only) enterprise behaves efficiently, both in the short and long run] the refusal of public authorities to apply the *first-best* is equivalent to they have imposed a *financial constraint* to the subsidy to be paid to the producer enterprise. Normally, this constraint consists simply of the subsidy be zero, S=0. Then, what would in this case be the way of complying such constrain, while minimising the loss of 'social utility' derived from not applying price = marginal cost? Since the usual reference framework in economics textbooks presupposes, as we have seen, 'one enterprise ≡ one product/service' a simplification that we come also maintaining so far, for the sake of facilitating comparisons, the *sbp* proposition, for S=0, was trivial: the *second-best* price to be set to the enterprise in question should simply be the average cost of the good – so that the enterprise operates without losses or profits. A logical and easy solution, certainly.

Therefore, the neoclassical economists advocating for the normative proposition of the *sbp* early posed the issue in a broader way, changing the question to a more complex one: «Let us suppose that the enterprise to which the prices have to be set produces and supplies the good in question, under *natural monopoly* conditions, to two or more groups of customers, and that these present different demand functions as for their degree of elasticity (of the quantity demanded in response to variations in price)[25]. How should the respective prices, to apply for each group of customers, be set to the enterprise, so that the financial constraint is met, S=0, while the loss of *social welfare* (in terms of *consumers surplus* – due to such prices be higher than the *marginal cost*) is minimised?»

This welfare loss to be minimised would consist, following the standard model, of the 'consumers surplus' under *sbp* being

[25] See footnote 28 below.

something lower than if *mcp* ('first best') was applied. Note that in this standard approach the fact that the *mcp* would also entail a parallel loss of *social welfare* because the corresponding losses of the enterprise should be covered out of public resources (by taxpayers), does not appear. Or, at best, this fact remains, implicitly, relegated to the background.

The way neoclassic economists answered the above question regarding *second-best pricing* was addressed along the 40-50s of the last century was by applying/adapting a theoretical formulation by Frank Ramsey[26] on optimal indirect-tax rates, published in 1927[27]. This seminal work did not refer, thus, to *sbp* itself but to define differentiated tax rates on the purchase of goods (as in our present VAT), so that the theoretical loss of social welfare (in terms of consumers surplus), generated by the 'distortion' in final prices such taxes entailed, would be minimal. The paper's core conclusion was, in short, that the different tax rates for each good should be inversely proportional to the price elasticity of the demand for each good[28]. The result from neoclassical economics theorists adapting this Ramsey contribution to answer the question about *sbp* was formulated

[26] Frank Ramsey was a brilliant student at the University of Cambridge in 1922 when, at the age of 19, made public a writing refuting an argument on the philosophy of science in an article published by one of his teachers, Keynes; who ended up by willingly admitting the rectification. Five years later, Keynes was precisely the editor of *The Economic Journal* at the time of publishing the Ramsey's paper referred here. Unfortunately, Ramsey died very young, few years later, in 1930.

[27] Ramsey, Frank P. (1927), "A contribution to the theory of taxation", *The Economic Journal*, 37: 145, pp. 47-61.

[28] Reminder: The Elasticity of demand for a good. Having observed a given reduction in the selling price,

Elasticity = (relative increase observed in the total units demanded) / (relative reduction in the price)

and the reverse, for a price's increase. So, e.g., if a 10% reduction in the price makes customers' demand to increase by a 10%, we say that elasticity –for that interval of price-quantity observed – is equal to 1. The more the value below 1, the less elastic (i.e., the more rigid –'vertical' in the graphical language as in figure 8–) the demand is; and the reverse if the calculation gives a value higher than 1.

and developed by Hotelling and Debreu, among others[29]. It can be summarised in the following generic proposition, called precisely 'Ramsey prices': «Given the financial constraint imposed by public authorities (usually that of zero subsidy, S=0'), the deviation of each price above marginal cost should be inversely proportional to the elasticity of the respective demands»[30]. This implies that the losses the enterprise will have with one (or more) of the group(s) will internally be compensated with the profits it raised with the other(s). (Let us take into account that in these theoretical works, it is someway implicitly assumed that the enterprise in question is publicly owned).

The same proposition is straight away applicable to a different imagined scenario where two o more goods – whose situation regarding unit-costs/demand is that of a natural monopoly – are jointly produced/supplied by a given enterprise; as well as to an alternative scenario where each of the above goods is produced/ supplied by a different (public) enterprise. In this case, the financial constraint S=0 would mean that the algebraic sum of profits and losses of these enterprises must be zero; which entails that public authorities would subsidise the loser enterprise(s) out of the profits collected from the other(s). The latter is precisely the alternative scenario later considered by Boiteux.

In 1956 Marcel Boiteux made an equivalent formulation when addressing the optimal price setting for public monopolies in

---

[29] Hotelling, H., "The General Welfare in relation to Problems of Taxation and of Railway and Utilities Rates", *Econometrica*, 1938: Vol. 6, n. 3, pp. 242-269; Debreu, G., "The Classical Tax-Subsidy Problem", *Econometrica*, 1952, Vol. 20, n.1, pp. 100 (original: working paper, *Cowles Commission*, Yale University, July 1951).

[30] Expressed it formally: $\frac{P_i - MC_i}{P_i} = \frac{k}{elasticity}$ where Pi is the price to set to the (publicly owned) enterprise to apply to the customers group '*i*'; (or, to the customers of good '*i*' produced by the enterprise. And *k* is (a constant) <1.

France[31]; where 'public' means *State-owned*. He does not properly speak of 'second-best', but the idea is exactly the same:

> " (cet article) Il concerne le probleme pose par l'incompatibilite de la regle de vente au cout marginal preconisee par les Welfare Economics, et les conditions d'equilibre budgetaire imposees par les Pouvoirs Publics aux entreprises nationalisees" (op. cit, p. 22).

Formally, the problem addressed by Boiteux was the setting of 'optimal management criteria' for (actually: 'optimal prices' to be applied by) nationalised enterprises managing *public monopolies*. (He refers, by way of example, to Electricité de France and to Charbonages de France). He assumes the usual hypotheses of the General Equilibrium model (or Welfare Economics, as he puts it), including, therefore, that of 'no income inequalities between customers' (= 'marginal utility of money is the same for every citizen'). And he assumes, implicitly, that a 'public monopoly' – like the two cited cases – has the characteristics that 'the marginal cost is lower than the average cost'. The latter is, however, shocking, because a public monopoly, as the ones he cites, is a de facto monopoly, by a State's decision. It is not a *natural monopoly* (type I situation, in figure 8) where the volume of demand does not even allow for a production plant with the *minimal optimal scale* to function at full occupancy – which is the case where inevitably marginal cost is below average cost, and the latter does not reach its minimum. But, let us park this for a moment.

The approach Boiteux draws on is the same as that before: to set prices, under the financial constraint S = 0, so that the loss in

---

[31] Marcel Boiteux, 1956 "Sur la gestion des monopoles publics astreints a l'équilibre budgétaire", Econometrica, 1956:(24)-1; pp. 22-40.

consumers surplus (compared to setting prices = marginal costs) be minimised. Therefore, his conclusion is practically the same: the difference between the price to set and the respective 'fictitious' marginal cost of each good should be inversely proportional to the elasticity of the demand for each good.

> "..: l'écart relative entre prix et coût marginal doit être proportionnel à l'élasticité du bien consideré. Le coefficient de proportionalité (k) est choisi de manière a réaliser l'equilibre budgétaire desire." (Boiteux, 1956, p. 37).

[Boiteux speaks of 'proportionality' instead of *inversely proportional* because he is using as definition for elasticity (p. 37) the inverse of the standard one, stated here before][32]

By 'fictitious' marginal costs he refers to a theoretical correction to the respective marginal costs – on the grounds that two or more of the involved goods might be partially substitutable. This theoretical precision is indeed the distinctive element brought about by his contribution. Nonetheless, in the neoclassical economics literature the expression 'Ramsey-Boiteux prices (or pricing)' has since been consolidated.

(d) 'Optimal prices' for Public Monopolies: four problems

The economic policy proposal of *second-best 'Ramsey-Boiteux (public) pricing'*, as well as its further developments, presents, however, serious problems. Firstly, the usual fact of it being (mis)used as

---

[32] Interestingly, Boiteux does not mention Ramsey at all in his article. Nor does he use the expression 'second best'. And, as pointed out, he defines elasticity inversely, as *(relative change in Price)/(relative change in Quantity)*; p. 37; except when he gives an account of the 'theorie des surplus', which is in fact the 'Ramsey prices' model as from authors as Hotelling , Hicks, and Debreu –to which Boiteux does refer to in his article.

applicable to any monopoly situation, when, in any case, it would be limited to *natural monopoly* situations; not, thus, to a *de facto* monopoly. If an enterprise holds a monopoly on, e.g., electricity in a country, by public powers' decision or simply because of market dynamics, that does not imply that the good 'electricity' responds to the unit-costs & demand conditions that define a natural monopoly (i.e., marginal cost below average cost, *in the long-run* (the situation *I*, in figure 8). We may replace 'electricity' in the above by 'gas', 'train transport', o any other good that currently or in the past has been entrusted by the State to an enterprise, as a public monopoly.

The above misinterpretation of the theoretical proposition itself seems often based on (or accompanied by) the implicit idea that 'if the production of a good requires significant fixed costs, the marginal cost will be lower than the average cost'[33]; which is simply a wrong assertion: The concept of marginal cost to reasoning on social efficiency, and therefore in the standard General Equilibrium model, is the *long-run marginal cost,* LRMC(q). Let us recap about this: the fact that a company, or the production of a certain good, requires 'considerable fixed costs' does not mean that the marginal cost of the good is lower than the average cost. All enterprises/ goods – and especially the industrial and industrial-services ones – require 'significant fixed costs'. Any production activity, at any scale of production, requires some fixed costs and some variable costs – *in the short run.* Every enterprise, therefore, has certain fixed costs, and every large company has 'very important fixed costs', *in*

[33] This is doubly surprising in the case of Boiteux, because, in addition to being already then a recognised academic, he developed a relevant professional dedication; especially in the area of French Publicly Owned Enterprises. In 1956, the year in which he publishes his seminal article, he was an engineer at the Service of Studies of Electricité de France (EDF); in fact, he signed the article as such. Two years later he became Director of the Service. And in 1967 he was appointed General Manager of EDF; a position he held until early 1979. His subsequent resume is even more notorious.

the short run. But this does not mean that the relevant marginal cost to reasoning on a social-economic optimum (long-run marginal cost) is lower than the corresponding average cost as we have seen not only in chapter 3 (empirical inductive approach) but also in chapter 2 (standard approach). Otherwise, all the enterprises/goods would be natural monopolies!

> Putting it schematically: in the following sequence, «'public monopoly' => considerable fixed costs; => the existence of these fixed costs makes the marginal cost (which comes from variable costs) lower than the average cost (which also includes the fixed costs)», the last statement is false. It even contradicts the economic theory itself which the *sbp* is based on (figures 1 and 3).

Seen the other way round, in the long-run practically all enterprises' costs are in fact variable; and theoretical considerations of 'social optimum' and 'equilibrium' do refer to the long-run. By way of example, if the leaders of a successful start-up undertaking decide to triplicate its activity, this can not be done the following week; it requires a given time (here the meaning of in-the-long-run). Once accomplished the expanding objective, the undertaking's fixed costs will likely be three times than before as we have seen through chapter 3; but its average cost will be similar (or perhaps a bit less, because of economies of scale). In short, only in cases where the demand is comparatively low situations type I, in figure 8 the composition of a firm's costs (variable, fixed) makes that the marginal cost does not coincide with the average cost but be lower than this.

Let us take, by way of example of price-regulation of an activity that (may be developed by a public monopoly but) is not a natural monopoly, the costs/demand situation for electricity in a given, even small, country:

> A thermo-generator or turbine that burns coal, oil, or gas (combined cycle) may produce just a minor part of the electricity-per-hour required by a country's network; or even by a medium city. With, e.g., gas-combined cycle technology, the *minimum optimal scale* of production (which entails that the average cost per KWh is minimum, and equal to marginal cost) is about two generator units (turbines). A power plant has usually 2-4 generators. And an electricity company uses to have several power plants in the country, connected to the network; a clear case, then, of *replicability* of the *mos* by a given enterprise. Thus, if all power plants in the country are under the umbrella of one only enterprise (publicly owned, for example), then we are simply before a *de facto* monopoly. That is, the cost/demand situation for electricity is rather that of type IV in figure 8: long-run *marginal cost* = long-run *average cost.*

Nevertheless, reading some academic references about *second-best pricing,* one draws the impression that the referred confusion of 'public monopoly/ nationalised enterprise' with 'natural monopoly' is due in some cases to the authors reasoning implicitly in terms of *short-run* (plus no full occupancy level), instead of long-run[34]. Leading scholars, such as Ray Rees and Ralph Turvey significant contributors to the field of public monopolies' regulation and public prices' setting argued (better and more rigorously) the above critical remarks decades ago[35]. Again, there is, thus, nothing original here on my part by highlighting the here referred incoherences.

---

[34] A more complete discussion regarding the above incoherence observed in the standard literature on *second best pricing* can be seen in Vergés, 2000: 90-95.

[35] Turvey, Ralph (1969) "Marginal Cost", *The Economic Journal*, 79(2) 282-299; p. 283; Turvey, Ralph (1971) *Economic Analysis and Public Enterprises*, London, George Allen & Unwin: pp. 57-58. Rees, Ray (1984) *Public Enterprise Economics*, LSE; pp. 45-54.

A second problem to add to this, regarding the *second-best pricing (sbp)*, is that a prices-discrimination based on differences in demand elasticity would lead to results lacking social-sense. Let us suppose the first Ramsey-Boiteux scenario: that of a public enterprise providing a single good, to two types of buyers: 'domestic' and 'industrial'. If the elasticity of demand for the latter is higher than that for the former, the *sbp* economic policy recommendation is that the price-cost difference be higher for the former; thus, a price higher for 'domestic' than for 'industrial' buyers – since marginal cost (as well as average cost) would be the same in both cases. This implies that, under the constraint of S=0, an income transfer from 'domestic' to 'industrial' customers will result. The nonsense of this lies in the fact that in principle there is no relationship between a higher elasticity of demand for a group of customers and social elements that might justify an income transfer to them, via prices, from customers whose elasticity of demand is lower. The same remark is applicable to the other two imagined scenarios referred to before: that of one (public) enterprise providing two or more goods (under natural monopoly conditions); and that of each of these goods provided by different (public) enterprises. More generally, as far as the demand for basic-necessities goods tends to be rather 'rigid' in relation to changes in the price (low elasticity), an application of the *sbp* could easily lead to recommend to politician decision-makers to set for those goods prices above-unit-costs in a proportion higher than for other non-essential goods.

A *third problem* arises because the *second-best Ramsey-Boiteux* is based on the neoclassical economics' concept of "consumers' surplus", as the measure for the (differences in) social economic welfare. And, in turn, 'consumers' surplus' relies upon the assumption – among others – that there does not exist income inequality among citizens. Consequently, insofar as such assumption is not fulfilled in the real world (nor as a crude approximation) but rather the opposite is true (income inequality has always existed; and they have even broadened throughout last decades, as Piketty, among many others has extensively documented[36]), the standard normative proposition 'Ramsey-Boiteu prices' for public monopolies lack of formal validity or relevance for our market economies.

To look at the matter from another side: the 'incongruousness' – or absurdities, if preferred – pointed out here as second and third problems are a consequence of the theoretical formulation itself. They com from the assumption, among the others of the GE's neoclassical model, of 'non-existence of income inequalities in the society considered'; i.e., that the marginal utility of 1 £ is the same for every citizen. Without such an assumption, a maximisation of the theoretical concept of 'consumers surplus' does not correspond with (or does not guarantee) any social welfare optimum. Its is, thus, a determinant assumption; which, by the way, Ramsey did not forget to mention at the beginning of his article. And so, in some way, did Boiteux at the end of his, though in more generic terms:

> ".. conclusions elles-mêmes fondées sur des hypothèses dont le réalisme est contestable . . . On pot se demander si l'aplication practique des resultats obtenues présente un réel intérét. .." (op. cit. p. 35).

But, unfortunately, these type of remarks or methodological precautions tend easily to be sort of ignored by subsequent scholars applying or developing seminal works such as those referred to.

Finally, a *fourth problem*; a practical or empirical one: to carrying out an application of the *sbp* to specific goods (which are under

[36] Piketty, Thomas (2013), *Le Capital au XXI siècle*, Ed. Les Libres du Nouveau Monde, Paris.

the situation of natural monopoly itself) would run up against an almost insurmountable practical difficulty: to determine, quantify, the *demand function* itself, in order to determine its *elasticity,* for each of the two or goods. In, principle, for a specific good, this measuring would entail observing what happens regarding the total quantity demanded when there has been a given change in the market price. However, it is not easy to identify changes in demand that are clearly associated with the change in price during the observation period. Mainly because changes in quantities purchased by customers do not depend only on the price, but also, simultaneously, on other variables; as the evolution in consumer purchasing power, the market dynamics of alternative (substitutes) goods', overall trends in the economy, economic expectations of citizens, etc; (and, in economics, we can not make *controlled* experiments, as, for example, to keep constant all independent variables except one).

This may explain why most of the empirical studies about elasticity measures are simply estimates based on data from surveys carried out for a given sample of people-as-consumers; spite the concept being one of the most used and useful for general, abstract, explanatory purposes, about a market's demand, in textbooks. It is also common in the specialised economics literature, regarding demand elasticity's estimates, to use a conceptual interpretation of the elasticity as, implicitly, a qualitative variable: certainly, an expert, by following systematically the evolution of the market for a certain good, and or carrying out a qualitative survey on a selected consumers sample, may reasonably conclude that the estimated *elasticity* of such demand is rather very-high, high, 'normal (E=1), low, or very-low (quite rigid) for the time period and interval of units/price observed. And these appraisals may result valid for building useful approximations, either for theoretical reasoning or for economic policy measures considerations.

(e) Theoretical inconsistency of the Marginal Cost Pricing proposition

Aside from what has been overviewed throughout the former pages related to the MCP paradigm, it happens that there is something else to this respect which could also have been placed early in this sub-section, after entry (a): At the theoretical level from which MCP is deduced, there is a problem of incoherence regarding it, which is internal to the standard model itself. Within the ESM's *general equilibrium* mathematical model, such a normative proposition of MCP is not valid as a mathematical condition (for a 'social optimum') *precisely for a 'technical' situation of natural monopoly*. To postulate such a condition implies, therefore, an inconsistency regarding the theory itself from which it is formulated.

To succinctly describe this inconsistency: in the *general equilibrium* model, the 'marginalist proposition' of «the social optimum requires that 'price = marginal cost', for all goods» comes out as a first-order mathematical condition from a constrained-optimisation of a *social utility function*[37]. But according to such constrained optimisation's simultaneous-equations-system, a mathematical second-order condition so that the first-order one, applied to a specific good, actually guarantees a maximum of *social utility* is, precisely, that the average cost for such good be not-decreasing for the volume of units for which the first-order condition is met (a more developed formal reasoning about this may be seen in Appendix D). Such a second-order condition is certainly met overall in the model, for the 'normal' cases: goods for which decreasing returns to scale beyond their respective optimal scale are assumed, these goods are produced by perfectly efficient firms, and no entry barriers to the sector exist;

---

[37] A complete formulation of the system of simultaneous abstract equations of the model, its definitions as well as the resulting mathematical deductions, can be seen, for example, in Vergés (2010:106-113).

conditions that makes that necessarily 'price = marginal cost = average cost'. But that second-order condition is not met precisely in a situation of natural monopoly since in such a case the average cost of the good is always decreasing (i.e., 'increasing returns')! Thus, in the context of the general equilibrium model itself, it is inconsistent or contradictory to postulate the criterion of *marginal cost pricing* for natural monopoly situations (in which average cost decreases when the volume of production increases).

It is not that this 'second-order condition' had remained hidden among the relative complexity of the mathematical formal deductions from the constrained optimization of the general equilibrium model. On the contrary, it has historically given rise to an extensive specialised literature within the modern-neoclassical economic theory. This academic literature is known precisely as 'the *increasing returns, non-convexities'* (theoretical) *problem*[38]. And it is also frequent to find in advanced microeconomics textbooks a chapter devoted to this *problem*. Yet, when in the same manuals, in previous chapters, the topic of *natural monopoly* is dealt with, the classical normative proposition of MCP is presented as the 'logical, well-known,' conclusion/ recommendation for these cases, thereby ignoring, in fact, the referred second-order condition, which simply invalidates such a proposition. This striking incoherence between the chapters of an economic theory manual simply occurs, as if they were like watertight compartments.

4.3.2 The 'natural monopoly' situations, according to an empirical inductive approach

Observational evidence from real economies shows us that the cost-demand situation type 'I' in diagram 8 – technically, *natural monopoly* – are much more frequent than is commonly assumed in mainstream

[38] An overview of this literature can be seen at Vergés (2010:118-120).

economics textbooks. In fact, the situation is particularly frequent for many 'ordinary' goods – in the sense of products or services that are non socially sensitive or strategic; for which, logically, the convenience of regulatory measures do not normally arise. This is the case, for instance, for most of the complex-technology equipment (such as a scanning electron microscope, a professional film projector, a turbine for combined-cycle power plants, any sophisticated industrial robot or a 'train' of automated machines, etc.). These are cases for which generic evidence shows that the technical-economic situation tends to be type '*I*': the total demand is not large enough for even a single company to produce at the minimum-optimal-scale level, i.e., that scale which would allow achieving the minimum average cost. The same is true for numerous luxury goods such as yachts, armoured cars, private helicopters, etc. Obviously, the unit cost of, e.g., a certain type of yacht would be much lower (and so its price) if it were sold and therefore produced by hundreds of thousands per year, as it is the case for most cars.

Of course, nobody would expect public authorities to be concerned and spend administrative resources regulating the price of these goods however much they are produced under technical conditions of natural monopoly. Although if the reasoning of the standard, orthodox, economic theory was to be followed, and one is consistent with its deductions, due to the fact that they are technically 'natural monopolies' (marginal cost lower than average cost), they should be regulated (and subsidised!), 'so that their prices were equal to their marginal costs, and thus to guarantee allocative efficiency within the whole economic system' all in accordance with the standard paradigm.

In some cases, as pointed out before, the technical-economic situation of *natural monopoly* occurs certainly for a good that is, in addition, a socially sensitive or strategic product or service. These are the cases for which there tends to be a socio-political consensus that such a productive activity should be subject to regulation by public powers, in order to avoid abusive prices and/or guarantee supply conditions. The usual historical examples in this regard are basic *public utilities* such as the distribution of water, electricity, and gas, as well as telecommunications for a given population. These are cases where the *natural monopoly* feature comes mainly from the fact that they are goods that require an important physical infrastructure, such as a distribution network (wiring, piping), which, in socioeconomic terms, it does not make sense to duplicate, triplicate, etc. In addition to these historical examples, there are those of public urban transport services, which also present, in whole or in part, characteristics of natural monopoly. In this specific case, mainly due to *economies of coordination*; besides their features of socially-sensitive *goods* regarding service configuration (which type and strategy of urban transport?), interrelationship with urban development, and ensuring service regularity.

The regulation for those goods 'with technical-economic features I' and that are also 'socially-sensitive or strategic' has historically been, and keeps being to a certain extent, implemented *directly*: the service is provided under a monopoly regime by a publicly owned enterprise, through which public authorities directly set up (order to the enterprise management) the price, service characteristics (as the quality parameters), and conditions of provision to users. And in other cases, this regulation is *indirect*: through a legal rule, or an administrative regulation, which establishes the same elements (price, service features, and provision conditions) to the enterprises -private or public- that provide the service; as well as, in some cases, the terms public powers must proceed to the temporary assignment ('concession') of the provision of the service to a company, through an 'ad hoc' contract. In the public administration and public agencies jargon, the latter is known as 'public tender & concession' procedures; and in the academic jargon, it is associated with the topic of 'contestable markets' or 'competition for the market' (private companies competing to get the public concession).

Whether this regulation or economic intervention by public powers is direct or indirect, what is in priority regulated (publicly decided) is the price – especially, as per mainstream economics' texts. But, as has been underlined above and tends to be neglected in standard academic approaches, on a *concession* contract a precise *definition* of the product/service to be provided uses to be formally established also: technical specifications, service scope, overall access conditions for customers, and, especially, quality parameters or attributes. Setting these 'qualitative' requirements is fundamental, taking into account the ex-post experiences historically accumulated about public tenders and concessions. For example, regarding some contractors' business practices like restricting somehow the access to some collectives (e.g., discriminating against 'expensive' customers), and/or reducing the quality levels of the product/service provided. These observed practices use to be a way for the private contractor to reduce its costs, and so since the price customers pay is 'officially' fixed– increasing its profits.

Furthermore, and returning to the initial paragraph of this point, it should be stressed that, although these cases in which both conditions occur (the technical-economic situation of natural monopoly and that of being a socially-sensitive or strategic good) use to be cases of high socio-political impact, these are not, even remotely, as has been argued, the most numerous cases of natural monopoly in practice. And the reverse: not all the goods that are the object of economic regulation in modern economies respond to the technical situation of 'natural monopoly'. In many instances, public regulation has to do with the fact that the production or consumption of certain goods has associated *social costs* or *social benefits* that are not reflected by the market (*externalities*). A decisive topic we will deal with in the next chapter.

Appendix D

The theoretical inconsistency of Marginal Cost Pricing

As stated in the main text: MCP stems from a first-order condition to maximise the social utility function in the simultaneous-equations-system of the standard General Equilibrium Model. But a mathematical second-order condition so that the first-order one, applied to a specific good, actually guarantees a maximum of *social utility* is, precisely, that the average cost for such good be not-decreasing –for the volume of units for which the first-order condition is met.

To express this in terms of the mathematics and terminology of the *general equilibrium* model:

> 'Given the *efficient Production-Possibilities Frontier* for any pair of goods, A and B, ($PPF_{A,B}$), Social - Utility Function constrained optimisation requires that the first derivative of $PPF_{A,B}$ –which in turn is the Marginal Rate of Transformation between both goods, $MRT_{A,B}$) – be, in absolute value, not-increasing. And that occurs when the $PPF_{A,B}$ – which is, in any case, a decreasing function, is ***concave*** (viewed from the axis origin) or straight. This condition is in turn met if, for both goods, their Production (Costs) Function, (Total costs, as a function of the total number of units produced) grows more than proportionally – for the relevant number of units – and therefore its graphic representation is a ***convex*** curve. This is equivalent to stating that the average cost of goods, A and B, are both increasing for the referred number of units (i.e., 'decreasing returns' in the production of both goods)'.

(A properly detailed argument of the above can be seen, for example, in Vergés (2010:110-113, and 75-78).

In the ESM and the specific literature on general equilibrium, the above rather cryptic chain of sentences tends to be compactly expressed as «the production function for every good of the economy is '*convex*'». Or, even more compactly, with the statement: «the condition of ***convexity*** must be met»; (this with the implied meaning of '... so that the first-order condition, Price=marginal cost, for each good entails a maximum of Social Utility)». And, certainly, using this terminology, a situation of natural monopoly is a case, or rather synonym, of ***non-convexity***.

I must apologise to readers for this long explanation on 'concavities' and 'convexities' as if we were dealing with geometry issues. These technicalities may be, however, justified. First, because they are consequence of the peculiar mathematical-geometrical language of mainstream economics. And mainly because of the traditional confusion the reading of mainstream economic texts on the topic usually generates: at a given stage, they speak of (the condition of) 'concavity', and then or simultaneously of 'convexity', while both terms are apparently used to refer to the same formal argument. The point is that the two expressions refer to two different functions/ diagrams of the theoretical model; though both simply respond to two ways of referring to the same objective condition: that the axiom of 'decreasing returns' must be met for (the volume of units traded of) each good.

Chapter 5
Dropping-out unreasonable simplifications

Taking into account the determinant realities of one-firm = several products, product differentiation, foreign trade, income inequalities, public sector, and 'externalities'

> " A competitive economy tends to produce the kind of goods people want at the lowest possible price because encourages entrepreneurship and technical dynamism through a restless struggle for advantage, a struggle that is not confined to price competition but includes *nonprice variables*, such as *new goods, better old goods, better-serviced goods, and more quickly delivered goods*. In other words, for Adam Smith and for the man in the street, competition is a type of behaviour by businessmen and not a market structure like "perfect competition", according to which business firms are purely passive "price takers" rather than active "price makers".
> (Blaug, 1998: 15)

So far – to facilitate comparison with the theoretical explanatory model of mainstream economics (ESM), summarised in Chapter 2 – we have maintained three usual strong simplifications, among others: that an enterprise is an entity that produces/provides one single good (product or service); that such a good can not be subject to differentiation in the market, in the face of customers; and that the economy we are considering is a closed one, without foreign trade. To which the unrealistic assumption of 'equality in income distribution' should be added, as well as the absence, in the whole theoretical scheme, of public powers' economic activity and of 'externalities'.

Certainly, when using explanatory schemes or models it is necessary, consubstantial, to make simplifications of the reality under analysis, to abstract certain aspects, without compromising the essentials of what is intended to be explained. The danger lies in falling into over-simplifications, in the sense of omitting elements that, rather than secondary or points of detail, constitute key elements to precisely explain or give a valid and useful schematic description of the reality under consideration. In that respect, the abovementioned methodological simplifications and omissions are indeed *oversimplifications*. Thus, let us take a further step toward a realistic formal explanatory scheme about how our economies work, to answer the following questions: How come the alternative, empirical-inductive, explanatory schemes – set out and argued so far (Chapters 3 and 4) – affected by removing the referred oversimplifications and omissions?

In short, let us see what should be changed in previous conclusions as a result of moving to take into account that, 1) the most usual is for a firm to regularly produce several goods, 2) that, for each of them, differentiation in the market, in the face of potential customers, is fundamental, a defining feature in our real market economies, 3) that foreign trade is a determinant piece in the whole picture, and 4) that income inequalities, public powers' economic activity, and 'externalities' are fundamental realities for explaining the workings of our market economies.

Let us start by the second topic.

5.1 Product differentiation – an omnipresent, and determining, reality

Looking at a 'firm's catalogue'

The existence, or simply the possibility, of *variants* for a given 'good', product or service (in terms of different sizes, or oriented to different uses, etc.) is a first 'natural' element of product differentiation. For example, regarding the *product* 'home refrigerator, there are large, medium, and small ones; or, regarding an 'accidents insurance policy', there are different *variants* covering more or fewer risks; etc. Also, the possibility of *different levels of quality* for a good, or a variant of a good, is another great source of differentiation, equally familiar and obvious to us. Thus, not all "medium-sized household refrigerators", or not all "40-inch TVs", available in the market have the same quality, technical features, use options, aesthetics, etc. Not all "4.4 metre 5-seats cars" have the same quality (materials, equipment), technology (gas, hybrid), performance and safety features; or the same aesthetics; (in these cases we tend to speak of different *models*). A specific "X-recovery-physiotherapy-session" can be performed with different levels of quality (efficiency, professionalism, timeliness, equipment, etc.). And so on.

The usual commercial policies of specific companies offering us this or that generic *product* in different sizes, characteristics, and appearance (variants), and/or different quality levels (*models*) –and therefore different prices– are direct examples of common product differentiation. The goal pursued by an enterprise through these business policies is not only to adapt to specific demands of potential customers but to also differentiate itself as a company, in the face of potential customers. Hence the importance of brands; as well as advertising: These business practices illustrate the determining relevance, as regards the workings and structure of markets, of the existence of product-variants and differences in quality attributes, since that gives rise to de facto *different products* produced by a single firm, spite they bear the same common-name; 'TV set', for example.

A first consequence of formally abandoning the traditional simplification that there is no product differentiation vis-à-vis customers/users is that it forces us to stop reasoning in terms of 'a good/product' meaning something like, for example, 'a private car'. Instead, we are obliged to assume that what really exists (i.e., is produced and sold by a firm, has a given cost and a given price, etc.) is different 'goods' with the same generic label – e.g.: *private cars* – of 4 or 5 different sizes, each of them in turn with different (say, 3 or 4) quality or performance levels. Thereby, *each one defines or is associated with a specific market*!

A second relevant element that 'soars' over all the above is, of course, innovation: It is a specific and relevant driver of product diversification. Especially when innovation is not simply cosmetic, it also allows the enterprise to (also) differentiate from competitors on the basis of 'being ahead' (at least for a certain time). This brings an added issue to the picture: sometimes it is difficult to discern whether the result of a given innovation is simply a new variant or model of this or that generic product/service of a company, or whether the differences that such innovation entails are so substantial that rather a distinctly different product has emerged.

Finally, a third element of differentiation is the subjective perception/ appreciation by potential buyers of a specific enterprise, regarding this or that product; or, in broader terms, the people's external perception about the overall 'quality' (prestige) of such an enterprise's products. Normally the actions that a firm carries out in that line focus on the intensive use of a brand that identifies itself. This brand becomes prestigious and popular, not only but mainly, through sustained and costly actions; basically, 'corporate' advertising campaigns and sponsoring. The effect of this companies' generalised strategy of influencing society to so gain market power (and thus the possibility of higher profit margins) stands out to any observer. By way of example, a typical case: a famous-logo sneaker can be sold at a price two or three times that of a lesser-known brand sneaker, even though as customers we may not be properly able to judge the difference between one and the other in terms of materials, manufacturing quality, or use-performance.

In any case, the fundamental issue for our overall subject the discipline of Economics as an explanation of how economies work is that moving to take into account these elements of reality forces us to modify the explanatory framework in the following sense: '*Product differentiation*' by companies normally entails a different unit cost for each *variant, model,* etc.; and, in parallel, logically a different price in the market. In practice, this leads to a *multiplication of the 'products' marketed by this or that company*. Each *variant* or *model* is technically and commercially a different 'product', and customers buy a certain quantity of it at a given price. Therefore, it defines (or belongs to) *a different, specific, market,* with its '*industry's cost function*' – and, thus, its *supply price function* – and its specific demand function. That is, each company's 'different product' would have its own figure 7's diagram!

Consequently, differentiation – whether in the form of *variants* of a good, relevant differences in quality or performance (*models*), or due to the subjective 'popular' prestige of the product/company, or thanks to a mixture of all that – ultimately generates a certain fragmentation/ multiplication/ segmentation of 'markets'. That is, it gives rise to inflation in the number of specific, different markets (market: where a certain 'price/quantity' relationship for a certain good takes place). In other words, a 'natural' (non-artificial) consequence of differentiation is certain *atomisation of the 'markets' of products and services*. This, among other consequences, facilitates the 'control' of these so-specific markets by one or a few enterprises; surely this is the most relevant consequence from moving to take into account product differentiation, as part of the task of contrasting standard *theory* with *observational evidence*.

Differentiation and firms' marketing policies: 'market share' and 'niche market'

The most commonly observed business strategy concerning the specific market or markets in which one company operates (or plans to operate) is that of tending to 'gain market share'– so to use the popular terminology of business schools, of MBAs. That means increasing the percentage of total demand for the product/ sector that is covered by the company in question. A given company may gradually achieve this as a result of certain commercial success, often based on some kind of product differentiation and marketing policies; or through a temporary low-price policy, aimed at driving competitors out of the market (predatory pricing). Another, complementary, way for a company to increase its market share for a given product is by 'leaps': buying up competing companies, or leading mergers; or, more generally, through a mixture of all these business policies.

Along the same line business strategies most commonly observed in this regard – there is that of trying to find, or generate (sic), a 'niche market'. This is a star concept that is taught also in the MBAs as one of the so-called *best practices* or *success' factors* in business management. This idea-concept means usually: finding up a new product, or a decisive differentiation; or obtaining access to a 'virgin' territorial area, etc. In any case, the term 'niche market' refers to situations in which – thanks to some elements of specificity involved – competition from other firms will be scarce and/or difficult, or even null in practice. Thus, as can be deduced, in terms of economic theory 'niche market' refers to a situation close to that of a *monopoly* – even if temporary.

These usual business management policies – 'gaining market share' and 'exploiting, finding (or generating), a niche market' – are enterprises' strategies aimed at creating or operating in situations where there is (/will be) little or no competition, because of factual business climate's conditions, even if these might be temporary. Ultimately, they consist of business strategies geared towards achieving market-power positions that allow for higher-than-usual profit margin rates. That is, they are situations that, technically speaking, are of an oligopolistic or monopolistic kind.

Conclusion: ***Products differentiation and innovation give way to markets segmentation.*** The consequence of taking product differentiation into account (and the related enterprises' usual commercial strategies regarding markets) is, in short, that it illustrates and helps to explain the enormous multiplicity of 'specific, real, markets' that we observe in our market economies. This, in turn, explains the 'normality' (statistically speaking) of situations of companies holding a certain (or a great deal of) market power –in the specific markets they operate; and, consequently, the 'normality' of relatively high-profit rates –we have seen in 4.1 and 4.2.

5.2 Multi-product (one firm = several products), the most common situation: repercussion on the formal explanatory scheme

A source of synergies in costs ('economies of scope')

An enterprise producing just one good is really an infrequent case[1]. The overwhelmingly general case in the business world is for a firm to produce several, different, products or services: It is quite normal for a company to produce different products that share the same common name; i.e., they are *variants* or *models* of a given generic good –in the sense of product differentiation discussed before: they are similar in terms of their use or function, but differ in size, features and/or quality. Consequently, they have a different unit cost, a different selling price, and a different demand; therefore (apologies

[1] To our (teaching economists) despair when searching for examples, even apparent cases such as a 'cement company' are not actually 'single product': in practice they tend to produce more than one type of cement, as well as other secondary materials.

for repeating myself) they are actually different 'products'. As complementary to the previous examples:

> Telecommunication services with different transfer speeds or coverage features. Or most clothing and foodstuffs: the possibilities of differentiation of products with the same name ('sweater' or 'wine') are obviously enormous; and constitute a fundamental characteristic, not necessarily artificial or forced, in the respective sectors.

It is also quite general for an enterprise to produce goods that are completely different, in terms of their use or function. This 'multiple' production is either in a sequential way (first a production section is dedicated to a product, then to another), or jointly: certain phases of the production processes, or certain pieces, treatments, or elements, are common to different productions of the enterprise (*joint production*).

> Examples: A manufacturing company that produces refrigerators, air conditioners and washing machines; a firm that manufactures cars, trucks, and motorcycles; a company that provides both passenger and freight transport services; a firm that provides both auditing and consulting services. And, as an extreme case, an industrial engineering company for which each project they develop on behalf of a client is a different 'product'.

Furthermore, it is also quite general for both situations (*'differentiated' products*, in the sense of being *variants* or *models*, and *clearly different products*) to occur simultaneously in the same company; for instance, in the case of the first example in the above 'paragraph'. We should also add, as an extreme (but not rare) multi-product situation, those cases of large companies with several divisions or subsidiaries –each of them, in turn, producing different goods or services, in the double sense above, which share corporate central services, such as top management, financing, legal department, etc. (we then tend to speak of 'business group', conglomerate, or corporation). One consequence of this is that it is not at all extraordinary to find companies whose catalogue of products/services contain tens or hundreds (or thousands, in the case of large industrial corporations) of items.

The main observational finding regarding this reality is that the fact that an enterprise produces more than one product is, in general, a source of *costs synergies*. Meaning by that that it is cheaper for the enterprise to produce several products together, *within the same organisation*, than if they are produced by several undertakings separately. This statement is widely supported by empirical observations; and no new in the academic field (both, orthodox and heterodox): 'costs subadditivity' is the expression used in economics to refer to this[2].

Mainstream economics does deal with the case of multi-product firms; although the reflection of this in standard textbooks basically focuses on the concept of *'joint production'*. More specifically, it concentrates on the issue of those operating costs that are common to several goods jointly produced. In this regard, its main thesis is precisely in line with the more general one mentioned above: that joint production leads to savings in total costs for the firm: *costs sub-additivity*, also referred to as *economies of scope*. However, the general approach taken regarding this issue of 'joint production' is usually to consider that this case of multi-product enterprises constitutes a very specific situation: rather an exception to the general case; (in much the same way as occurs in a manuals' section devoted to

[2] This is the concept coined for those situations observed where an enterprise that moves from producing 1 product to producing 2, 3, 4 etc. – e.g., through the successive acquisition of other companies that produce those products – registers total costs lower than the sum of the total costs of the precedent firms, even though these were operating, as single-product companies, with perfect efficiency (minimising costs, in the short-run; and well-dimensioned – in the sense of having achieved the 'industry's minimum average cost' at the time).

'imperfect competition'). Or, simply, the topic uses to be dealt with in mainstream textbooks in a lateral way, disconnected from the central theoretical paradigm (ESM). Thus, it is likely we may find that the issue of 'economies of scope' is discussed in a certain advanced section of a standard manual, but the resulting implications do not lead the authors to revise their previously assumed hypothesis of 'decreasing returns (growing average-cost)' which nucleates the core chapters of the manual in question.

In any case, in real economies it is easily observable that the vast majority of enterprises are multi-product: they produce/supply several goods or services each with a different unit cost and a different selling price. This, moreover, tends to generate some type of synergies which translate into savings in total costs at the enterprise level (*costs sub-additivity, economies of scope*); which in turn accentuates the tendency towards indefinite economies of scale for the different goods produced by an enterprise.

Conclusion: By moving on to consider the reality that *the vast majority of enterprises are multi-product* we come across an additional element to the arguments developed before (in sections 3.4 and 3.5) regarding the relationship between the *size-of-the-firm* and the '*unit-cost-of-its-product*'. This is specifically in the sense that the ubiquitous multi-product situation is an element that contributes to the fact that, as an enterprise follows a path of growth, its average cost (for this or that product in its catalogue) tends to be either constant *or rather somewhat decreasing*.

On incorporating this into the previous graphical-conceptual explanatory schemes, in general, the multi-product feature of firms makes it more likely that – as the size of an enterprise increases while expanding its range of products – *the unit costs for each specific product will tend to go down somewhat* (dashed tilted line for *long-run average cost* in diagram 6a), rather than be constant. This is consistent with the pattern persistently observed of *seemingly indefinite economies of scale* in certain manufacturing sectors. This can be illustrated by the fact that well-known products – such as high-definition flat-screen TVs, standard photovoltaic panels, or high-performance personal computers– have become cheaper and cheaper (for a given performance/quality level) over the years as they began to be jointly produced and on a scale each time higher, reaching to millions of units per year by this or that multinational corporation, *as part of its product range.*

5.3 Foreign trade; what changes into the explanatory scheme when moving on to take it into account

Real market economies are certainly not closed economies as, to simplify, the standard theoretical model of *competitive markets and general equilibrium* assumes. Foreign trade is really something almost as old as civilisations. Since the first industrial revolution and the subsequent development of maritime and rail transport, import and export transactions have largely ceased to be a mere complement to the overall turnover of a market economy. For practical reasons, as well as to make comparisons possible, the premise of 'let's assume a closed economy' has been maintained here so far; also within the alternative explanatory scheme. It is now a matter of seeing how these explanatory schemes change by abandoning this oversimplification.

The same path towards realism would certainly be needed to follow as regards the reality of *unemployment;* that is, we to move towards removing the ESM simplification that "there is full employment"; something that is partially addressed in this section with regard to foreign trade dynamics. Moving to full addressing the so relevant multifaced issue of unemployment goes beyond the planned scope of this text. Thereby, the following focuses on what changes, for our explanatory scheme of the functioning of our economies, when abandoning the over-simplification that these are closed economies

5.3.1 Foreign trade, concerning the structure of domestic markets (degree of competition)

There are more and more companies for which 'their market' refers to local plus international demand; and/or to local plus international suppliers. This is especially the case since the last third of the 20th century, with the spread of globalisation; i.e., the strong increase in world trade. Exports, as well as imports, have overall reached a significant relative weight in a country's economic activity.

Gross Domestic Product (GDP) can be used as a rough measure of the value (at market prices) of all goods and services produced by the whole country's undertakings over a period of time. Thus, if we compare the value of exports with GDP figures we can obtain an overall idea of which part of the production, of the activity of the enterprises in a country, is sold to customers in other countries. By way of example, for several European Union countries, the part of the country's production that is sold abroad represented between one third and almost half of the total, over the last few years:

	EXPORTS % of the respective GDP			IMPORTS % of the respective GDP		
	2010	2014	2019	2010	2014	2019
Germany	44.8	45.6	46.9	37.3	39.0	41.1
France	26.8	29.7	31.8	28.1	30.8	32.8
United Kingdom	28.3	28.5	31.6	30.3	29.4	32.7
Greece	22.1	32.4	37.2	30.7	34.8	37.2
Spain	26.0	33.5	34.9	27.0	30.4	31.9
Italy	25.1	29.1	31.5	26.9	26.2	28.4
The whole EU (28 countries)	38.6	43.0	46.6	37.5	40.0	43.6

Source: Own elaboration, based on information from *Eurostat Database: Dataset code tet00003, (Esports); Dataset code tet00004, (Imports)* - Last update as of 01/10/2020.

In any case, foreign trade is a relevant proportion of domestic economic activity, as we can see. However, this part of the economic reality is not conceptually contemplated – for the sake of simplifying – in the explanatory schemes of previous chapters regarding the market structures that could be expected to be observed for a given good or industry: those conceptual schemes implicitly presupposed that the 'demand function' for this or that good is determined by the socio-economic conditions and preferences of the country's citizens, i.e., that it refers just to the local (domestic) market.

What changes in these schemes when we include the reality of exports and imports in the picture?

Domestic exporter companies

Let us consider a specific product or service that, if taking just the domestic market into account, would technically qualify as a *natural monopoly* situation (type I in figure 7): such good might lose this connotation if it is exportable. (Certainly, not all goods are exportable: passenger transport, and vehicle repair services, for example, are not). In the case of an exportable good with a 'domestic' type I situation, the (only) producing firm may increase its volume of activity by exporting, thus reaching or exceeding the corresponding *minimum optimal scale* of production, and thereby operating at the lowest average cost. As a result, the technical-economical situation for that good would cease to be that of 'natural monopoly'.

Nevertheless, the recourse to foreign markets does not always entail such a change. For certain goods, such as aircraft or highly sophisticated scientific or industrial equipment – which are clearly associated with type *I* situations when considering only domestic demand – in most cases they still present such a situation even when foreign demand is added. In some of these cases (e.g., big-high-technology medical equipment) because even such international demand is comparatively low; and in others, because the *product differentiation* elements e.g., for technically sophisticated consumer products/services – turn out to be very important to potential foreign buyers. This explains why, despite being a *priori* 'type I situations even on a global scale', we may observe that more than one producer company coexists in the global market for some of these goods – and even these companies obtain high margin rates. This would be the case, for example, for armoured cars: the country of origin of the manufacturer car company – or simply the prestige of this manufacturer – is itself one of the *product differentiation* elements for those who have to make the purchase or import decision.

More generally, regardless of whether the domestic demand situation is a type I, II, III, or IV in figure 8, the fact that a good is exportable means that effective demand may be greater than domestic demand, which enables the companies supplying the good in question to produce and sell it on an even larger scale than otherwise. This is a strategy i.e., also to export, as a way of achieving greater growth– that observation shows is followed by a significant proportion of enterprises, which allows them to produce at a larger scale and thereby reducing their average costs; and so to secure or increase their profits.

In short, removing the simplification that the market 'demand' for a good is only that of the domestic market adds one more element regarding the overall prevalence in our economies of *constant-or-decreasing average costs* in the operation of companies; that is, the opposite to the standard axiom of 'a firm is faced with decreasing returns to scale when producing beyond a given (relatively small) quantity'.

Imports: Increase domestic markets' competition?

The fact that it is or becomes possible to import a given good basically means that some foreign enterprises are added to the 'domestic' ones that in principle would compete in the market. The consequence regarding the type of market situation that will tend to prevail (irrespective of whether total demand for the good in question is type II, III, or IV) is not predictable. This is for the same reasons set out in section 4.2: the resulting market situation will depend on the market strategies of all competing firms, domestic *and foreign*. In that respect, generic evidence shows us that *the entry of a (new) foreign company offering a given good may represent either a certain increase in the degree of competition in the sector, or just the opposite*. The latter is more likely if the foreign entrant is a large international company that uses its financial power and distribution channels to implement an aggressive strategy of gaining market share, that is, a predatory marketing strategy aimed at driving pre-existing companies out of the market.

To sum up: taking into account the reality of international trade- on the one hand the existence of external demand for this or that good or service, and on the other hand the presence of domestic plus foreign suppliers is one more element that makes the ESM's core postulate unrealistic and artificial: The postulate of the 'natural' tendency to competitive markets equilibrium, to *perfect competition*: markets in which – let us recall – a multitude of modest companies are supposed to compete, each one taking the selling price of the product in question as an external data, set by an abstract entity, 'the market', and obtaining as profits just what those companies' owners would have obtained if the money they invested in their undertaking had been deposited in a bank.

5.3.2 The standard *Theory of International Trade* and its implications on Economic Policy

In addition to the above incidence on the type of market structure resulting for this or that good, there is another key issue to considering foreign trade as decisive for an explanatory scheme, even if general, of the workings of our market economies: its overall social-economic impact. For a given country, trade with other country/countries occurs within the framework of certain terms of trade. Normally some kind of 'Exports–Imports' disequilibrium (the *trade balance*) of one or the other sign, greater or lesser, is associated with it. This *disequilibrium* has socio-economic repercussions, not considered in the *general equilibrium (GE)* model – you will forgive the implicit redundancy. For example, a *deficit* in the *trade balance* generally entails some kind of costs for the country, and therefore certain negative repercussions on the macro-variable to be optimised in the system of simultaneous equations of the GE model: *social utility*, which stands as a synonym for the measurement of the economic social welfare of an economy, a society.

Let us, therefore, go on to consider foreign trade as a whole. Specifically, let us start by analysing what the conventional *model, theory,* or *doctrine of free international trade* i.e., that based on the *comparative advantage* – tells us; and then contrast this standard theory with the main empirical evidence historically accumulated on the matter. Some reasons make this purpose of special interest. First, such a traditional explanatory *Theory of International Trade* has a decisive link with the *GE* model. Second, it is also based, as we will see, on deductive assumptions. And third, because its central postulate ['free foreign trade benefits all parties'] (also) has a traditional and notable presence in economics textbooks and beyond: in the political and media arena. Its use to defend foreign trade liberalisation policies all over the world is the most notable aspect in this respect. This idea-proposition has been, and remains, pervading economic and political debates on international economic relationships; (where 'free trade' stands for: each country reduces drastically, or simply eliminates, its tariffs on imports). In the words of Robert Skidelsky, 'The theory of comparative advantage has been the most influential doctrine in the whole economics'[3].

To put it briefly, the GE model generates the paradigm, widely spread beyond economics, that free markets in general (both for products/ services and for labour and the other factors of production) is an ideal guiding principle for social organisation in an economy: the generic idea of 'Perfect Competition' as a condition for the better economic results for everybody. This framework idea pervades much of the reasoning of economic and political professionals that are based – consciously or unconsciously – on orthodox economics. And such core idea of 'the intrinsic goodness of free market and competition' was extended early (since David Ricardo and other classical economists) precisely to international exchange, to foreign trade, with the *theory of international trade* or of *the* ***comparative advantages***: 'international free trade as a source of mutual economic advantages for the countries involved'.

From this perspective, the aim of what follows in this section is, first, to summarise this 'popular' theory or standard model, as well as the assumptions on which it is based; and then to develop the main conclusions derived from contrasting such assumptions with the abundant observational evidence on the subject, paying special attention to analyse the current real relevance of the idea of comparative advantage itself in a globalised worldwide market.

(a) The classical theory of (free) international trade, or of comparative advantages: specialisation & exchange

The theory or model of 'free foreign trade and *comparative advantages*' between two countries – which leads to the proposition that the outcome will be an economic gain for both – was fundamentally

---

[3] Skidelsky, p. 37.

developed by David Ricardo, in his book *On Principles of Political Economy and Taxation*, published in 1817. Although the expression '*comparative advantage*' was later coined (1844) by another classic economist, John Stuart Mill. Later on, especially during the last century, modern neoclassical economists have introduced a number of modifications to it – to make it less simplified and closer to the real world of international trade; but also as a result of introducing neoclassical economics' premises, tools and language, this theory or model is essentially the one till explained or taken as a base in most of today's reference textbooks[4].

This *Ricardo's model* or argument is based on a simplified scheme of foreign trade in which it is assumed that there are only two countries, England and Portugal, and two products, cloth and wine, in the production of which both countries present a difference in productivity. The reasoning uses an illustrative numerical example which – probably because of its simplicity (not trivialness) – became famous in the economics' profession: that of Ricardo's 'four magic numbers', still used in many first-year standard manuals today:

WITHOUT
FOREIGN TRADE:
Hours of Work necessary
to produce **1 unit** of each
product

	Cloth	Wine
England	100	120
Portugal	90	80

Alternative situation :
FREE FOREIGN TRADE:
Each country specialises in producing
the good for which has a comparative
advantage, and exchanges (trades) the
surplus with the other

Cloth		Wine	
220 h. work	= 2.2 units		
		170 h. work	= 2.125 units

[4] Gilpin, 1987, pp. 177-179; Schumacher, 2013, pp. 86-87.

As can be seen, the example assumes that Portugal is (was) more efficient (has higher productivity) producing both cloth and wine: it has an *absolute advantage* in both regarding England. However and this is the key issue – its productivity advantage is comparatively higher in wine: i.e., *it has a comparative advantage in wine*. Alternatively, the other way round: England has an *absolute disadvantage* regarding Portugal in producing both goods, but its *comparative disadvantage* in cloth is notably lesser. It is easy to deduce from such a numerical example[5] that if each country specialises in what it has a *comparative advantage* (or a lesser *comparative disadvantage*) that is, England in the production of cloth, and Portugal in wine, and they exchange their respective 'surpluses' with the same resources (total hours of work, in one and the other country) the joint production of both goods will be greater than if each country produces both goods separately (each country one unit of cloth and one unit of wine): under the *specialisation and exchange* binomial, the joint production of cloth will go from 2 to 2,2 units; and that of wine from 2 to 2,125 units. Therefore, (following the reasoning of the Ricardian example-model) with free foreign trade (and, therefore, *specialisation*) England could export 1-unit of cloth to Portugal, at a price equivalent to, e.g., 100 work-hours, and import from Portugal 1-unit of wine, at a price, for example, also of 100 work-hours (thus, the trade balance in equilibrium). This would mean that England would have

---

[5] In fact, Ricardo, in his explanation (pp. 90-91 of the cited book, reprinted edition by Batoche Books/Kitchner, 2001), does not refer to these 'fours numbers' as *technical coefficients*, as above; (i.e., work-hours per yard of cloth, and work-hours per gallon of wine). He refers to: the *work of 'x'*, (100, 120, .. etc.), *men over a year*, to produce *a given* (not precise) *quantity of cloth (C) and of wine (W), per year*, both in one country and in the other. That is, C yards of cloth, and W gallons of wine, to be produced in one and in the other country. Thus, for example:

To produce C yards of cloth in England requires the work of 100 men over one year =

= 100 x (*annual working hours, per man*) = 100 x (awh) = *Total work-hours* ≡ TWH

Thereby: TWH/C ≡ ***work-hours required per yard of cloth = 100x (awh / C)***

Thus, if – as Ricardo assumes – *Annual Working Hours* – as well as *C* – are equal for both countries, we may consider the quotient in the right as a constant –in the example. Therefore it is indifferent, and practical, to take (or refer to) the number '100' (or '80', '120, '90') directly as (a given multiple of) *work-hours per unit of product*. That is, as *technical coefficients* – as later authors have actually been doing–, since this simplifies the argument.

0.2 more units of cloth than before, and Portugal would have 0.125 additional units of wine, plus 'profits' (in cash or in kind) equivalent to 20 work-hours.

This quantitative outcome from free trade, as for the distribution of the gains, would be just a possibility, among others, depending on the respective 'international' prices (100, 100, in the above case). Any combination of Price-of-wine ≥80, Price-of-cloth ≥ 100, could be given. The resulting exchange prices will depend on the respective domestic demands (preferences) and bargaining power of both parties. (Here Ricardo, and followers, implicitly assume that this is an exchange between equals: between traders of similar importance and behaviour in both countries; i.e., a kind of 'perfect international competition'). In any case, following the reasoning of the model-example, both countries will be somewhat better off with the combination of *specialisation and free bilateral trade* than without it. The trade arrangement, the commercial bargaining (on prices), is equivalent to reaching, in a certain way, a given sharing of the net increases in production achieved through specialisation (0.2 additional units of cloth and 0.125 additional units of wine, in the example) between the two countries. To sum up, the thesis that flows from the Ricardian example/model is therefore that, under the assumptions implied by its argument (which are specified in the next point), the foreign trade between two countries that have some comparative advantage will bring benefits for both.

We may well consider this as a model, formulated using an abstract numerical example not based on a real observed situation. An explanatory model grounded moreover on deductive assumptions. It was not intended to reflect a real situation in terms of 'productivities' observed in England and Portugal when Ricardo was writing, but an abstract reasoning illustrated by an *ad hoc* numerical example. In any case, we may find it surprising that in his example Ricardo makes Portugal appear more 'efficient' (with higher productivity) than England not only in the production of an agricultural good (wine) but also in that of an industrial good (cloth), since, certainly, economic history indicates that the situation regarding 'cloth' was the opposite. Ricardo obviously knew this well (page 90 of the text cited), thanks to family tradition, and as a merchant himself[6]. His reverse, instrumental, supposition responds to the fact that his aim is (was) to argue, to demonstrate, that it was not only in the case of a symmetrical situation of *absolute advantages* (England more 'efficient' in cloth, Portugal more efficient in wine) that the trade between the two countries benefited both parties (something that Adam Smith had already argued a few years earlier). He wanted to show that, *even in the case* that Portugal had an absolute advantage over England in both productions, the commercial exchange – based on specialising – was still beneficial to both countries (also to Portugal). This, in a way, could also be interpreted as a way of justifying the de-facto situation at the time (Portugal surrendering cloth production to England) as the better one for both countries[7]. In short, Ricardo (like other later economists) wanted to show that the decisive point in this respect would be whether there were *comparative* advantages. Which he does elegantly demonstrates with his example.

(b)The assumptions behind the model of comparative advantages

---

[6] David Ricardo belonged to a Sephardic family originally from Portugal, which first settled in the Netherlands and later generations in England. Born in London, his activity as a merchant gave him direct knowledge of the English-Portuguese trade of his time. In this trade, the export of wines from Portugal to England and of textiles from England to Portugal was indeed dominant, as Ricardo himself begins by commenting in his book (pp. 89-90 of the edition cited in the previous note), some lines before starting to argue the issue of *comparative advantage* by means of his example (pp. 90-96). We could interpret that, starting from the reality of his time regarding the existing trade between Portugal and England, what Ricardo wants is to demonstrate, with brilliant abstract reasoning supported by a simple (not simplistic) invented example, that this trade, which already existed between both countries, benefited both (not only England). He moreover, of course, uses his example/model to generalise the argument; that is, to defend, to illustrate, the general validity of the argument regarding the benefits of international trade between (any) two countries when comparative advantages are present.

[7] Skidelsky, 37-8.

As an explanatory model, it relies upon a number of assumptions and simplifications. Regarding the latter, the main one is obvious: trade is considered to be only between two countries, E and P, and limited to two generic goods: 'wine' and 'cloth'; and considering only one production factor, Labour. As for the assumptions themselves – those that make it possible to assert that the result of free foreign trade between two countries will be beneficial to both parties, they are basically:

a. *There is no Capital mobility* (between the two countries)* *nor Labour mobility.*
   (*): e.g., it is not possible for *E's* merchants to invest in *P's* 'cloth' industry)[8].

b. *There is full employment* in both countries; or, as an approximation, there is *constant* employment (before vs. after specialisation and exchange)[9]

c. *Wages are equal in each country* (taking into account the exchange rate), or they *tend to equalise under free trade*. That is, the comparative differences in terms of labour-hours-per-unit-of-product (Ricardo's 'four numbers') someway translate into proportional differences in *trading prices*.

   This assumption is a translation of the fact–illustrated in the previous point that the model's logic implicitly considers that trading prices for cl and w are expressed in or are proportional to the respective labour's technical coefficients (hours-per-unit-

[8] Obviously, Ricardo takes into account that, in addition to Labour, both wine and cloth production require a certain amount of Capital. He himself makes explicit this assumption of the non-mobility of Capital (page 91, of the cited edition), and why he considers that it is obvious that such assumption is actually met –in his time.

[9] This, in the sense argued by Krugman, in his 1996, "Ricardo's difficult idea", p. 7.

of-product), that wages spontaneously adjust to differences in productivity; and that Labour initially occupied in the production of cloth and of wine is interchangeable between both. Therefore "(according to the standard theory) comparative production costs advantages are transformed into absolute price advantages" (Schumacher, 2013, p. 87-8).

d. As a result of specialisation and free trade, there is monetary *equilibrium in the Trade Balance* between the two countries.

e. *Capital resources employed under autarchy* (each country producing both goods) *are equal to those required to specialize in one of the goods for then proceeding to exchange the increase in production.* Additionally, (e2) *Capital cost in each country is not relevant to determining goods' trading prices* – since these are supposed (c) to result just from the comparative advantage in terms of labour hours.

f. *Transportation costs are not relevant*; more precisely, they are not considered in the classical setting.

Other implicit assumptions should, however, be added to these when the model is extended to worldwide trade (any number of countries): (g) *each country in the world has a comparative advantage to exploit, in which to specialise*; (h) trade between countries is carried out by companies with similar bargaining power; i.e., there is *perfect (international) competition*. Finally, all of the above is considered in the framework of a comparative-static equilibrium analysis: observed comparative advantage/s are deemed constant over time. Technical change is, thus, absent in the standard formulation of the theory (Schumacher, 2013, pp. 92-6).

(c) Mathematical modelling and the Leontief Paradox

The further mathematical formulation of this Ricardian model logically brought the possibility of expressing the concepts handled by the model (comparative advantage, gains of each country, relative prices, etc.) in more general terms for two or more countries, more than two goods, etc. as well as in a more rigorous way. (A summary presentation of the original model in a mathematical formulation can be seen in Annex E at the end of this chapter). A significant step in this regard is the development by Eli Heckscher, in 1919, completed by Bertil Ohlin, in 1933. They refined the Ricardian model by applying the then relatively-new general-equilibrium paradigm and its methodology (mathematical diagrams), giving way to what is known as the neoclassical Heckscher-Ohlin theory (of international trade)[10].

This refined theory was later the object of criticism, especially after a study by Wasilly Leontief where he carries out a thorough empirical test of such a theory, by taking the case of the U.S. for a notably long period (1919-1939)[11]. The results of this study showed not only that the prediction of the theory did not hold in such a case but that just the opposite was true: the nature of the U.S. imports and exports were exactly the opposite to the prediction of the theory. This Leontief's result has since been known as the 'Leontief Paradox'. What is significant as regards the preconceptions of modern-neoclassical economics: An empirical contrasting than refutes a theory (with one only case, but a notable one) becomes 'neutralised' within the academic mainstream economics literature by considering it not a (provisional) refutation of such a theory but a 'paradox'. That is, as a curious or abnormal empirical observation insofar as it is contrary to the Ricardo-Hekscher-Ohlin theory. A theory that, thereby, remains

[10] The main proposition from it is that countries endowed with comparatively more Capital than Labour will tend to specialise in capital-intensive goods, while countries with comparatively more Labour than Capital will focus on Labour-intensive goods, so developing their respective comparative advantage on which to base their exchanges, for the benefit of both parties.

[11] Leontief, Wassilly, (1953).

untouched, as if shielded against empirical evidence. Indeed, Leontief himself assumed this epistemological approach in the referred work: since according to his statistical findings the foreign trade of the U.S. did not meet the proposition of (i.e., 'the optimality condition' required by) the standard theory/doctrine, he ends his article by concluding that the U.S. would increase its social welfare by changing the composition of its foreign trade (exported and imported goods), according to the theoretical proposition regarding the Labour vs. Capital ratio within both exported and imported goods[12].

As the above case illustrates, the step of formulating an abstract, mathematical model opens up (or in any case facilitates) the possibility to carry out empirical contrasting. The problem in these cases, however, is that since the model is so simplified and has such restrictive (or unrealistic) assumptions, its empirical verifications or simply that of its prediction that 'free foreign trade based on exploiting the respective comparative advantage/s, via specialisation, will benefit both parties' are in practice a difficult to impossible task. Perhaps these limitations have something to do with Schumpeter's lapidary sentence when referring to what he called the 'Ricardian vice' (to take so many things as given): "(the theory of comparative advantages) It is an excellent theory that can never be refuted and lacks nothing save sense", (in his 1954's *History of Economic Analysis*, p. 448).

In either case, especially since the 1950s, academic economists have developed the basic mathematical formulation of the Ricardian model, extending and generalising it: not only to more than two goods between two countries, and more than one variable factor (not only Labour) but also to more than two countries (multilateral trade); also by to relaxing assumptions, as that of the non-mobility of Capital between countries, taking into account transportations costs

---

[12] Leontief, 1953, p. 349)

as well as the dynamics of comparative advantages, substituting monetary costs with the concept of opportunity costs, etc. (see note at the end of Annex E). These more general neoclassical mathematical models[13] inevitably require the introduction of new *ad hoc*, more specific, simplifications and assumptions since the reality of international trade and the different socio-economic conditions of each country draws such a complex picture: it is a multi-face *and changing* reality. Thus, along this path of increasingly sophisticated mathematical models, there has been a tendency for specialised scholars to use or introduce axioms and postulates typical of the General Equilibrium (such as: 'price=unit cost'; the standard concepts of supply and demand functions; spontaneous free-market equilibrium (at international level), etc.). Understandably, this specific literature speaks of 'Ricardian General Equilibrium mathematical models' (RGEM). Nevertheless, these mathematical models –formally less schematic although quite more complex– still encounter serious difficulties to allow for empirical testing of their specific assumptions, propositions, and predictions. This leads to the fact that the application of these models cannot normally provide analytical results with significant explanatory power. This, in the sense that these theoretical mathematical developments hardly yield conclusions with possibilities of explaining, for example, why about such and such socioeconomic *consequences* and/or results observed across time for specific countries after they have opened up to international trade.

[13] A complete presentation of current mathematical models of *international trade/ comparative advantages*, as well as a historical overview in this respect, can be found in the popular manual *International Trade, Theory and Policy*, by Krugman, Obstfeld and Melitz (2017; 10th. Ed., Chapters 3 to 6).

Standard mathematical modelling' outcomes

A typical contribution addressed to refine the standard theory of international trade may consist, for example, in qualifying the assumption/prediction on the long-run equalisation of wages in a bilateral trade situation, in relaxing the simplification with respect to the type of goods by (also) considering intermediate goods, etc. The epistemology of these theoretical innovations usually involves developing or adapting a mathematical model based on the referential framework of neoclassical economic theory (marginalist equilibrium analysis, production possibilities function, a deductive wages/ costs/ prices relationship, indefinite technologies, perfect information, etc.). And their results or conclusions usually consist of theorems; that is, the results formally refer to the issue introduced (a more elaborated prediction on wages equalisation in the long run, the formal repercussion from also considering intermediate goods, etc.) but in highly abstract terms –a feature that is enhanced by the reflection of the additional, specific deductive assumptions that were introduced to make possible the novelty's math-modelling. In a way, something similar to the outcome of a complex exercise in deductive logic. Consequently, empirical verification of the theoretical assertions, of the theorems, becomes virtually unfeasible.

This is not entirely a shortcoming but a matter of objective difficulty associated with the use of math models in modern neoclassical economics. Basically, because the key economic variables showing the referred socio-economic consequences (Employment, Unemployment, Salaries, Prices, Trade Balance, Foreign Debt, ...) are in the economic reality simultaneously co-determined both by macro-variables other than those included in the corresponding RGEM model (other variables that, moreover, are not always quantitatively 'controllable'), as well as by the economic policy measures the country under consideration applied along the studied period.

Empirical standard research's constraints

Let us consider what an empirical contrasting of a theoretical result on the topic would entail. For example, to contrast a specific conclusion or prediction about the relationship between *foreign trade liberalisation* and *Employment* (or *per-capita income*, .. etc.) resulting from having applied one of such complex mathematical models:

It is possible (1) to obtain time series covering many years, and for one or more countries – on exports, *imports, employment, unemployment, per-capita income,* (and other model's variables that be quantifiable and available; e.g., foreign capital inflows, prices indexes, ...). And (2) then carrying out the best econometric analysis these data allow for.

However, the involved research team will be well aware that the annual variations of, e.g., *employment* in the time series depend *simultaneously* on different variables (whether or not included in the model) as well as on economic policy measures taken by the respective governments across the years analysed. Hence, even squeezing in depth the possibilities of econometrics' multivariate analysis, it is not usually possible to know with a minimum valid approximation which part of the *variations* in employment come explained by the set of these co-determining elements different from the foreign trade flows unless subjective estimates are made. Therefore, it cannot be deduced in fact to what extent and in what sense the *variations* of employment shown by the time series are related to foreign trade flows. Of course, specific, partial approximations might be drawn; the problem then lies in the degree of ir/relevance of them.

Let us consider this example-argument simply as illustrative of the objective difficulties for researchers, pointed out above.

Considering the issue from a different perspective, these mathematical less simplified models that might entail more realistic assumptions yield complex partial deductive results about specific sub-topics of the theory of international trade. One consequence of this feature is that such results tend to remain within the domain of the specialised literature and professionals. This, in turn, may contribute to explaining the fact that the Ricardian paradigm ('free international trade allows exploiting comparative advantages for the mutual benefit of the involved countries') continues currently being widely assumed as a generally valid guiding idea. Or, in the case of the mainstream academic world, at least as a valid simplification. Nevertheless, modern neoclassical theorists defending the intrinsic goodness of free international trade do tend to nuance the argument by rather talking in terms of *potential* gains *in the long run*; also, they do not specifically assert that every country will gain *equally* (or *fairly*), but simply that the sum of the units of each good produced by the involved countries will be higher. In either case, "Regardless of theoretical differences, however, liberal economists maintain their basic commitment to the mutual benefit of free (international) trade ..." (Gilpin, 1987, p. 179).

In short, socio-economic dynamics (simultaneous changes in macroeconomic variables) make it hardly possible to test current mathematical theoretical models as to assessing the effects on the social welfare of a given country, some years after it has dismantled its tariffs on imports. (Schlefer, 2012:75-6). An alternative strategy for empirical contrasting of the standard Theory of International Trade is to focus on confronting not directly its predictions but its assumptions with the respective more-obvious empirical observations regarding them. What follows respond to this idea.

5.3.3 Confronting the standard model on international trade with available generic evidence

(a) Generic findings

From a historical perspective, one of the main remarks to this respect has been that, under the banner of free trade, the more or less 'forced' *opening to international trade* (i.e., significant reductions or elimination of import tariffs) has in fact prevented industrialisation – or sufficient industrialisation – in many less developed countries. In this sense, there is also a certain overall acknowledgement that most of the 20th century industrialised economies did not manage to become so by means of symmetrical, equalitarian, opening up to international trade, but rather by means of *de facto* protectionist measures (or imperialist ones: the case of England with regard to India in respect to local textile production, for example).

> "the imposition of free trade on Portugal killed off a promising textile industry and left her with a slow-growing export market for wine, while for England, exports of cotton cloth led to accumulation, mechanisation and the whole spiralling growth of the industrial revolution"
> (Joan Robinson, in "Aspects of Development and Underdevelopment", 1979, *Cambridge University Press*; p. 103).

A variant of the above assertion is the remark that the existing *comparative advantage* for a given country may simply be a consequence of its level of technological development being higher than that of another country to which it exports; and that in many cases free trade has tended to consolidate, or even accentuate, these differences in the degree of development. 'As soon as 'catch-up' became the name of the game, countries looked to exploit dynamic, not static, gains from trade. This means developing higher-value industries shielded from premature competition. Friedrich List claimed that free trade can be an instrument to entrench existing trade advantages, and, via these, existing power advantages.' (Skidelsky, 2020, pp. 37-38). This would be an aspect of what is known as *unequal exchange*. In the words of another well-known economist:

> Ricardo's theory is absolutely right within its narrow confines. His theory correctly says that, *accepting their current levels of technology as given*, it is better for countries to specialize in things that they are relatively better at. One cannot argue with that. His theory fails when a country wants to acquire more advanced technologies that is, when it wants to develop its economy. It takes time and experience to absorb new technologies, so technologically backward producers need a period of protection from international competition during this period of learning. Such protection is costly, because the country is giving up the chance to import better and cheaper products. However, it is a price that has to be paid if it wants to develop advanced industries. Ricardo's theory is, thus seen, for those who accept the status quo but not for those who want to change it.
> (Ha-Joon Chang, in his book *Bad Samaritans*, 2008, Bloomsbury Press NY; p. 29).

In a more colloquial expression by the same author at a lecture: "... by recommending to (or even forcing upon) developing countries the free-trade, free market policies that they themselves never used when they were developing, the rich countries that have reached the top are 'kicking away the ladder' to wealth that they themselves climbed".

It is significant in this sense the fact that 'only after World War II did the United States seriously liberalize trade' (Schlefer, 2012: 184, 187-8).

Linked to the above, there is the non-trivial question of the *risk of dependency or vulnerability*: to the extent that *specialisation-and-exchange* entails for a country to import certain goods, practically ceasing to produce them at home, this places the country in a certain situation of dependency and/or vulnerability with respect to the outside world. This vulnerability becomes especially relevant when it affects essential goods, such as certain foodstuffs or medicines, or to socially strategic goods for the country. An international crisis, a disruption within international trade in general, in the clock-mechanism-running of globalisation, can have particularly serious consequences for a country in such a situation of vital dependence on the outside world.

(b) Evidence on specific assumptions

Another element that stands out when confronting the standard model of international free trade with the observational generic evidence is that of *recurrent deficits in the trade balance* of many countries. Formally, this is a case where the model's assumption *'**d**'* that of 'free trade automatically leads to a monetary equilibrium of Imports - Exports'– is not fulfilled. (Of course, we are not referring to non-fulfilment in the strict arithmetical sense of the difference being exactly zero but rather that such an imbalance is proportionally significant). In many cases, this non-fulfilment is moreover observed in a reiterative manner, even if measured as in the Ricardian model: in terms of work hours. In this regard, for economically weaker countries the fact of opening up to international trade, i.e., to implement a drastic reduction or elimination of 'tariff barriers', has often resulted in recurrent deficits, over a large number of years (see Annex F). And these deficits in the *trade balance* have a cost for the country as a whole. Mainly, the costs derived from the indebtedness that such an external imbalance forces to, as well as those costs associated with the increase in unemployment that these imbalances might generate.

Thus, the sustained trend, especially since the last third of the twentieth century, towards opening up to international trade – that is, to a substantial reduction in import tariffs has in many cases been accompanied by an *induced increase in* countries' *unemployment.* This formally means that assumption *'b'* of the theoretical model is not fulfilled. In some cases we can, alternatively, observe what is somehow equivalent: that a kind of substitute for unemployment arises, in the form of degradation of employment conditions, of a high level of labour precariousness; i.e., more presence of part-time, temporary, on-call, jobs, fixed-term contracts, worsening of workers effective rights, etc; (formally: assumption 'c' on real salaries does not hold). This, because for a larger than promised time stretch, there are fewer job opportunities in the concerned country, due, in turn, to the fact that certain goods are no longer produced in it, but imported, while the expected compensation – new productions, for exporting – did not properly develop. In other words, the automatic adjustment in (un)employment, that orthodox economics tends to assume, is not actually so automatic in many real cases.

The prediction that the people displaced by 'new imports', the new unemployed, will move in a reasonable time to other jobs (or even 'better jobs') in other economic activities, is in many cases not met. In the favourable instances, such spontaneous adjustment tends rather to occur in the medium/*long-run*; though the *long-run* may become too long – even not going so far as Keynes' reiterated phrase "in the long run we are all dead" – referring to his academic colleagues' habit of talking about long-run *equilibria.* This means that in any case there are certain social costs derived from such adjustment delay. As for the not so favourable cases, the unemployment increase may become entrenched. In any event, all this entails some given social costs, induced by persistent foreign-trade imbalances; whether in the form of public expenditure on unemployment benefits or if the country concerned does not have an effective social safety net to support the unemployed– in the form of increased poverty.

Moreover, as for assumption *'c'* on 'the trend towards equalisation of real salaries among trading countries', besides that pointed out above, there is the overwhelming evidence on the contrary illustrated by the last decades' flourishing of off-shore outsourcing by developed countries' firms (an issue dealt here with further on), which is based precisely on persistent differences in salaries. This non-fulfilment of the assumption on wages can, however, be waived if as some modern-neoclassical authors do– we move to consider the fact of persistent lower wages in this or that country as a comparative advantage itself.

These critical remarks (which are neither new nor original on my part) regarding the fact that the assumptions of the standard theory or model of international trade especially assumptions *(b)*, *(c)* and *(d)*, because of their major implications are mostly not met in the foreign-trade real world, have nevertheless been questioned by relevant academics such as Paul Krugman.

Thus, regarding the above critical remark about the non-fulfilment of the *full employment* condition [assumption (b)], Krugman argued in his 1996 essay[14] that this objection should be discarded because the decisive point, to continue considering the standard theoretical model to be useful, is that this condition does tend to be met in the long-run.

He also rejects the previous remark on the non-fulfilment of assumption ***(c)*** on wages equalisation between countries on the

[14] He defends that the classical Ricardian answer to this would be "..International trade is a long-run issue, and (..) in the long run the economy has a natural self-correcting tendency to return to full employment"; and adds, in modern-neoclassical language, that ".. 'constant' employment is a reasonable approximation to full-employment (condition)", as well as that 'constant' employment is, in turn, a reasonable assumption because ".. countries have central banks, which try to stabilize employment around the NAIRU (Non-Accelerating-Inflation Rate of Unemployment) .... and they (central banks) are successful in this endeavour". (Krugman, 1996, point 3).

grounds that, again, this equalisation is actually fulfilled *in the long-run*. His overall root conjecture in this respect, in the referred essay, is that wages at the national level adjust to increases in productivity (neoclassical theory on *labour marginal productivity*), at the time that foreign trade makes *productivity levels converge between countries*, and thus wages tend, 'in the long-run', to converge between the involved countries, as a consequence of their foreign trade. As an example of this, he cites the historical case of Japan[15].

Moreover, Krugman also rejects the above remark that assumption ***(d)***, on *spontaneous trade-balance equilibrium*, does not actually hold regarding many countries. He defends the point that there are in fact *automatic adjustments* that do equilibrate trade balance (again, in the medium/ long-run). His argument in this respect assumes the classical economics' thesis, '(foreign) trade imbalances are self-correcting via domestic price adjustments', to which he adds the neoclassical argument regarding government intervention through monetary policy, as an action effectively enhancing the above automatism[16].

Note, regarding Krugman's above point on assumptions 'b' 'c' and 'd', that while his considering *changes in productivity* over time for this or that nation is something pretty realistic, within the logic of the standard model these changes would properly mean changes

---

[15] Though, precisely Japan was already an industrial power before World War II.

[16] More precisely, his conjecture or thesis regarding the topic is (Krugman, 1996: 3): a country with recurrent trade surplus will experience an increase in domestic prices (inflation), and thus in its exporting prices, which will cause an exports reduction. On the other hand, a country registering recurrent deficits will experience a fall in domestic prices (deflation), thus also regarding its exporting prices, which will make its exports internationally cheaper and thus increase. As regards the modern-neoclassical argument that he adds, as a complement to the above, it refers to governments intervention through monetary policy: "..when monetary policies target the unemployment rate, exchange rates do the adjusting (of foreign trade imbalances)". This assertion would imply, in the case of a country trying to fight trade-balance deficits, to take for granted the following cause-effect chain: «(monetary policy aimed at Unemployment) → (generates) domestic prices (inflation) → exchange-rate devaluation → Exports → Equilibrium in the trade balance.

regarding countries' *comparative-advantage-position* itself; what modifies the analysis perspective on the overall topic.

Continuing on assumption 'c' on the equalisation of wages, it is the case that rarely theorising statements – as the former one – take case observations as a departure step. We might well ask why? By way of case-example: bilateral trade between Mexico and the US has been significant for both countries for decades. About 80% of Mexico's exports go to the US. As for the US's exports, Mexico is being its second country partner – after Canada[17]; (the North American Free Trade Agreement, between the three countries, came into force in 1994). Moreover, the volume of this bilateral trade has grown strongly over the last four decades, in line with the boom in international exchanges (globalisation)[18]. Taking into account the above, were we to follow the neoclassical assumption of a trend to wages equalisation between the US and Mexico (taking the exchange rate into account) as a result of a free bilateral trade based on comparative advantages, then we should expect that a clear tendency in that sense is observable along last decades in this case. However, overall empirical data in this respect do not support such a prediction/assumption at all. In 1990 the average wage in Mexico was equivalent – in ppp, 'purchasing power parity', terms) to 31% of the average wage in the US, in 2000 it was still 31%, in 2010 27%, and in 2020 23%. Thus, not only has Mexico's wage rate differential with respect to the US not decreased in four decades, but it has increased. This facts-finding suggests the usefulness of possible theoretical

[17] "U.S. Relations With Mexico", *U.S. Department of State - Bilateral Relations Fact Sheet, Bureau of Western Hemisphere Affairs*, September 29, 2020; (www.state.gov/u-s-relations-with-mexico/; retrieved as of 9/08/2021).

[18] From 1980 to 2020 US total exports increased by a factor of 2,6 in real terms (amounts adjusted by the overall consumer prices index); and from 1990 to 2020, by a factor of 2. (Own calculation based on data from "U.S. Trade in Goods and Services - Balance of Payments (BOP) Basis", *United States Census Bureau, Foreign Trade*. https://www.census.gov/foreign-trade/statistics/historical/index.html ; retrieved as of 9/08/2020).

research, following an inductive approach (instead of the usual deductive epistemology of mainstream mathematical modelling commented before in 5.3.2c), which could contribute to somehow modifying the standard paradigm in this respect; this in the sense of providing a better theoretical explanation about the socio-economic implications of free foreign trade within a given country.

Admittedly, the above entails making a notable simplification insofar a country's comparative *average-wage* does not only depend on its foreign trade – as implicitly assumed by the standard formulation (assumption 'c' itself) of the 'theory/doctrine of international trade'. Nevertheless, whether a wages-equalisation effect exists – stemming from that part of Mexico's economic activity related to bilateral trade with the US, we should expect such an effect would show statistically up to some degree. In this vein, a theoretical research work oriented to elucidate why the result predicted by standard theory is not observed in this case (*one case*; but a significant one) would likely be more useful – than those resulting from mainstream mathematical modelling as mentioned before, in 5.3.2 in terms of explaining/ understanding the economic reality of the practice of 'free' foreign trade, and its effects on social welfare indicators of the countries involved.

Last but not least (perhaps we should have started by underlining this), there is a general agreement among economics scholars that assumption ***(a)*** of the classical model, on the *no international mobility of Capitals,* is not met overall[19]; something that would by itself undermine most of the standard proposition significance.

---

[19] A more complete and systematic overview on confronting the assumptions and predictions of the standard Theory of International Trade with empirical evidence (presented, moreover, also for non-specialists) can be seen in: Reinhard Schumacher, 2013, "Deconstructing the Theory of Comparative Advantage", *World Economic Review*, no. 2: 83-105.

5.3.4 Are there actually so many comparative advantages worldwide?

'Natural' and 'acquired' comparative advantages

Let us now focus on the (implicit) assumption **'g'** of the standard model: that of 'every country has a comparative advantage'. Since 'exploiting' a *comparative advantage* entails specialisation, are there actually as many opportunities in our economies, at a worldwide level, as for every country to specialise in something specific? Can we speak of comparative advantage as something that 'by nature' any given country has or can develop or acquire? In this respect, one of the characteristics of today's economies, even before having reached the present level of globalisation, is that the so-called *'traditional' comparative advantages* of one country in relation to another have somehow largely disappeared. This is the case unless we consider as such the fact that a country has persistently comparatively very low wages. In which case the assumption *'c'* of the classical model – that of 'wages are equal in the (two) countries involved, or that with free foreign trade they tend to be so'– is, however, not met either. In some researchers' complex mathematical models this assumption *'c'* is relaxed; however, ultimately it is the classical basic model that socially transcends beyond specialised economists' fields.

Let us recap in this respect. According to the classical paradigm of the *Theory of International Trade* reviewed here, it is the bilateral comparative advantages that make it possible to recommend each country or region to specialise in that activity in which they have a comparative advantage (comparative higher productivity). As we have seen, the topical reference in many textbooks is still David Ricardo's example: that of England focuses on textiles (as a metaphor for an 'industrial product') and Portugal on wine (as a metaphor for an 'agricultural product'), and their respective surpluses are then exchanged. The problem, however, is that international trade over the last few decades even more so with globalisation– is characterised by the existence of if I may say so dozens of 'Englands' and dozens of 'Portugals'. And, obviously, what might make sense when we imagine only two countries and two products (one country specialises in 'A' and the other in 'B') is not necessarily the case when many countries are importing and exporting. A realistic look at the matter shows us that there are not enough comparative advantages for each country to have an exclusive one on which to base its foreign trade.

To some extent, only *'natural'* comparative advantages based on specific 'primary' goods remain today; (notably the cases of countries with certain mineral resources). And as for 'acquired' advantages, mainly those in favour of countries or regions that develop innovations and protect them through patents remain as such[20]. In general, these are the countries that historically started, as for the international trade arena, from an already higher technological-industrial level. In this regard, thinking of the Ricardian model, certainly from the beginning of the 19th century until now the panorama regarding the triptych of *foreign trade/enterprises/technologies* has substantially changed: Regarding the first element, as for transport; for the second, in regards to which is actually the corresponding home country (multinationals, subsidiaries, etc.); and as for the third, regarding the accelerated innovation pace. In short, the panorama has become even more multifaceted.

Thus, as for the 'acquired' or 'attainable' comparative advantages, for years now most industrialised countries say, the OECD members

[20] "... Ricardo's was a doctrine of static equilibrium: it called on countries to specialise in what they could do best in the present. This might have made sense when advantages were in natural endowments, but not in manufacture. As soon as 'catch-up' became the name of the game, countries looked to exploit dynamic, not static, gains from trade. This meant developing higher-value industries shielded from premature competition.", Skidelsky, p. 38.

have indeed been in a position to produce almost any kind of manufactured product at a more o less similar cost. This is basically because knowledge of the procedures and technologies to be applied (know-how) is in fact internationally available and widespread. This is occurring increasingly rapidly and extensively except, of course for those innovations protected by patents; though, certainly not in a homogeneous way. Not all industrialised countries are in this respect at the same level. Production activities regarding goods with a high technological content –as well as technological innovation itself have a greater weight in the economies of some of these industrialised countries (e.g., USA, Germany, Japan, or China). In addition, there are persistent significant differences among nowadays industrialised countries as regards average wages, or, more precisely, labour costs.

In parallel to this, most developing countries –and we are speaking of several dozens of them can produce if an international body convinces them that they will be able to export it almost any agricultural production (cotton, palm oil, melons, flowers, soy, sugar, coffee,...). Or they can produce almost any component or part for manufacturing industries of more developed/industrialised countries. Or they can produce clothing or sneakers for this or that multinational; etc., etc. In short, we have that familiar picture offshoring in which companies of highly developed countries technically specify some given products in order to be produced by manufacturers in less developed countries, order them how each product must be produced (know-how and technical equipment), and afterwards import the products from these manufacturers, at a lower cost price than if were produced at home, precisely because wages are considerably lower in those less developed countries.

This drawing is complete if we consider in it that, moreover, international markets are saturated in many industrial sectors, due to the over-capacity of production of the existing big firms. Think, for example, of the great marketing efforts by large carmakers companies to place their production into markets on an international scale. Should this over-capacity/saturation not exist, it would not be the lack of know-how (about technology, procedures, ..) and fitness (workers' training, country's industrial environment) to produce computers, planes, DVD players, bulldozers, micro-chips, sophisticated medical diagnosis instruments, etc., which would prevent dozens of industrialised countries from being added to the list of those currently producing these goods.

To sum up, it could be said that *comparative advantages* – in the way mainstream economics textbooks still refer to them: almost in the same terms as at the beginning of the 20th century – have virtually faded away. This is the case for both, the 'natural' ones (the classic: 'wine in Portugal') and the 'acquired' or 'attainable' ones: specialising in a certain crop (cotton, e.g.), in a certain auxiliary industry (e.g., parts for car manufacturers), or simply in some 'mature' manufacture. Insofar as the scenario described above is significant, it depicts a relatively new situation, which makes the very concept of 'comparative advantage' fuzzy. There has not yet been a serious movement of awareness about this new situation: To the extent that it is not possible for every country to have 'one' specific comparative advantage on which to base their international trade, the theoretical statement that with free international trade *all* countries involved *always* gain cannot be sustained.

5.3.5 *Free-foreign-trade* implications neglected by standard theory

(a) 'Comparative advantage' because of exploiting 'increasing returns'

A specific successful type of apparently 'acquired' comparative advantage is that resulting from (firms from) a given country producing at an unbeatable low cost by *exploiting increasing returns* at an international scale, i.e., cases of indefinite economies of scale: they produce a given good literally 'for the entire world'. A few scattered words are enough to set such a scenario: China, South Korea, TV screens, globalisation, toys, Amazon, mobiles, ... Let us note that in this scenario the causal relationship is the inverse of the theoretical reasoning in the classical, Ricardian, model. In this, a pre-existing comparative advantage (England, in textile) leads to the recommendation that the country specialises in that product. However, in our present real economies, the reverse seems to be more common and not only since the era of globalisation: if a country decides (i.e., there are companies in it that decide) to specialise in something, it acquires, as a result, kind of a comparative advantage, thanks to (its involved companies) exploiting increasing returns to scale. That is, they are achieving a much lower unit cost than any other country('s companies), and thus being able to offer the product internationally at a lower price than any other country; '*be more competitive*' is a commonly used synonym for referring to that. If, in addition, wages in that country are comparatively lower compared to the international context or/and such country has few or no labour and environmental protection regulations the 'international competitiveness', in costs, of the product concerned will even be greater.

(b) When comparative advantages 'do not work' as predicted

On the other hand, what can we conclude regarding those traditionally considered 'natural' comparative advantages of specific countries, that now appear 'not to work'? Let us take a specific case. In the 60s, probably, any neoclassical economist may have concluded that although Senegal seemed to have rather absolute disadvantages regarding international trade, its disadvantage in rice was comparatively lower, i.e., that it had a *comparative advantage in rice*; and, therefore, they would have predicted that, under free trade, Senegal would end up exporting rice, etc. etc. Nevertheless, this is not precisely what has happened. Over the last few decades and on the wave of international liberalisation policies, a great part of the country's ricelands have become uncultivated, while the country has moved to import more than half of its consumption of rice from India because Indian rice is internationally 'more competitive'. This is, of course, a specific case[21]; we cannot generalise; but it is not without significance.

More in general, a review of the observational evidence, trying to search for more o less clear patterns regarding international trade, shows that those comparative advantages 'acquired' or 'attainable' through specialisations in some product or service are of less and less entity: given the easy mobility of Capitals and know-how, almost any country can specialise in anything. Within this scenario, the problem is that if several of these countries specialise in producing 'x', the ephemeral comparative advantage for the country that took the first step vanishes. What could be true when it is supposed that only one country will specialise in 'x' (as the standard paradigm does: assumption 'i') ceases to be true when the same strategy of

---

[21] ... Rice growing in Senegal has traditionally been one of its main agricultural productions. However, for years –and as a result of having dismantled its institutions and instruments of support for the development of rice crop, in the framework of liberalisation policies– Senegal has been importing more than half of the rice that it consumes from India; because it is cheaper. In India-Senegal bilateral trade (which is normally in deficit for Senegal*) rice is India's main export item. On the other hand, according to the FAO**, around ¾ of the lands suitable –and traditionally used before– for rice crops (basically around the mouths of its two rivers: the Senegal River on the northern border and the Casamance River on the south) is not cultivated. Also, there is no evidence that the Labour that rice imports have displaced in those regions has largely found employment in other productions (probably for the same reason that it would be difficult to grow anything other than rice in the Mississippi Delta). Moreover, indeed, the country's overall Trade Balance has persistently been showing deficits since the 80s (according to the World Bank; see Annex C, at the end of this chapter).

(*): *https://embassyofindiadakar.gov.in/relationpages.php?id=81 (retrieved 30-04-2020)*

(**): *http://www.fao.org/fileadmin/user_upload/spid/docs/Senegal/Riziculture_etatdeslieux_SN.pdf*

specialisation is followed by several countries that are in a similar situation. A well-intended recipe (e.g., 'specialise in 'x'', or 'focus on quality', or '... on excellence') that could become effective for one only country, is not necessarily valid –and generally is not – as a simultaneous solution for several countries; precisely because if many countries follow the same strategy, it is no longer effective for any of them. The encouraging idea of 'you should develop a comparative advantage' is contradictory to recommending the same option to dozens of countries – which is something that international institutions such as the WB and the IMF have been doing to some extent until recently: a country can be 'saved' by applying such a well-meaning recipe, but only provided that it has no (or not many) imitators.

(c) Delocalisation (and Offshoring): winners and losers

In the abundant literature on foreign trade and the standard theoretical model/s on the topic, we often seem to forget that foreign trade is mostly carried out by *enterprises*, not countries. Enterprises are the basic agents that decide what is imported and exported, and from/to where; and they employ a certain (changing) number of *workers*, who receive a given *salary*. However, it is the countries (their institutions) that have to manage and cover the *social costs* associated with the possible imbalances in foreign trade, discussed before.

Let us focus on the practice of *delocalisation* and its cousin, *offshoring*. Or, more generally, on a particular kind of foreign trade with countries that exhibit the 'comparative advantage' of '*persistently* lower wages' (including lower or no social charges) as well as usually lower environmental charges on companies (asymmetry in *externalities* policy between the two countries involved). Following a usual conceptual distinction, *delocalisation* is used here to mean companies of industrialised, developed countries ('guest') proceeding to move their production plants to another 'cheaper-production' country ('host'), usually a less developed one. While *offshoring* refers here to when a company moves to outsource the production of some of its products, or production processes, to a *foreign country's company* (offshore outsourcing). Although accepting that, inevitably such distinction is not always clear in practice.

Regarding this wide topic, it is worth starting by underlining the empirical evidence that, over the last two decades, thanks to this particular 'unequal' trade delocalisation/ offshoring, millions of people within 'host' countries have risen out of poverty even though not without contradictions[22]. At the same time, it is self-evident that if *guest* countries' *companies* have engaged in delocalising/offshoring to these less-developed host countries it must be because it was convenient for such companies. This binomial might be interpreted as evidence that international trade or at least a specific type of it: delocalisation and offshoring is mutually beneficial. Or, more precisely, as evidence that with free international trade (no barriers for delocalising or offshoring) both, the 'host' (the countries with lower salaries and, in general, with lower costs for firms) and the 'guest' countries (the ones of the 'delocaliser' companies) benefit. In other words, it might be interpreted as a kind of virtuous effect derived from the pure profit-seeking behaviour in business; i.e., that of the companies that delocalise factories or productions, and/or manage this specific kind of international trade.

However, we can not properly speak of a win-win result *for everybody*. A closer look at the whole picture should be made; certainly, in the (guest) developed countries, those companies that delocalise or engage in offshoring -or its equivalent: close all their factories and switch to importing and simply marketing the

[22] An account on the debate in this respect can be seen in Skidelsky's point 'Who is right?', pp. 45-48.

product in their own country and around- improve their benefits (otherwise they would not embark on such a business strategy). This, nevertheless, comes at the cost of reductions in production activity and employment at home, for an uncertain time stretch. Thus, it is not an exchange in which 'everybody gains'. We should differentiate between collectives, in both countries: low-wages (host) countries use to gain: local employment increases, wages increase to some extent, and the profits of local exporting companies increase. As for the companies in the industrialised countries which, thanks to delocalisation/offshoring, have the goods produced at a notably lower cost also gain. However, the workers that, as a consequence, become unemployed in the 'guest' country suffer a personal loss; (it is rarely a joy to lose one's job, even if part of the former salary is received as unemployment benefits). And the public sector of this 'more developed' country also loses, since it has to confront the unemployment costs.

In both instances – new unemployed people and the public sector, the referred consequences last *for an uncertain period of time*. Because the standard liberalist argument that 'the dynamism of markets will do that in a *reasonable period of time* these workers displaced by delocalisation/ offshoring – or more in general, by the expansion of imports from low-costs-for-companies' countries that accompanies globalisation – will find employment in other, new, economic activities', is unfortunately not confirmed by unemployment statistics in most cases. In other words, this 'reasonable period of time' of the classical argument turns out in most cases to be too long; too long a period of time to consider that 'nobody loses' with this specific asymmetric international trade based on the comparative advantage of countries with lower business costs (wages, social security and environmental standards).

5.4 Economic inequalities, public sector, and externalities: issues relegated in the mainstream

Let us now focus on three issues that, though they are dealt with in mainstream economics as independent, monographic, topics in advanced chapters or textbooks, are absent in the core standard economics' model on the grounds, we could guess, of simplifying. These are *Inequality* in income (and wealth) distribution; economic activity of *public powers;* and *externalities* (those social costs or benefits that are not registered by markets' transactions). The objective here, in this respect, is not properly to develop these issues but to show the explanatory consequences from they do not be considered in the core paradigm of mainstream basic economics texts and courses, which are intended to explain the key elements and workings of the economic world. An absence that is indeed rather difficult to justify on the grounds of simplifying, of abstracting 'secondary' or of-detail points. Notably regarding the two first realities above mentioned.

The point in what follows is, thus, to develop the consequences of these three realities not being present in the theoretical picture of the economic world that orthodox economics texts and courses deploy; and that is the default economics' corpus most students will be taught to or remind about. As a result, the unrealism of an economics paradigm intended to provide an analytical description of our economies but that leaves out of such formal description realities like the above-cited is underlined. By way of example: the unrealism of assuming equality in the distribution of income & wealth; something that affects the core of the General Equilibrium model itself: its definition of 'social-economic wellbeing'. As well as it is something more than distorting to develop an economic explanatory model that talks about 'the optimal basket of goods at the whole economic level' but abstracts the existence of nothing less than 'taxes' and 'public expenditure' eventually relegating that part of the economic reality to isolated advanced courses; or to provide an anecdotic presence of this reality by, for example, using the standard diagram of 'market equilibrium point' (figure 4a, Ch. 2) to explain how a tax, on production or consumption, 'distorts' the otherwise 'optimal market equilibrium point'.

As already pointed out, the three mentioned realities inequalities, public sector, and externalities do are the object of specific attention in mainstream economics as sectoral topics; as specialised fields of study in either latter chapters of advanced manuals or specific upper courses. However, this subsequent addressing does not significantly give way back to consequently rethink the paradigm of the 'GE of competitive markets'; spite (or perhaps because) considering such topics would invalidate some of its propositions.

Taking into account *inequality in income & wealth distribution*

The ESM's assumption of 'equality in income & wealth distribution among citizens' is an *explicit* premise in the model, rather than an (over)simplification. Such assumption is formally necessary for the model's definition of the concept 'social utility', or 'social wellbeing': the fact of assuming equality in the distribution of income and wealth allows the model to postulate that the economic utility of, say, an additional £5-banknote in the hands of an individual is the same for everyone in the society; (in technical terms: the 'marginal utility of money' is the same for every citizen). A statement that is, in turn, necessary for postulating that individual monetary utilities consumers' surpluses and producers' surpluses (firms' profits) can be arithmetically aggregated, to so giving place to 'social utility', as the measure of *social-economic wellbeing*; which, in turn, is a core concept since its maximisation defines, in the standard model, the idea of *optimisation* (of social wellbeing) as a result of the General Equilibrium of competitive markets. Additionally, the premise of *equality* among individuals is also necessary to, in turn, justify the GE model's instrumental assumption of 'no entry barriers' for anybody in the society to become an entrepreneur, a new active firm, in the sector of this or that product or service.

Looking to it the other way round, since such assumption of 'income and wealth equality' among citizens is undoubtedly not met at all in our real market economies, the idea-proposition of «free markets overall leads spontaneously, without any public powers' intervention, to an optimisation of Social Wellbeing» simply cannot be sustained.

The economic activity of public powers

Production of services, and income transfers

The public sector provides services that represent a significant share of total GDP; which, therefore, constitutes a substantial element to formally elaborate (and teach) about the sphere of Production, the idea of 'social-economic wellbeing', as well as about the functioning itself of market economies.

Public powers' economic activity entails, in short, *Taxes Collection* (including social security contributions) and *Public Expenditure*; the former being eventually complemented by resorting to 'public borrowing'. Both sides of this economic activity affect thus the overall results of the economic system as for talking about 'social-economic wellbeing' –whatever the meaning we would assign to such expression. To start with, the interplay of taxes collection and certain public expenditure entails (and is intended for) income transfers from upper-income tax-payers to lowest-income people.

Overall, the economic relevance of public-powers' spending in many cases approaches half of the total economic activity of the country (GDP). By way of examples:

Public powers' spending (% of GDP)			
	2000	**2020**	**(2019)**[23]
EU	47.1 %	53.1 %	(46.5 %)
United Kingdom	35.3	51.5	(40.4)
USA	34.2	47.8	(38.2)
Australia	37.4	46.6	(44.1)
Japan		47.3	(38.9)

Own elaboration, from Eurostat and OECD databases[24]

This public expenditure basically entails public *production and provision of services*, together with money transfers to specific citizen groups. Regarding the first block, it is useful, for our purpose here, to distinguish between *institutional, or collective, services* and free *ordinary, or individual, services* granted by law. The former refers to those Administration's services addressed to fulfil the usual commitments of Public Powers; to name the more common ones: Collective decision-making system (Parliaments: central, regional, and municipal); management of collective issues (Government bodies: id.); Law Courts; Law-enforcement services (police); public infrastructures (roads, first-mile of internet, ..); national defence; coverage of collective protection against natural phenomena; etc.

As for the free *ordinary (or individual)* services granted by law, the more relevant ones we may observe are those of the Public or National health system; the Public education system; National cultural & scientific institutions (museums, research institutes, ..);

[23] Year 2019 has been added because year 2020 shows, in general, a circumstantial climb in public expenditure, as a consequence of measures to fight the covid-19 pandemic. This is mainly regarding Health, Subsidies to business, and Social protection programmes.

[24] For EU: Eurostat, "Government expenditure by function", accessed as of 6/13/2022; the rest: OECD, "General government spending", *https://data.org./gga/general-government-spending.htm*, accessed as of 6/13/2022.

etc. Different from the former (collective services), regarding those *ordinary individual services* their comparative relevance within the economy is significantly different among different countries: higher for those countries which opted for what conventionally is termed as 'a welfare state' framework.

Regarding *money transfers* to specific citizen groups, the quantitatively more significant ones observed could be grouped into Public old-age pensions system, Granted unemployment benefits, and Personal transfers for social exclusions and poverty mitigation. Again, the quantitative relevance of this part of public expenditure uses to be quite higher for countries that have developed to a significant level a 'welfare state' system; in this case, mainly regarding a Public pensions system and a system of *Unemployment benefits*.

Public powers as producer & provider of individual services

Public production of services is a relevant share of total domestic production (GDP) and, thereby, Employment. This, even if we refer just to the *ordinary, individual, services*.

Over the last two decades, these ordinary or individual services amounted, in the case of the EU, to 14-15 % of GDP; (one more percentage point in 2020, due to a higher effort in Health services, because of the Covid-19 pandemic). A similar relevance of these individual services is observed for the UK and the US: 13-15% of GDP (also excluding 2020's data). More in general, regarding the OECD countries, in the statistics upper quartile appears, for example, France, with 15.5-17 % of GDP; and in the lower quartile Switzerland with 8-9.5 % of GDP; (in both cases also excluding 2020's data).

The whole or a relevant part of these basic *ordinary services* like Health and Education are produced and/or provided through a mechanism different from that of prices & markets the mainstream economics focus on; this, with minor exceptions (tolls, levies, cases of co-payment, ..). Therefore, a relevant part of the economic activity within a country (GDP) comes not explained by the standard economics' paradigm; i.e., by most reference generalist textbooks and manuals.

To this we should add *income transfers* by public powers mainly public expenditure on retirement pensions and unemployment benefits (plus social protection against social exclusion's abatement), which represent an even higher share of the GDP:

The EU, 18-19%; the UK, 13-14.5%; the USA, 6.5-12.2%; France, 20.5-24.8%; Switzerland, 13.5%.

Taking into account the percentages above, certainly it has not much sense a theoretical model to explain the functioning of our market economies, as the orthodox one, that talks about equilibrium, social optimality, etc. in an economy, when around 15% of the production and consumption activities, plus around 18% of people's income, are not taken into account in such a model. In the political arena, the old liberalist lemma 'the less State the better' uses to also be expressed through claiming for a 'hands-off policy'; i.e., for 'State (Public Powers)'s hands-off of the economy'; meaning by that to reduce taxes and public spending especially these above: *free individual services and income transfers*. It would be an unfair extrapolation to state that orthodox, modern neoclassical economic theory (ESM) obeyed since its inception to provide the adequate scientific basis for a hands-off policy. However, what does can be stated is that for those that advocate for such a liberalist economic policy, the orthodox economic theory offers them an ad hoc, as familiar as 'scientific', elegant reference support.

In this regard, the fact that the economic activity of public powers is the object of wide specific attention in later specialised or upper courses in economics does not change indeed the above diagnosis.

'Economics of the Public Sector', as a speciality in standard economics

The economic activity of public powers is indeed widely dealt with in mainstream economics, but 'afterwards', as a side-issue or matter of study, in upper courses and specialised texts. This is usually under the terms of Public Economics, The Economics of Public Sector, or Public Finance; a relevant subject that in turn encompasses several sub-topics like Fiscal Policy, Public Goods, Public Choice, National Budget, Cost-benefit analysis, etc. This formal analysis of the economic facets of the public sector tends, however, to be developed like autonomous, monographic, topics. Their development tends to be mostly aside from the theoretical basis of the economics' paradigm students have been trained on along first or introductory courses, and corresponding manuals. Thus, the fact that taking into account this 'especial' area of our economies leads to invalidating the ESM definition of, for example, 'social-economic wellbeing' does not apparently receive much retrospective attention; in particular, as regards reformulating the standard paradigm of <the General Equilibrium leads to a social optimum>. Such a coming-back pathway of the scientific method to revise and modify or discard cornerstone assumptions when they are not supported by empirical observation is not, or rarely, addressed. The task of revising, reformulating, or discarding basic statements of the standard paradigm itself is in practice simply avoided.

Instead of that, what is a common academic practice in this regard is, in some way, the reverse: to directly apply the conceptual-graphical construct of the ESM to introduce in it a given specific element of Public Economics in basic courses and manuals. By way of example, that referred before: to use the standard diagram of the 'market equilibrium point' (figure 4a, in chapter 2) to schematically represent, in abstract graphical language, the change upon it the existence of an indirect tax (say, VAT) entails; and thus to teach to readers/students about the deviations from the *optimality conditions* ('consumer surplus' and 'producer surplus') that such a 'real-world' element (VAT) entails.

Costs and benefits not registered by markets

The no-considering of the ***externalities*** in the standard model has a different character since such absence might be considered as an implicit simplification that of 'let us assume that there are no externalities in the economy'; that is, *indirect social costs or benefits, in the sense that are not registered by markets' functioning*. It is indeed an economic reality that has important social impacts in the case of certain activities. But many products and services have no significant externalities associated with their production or consumption. In any case, the ESM (implicitly) assumes that there do not exist externalities, either in production or consumption. And, in this case, such a methodological simplification may be acceptable to some extent.

Likely, the more relevant cases of externalities in practice are the *negative externalities in production*: indirect social costs, of a given product or service, which are not supported by the corresponding producer. Thereby the cost of the product or service for the provider firms is actually lower than its social, real, cost; which, in turn, means that usually, its consumers are not paying the real (social) cost of what they are buying. The case of a firm's functioning activity causing nuisances to the nearby population is a typical example. Although most of the more relevant ones in this regard can be signalled with a few words: environmental pollution, local natural resources' depletion or degradation, side-effects on public health and security, etc.

A wider economic dimension in this regard appears when we consider well know common situations where the pollution or degradation generated as a consequence of a specific production process or activity is not limited to the domestic territory (a country) but affects worldwide, the whole planet; as is the case of CO_2 emissions mainly generated by enterprises' processes that burn fossil fuels, and its effects on overall climate degradation.

These so common cases of negative externalities in production mean as regards to the standard general equilibrium model that, if not public powers' action is taken, the corresponding enterprises' production costs, and therefore their selling prices, are not good signals of the actual social costs of the goods in question contrarily to what assumes the standard economic paradigm.

Another important economic situation in this regard, though with not so wide extension, is that of *negative externalities in consumption*; i.e., when the consumption of a given product or service, by all or some of its buyers, causes regularly significant nuisances to other/s people alien to those involved in its production or provision. The point here, as the standard paradigm is concerned, is that its assumption of perfect (or, by approximation, reasonable) information of citizens as buyers is not fulfilled: As consumers, we do not always have enough information to evaluate a possible des-utility from using/consuming some specific product; for example, psychotropic drugs, tobacco, etc., (self-infringed negative side-effect). Or we are not always aware of the negative side-effects such consumption causes to other people, (negative side-effect, infringed to others); for example, in the way of heavy noise, smoke, insecurity, etc.

We also talk about *positive externalities in production*, even if this is rather an anecdotic situation: it would be the case where the production activity of a given firm generates some (unintended) indirect effects that are beneficial to other firm/s or people without commercial relations with the first firm. Compared to the above-referred situations, the socio-economic relevance of these possible externalities is rather low. Although, for some reason, the case uses to receive notable attention in mainstream textbooks; something that comes illustrated by the so-casuistic imagined cases used to talk about such positive externalities; for example, the classic one of a farmer that crops fruit trees, its neighbour that farms honey beehives, and the two-way issue of the pollination of the trees' flowers by the neighbour's bees while these feed themselves.

Finally, there are cases of *positive externalities in consumption*: when the consumption of product or service 'X' by a given buyer also benefits marginally other/s people alien to the former. A relevant example in this sense is that of vaccines, insofar the fact of it being 'consumed' by a person generates a positive effect (utility) for her, but also a possible positive side-effect for other people to the extent that their possible infection is avoided, even if these are not aware of that. As can be seen, these cases also involve an informational issue in the sense that the standard assumption of «consumers have perfect information and knowledge» is not fulfilled. Even for 'direct' consumers, estimating the utility that derivates from consuming the product in question may be either difficult/doubtful or beyond their ordinary possibilities; and more even so for people that might be passively-benefited.

Externalities lead public powers to intervene in the economy

As the reader may have guessed, historically the political awareness and concern on the existence of relevant cases of externalities have led to public powers intervention, through establishing specific *regulations*. This, notably regarding the negative ones: those *social or indirect costs* not registered by the market mechanism. Such regulations mainly refer, for example, to environmental rules and taxes to producers, as well as over-taxing or just forbidding, the consumption of some goods (either absolutely or by applying age discrimination). As for the case of positive externalities in consumption, regulations use to entail subsidising to some extent the selling price of the goods in question.

Seen in another way, the existence of significant *negative externalities in production* means that markets do not always register the real cost of a product or service but under-valuate it. This is mainly related to industrial waste disposal, environmental pollution, natural resources, and common goods' depletion, etc. Regarding *negative externalities in consumption,* their existence entails that the ESM assumption regarding perfect information for citizens as consumers does not hold; which leads governments to regulate the production or consumption of the products/services in question, or, in certain cases, to ban them. More in general, taking into account externalities also affects the formal appraisal and definition of 'social-economic wellbeing' itself since such a theoretical concept should encompass that with a monetary reflection plus that without. In other words, where negative or positive externalities exist without any regulation addressing them the respective market prices cannot be considered the real (social) prices and costs as for social wellbeing considerations.

As for *positive externalities in production,* they are not actually relevant, as far as our present discussion: for the traditional case (bilateral positive side-effects), because of its trivialness, as argued before. However, the concept could suggest, because of proximity, a wider topic: we could talk about 'multilateral positive side-effects in production' because, paradoxically, a kind of positive multilateralism is an overall feature of any market economy. The whole firms' ecosystem in an economy, works, by nature, full of synergies; hence the usual positive connotation, for economic development objectives, of the expression 'local business-environment'. By way of example, the fact that a given concentration of firms in a given territory, each one producing or providing different products and services (industrial parks, business districts), attracts other firms to establish there because of perceiving some advantages. We could state that this would be a situation of diffuse 'multilateral positive externalities in production'; though it would be doubtful the informational usefulness of such labelling.

As in the case of the two previous subjects income inequalities, and the public sector's economic activities, the topic of *externalities* is also dealt with in mainstream economics as a stand-alone topic; as a parcel worked on isolated from the standard core paradigm; usually under the heading of Economics of Regulation. It is in a way implicitly assumed that externalities analysis does not relevantly modify the validity of the paradigm of the GE *of competitive markets* as an explanatory framework construct about the essentials of the workings of a market economy, for generalist teaching and textbooks.

Appendix E: The basic 'Ricardian' model – of comparative advantages and international trade – in mathematical language

	'cloth'		'wine'	
	Labour hours per unit	units	Labour hours per unit	units
'England'	(e)Hc	1	(e)Hw	1
'Portugal'	(p)Hc	1	(p)Hw	1
Sum of productions under autarchy		2		2

Definitions:

- *'England', stands for 'a given country* ***(e)****'*
- *'Portugal', stands for 'a given different country,* ***(p)****'*
- *'cloth' stands for 'a given (industrial) good,* ***c****'*
- *'wine' stands for 'a given (primary) good,* ***w****'*
- *1 'unit' (pack) of 'c', and 1 'unit' (pack) of 'w' are defined such as : (p) Hc > (p)Hw, and (e)Hc <(e)Hw*

Initial assumptions and definitions:

- There is an *absolute* advantage of country 'p' in good 'w' when: *(p)Hw < (e)Hw*
- There is also an *absolute* advantage of country 'p' in good 'c' when *(p)Hc < (e)Hc*
- There is a *comparative* advantage for country 'p' in good 'w' if:

$$\frac{(p)\,Hw}{(e)\,Hw} < \frac{(p)\,Hc}{(e)\,Hc}$$; or, which is equivalent,

- There is a *comparative* advantage for country 'e' in good 'c' if:

$$\frac{(e)\,Hc}{(p)\,Hc} < \frac{(e)\,Hw}{(e)\,Hw}$$

Alternative situation, ***under free trade*** between 'e' and 'p' for goods 'c' and 'w':

Production of good 'c' if country (e) specialises in it:

$$\frac{(e)\,Hw + (e)\,Hc}{(e)\,Hc} > 2\ ;\ \text{since,}\ \frac{(e)\,Hw}{(e)\,Hc} > 1;\ \text{thereby, 'c'} = \frac{(e)\,Hw}{(e)\,Hc} - 1,\ \text{units}$$

Production of good 'w' if country 'p' specialises in it:

$$\frac{(p)\,Hw + (p)\,Hc}{(p)\,Hw} > 2\ ;\ \text{since,}\ \frac{(p)\,Hc}{(p)\,Hw} > 1;\ \text{thereby, 'w'} = \frac{(p)\,Hc}{(p)\,Hw} - 1,\ \text{units}$$

Results of the free-trade (barter) of goods 'c' and 'w' between countries 'e' and 'p', (assuming that the consumption of each good in each country is not lower than without trade)

Exchange 'prices'*, $\boldsymbol{\Pi}$: $(e)Hc \geq \boldsymbol{\Pi c} \geq (p)Hc$; and $(e)Hw \geq \boldsymbol{\Pi w} \geq Pw$

(*) in terms of Labour-hours

Traded units, $\boldsymbol{T}$: $\dfrac{(e)\,Hw}{(e)\,Hc} \geq \boldsymbol{Tc} \geq \boldsymbol{1}$; and $\dfrac{(p)\,Hc}{(p)\,Hw} \geq \boldsymbol{Tw} \geq \boldsymbol{1}$

About further steps in the model's development: To make the above *terms of trade* and their implications precise it requires, as a first step, introducing additional assumptions; mainly about: 1) demand and supply functions for each product in each country; 2) market conditions in the competition/ monopoly axis especially for the export-import companies in both countries; 3) equilibrium (/lack of) in the bilateral '*trade balance*'; etc. . And a second step in this direction of generalising the model by bringing it closer to situations in the real economic world requires extending the model in question to more than two goods, more than one factor of production, more than two countries, Capital mobility; etc.

For an overview of the more common specific steps and options along the previous lines, that have been developed by scholar specialists in this field, see some reference manual on *international trade*, like, for example, the one by Krugman et al. (2017) aforementioned; or (also) some more specific text such as *A New Construction of Ricardian Theory of International Values; Analytical and Historical Approach*, by Yoshinori Siozawa, Tosihiro Oka, and Taichi Tabuchi, (Ed.), 2017, Springer.

Appendix F: Historical data on Trade Balance for populated countries in three specific worldwide regions; 1975-2020

Source: The World Bank https://data.worldbank.org/indicator/BN.CAB.XOKA.CD?end=2018&name_desc=false&start=1977&view=chart ; (retrieved as of 13/07/2021)

Region: Latin-American* Current account balance (% of GDP): Argentina, Brazil Chile, Colombia, Mexico, Peru; 1975 - 2020

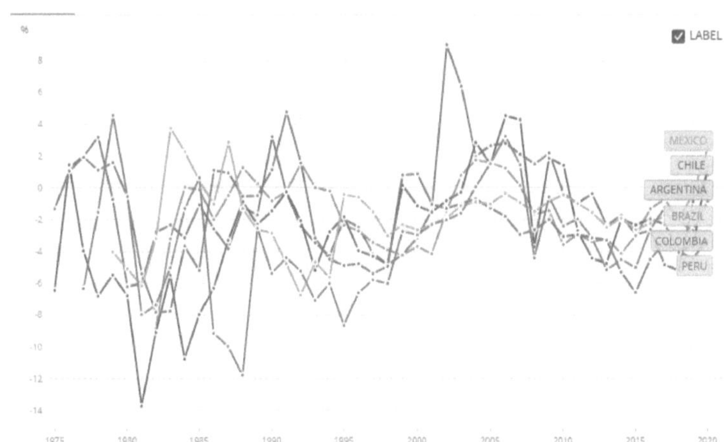

(*) Large oil's exporters excluded

superavit

↑

→ Trade Balance = 0 , (balanced) ←

↓

deficit

Region: Centre/Southern Africa* Current account balance (% of GDP): Congo, Dem. Rep., Ethiopia, Mozambique, Kenya, South Africa, Tanzania, Uganda; 1975 – 2020

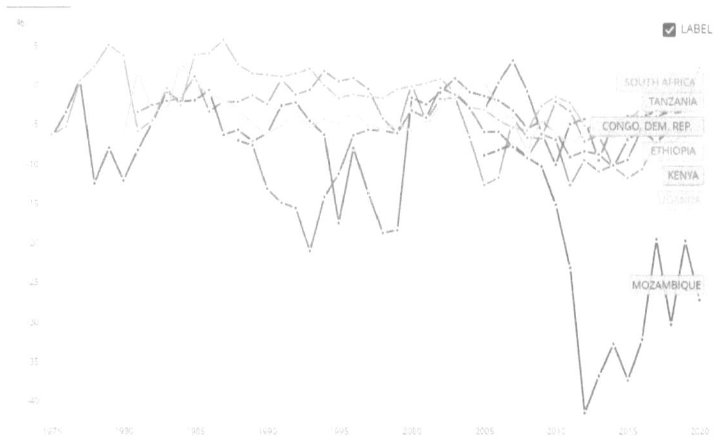

Region: Southern/Centre Asia-Pacific* China, Korea and Japan also excluded) Current account balance (% of GDP): Bangladesh, Cambodia, Myanmar, Vietnam, Indonesia, India; 1975 – 2020

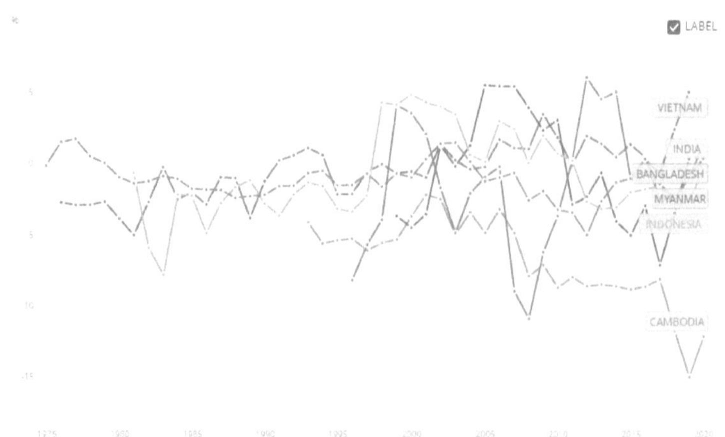

Chapter 6
Towards a really explanatory discipline

In the previous chapters we first saw the basic elements of the main explanatory paradigm of the standard (mainstream, orthodox or modern-neoclassical) model in Economics. Then, a systematic confrontation of these elements with the main historically accumulated observational evidence has been presented. As a logical derivation of the latter, in parallel an alternative formal explanatory scheme has also been set out.

For methodological reasons, the different core topics have been discussed separately, following a given, usual, sequence. In order to achieve a more coherent overall insight it seems useful to devote this and the following last chapter to presenting an overview, connecting and summarising the different key findings and assertions resulting from the previous pages. It is a matter of ordering and linking up the evidence, arguments, and formal explanatory schemes (those related to both the standard model and the alternative empirical inductive 'explanatory model') which, for practical reasons, have been addressed separately thus far. This means that the thematic order in what follows is not necessarily the same as in the previous chapters.

6.1 Unnecessary unrealism to be overcome

After the empirical-inductive approach developed in chapters 3 to 5, let us go back, with more elements now, to the starting point: the acknowledgment that i) the last-decades mainstream economics, or modern-neoclassical economics/*microeconomics*, is mainly developed around an explanatory model whose core conceptual pillar ('*general equilibrium of competitive* markets') mostly relies upon axioms, hypotheses, or deductive assumptions regarding key elements of the workings of a market economy; ii) these axioms and theoretical assumptions cannot be sustained according to the empirical evidence provided by observations from our market-economies; and iii) this is a mismatching that occurs both in the present time and historically; thus, as we have already seen, the above assertions i & ii are not exactly new in economics literature or original from my part. Yet, from such a mainstream *economics' standard model* (ESM) comes out the *perfect competition & efficient (free) markets* paradigm, which pervades a great deal of economic thinking, not only in scholarly economics/microeconomics but also and especially in socio-political life with regard to economic-liberalism stances. This standard core paradigm has been analysed in detail and discussed at the beginning. Let us briefly recap it here:

> Provided there is not any intervention or regulation by public powers on the market of a good (product or service), it happens that in such a market there ends up being a large number of producer/supplier enterprises; all of them perfectly efficient and practically identical the same size, and producing with the same technology, whereby they are achieving the same unit (average) cost: the minimum possible one. That gives way to a situation of *full, perfect competition* (none of those firms holds any market power). This, in turn, makes that the selling price of such firms end by being equal to the referred unit cost (market equilibrium price). Therefore, they will operate without obtaining profits. This *market equilibrium* (perfect competition) occurs spontaneously and for all the goods in the economy – with a few exceptions (cases of *natural monopoly*). If, moreover, the same free-market's prices conditions prevail for Labour (and the rest of the production factors) the result from this free play of markets overall the 'general equilibrium of competitive markets' will entail an optimum of social-economic wellbeing.

That is, a theoretical paradigm that is easily, and frequently, condensed into a 'high level' thesis, of broad implications regarding economic ideas and beyond: nothing less than the recipe of free markets for both every good and factor, as a *generator of an optimal social-economic welfare*. This 'high level' paradigm is based, however, as seen in the first chapters, on an explanatory theory on the workings of our market economies which, on the contrary, builds on rather 'technical' elements which induces the idea of an aseptically factual approach. These elements consist specifically of theoretical explanatory models on the patterns of production costs (in general) and on the enterprises' behaviour in this respect; (*production theory*); as well as on the workings of markets (*prices* determination, and supply/demand equilibrium). But, in turn, this set of theoretical postulates of a 'technical' nature are based on *axioms and deductive assumptions* as we saw at the beginning, in chapters 1 and 2 – which come out to be clearly unrealistic: they are not supported by the most obvious evidence that economic reality has come showing to us as it has been developed along (chapters 3 to 5). And this is not regarding matters of detail (those that normally justify simplifications), but regarding fundamental aspects of the functioning of a market economy based on private enterprises.

A theory on an imagined economy

Relevant implications

The problem we face does not stem from the fact that such a paradigm – the 'automatic' *general equilibrium of competitive markets* – makes use of certain simplifications of the economic reality to be explained. Simplifications are, of course, needed in any theoretical setting to schematise and abstract details; even more so in the case of social sciences, with their multi-related and casuistic reality. Nor is the problem specifically that the ESM suffers from some oversimplifications – as it indeed does, or that it makes certain questionable assumptions about variables or elements of the economic reality that are difficult or impossible to observe or evaluate in the real world. The problem actually is that the ESM's simplifications relate to an imagined, rather than observed, economy (Komlos, 2019:6-7); and that, thereby, some of its key assumptions are clearly unrealistic. These are assumptions about easily observable variables and elements of a market economy; however, the corresponding empirical contrasting became relegated time ago in mainstream neoclassical economics. When professionals engaged in such empirical testing, the referred lack of realism stands out. The consequence of these ESM's features is that it the does not actually explain schematically the reality as regards how a capitalist market economic system works (dynamics and patterns of firms' behaviour and decision making, production activities, unit costs, prices, markets, etc.), but rather speaks schematically to us about a sort of unreal, alleged, economy.

This is not only an epistemological bias. It has decisive consequences; first of all, in the academic and professional sphere. It affects how economics, the workings of market economies, is explained in textbooks and in the classroom. What is transmitted to readers and students is a theoretical description – which pivots around the 'construct' of *perfect competition* – characterised by oversimplifications and deductive assumptions, concerning key aspects, that do not correspond to the economic reality of our societies. And if the *economics* that is taught and one reads about is not realistic, the conclusions that will be drawn for specific situations – as well as the diagnoses on this or that economic situation developed by economics professionals (from government or economic institutions) – are at risk of being wrong or unfocused. Moreover, as a result, economic policy measures based on such diagnoses may be unhelpful if not counterproductive. Unfortunately, the global economic crisis that exploded in 2008 showed us significant examples in this respect.

Furthermore, the above remark is also significant outside the economic discipline. In the political arena, neoliberalism arguments rely on this basic paradigm of mainstream economics to defend their principles of no (or minimal) intervention of governments into the economy; of no (o minimal) regulation of markets (think of the motto "free markets are self-regulating"), and, ultimately, to defend what is behind the well-known expression of "the less State, the better": minimal public expenditure, minimal taxes "because they distort the *general equilibrium*, which is what guarantees a social optimum". These economic policy recipes, which are somehow held upon the standard paradigm, obviously point towards a particular political-economic organisation of society (free markets, in the sense of zero or minimum economic intervention and regulation by public powers, etc.). All of this, despite such a standard economics' paradigm, which these *theses* rely upon, cannot actually be sustained if we don't neglect the testing phase of the scientific method.

The attempt of 'imperfect competition'

Standard or mainstream economics also encompasses indeed the topic of 'economics of *imperfect competition*'. This specific line responds in principle to an attempt to modulate or correct an element of orthodox economics: the assumption on *perfect competition*. That is, to bring (certain parts of) neoclassical economics/microeconomics closer to the real economic world. However, as an academic topic, considering its actual scope in textbooks, and adopting a time perspective, it has not substantially modified the panorama described above. On the one hand, the topic of 'imperfect competition' has not gone in fact beyond of appearing as a complementary chapter or section in reference economics' textbooks; or as a matter of upper courses texts. This, besides of being, of course, a line of specialisation within academic literature – especially since the book by Joan Robinson *The Economics of imperfect competition* (1933). Overall, the presentation of 'economics of imperfect competition' in manuals tends to generate in students and general readers the idea that by '*imperfect competition*' the text (or the classroom teaching) refers rather to special, non-majority, economic situations; which contributes to reinforcing, as for readers and classroom attendants, the idea that '*perfect competition*' is the default economic situation. On the other hand, textbooks (and academic literature in general) on the *economics of imperfect competition* suffer from the handicap of being mostly constrained to the same methodological/epistemological framework of the ESM; that is, predominance of deductive reasoning, lack of empirical inferences, etc. This, in addition to a curious ontological element: the involved scholars implicitly considering (or in any case, talking about) economic reality as *imperfect* because it does not fit with what the theoretical standard paradigm states.

In short, the economics' standard model, ESM, does not explain well the economic reality for the vast majority of cases, goods, sectors, or markets. A significant part of the preceding pages of this book have been dedicated to arguing this statement. Before such a scenario, when a theory does not explain well the reality it intends to describe, its key assumptions and hypotheses do not hold in the reality under consideration, and some of its predictions are not verifiable – or they are not confirmed by the accumulated empirical observations, then such a theory should be modified, reformulated, or replaced by one that allows us to explain this reality reasonably well as to make verifiable predictions.

Towards an explanatory theory on real market economies

With this driving idea in mind (empirical testing), the logic raw material in this text has been the last-decades' (rather scarce) empirical academic works, and the historically extensive, fairly affordable, generic empirical evidence that the direct observation of the workings of our market economies based on private enterprises – or capitalist, if preferred offers to us. That is, that observational evidence – which, to a large extent is 'common business knowledge' related to the sphere of production, firms' operation, and markets dynamics. And then, from such an empirical basis, proceed to infer patterns of behaviour as for enterprises behaviour, unit-cost/prices relationship, and the prevailing type of markets in the competition-monopoly axis.

The reason why it is worth devoting substantial attention to those seemingly so 'technical' parts of the economic reality is that the 'technical' axiom or 'law' of *decreasing returns* that is assumed in the ESM with respect to the sphere of Production is actually one of the pillars that underpin the standard model itself – as was argued in chapters 1 and 2. In the same way the paradigm of the 'homo economicus'[1] is another of these pillars; like it also is the 'simplifying assumption' of 'there are not appreciable inequalities in income distribution' in the society of the economy under consideration (sic); as well as the fact that the ESM's general equilibrium model ignores the existence of social, non-monetary, costs and benefits (externalities).

From this outlook, if we focus on the aforementioned apparently uninteresting 'technical' 'pillar' of the *decreasing returns* to scale i.e., on the patterns of behaviour of business establishments' unit costs the discussion requires, as a first step, identifying the ESM's key axioms, assumptions, and hypotheses about such a theoretical 'pillar.' This is much close to a lay reader environment than it might seem since such a pillar refers in fact to social activities that most of us, directly or indirectly, participate in –whether as employees, entrepreneurs, customers, etc. Let us synthetically overhaul those key hypotheses:

---

[1] In short, that abstract image of considering people in general as individuals perfectly informed and purely rational –regarding economic issues and decisions–; simply as maximisers of their personal utility when deciding what to do with their income and wealth.

An ESM's conceptual pillar without a base: the '*law* of decreasing returns to scale'

The aforementioned ESM's core postulate free-market-play overall leads by itself to a *general equilibrium of competitive markets* associated with an optimum of social wellbeing has two cornerstones as has been developed in chapter 1: a purely deductive assumption (i.e., a theoretical premise, not based on systematic observations of the economic world) and an auxiliary hypothesis; both apparently of a rather 'technical' character. The former is the backbone of what in standard manuals usually appears as Theory of the Firm, Theory of Costs, or neoclassical Theory of Production': the deductive assumption of the appearance of 'decreasing returns to scale' in the production of any good (product or service) by a firm, as something of a general, universal, scope. An assumption that can be summarised in plain language as follows:

> In the long-run in the sense that the size of a producer undertaking may change, in the production of any good ('A'), *increasing returns to scale* (lowering average cost) are observed when, starting from relatively small firm's size, an efficient firm grows in size. But this, up to a given size or production structure, associated with a specific volume of production, q^{os} units. For higher firm sizes -and therefore, volumes of production higher than q^{os} units *decreasing returns to scale* appear: the average cost of 'A' becomes ever higher the higher the firm size. Thereby, a producer enterprise achieves the *minimum average cost* (productive efficiency) when it is dimensioned to produce, and produces, just q^{os} units of 'A'. Therefore all enterprises engaged in the production of such a good tend to grow just up to this optimal size/scale, but never to exceed it. ('*law (sic) of decreasing returns*').

It is worth underlining that this *assumption* is not usually presented in textbooks as such, but rather in an implicit way. It is introduced using an exposing register that simply suggests: 'that's the way things are'. Most often we will not even find it expressed or argued in a narrative way (in the line of the above statement) but basically in graphical language. Mainly through the traditional diagram used to represent the behaviour of the 'long-run average cost' (in relation to the volume of units of output) like an 'ample' U-shaped curve, (figure 3, in chapter 2).

As for the *auxiliary hypothesis* – a *conjecture,* in fact – again it generally also appears in an implicit way in standard economics/ microeconomics textbooks; as if for some reason it were something obvious. It can be summarised as follows,

> The units demanded in the market for a (any) specific product or service – at a price close to its minimum-average-cost, Q units of product, is many times higher than the volume of units associated with the *optimal scale* (size) for an enterprise producing such good: q^{os} units of product. Therefore, there will be many enterprises, with the same optimal size, efficiently producing such product/service and covering the market demand for it; (as many firms as Q/q^{os}). The same applies to any good/industry – with a few exceptions, natural monopolies

And, certainly, when both assumptions are brought together – the *deductive assumption* about the enterprises' size and unit-costs, and the *auxiliary hypothesis* on the relative size of market demand for any good– then the central theoretical proposition or postulate of the ESM summarised at the beginning of this section formally emerges as a simple deduction:

> There will be 'many' identical enterprises producing the good 'A'; all of them producing efficiently, at the same average cost, and, therefore, competing fiercely in the market.

A postulate – the definition of *Perfect Competition* for a good – that is then assumed as valid for any good in the economy. This is, then, the ESM's theoretical discursive path towards the upper-order postulate of 'perfect efficiency and competition, as a result of free markets overall'.

In short, the above summarised formal analysis has allowed us (chapter 2) to bring out the underlying basis of the standard model paradigm, by making its starting assumptions and hypotheses explicit; thereby showing that a key theoretical premise underpinning the mainstream, modern-neoclassical economic theory of the *general equilibrium of competitive markets* is indeed that of 'the *law of decreasing returns to scale*'. In turn, this premise is usually based – in the texts where it is actually argued – on two traditional second-level assumptions. One is that of (in the production of any good) there is always a limiting, non-expandable, *fixed-factor* of production. The other is as a firm grows, there is a point at which it becomes difficult to manage, to control, and thereby becomes less efficient because it is too big: it starts to produce at a higher and higher unit cost. These two explanatory hypotheses are, nevertheless, of a deductive nature reasoning too; this, in the usual sense of they not being presented as the result of a systematic observation of real cases, but as if the reality to theorise on was actually not observable, or it was so in a very limited way.

However, the above theories the first-level one, regarding 'decreasing returns to scale', and the two second-level related hypotheses of 'a limiting fixed factor' and of 'big firms become less costs-efficient' – refer in fact to realities that are, obviously, quite easily observable: the firms' size, the volume of production, and their respective unit costs are observable variables. And when such a chain of deductive reasoning is subject to an empirical analysis we find that its theses are strongly at odds with observational evidence from the real world of business and usual mass production by large firms. The empirical evidence in this regard is both widely accessible and historically overwhelming – as shown in 2.3, 3.4, and 3.5; a remark that, on the other hand, I am far from being the first to point out.

This is certainly a decisive conclusion since without the axiom of 'the law of decreasing returns to scale' the central deductive proposition of the economics' standard model – that of an automatism leading to perfect-competition markets in the whole economy (the general equilibrium of competitive markets) – cannot be sustained. It is on the grounds of the above paragraphs that it could be said that such a mainstream paradigm on the functioning of a market economy describes rather an alleged, imagined, economic world.

Math-type diagrams as language, and marginalism as epistemology

The abovementioned axiom of *decreasing returns* to scale in-the-long-run is the basis, in the ESM, to derive or define the specific model for the behaviour of the long-run average *cost* in the production of any product or service. In turn, this specific 'so technical' model is used, throughout a theorising chain, to build the upper model of the *general equilibrium of competitive markets.*

Such standard sequence starts by introducing the *'decreasing returns to scale' axiom*; which is made basically through graphical language: by means of a diagram representing the behaviour of long-run *average cost* (*lrAC*) as a function of the units produced, q, by an enterprise. This representation consists specifically of drawing a vertical parabola, whose minimum value (min. *lrAC*) would mark the volume of units of product associated with the aforementioned *optimal scale* for any firm: $q = q^{os}$. And, from this 'graphical' definition, the ESM leads us to the following step: the concept of the *market equilibrium point*, where the *Price* of the concerned good equals its long-run *Marginal Cost*; which is precisely the condition required by the *general equilibrium* model to talk about a *social optimum.*

As already pointed out, the ESM's particular graphical language plays a determinant as well as conditioning role in textbooks and teaching practice. This, not only as a way of describing or schematising relationships between variables (such as, for example, that mentioned above: *unit cost*, in relation to the volume of units produced/supplied) or because the specific type of graphs and diagrams that are drawn implicitly suggest specific mathematical relationships (mainly quadratic functions). It is also because in many cases the aforementioned deductive assumptions come simply implicit in the way those diagrams are drawn – rather than these assumptions being made explicit and argued in a narrative way by the author in the text or manual. Thus, for instance, the *decreasing returns to scale* axiom is usually introduced implicitly by just presenting a diagram for the relationship *lrAC(q)* where a big, open, parabola envelops several small parabolas, each one representing the short-term average cost for a firm with a given size (production structure) successively larger (figure 3, in chapter 2).

That makes that one way to point out the main axiomatic cornerstones of the standard model is to refer to its key typical diagrams; notably to four of them:

- The way (the pattern of behaviour assumed for) the *average cost in-the-short-run* is drawn – as a function of the volume of units produced – is itself the formal statement on the topic: a 'U-shaped' curve (vertical symmetric parabola): fig. 1, in chapter 2.

- The star diagram already mentioned: The way a set of successive 'small' U-curves are drawn (each one representing the *short-run* average cost for a good, according to alternative possible sizes for a producer company) is itself a core formal statement. A set of curves that is completed by drawing a curve that tangentially envelops them, to so represent the average cost in the *long-run* (fig. 3). That is, the traditional big 'U-shaped' curve ('salad bowl profile'). This diagram is definitely, as we have seen, central to the ESM since it is the one that introduces/illustrate/'draws' the axiom ('law') of *decreasing returns to scale*: from the volume of units/size-of-firm where the wide big symmetric vertical parabola has its minimum. This point (q^{os} units') uses to be visualised, logically, towards the middle of the diagram; which easily conveys to the readers the idea of it signposting a rather mid-size, modest, firm; a firm size beyond which – the diagram says the average cost of the good (any good) becomes ever higher.

- The diagram for the *sum of the units (q)* that every sector's firm is willing to offer at a given *price* (P_s). That is, the *supply function*; traditionally conversely formulated: $P_s(q)$. This is drawn as an upward curve (see figure 4) because the concept P_s is *defined* through the hypothesis of it being equal to the growing part of the *long-run marginal cost* (*lrMC*) in the previous diagram.

- And the diagram for the *market equilibrium point* (figure 4a), which may well be considered as the 'co-star' diagram/concept in economics' texts. It is built or defined by overlaying to the former (the *supply function*) a representation of the *demand function* for the referred good, $P_d(q)$, as a simple downward line. Thus, according to the ESM, the *market equilibrium point* for a product or service ($P_{equilibrium}$, $q_{equlibrium}$) is defined/ explained (represented): as the crossing of both curves, the *supply function* and *demand function*, for the good in question (fig. 4a); a point for which – the diagram tells the reader – *Price* = (long-run) *Marginal Cost*.

Finally, in the ESM it is assumed that the explanatory scheme made up of the above graphical/discursive sequence – or, more properly, by the set of assumptions embedded along the sequence – is valid for any good produced in the economy; except for some exceptional cases (situations of *natural monopoly*). The implicit overall assertion is, thus the 'condition' *Price* = (long-run) *Marginal cost* is met (in the model) for practically every good.

On the other hand, the mathematical formulation of the *general equilibrium model* (a conditioned optimisation in a system of simultaneous equations) leads to demonstrate that the optimization of the system's core variable, which stands for an abstract *social utility*, occurs when *price=(long-run) marginal cost, for every good*. A conclusion, however, that has previously required, when defining *social utility*, to make the unrealistic assumptions, or oversimplifications, of //there is no inequality in the income and wealth distribution among the citizens of the economy considered\\ (sic); and that //there is full employment of Labour and the rest of production factors\\. Thus the circle is closed: the standard theory on costs, returns to scale, and firms' behaviour tells us that, 'in equilibrium, prices are equal to their respective (long-run) marginal cost'; and the mathematical result of the *general equilibrium model* teaches us that 'an optimum of social wellbeing requires mathematically *price = marginal cost* for every good'. In the usual shorthand expression: "free markets overall lead to a general equilibrium of efficient competitive markets, which corresponds to an overall optimum of social wellbeing"

Once the circle has been completed in the former overhaul, let us stress a fact that reiteratively appears through it: in the ESM arguments, the *marginal cost* rather than the *average cost* of a good is the protagonist concept or variable. This is even though the model itself assumes that both will be identical, on the grounds that 'the always-efficient behaviour of the producer enterprises means that the (*l-r*) *average cost* is the minimum one for each of them'; thereby the respective (*lr*) marginal cost will, mathematically, coincide with it (fig. 3). The explanation for this semantic/conceptual prominence of *marginal cost* over average cost must be sought in the background-method of the mainstream economic theory itself: *Marginalism*. This is because, in the formulation of the '*general equilibrium of competitive markets*', the concept of *marginal cost* is the one that, in mathematical terms, links (from the 'production' side) with the concept of consumers' *marginal utility*, which in turn is the protagonist in the definition of the *demand function* and, therefore, in the 'consumers side' of the General Equilibrium's system of simultaneous equations (as seen in detail at the end of 4.3.1).

To sum up, the ESM's paradigm around the *competitive equilibrium* in markets of products or services, the *perfect competition*, and more precisely the *general equilibrium of competitive markets* in the economy, conveys the thesis that the overall result of such *general equilibrium* is nothing less than an optimum of (economic) social wellbeing. However, and in contrast with the *transcendence* of this postulate, the theoretical sequence that leads to it rests upon a 'rather technical', aseptic, base. It is basically sustained by deductive reasoning and hypotheses about, on the one hand, the overall behaviour of the unit-costs of products and services (average cost, marginal cost) – in relation to the volume of units that an efficient company produces, and, on the other hand, about the behaviour (decisions) of companies in this respect (company's size, production capacity) and regarding their respective markets (prices determination).

The *Economics Standard Model* also extends to macroeconomics

The ESM, in the terms and with the scope referred to so far, and discussed throughout former chapters, basically deals with the economic world of production, unit costs, firms' behaviour, determinants of prices and profits, and market structures (in the competition/monopoly axis) prevailing in our economies. But this scope is not, of course, the whole of mainstream *economics*. Nevertheless, the ESM permeates and conditions somehow the rest: mainly specific theories on causal relationships between variables relative to the dynamics of an economy as a whole. These cause-effect relationships have been mentioned earlier, in the Introduction; but have not been properly addressed here (except the economic analysis of foreign trade). They are descriptive models concerning certain macro-variables and their interrelationships; and, obviously, make up the bulk of the content of *macroeconomics* texts.

Let us return briefly to this question to underline the indirect dependence on the ESM of most macroeconomic theories; but now with the background of having reviewed the elements of the ESM across previous chapters. To be more precise and also bearing non-economist readers in mind – what follows in this point refers to specific theories on *cause-effect relationships* in the macro-economic sphere, such as, to cite some of the most common in macroeconomics textbooks:

Functional relationship			Theoretical model about, or associated usual label
(change in ↓)		(change in ↓)	
(*Public Expenditure* under Public deficit)		(*Gross Domestic Product*, GDP)	'Public Expenditure multiplier'
→	-->	→	Ricardian Equivalence theorem
(Rate of Interest)	→	(Business Investment)	The *IS* model
	→	(Savings)	
(Money Supply)	→	(Rate of Interest)	The *LM* model
(Rate of Interest)	→	(Demand for Money)	
(Money Supply)	→	(Inflation Rate)	Theory of Money (part of)
(Income-Tax level)	→	(Business Investment)	
(Legal Minimum Wage)	→	(Employment)	Unemployment Theory
(Unemployment Rate)	↔	(Inflation Rate)	Phillips Curve; NAIRU
(codetermining variables)*	⇨	(Economic Growth)	Economic Growth
(codetermining variables)*	⇨	(GDP, Employment, ...)	Theory of Economic Cycles

(*): according to certain hypotheses

This is just a simplified scheme, of course. Especially because, for most of those functional relationships, there are other macro-variables, not only quantitative ones, that co-determine or condition the respective 'effect'. Regarding these *theories* (right-hand column), the plural must also be understood in the sense that, for some of these relationships, there may coexist more than one theory in the standard macroeconomics playground. The degree of academic uniformity on macroeconomic issues is not as monolithic as in the case of the ESM topics reviewed and discussed in previous chapters. Regarding these macroeconomic topics, more room for alternative approaches can be observed. This can likely come explained by the fact that these autonomous theories are somehow less abstract; but especially because they are the basis for developing propositions/ recommendations for *Economic Policy* measures. That makes that, though these macroeconomic topics are normally understood and worked on by scholars mainly in terms of *positive economics*, a certain tendency to express them in terms of *normative economics* is somewhat inevitable –and even understandable. This feature, in turn, is directly related to the aforesaid fact that sometimes there is more than one theory in the academic field (right-hand column) for a given cause-effect relationship (left-hand column); and, therefore, different economic policy recommendations. By way of example, this is the case for the first functional relationship in the list above:

The causal relationship Public deficit → Economic activity

In this case, we have on the one hand, the mainstream economics theory in this respect, which, following the 'Ricardian *equivalence theorem*', postulates, in essence:

> In a situation of economic crisis, an *increase of public expenditure (and deficit) financed by public debt* has not in fact any net effect at all on the level of economic activity (GDP, and, thereby, Employment). This is because citizens become aware that the

> new public debt will have to be returned sooner rather than later, and that, thereby, the government will increase taxes in the near future in order to pay back this debt. Consequently, citizens react by saving more (reducing their present consumption and/or investment), so as to be prepared to face the extra taxes they expect to have to pay in such a near future. Therefore, that citizens' feed back counterbalances, neutralises, the direct effect of the new public expenditure.

And this theory/postulate about the existing causal relationship is what is wielded as base-argument for a well-known recommendation of neoliberal economic policy:

> 'Seeking recovery of economic activity by increasing public-budget deficit, and thereby, public debt, is a useless, if not counterproductive, policy. Instead, if the rule of budget equilibrium is applied, even if this implies cutting public expenditure in the short term then a healthy economic recovery will eventually end spontaneously by developing' ("virtuous austerity")].

On the other hand, we have the alternative, opposite, theory regarding the same cause-effect relationship, which can be summarised as:

> The outcome we can expect from an increase in *Public Expenditure* (and, thereby, *Public Deficit*) within a situation of economic recession will be an increase in economic activity (GDP) equal to the increase in *Public Expenditure* multiplied by a factor greater than 1 (public spending 'multiplier'). Therefore, the standard neoclassical assumption (the above one) regarding a neutralising citizens' behaviour can be discarded because implausible.

Obviously, this alternative theory/postulate translates into an *economic policy* recommendation opposite to the 'neoclassical' above, which can be summarised as:

> Under a recession situation, in order to foster economic recovery (GDP, and thereby, Employment), public expenditure should be maintained or increased, and thus public deficit, so to generate the 'multiplier' effect. The deficit may be financed by public debt (as-long-term-as-possible) and/or an increase in monetary supply by the central bank.

The reason for the above touching upon macroeconomic topics and theories (such as those listed above) responds simply to underline the macroeconomics epistemological dependence on the ESM here reviewed. These connections mainly occur throughout the premises and hypotheses that such macroeconomics theories tend tacitly to rely upon; especially that of the assumption of the economic hyper-rationality of people: individuals, households, entrepreneurs, and firms' managers; (Komlos, 2019:57-56); i.e., the *homo economicus paradigm*. As well as that of 'all people enjoy *perfect information and foresight* when making their economic decisions'; which, in turn, implies assuming that all of them have *identical training backgrounds* as regards economic decision making. Regarding the implications of such theoretical dependence, think, for example, of the argument behind the 'equivalence theorem' mentioned above: the presupposed behaviour of ordinary people as consumers/savers, investors, and tax-payers; specifically, when the government engages in a public deficit policy as a means to foster economic recovery in a crisis situation.

Such an argument invites us to imagine a social scenario in which people (or households) in general normally keep an eye on the financial pages of newspapers, paying special attention to the news about the government's economic policy measures; specifically in the case of an increase in public expenditure that implies a certain budget deficit, and thereby a new public indebtedness; and even they get aware of the maturity year for this new debt as well as the interest rate. As a result, they come to the conclusion that in a rather forthcoming year the government will have to raise taxes in order to repay such debt; and work out what part of that future tax-increase everyone will have to pay (perhaps by making an intuitive mental calculation according to the amount of debt and the number of people who pay taxes; or, more professionally, with the help of an excel sheet?) And so, placed before the expectation of having to deal with such a forthcoming payment, they decide to reduce their present consumption in order to start saving now so to be prepared to cover such an additional tax.

[Rather surreal, indeed; it is even hard to believe that the very economists who take this assumption of 'precautionary saving' for granted really behave in such a way. Indeed, I presume they don't. They may take illogical assumptions for granted, in their papers and books, but they are not usually illogical people.]

The links between the referred macroeconomic theories and the theoretical corpus of the ESM are also reflected in the prominence the idea of equilibrium has in their approaches; as well as in the use of the traditional graphical-mathematical language. For instance, the macroeconomics' IS-LM model: in mainstream textbooks, it is in principle presented in terms of a descriptive theory developed mostly through an also-traditional diagram. But its theoretical formulation builds in fact upon the premise of a certain idea of 'macroeconomic *equilibrium*'. Somehow in parallel to the ESM-microeconomics' general equilibrium of competitive markets.

If I may use a graphical image, mainstream economics could be described as a compound of buildings where the ESM's imposing construct occupies the main entrance area, whereas the buildings of the specific, more or less autonomous, theories and descriptive models of macroeconomic topics (such as the aforesaid IS-LM model) would be distributed across a wide area behind and around; although each of them sharing, to different degrees, the same basic architecture and design (homo economicus, perfect information, equilibrium, etc.) as well as the inner layout (deductive reasoning, marginalist approach, etc.), signposting, and operating system (graphic-mathematical diagrams as language).

After these, rather unsystematic and generic, / references to the mainstream economics map as a whole, let us continue by focusing on the realm of the standard economics/ microeconomics topics discussed in previous chapters.

6.2 Empirical-inductive models of the world of production and of firms' behaviour

In the face of any explanatory theory – with its specific axioms, conjectures, assumptions, or hypotheses a permanent task of the involved professionals is/should be to contrast them with the accumulated empirical data or observations available about the respective area of the real world under analysis. That is, to check the degree of validity of such conjectures, assumptions, hypotheses, etc. More even when these are of deductive reasoning in nature, as is the case for mainstream economics.

An attempt in this vein has been carried out throughout chapters 3 to 5. The theoretical explanations, axioms, and assumptions of the standard model in mainstream economics have been systematically contrasted with the corresponding extensive observational evidence available. As a result of this empirical testing, the logical strategy has been to simultaneously formulate, for each topic, an alternative formal explanatory scheme/model that would reflect such evidence.

The referred extensive empirical evidence from the observation of the workings of the real business-economic world – used here for the abovementioned contrasting – can be grouped into three types: 1) *Generic evidence*, meaning by that easily-available-to-who-wants-to-observe: that rather obvious, easy to gather, evidence derived from the simple direct observation of the general ordinary workings of enterprises; especially that from inside, by 'observers' working within them. This means evidence resulting from firms' internal professional practices and activities as common as those associated with, for example, *cost accounting*. Or that evidence derived from employees ordinarily 'witnessing', or being an agent in, business transactions of purchasing and selling; or in investment decisions. *Generic* evidence also includes that coming through the observation of companies' activity from outside. Notably regarding those behaviours/decisions that are publicly disclosed on a regular basis, via companies' regular reports and releases; for instance, the average relationship price/unit cost (profitability), the pattern of behaviour regarding companies' strategic decisions on growth, marketing policies, or financial strategies. 2) *Indirect evidence*, derived from the ample dissemination in terms of both volume of publications and temporal coverage – of professional experiences from business managers, executives, and consultants – which has generated a wealth of literature on *business management and strategy* – as well as from professional sectoral periodicals. Finally, 3), of course, *direct evidence* brought about by the empirical studies available in the academic literature.

The outcome from this task of empirical contrasting regarding the field of production and firms' behaviour in this respect (chapter 3), is synthesised and presented in a more orderly and interrelated manner below in this section. This is especially relevant since this is the field related to the ESM's core thesis of 'decreasing returns to scale'.

General pattern regarding 'returns to scale', according to observational evidence

Let us firstly focus on the prior empirical discussion on the overall patterns of behaviour of the unit-costs of goods (products, services, commodities) in relation to the volume of production of an enterprise, and thereby the mainstream economics' core issue of '(decreasing) returns to scale'.

Summary of the observational evidence

On contrasting the axioms, assumptions and propositions of the standard, mainstream explanatory model with the respective observational evidence (chapter 3), the main conclusions derived can be summarised as follows:

a. Considering a *short-run* horizon i.e., a producer enterprise with a given size or production structure, at a given time – the most general pattern empirically observed for the *average cost* of a good, in relation to the units produced per period is that *it remains constant* (or decreases slightly, due to the decreasing of the fixed average cost) for a wide *range of units of product*. This interval tends to encompass the usual variations in the firm's monthly or quarterly production volume. It is, in short, the firm's normal-activity interval (see 3.2, 3.3); and comes framed between two extreme situations: on the one hand, that associated with the enterprise operating at a level well below its installed *production capacity* (in which case the average-cost is higher than when operating at a more-normal level of activity); and, on the other hand, the opposite situation: when the firm forces the flexibility of its installed capacity to its maximum (for example, resorting eventually to operating with more than two work-shifts, and/or 365 days a year, and/or to outsourcing some parts of its production process to other companies); in such an event, the average cost turns to grow.

To express this in the usual graphical/mathematical language of standard economics/microeconomics: in the diagram representing the plot of unit costs (vertical axis) and volume of units produced (horizontal axis), the relationship between both, for a firm, does not respond to a 'U-shaped' curve (i. e., a vertical parabola) as the ESM postulates, but rather to a, say, 'tray profile' mixed line. More precisely, such a relationship exhibits generally a behaviour as that schematised in figure 5: starting from abnormally low occupancy rates on, the average cost decreases; then moves to approximately constant for a relatively large interval of units to produce (normal range of activity of the enterprise), and turns to increasing for possible volumes of production greater than the firm's installed capacity.

b. This installed capacity, firm's dimension, or production structure (as well as the specific technology of this), constitutes a firm's decisional variable, but whose change requires a given time, and investment. This dynamic perspective leads to a *long-run* scenario as for a firm's operation. And this is the relevant one as for the decisive issue, in the ESM, of "decreasing returns *to scale*". The key concept to consider in this respect is, thus, the *average cost* of a good in the *long-run*, in relation to the volume of production, *lrAC(q)*. That is, the average cost of a producer enterprise as it grows in size, successively adopting more economical technologies associated with larger production structures. In this respect, the extensive empirical evidence shows (3.4 to 3.7) that the more general pattern is:

> As an enterprise follows the path of growing in size, and thereby in capacity and volume of production – it tends to achieve a lower and lower average cost, until it reaches a certain production dimension: that which, at the time, allows to use the most economical technology for the good in question (degree of

mechanisation, automation, digitising, work division, purchasing scale in the face of suppliers of materials, energy, parts, services, etc.). This size/dimension is, therefore, the <u>*minimum*</u> *optimal scale* (***mos***); in other words, the *optimal production plant or unit*. It is associated with a given production capacity, q^{mos} units, which is the volume of units for which the average cost of the good may be the lowest possible (at that time, since the state of technologies, salaries, and production factors prices change over time). A given firm may, certainly, have in operation more than one *optimal production unit*. This explains why, for company's sizes i.e., production capacities several times larger than q^{mos} units, the average cost tends to remain constant indefinitely (*constant returns to scale*), or, in certain cases, to be further reduced to some extent as the volume of units produced increases more and more (*increasing returns*; indefinite economies of scale).

In short, what is observed as a general pattern in the production world are ***constant returns to scale*** starting from that company's size associated with the corresponding *optimal scale (optimal production unit)*, or ***increasing returns***, in the case of some products or services that are produced/ provided at a very large scale.

The little surprising explanation of the above empirical acknowledgement – non-decreasing returns – lies in the obvious resource any enterprise generally has to double, triple, ... replicate several times the respective minimum optimal scale for its product, i.e., the corresponding optimal production unit (line, workshop, or production plant) that allows the firm to reach the *minimum unit cost* of the product at the time. Any enterprise producing a given good can ***replicate*** the corresponding *optimal production unit* as many times as its possibilities of placing more units in the market – while keeping or improving its profits expectations – allow (3.4). The possible exceptions to this overall pattern – such as the mining of 'rare' metals/earths, sometimes pointed out in standard advanced manuals, would in any case be of quite limited relevance (3.5.2). In fact, the remarks in this respect tend to be referred to supposed examples (stylised facts) that do not refer real cases. Moreover, the decisive issue regarding these possible exceptions is that they use to be products whose market is not properly that of 'one economy' (one country) – which is the conceptual framework of the theoretical paradigm of the ESM – but rather the global market.

c. The translation to the graphical language of the abovementioned overall pattern observed for the relationship [***average cost (in the long-run)***] ← [***size*** of the producer ***enterprise*** (in terms of ***production capacity, q units***)] responds to a plotting line not with the form of a large enveloping parabola, a large 'U', ('salad bowl' profile) but rather an enveloping line in the form of, say, a 'laying golf club', as in the following diagram (which condenses figures 6 and 6a in chapter 3).

Figure 6b: *OVERALL PATTERN OBSERVED for the Average cost of a good in the long-run*, (lrAC) or Industry's average cost (IC)*

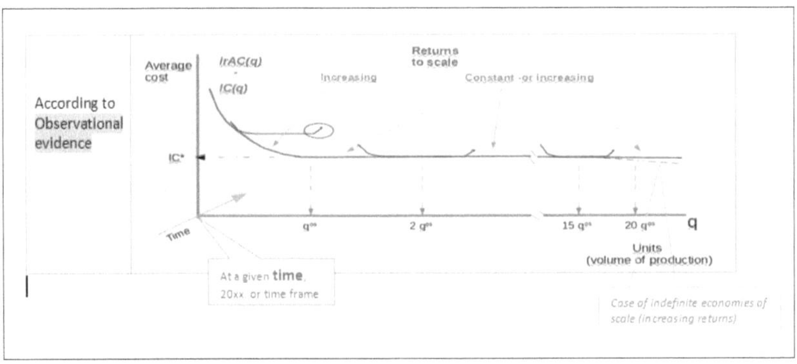

In order to highlight, also in graphical language, the contrast of the above with the standard postulate of "decreasing returns", the parallel traditional diagram of the ESM i.e., that of the 'U-shaped' hypothesis, as the plot representation of the general relationship [*average cost*] ← [*volume of units*], in the long-run, (figure 3 in chapter 2) is reproduced below.

Figure 3b: *According to the traditional axioms of the standard theory*

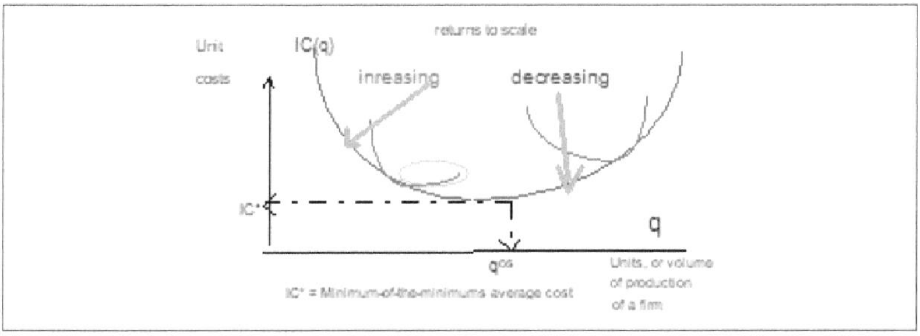

As we have already seen, this diagram/postulate plays a decisive role in the ESM: it is the main way of expressing its tenet of the 'law of decreasing returns'. Its right-hand side is then taken to formulate the ESM's supply function, the *supply curve* precisely as an increasing arch (lrMC, line in blue, figure 4, chapter 2). And this *supply curve* is then used to graphically define the '*market equilibrium point*'. Therefore, such a diagram/postulate of figure 3 is ultimately a core piece in the paradigm of the *general equilibrium of competitive markets* (3.6).

d. In mainstream economics/economic theory, a certain inconsistency is generally observed when the concepts of "average cost in-the-long-run", *lrAC*, and "Industry's average cost", *IC*, are used interchangeably in textbooks while they are not so.

The generally accepted definition for *IC(Q)* is: [the *mean* of the average-cost of every producer/offeror enterprise in the 'industry' of the good concerned)], in relation to (as a function of) [*the sum of all the units of good produced*/offered by them, ***Q***]. On the other hand, the definition for *lrAC(q)* is: [minimum average cost of the good *for one enterprise*], in relation to [its size or production capacity, measured in terms of the units of product allowed by full use of such capacity, ***q***].

Certainly, according to the overall pattern for enterprises' unit-costs observed in the business/production world, schematised in the first of the two previous diagrams, both concepts may be used indistinctly. Therefore, such a first diagram derived from observational evidence may indifferently be labelled either as *IC(Q)* or as *lrAC(q)*. But, on the contrary, the two concepts, *lrAC(q)* and *IC(Q)*, are not equivalent or synonymous precisely under the axiom of 'decreasing returns (at the firm level)' (second diagram, 'salad-bowl profile').

Such an axiom implies, as we have seen at 2.2.2, assuming that the minimum average cost of a good for an enterprise with a size beyond the corresponding *optimal scale* (production capacity of q^{os} units of the good) will be higher the larger the size/production dimension of the enterprise be; that is, that *lrAC(q)* grows progressively for volumes of units past the optimal scale for the good in question. This is precisely what the traditional 'U-shaped' hypothesis (right-hand side of the enveloping line, in the second diagram above) is 'saying' to us. However, when talking of the *Industry's average cost, IC(Q)*, another axiom of the standard model is involved: that of the 'full-efficiency behaviour of (private) firms'. According to this, none of the firms in the corresponding industry/sector will be interested in exceeding the size/volume of the optimal scale of production, q^{os} units, since it is the scale that allows them to operate with the corresponding minimum-absolute average cost, *IC** monetary units. Thereby, the average cost would be the same for all active firms in the industry/sector: IC* ,= *lrAC*(^{qos}). Consequently, the mean of *the average cost of industry's firms would simply be such a value.* That is, *IC(q)* would be a constant value, *IC** monetary units (for industry's volumes beyond qos). Thus, within the standard model, *lrAC(q)* and *IC(q)* are different for volumes of units past the corresponding optimal scale. And is the latter, *IC(q)*, the relevant concept to speak of the respective supply function.

Nevertheless, despite the above, in most reference textbooks – which assume the axiom of 'decreasing returns – the two concepts, *lrAC* and *IC*, are used indifferently, as if within the standard model they could be considered as synonymous. Moreover, this problem of internal incoherence has consequences, since it is transferred to the standard definition of the corresponding *supply function*. Here, the internal coherence would lead to the conclusion that, if we aggregate the data on 'quantities' and 'average cost' for each of the companies in the industry, the result for the mean of those average costs would obviously be a *constant value* (*IC** monetary units); and, therefore, the corresponding *marginal cost* would, mathematically, also be constant: the same value. As for the sum of quantities, it would simply be equal to q^{os} x (*number of active enterprises in the Industry*). Therefore, an internal coherent deduction for the *supply (price) function* should be a 'flat line', from q^{os} units on. However, when defining/drawing the *supply function/curve*, the standard model takes as such the hypothesised *lrMC(q)* in figure 4: the usual drawing of an increasing arch for $q > q^{os}$ (2.5.1). This obviously constitutes an internal incoherence in the model; or a contradiction between its axioms; which, moreover, affects the definition/ representation of the 'market equilibrium point' (as described further, in section 7.2).

Again, I should point out that to here showing up this internal inconsistency is neither properly new nor original: it is the so-called 'aggregation problem' regarding the *supply function*. Prestigious scholars have since long already pointed out this inconsistency (for instance, Sraffa, 1926:540-541); Morgenstern, 1972: 1176; or Keen, 2011: 128 and 136). Though certainly without too much echo, so far, in mainstream textbooks.

No evidence of a 'law of decreasing returns'

Consequences regarding mainstream paradigm

Given the implications the above assertions have concerning the standard paradigm in economics, let us recapitulate this core issue.

For a given good, the pattern generally observed, from its producer/provider companies, is *constant returns to scale* from the corresponding *minimal* optimal scale on. Except for certain goods/industries whose companies show a certain lingering trend of *increasing returns*, thanks to mass-production; that is, their *average cost* in-the-long-run, *lrAC(q)* continues slightly decreasing beyond the minimal optimal scale (remnant seemingly-never-ended economies of scale). To express this in the traditional graphical language: the linear section of the 'lying golf club' (first diagram above) is in these cases somewhat downward tilted. As for the theoretical marginal cost associated with the observable average cost, i.e., the long-run *marginal cost, lrMC(q)*, it would generally have the same pattern of behaviour: also constant from the minimal optimal dimension on; or, in the case of the referred exceptions, somewhat decreasing.

These statements are just the opposite of what the paradigm of the standard economic theory relies upon: that 'in general, for each good/industry/sector there exists an optimal size of company, comparatively small regarding the respective market demand; a company size that none of those in the sector will be interested in surpassing'. This is a deductive assumption that does not hold up at all in the face of the most obvious empirical evidence. Rather the opposite occurs: what we can observe is that, in general, companies in this or that sector or 'industry' actually tend to grow, and that this provides them with economical advantages (3.4 to 3.6).

These statements on the empirically observed patterns – regarding the average cost of goods in-the-long-run and firms' size in relation to this are, thus, of key importance since they invalidate a cornerstone of mainstream economics. Empirical evidence has shown that the ESM's deductive assumption or axiom of 'from a certain production capacity or company size, the production of any good is subject to the *law* of decreasing returns (increasing average cost in-the-long-run)' does not correspond at all with overall reality – with, perhaps, the exception of some specific case (which, sincerely, I have not come across in my professional work)[2]. As a consequence, the mainstream theory to describe the world of production, economies of scale, and firms' behaviour, does not explain such realities even approximately well. It is a theory that clashes with reality. Its predictions (for example, 'firms will not be interested in growing beyond a modest size, compared to the corresponding market size') do not correspond with what can easily be observed about the workings of firms in the real world of our market economies. The overall pattern observed in this respect is *constant returns* (or even *increasing*, in some notorious cases) for production volumes far beyond the corresponding *minimum*-optimal-scale, *mos*, indefinitely. Which is simply explained by the obvious fact of the *replicability* of the *mos* by any active firm in the sector; that is, that a firm may continue to expand and operate with two, four, twelve, .., etc., mos production units. (3.4 to 3.6).

A possible cause: The occupancy level is a key concept, neglected in mainstream economics

An enterprise in operation has a given available technology installed, to produce its product or service. This means it has set up a given production unit, or plant, endowed with machines, automated chains, digitised processes, etc., and fixed installations, within some given premises. That is, certain equipment set ('capital goods'), associated with a given *production capacity*: a certain number of units of product per period. This capacity will also depend on whether there is for the enterprise the possibility of operating with more than one work shift. Whatever the case, the firm will have a given team of workers hired to run such equipment, such a production capacity.

[2] In any case, not a single case of real firm or good, exemplifying a situation of 'increasing lrAC', can be found in any of the manuals referred to in foot note 6 in chapter 2. In those (few) cases where an example is used at all in the text, this is actually an abstract, imagined example (see foot note 7 in section 2.3).

This picture defines what is usually termed the *short-run* scenario for an enterprise. Of course, it may decide, regarding its more or less near future, to expand its installed production capacity. This by either, (a) simply to duplicate (triplicate, .. etc.) the equipment-set and workers-team it has in operation, so to be able to produce two, three, ... , more times per period than what its installed capacity at the time allows for; or (b) to carry out a technological leap in the sense of moving to an available, 'superior', technology (provided such a possibility exists). Superior technology in the sense of more automated/ robotic/ digitised (high-tech), entailing a larger production capacity (scale), and even allowing to operate at a something lower average cost (increasing returns to scale). This 'looking to the future' outlook drives us toward the middle/long-run scenario for the firm; within which as we have seen before – there is no place to talk of decreasing returns to scale, but to constant or increasing returns (constant or decreasing average cost, in the *middle/long-run*). Thus, the tenet of mainstream model in economics about postulating diminishing returns in that scenario, that is 'in equilibrium', has not any sense.

As pointed out before, in some authors' texts this standard tenet seems to respond to a sort of confusion as if implicitly they were arguing regarding a short-run, 'not in-equilibrium', scenario: As we have seen (section 3.3), a firm may temporarily decide to produce each week beyond what a 100% occupancy level allows it; i.e., running under normal working conditions. But such over-running will certainly entail something higher unit costs -because of forcing up the equipment and/or the workers' regular work conditions, and/or having to outsource some production phases/activities to other firms.

In short, it is not observed that, in a market economy, there is something technical-economical that prevents a given firm from growing and thus from covering a growing proportion of the demand for the good in question. If the firm's strategy, financial resources, and commercial abilities allow that and point in this direction, there is no element preventing such a firm from gaining market share and thus market power. Which is just the opposite of the cornerstone assumption of the ESM's model of the *general equilibrium of competitive markets* that postulates: 'since producer/supplier companies of a certain good will not be interested in growing beyond the corresponding *optimal scale*, there will end by being 'many' companies, all of them perfectly efficient, competing among them in the market for such a good'.

What may come as a surprise regarding this is that, as pointed out in previous chapters, the former conclusions/observations (argued along 3.4 to 3.6) are in fact nothing new or original. At least since the beginning of the 20th century, prestigious academics have been pointing out that empirical evidence overwhelmingly shows that, in the real world of 'production and business', there are generally no 'decreasing returns' in relation to the enterprise's dimension or production capacity (3.6). To quote just three of those economists: Sraffa, 1929; Lancaster, 1976 and 1981; and Mansfield, 1994[3]. Nevertheless, these statements have mainly been sort of neglected.

A long-standing curious academic impermeability to empirical evidence

Despite all of the above referred reiterated observational evidence and empirical studies – which leads towards the pattern graphically represented a few pages ago by the diagram in the form of a 'lying golf club', and despite this evidence having been pointed out long

[3] Blaug (1968 and 1985), Cohen (1983 and 1996), and Shepherd & Shepherd (2004) may be added to them; as well as some well-known authors of microeconomics textbooks, such as: Zamagni (1987), Hague (1974), and Koutsoyiannis (1977). Also, other authors that eclectically present both theoretical possibilities, *constant returns* and *decreasing returns*, in their manuals, as is the case of Varian (1992). Also, others that add a third possibility, increasing returns, such as Quirk (1980), Morgan et. al. (2009), and Eaton & Eaton (1996). Even Arrow himself – one the 'fathers' of the mathematical formulation of the general equilibrium model – could also be added, since he actually paid great attention to the evidence on constant and *increasing returns*: Arrow (2000).

ago and reiterated by renowned economists (at least since Sraffa), it is nevertheless (or continues to be throughout the years and textbooks' editions) the diagram-postulate in the form of a large 'U' ('salad-bowl' profile) what continues nucleating the reference mainstream manuals. How to explain this? To develop an answer, we should return on three key elements of the standard model that underpin its axiom of *decreasing returns*. The three of them have been discussed and argued in detail in sections 2.3, 2.6, and 3.5. Nevertheless, given the weight that these traditional theoretical tenets – decisive in the ESM– continue to have, both in the academic world and in mainstream reference manuals, it will be useful to synthesize, here in a more direct way, the empirical conclusions invalidating them.

First, the fact that the mainstream economics setting mainly ignores the possibility and, certainly, the reality – for any enterprise of a given industry to *replicate* several times the corresponding *minimum*-optimal-scale's production unit (*mos*). Second, the outstanding unrealism of the two arguments traditionally used in mainstream economics to, in turn, justify the reason for postulating the inevitability of 'decreasing returns', as an overall 'law' in the production of goods: on the one hand, the *Ricardian* or classic argument of "there is always a limiting fixed-factor of production, for volumes of production beyond that associated with the *optimal scale* (q^{os} units) for the good concerned"; and, on the other hand, the more neoclassic one of 'for larger volumes of production, a company becomes "too big", too complex to manage; to the point that it loses efficiency and/or its management and control costs soar' (2.3). The first argument may be found in some textbooks; the second, or both, in others.

Regarding the first issue that of ignoring the logical and overwhelming reality of the 'replicability', by producer/supplier firms, of the respective *minimum* optimal scale for the production of a given good, it is indeed particularly surprising: if such *mos* – which allows a firm to obtain the minimum-absolute average cost at the time– corresponds, for example, to q^{mos} = 1,200 units of good/ per-month, that production line, workshop, or plant may logically be duplicated, quadrupled, ..., replicated n times by this or that enterprise in that industry, so as it to produce 1,200xn units-of-product per month, *at the same minimal average cost*. And this is indeed what is observed overall in the business world (2.6 and 3.4). This acknowledgment, on the other hand, is nothing new in the economic literature[4]. To ignore all of this is, at best, to confuse the concept 'production unit/plant' with that of 'enterprise'. Obviously, nothing prevents a *legal entity* (enterprise) which is what operates in the market from owning several *production units* (lines, workshops, factories, production centres, subsidiaries, etc.).

As for the specific deductive assumption of the *'limitative fixed factor'*, the conclusion from the generic empirical contrasting developed here (3.5,II) is that it can not be sustained at all. There is no evidence that in general for this or that good there is a (comparatively small) *optimal size* for the producer enterprise, beyond which it confronts the impossibility of increasing the purchase or contracting of a certain production factor.

The assumption, inherited from Ricardo ("there is always a fixed factor of production that cannot be expanded; hence, when this limit is reached, to produce a greater volume of output the enterprise has to increase the other factors more than proportionally") is not observed to be met in business production activities (2.3 i, 3.5.II) There is no evidence than in real economies companies encounter a *limiting fixed factor*, in the sense that, as they follow the path of grow, increasing their scale, capacity, structure of production, they end up by experiencing decreasing returns, i.e., by their average cost becoming ever higher. Nor is such a limitation observed at the level

---

[4]To quote a few examples: Lancaster, 1981: 200; Blaug, 1968: 465-6 and 1985: 457; or, more specifically, Beckenstein, in his 1975 pioneering work

of a sector or industry (i.e., the set of enterprises producing a certain good, in the country[5].

In some manuals, the reasoning –when talking about "the inevitable presence of a given limiting fixed factor-of-production" to postulate the appearance of 'decreasing returns' seems to suggest that the author, instead of referring to the average cost *in the long-run*, is implicitly (perhaps, inadvertently) referring to the average cost in the short-run. In this latter scenario, the enterprise has a given size/structure (a 'fixed factor', *in the short-run*) and, certainly, if it tries to increase its production volume beyond its installed capacity at that time, the average cost will start to increase (in the standard graphical language: the section of the short-run average-cost curves rounded in green in the two previous diagrams). However, in the competitive-general-equilibrium model, the long-run average cost is obviously the relevant one; and in this scenario, the size, the productive structure/capacity of the enterprise, is a *variable*, decided by the enterprise's management, subject to changes over time; usually towards growth.

Neither is it possible to sustain the alternative or complementary neoclassical assumption about the appearance of diseconomies of scale 'because *the company becomes too big*' (2.3 ii, 3.5.I). That is, the tenet that 'for volumes of production greater than that of the corresponding *mos* the management, administration, and control costs of the company rise more than proportionally regarding the level of activity, at the time that the firm's operating efficiency decreases, 'because the company becomes *too complex to manage*'.

[5] Except, perhaps, for some possible specific situation (such as 'rare earths' mining, as it is sometimes pointed out) which, however, would be cases referred to international markets, not to a domestic market which is the reference scenario of the ESM. Nor is such a limitation observed specifically, for example, in the oil sector, which is sometimes taken as a reference about the topic: the corporate structure observed in that sector, in the principal producer countries (2.3,i), and the empirical evidence on the relationship [total volume-of-production] vs. [market price] speaks for themselves (appendix C).

This is a clearly unrealistic assumption –as we have already seen (3.5): there is no empirical evidence that, for a given good/industry, there exists, as a general pattern, a firm's size such that no firm in the industry is interested in surpassing 'because then the company would experience *managerial diseconomies of scale,* in the form of relatively higher management costs and lower overall efficiency – due to it becoming too big an organisation'. Indeed, the opposite is true: what economic reality shows us in this regard is that, in our market economies based on private firms, these generally tend to grow as much as their selling possibilities allow insofar as that increases or ensures somehow their profits expectations.

Large business chains such as Zara or Ikea, big business groups, and multinational corporations in general, may illustrate this; as well as the majority of mergers and take-overs of a company by another since these seek to obtain economic advantages from such operations if we pay attention to their protagonists' public statements. Advantages that include cost savings, precisely in management and administration's costs! We could, in any case, infer that if some management costs of the companies involved in a take-over or merger increase more than proportionally, this is in practice more than offset by savings in other costs.

To take this argument further on, when we drop the usual simplification in economics/microeconomics textbooks regarding "one company = one good" (an oversimplification, indeed), a well-known reality comes to the forefront: the vast majority of firms are multi-product. They produce/ supply several products or services on a regular basis, each one with its own costs and selling price. What has been historically observed in this regard is that this multi-product reality usually means that the enterprise, rather than run into '*diseconomies of scale* because of becoming too large', obtains savings in the sum of total costs (5.2): i.e., joint-production generates synergies in the form of *lower total costs* for the firm's set of products. This inference is indeed also featured in most standard microeconomics textbooks. And it even has a specific technical term there: *Subadditivity of Costs*; or, also, *Economies of Scope*. This subadditivity plays indeed a role as regards the observed trend towards more or less *indefinite* economies of scale (decreasing average cost in the long-run) for this or that product/service of a company's production range.

Other theoretical assumptions maintained against all evidence

The ESM's so-transcendent though unrealistic standard axiom of 'decreasing returns to scale' widely discussed so far is not, of course, the only instance of a thesis maintained against all evidence. Another example of deductive suppositions that have endured as axioms and ended up being used as if they were verified 'laws' to explain the workings of our economies in classrooms and economics and business-economics manuals is that regarding public (hostile) takeover bids (PTB).

Explaining take-over bids on companies

The standard theoretical explanation about why a PTB launched by a company or investment group over another company – takes place. According to the orthodox assumption (or standard theoretical explanation) in this respect, a takeover bid would be the result of certain investor/s becoming aware that a given company is underperforming because of being badly managed, in the sense that it could be operating at a higher profit. Based on this insight, such investors decide to purchase (to obtain the control of) such a firm in order to improve its management, so to increase its profits and thus benefit from the realisation of those 'latent profits'. In the words of prestigious authors:

> "The idea in a hostile tender-offer takeover is that the raider (the bidding company), having obtained the firms' stock,

> will vote to replace the existing board. The new board will then order management to implement a new strategy designed to generate better performance. Often, the current management will be replaced, and new management brought in to implement the strategy (...). The promise of the better performance means that the raider can bid more than the current price of the shares". (Milgrom & Roberts, 1992: 508)

This theoretical statement/description formally stems from the standard *theory of the firm* reviewed here in previous chapters. This theory, in short, is based on the perfect-competition-related assumptions of the standard model: perfect information and foresight for everyone as an economic agent, homo-economicus' behaviour, no entry barriers to any industry, efficient markets, etc.

Following the scientific method, this descriptive theory about PTB should long ago have been tested by verifying whether or not it corresponds to most of the cases that can be observed in the real economic world. Were the theoretical statement generally confirmed by empirical evidence, then we could conclude that it explains reasonably well such an element of the functioning of our market economies, and that such a theoretical statement would therefore be useful as a tool for schematic knowledge transmission in the classroom and textbooks. However, what empirical observation has since long been showing us is not that, but somehow the opposite: in general, neither the situation or profile of companies' object of a PTB nor the objectives of 'bidding' investors fit in with the standard deductivist theory (Jones, 2004:389-90). In fact, for anyone at all concerned about this market-economies' reality be it through economic media, the pervasive news about stock markets, or statistical studies on the matter – it will become obvious that 1) public takeover bids are in the vast majority of cases the result of strategic decisions by the bidding company to expand its markets (diversification of activities), to eliminate a competitor, or simply to grow: to purchase (or take a control position in) another company in the same sector of activity, as a quick way of gaining market share, entering a new market/territory, controlling a certain technological development, etc. (Samuelson and Marks, 2012:6); and 2) the firms that are subject to a takeover bid are typically companies that precisely operate at good profitability and/or with excellent prospects for the future which, among other reasons, is precisely what makes their purchase, or control, attractive for the bidding company or investors group.

To put it the other way round: admitting that there may have been some cases of takeover bids that correspond to the theoretical standard assumption/prediction (investors seeking to revamp underperforming companies), the fact is that no substantial empirical evidence has been provided so far in the academic literature to support such a mainstream theoretical postulate. Broadly speaking, the picture empirical observation on takeover bids shows to anyone interested in 'reading' the, otherwise easily observable, reality in this respect, is that the standard deductive assumption/prediction is not confirmed in the vast majority of cases. However, against what could be expected according to the scientific method, neither has such a theoretical explanation ceased being used as an axiom in textbooks and university classrooms, nor any mainstream theorist seems to have been interested in reformulating or changing it; that is, in revising published works as for the explanatory model based upon such a deductive assumption.

On firms' labour policies

We could continue in this way regarding other tenets in mainstream economics that are in startling contradiction with the easily available empirical evidence, asking ourselves about the underlying academic reasons in this respect. To mention just one more example: the standard assumption of: 'companies will reduce employees' wages in the case of an economic recession'.

" ... Truman Bewley (...) interviewed about 300 business managers (in 1999), asking why they don't lower wages in a depression. (...) The failure to do so, (...), has long been a subject of speculation among economists. (...). They (business managers) told him that to lower wages would create severe morale problems, and so would interfere with the operations of their firm. (...) . A few years ago I had occasion to ask Truman Bewley whether he was training students at Yale to carry on research like that he did on wages. His answer, I am sorry to report, was, "No, that would ruin their careers." (Bergmann, 2007:3-4)

6.3 A look at current research in micro-economics: the empiricist paradox regarding mainstream economics

Lack of empirical contrasting of assumptions, along with micro-empiricism

The above examples, plus those more systematically discussed earlier, allow us to highlight the fact that mainstream economics General Equilibrium, microeconomics-based, economic theory) has surprisingly been suffering from a sort of forgetfulness of the phase of the scientific method concerning the empirical contrasting of the hypotheses, premises and deductivist assumptions that its central model, the *GE theory*, relies upon. This, has especially been the case after the Second World War along with the rising dominance of mathematical modelling as a discursive method (Lawson, 2017:28-33), thus somehow neglecting earlier notorious warnings:

"§ 2. There is however no scope in economics for long chains of deductive reasoning; that is for chains in which each link is supported, wholly or mainly, by that which went before, and without obtaining further support and guidance from observation and the direct study of real life." (Marshall, 1898:43)

In a way, it could be said that modern neoclassical economics abdicated to a large extent the scientific method's stage of contrasting its presuppositions with empirical observations. This lack makes mainstream economics a theoretical structure that explains the economic world in a surprisingly unrealistic way; unnecessarily unrealistic, in fact. Certainly, any explanatory theory requires making abstractions and simplifications, and in that sense, it is of course sort of unreal. However, from the old Friedman / Hayek debate about positivism in economics, it seems that, in practice, a professional consensus has broadly been reached towards the latter's position: there may be room for unrealistic assumptions in economic theory but not so when the assumptions are empirically verifiable ... and are eventually refuted; "if it is possible to examine the reality of assumptions, then we should do so" (Swann, p. 6).

> ".. is there any other discipline which leaves its theory littered with masses of elegant hypotheses which are testable against observation, without so testing them? Do we have any testable hypothesis about why economists collectively behave with this lack of regard for scientific method?" (David Heighman, "Why Are Economist So Unscientific?"; Economists' Voice, May, 2007:1)

Nevertheless, the above statements will probably be dismissed by most scholars adhering to mainstream tradition. They could argue – and rightly so – that a great deal of the thousands of research papers annually published in prestigious journals within their economics fields are characterised precisely by introducing specific economic situations, subjects, cases, or aspects (stylised facts) into the framework of the mainstream general-equilibrium model; and that this makes such standard economic theory's works tend toward less-abstract, more realistic, explanations of the functioning of our economies. This, in addition to the fact that part of such published research also has an econometric content, thereby using quantitative data to determine models' parameters and their degree of confidence, etc. regarding specific causal relations.

To schematically tackle this, there is certainly a substantial part of the published research in economic theory that responds to a mathematical micro-modelling type of work. Even if they normally do not use quantitative data, they usually start by referring to very specific economic situations or aspects. Mainstream scholars can thus argue that such works in a way have an empirical character, as far as their approach and method or epistemology are based on considering or introducing specific aspects or cases concerning the economic world. The typical contribution in this line usually entails math modelling such a precise issue within the general framework of the standard *General Equilibrium* model, GE, or one of its strands. This means mathematically building a micro-model based upon the usual axioms and assumptions of the GE theoretical construct. This micro-modelling normally requires additional specific presuppositions about the particular economic issue under consideration, thus somehow following the deductivist pattern of the general model. On the other hand, there also are, of course, those economic theory works which basically have an econometric content, though they tend to also have a first micro-modelling part, within whose framework the econometric, quantitative, part itself is developed. The latter normally consists of defining and applying a given multivariable regression model -and/or a variance analysis, the corresponding estimation of the parameters, and working out the statistical tests regarding the degree of confidence of such parameters. Therefore, the outcomes from these research works might be considered as an 'empirical contrasting' of the specific theoretical micro model previously developed in the paper in question.

Here we have thus the paradox: heterodox economists denounce the lack of realism, an absence of empirical contrasting, in orthodox approaches, while a large part of academics working within mainstream economics lines understands and claim that most works and results within their research lines actually have clear empiricist contents. What follows in this section is an attempt to develop the elements of this paradox.

The 'mode of scientific production' in mainstream economics

This overview will focus here on academic published *production* in economic theory, though, on the grounds of coherence, skipping those journals specialised in macroeconomics. In other words, we will focus on economic theory works mainly related to the topics addressed in the previous chapters. Most theorists working on these lines will likely agree on labelling their works as 'research in *microeconomic* theory', although they usually tend to simply phrase them as 'research in *economic* theory', somehow taking the restrictive particle 'micro' for granted. This factual naming makes sense, insofar as topics like 'markets equilibria', 'social utility function', 'social-economic welfare', and, in short, 'general equilibrium of competitive markets' do not properly fit in well with the term 'micro' since they do indeed refer to the functioning of the whole economy. Thus, to follow the conventional wording, below we focus on academic research within microeconomics-based economic theory.

Since the 1940s, most of the research activity in economics has consisted – to be judged from what is published, which is a great deal – of modelling; i.e., mathematical modelling; this also applies to works with econometric contents. In principle, this math modelling tends to be presented in academic works as the result of introducing a specific case, situation and/or state of affairs regarding a given component of the general model. The so-planned more precise or enlarged model is then developed mathematically, seeking either to complement the general theoretical framework in some sense or to use such a framework for deducing formal conclusions regarding the specific situation considered. Thus, the basic strategy in this standard research programme leads to formal (mathematical) descriptions and explanations of particular economic situations, aspects or stylised facts of the economic world; be they observable or simply possible. The formal (theoretical) analysis of the particularity under consideration is developed within the framework and premises of the general standard model, which implies adding specific assumptions about such a particularity, since it is mostly addressed in abstract terms. That is, the specific casuistic introduced is made precise in mathematical-modelling terms.

> The general pattern in this line of academic production tends to be that, once the specific aspect of a real economy has been introduced, the paper develops the mathematical mechanics of the new or reformulated model, aiming specifically to find out whether or not the supposed economy (that of the GE model, with the micro-variant introduced) will also tend, spontaneously, to an equilibrium, or what the nature of the deviation would be. Or, conversely, the strategy consists of determining which other specific mathematical conditions such a 'redefined' economy should fulfil so that the equations-system of the new *general model* will have an *equilibrium* solution, an optimum of social welfare. Translated, this means that were such conditions met, the usual abstract economy of the GE model, with the added element of empiricist detail, would necessarily tend towards a 'general equilibrium of competitive markets'. In this respect "the set of fictitious assumptions does not reduce to those (if any) that are inessential to the results of the analysis. Rather fictitious constructions are usually vital in generating the results obtained" (Lawson, 2003:19).

For the illustrative purpose in this respect – also bearing in mind non-specialist readers, a small experiment about published research papers in economics/ economic theory over the last decade has been carried out. It has consisted of simply selecting ten of the usual leading journals in the field – skipping those specialised in macroeconomics, scattered along JCR-impact-factor 6.81 to 1.12[6], and then taking from each one the second paper of the second issue of 2012, plus the fifth paper of the second issue of 2020, a total of 20 research papers. A first descriptive analysis of this 'arbitrarily-at-random' sample of research literature shows that both types of works mentioned above – those basically *economic-theory mathematical-modelling* oriented, on the one hand, and those of a *predominantly econometric content*, on the other represent a similar proportion. Also, almost all of them, certainly, state in some way that they address a very specific real-economic-world slice, aspect, or situation.

(1) Basically economic-theory mathematical-modelling works

Regarding the first type of research papers i.e., those which are basically theoretical (mathematical modelling), most of them do not properly consider a specific empirical case, situation etc., but rather a given specification/modification within the standard GE model, by simply introducing deductive micro assumptions into it. This is intended -or presented- to make some element or strand of it somehow more precise. By way of (a real) example of specificity (from the referred sample):

> to assume 'an economy – such as the GE models, but with one non-profit firm producing a public good (...) whose inputs (production costs) are financed by voluntary contributions (subscriptions) of households'.

---

[6] The Journal of Finance, American Economic Review, American Economic Journal (Micro), Review of Economic Studies, The Review of Economics and Statistics, Econometrica, Journal of the European Economic Association, The Economic Journal, Econometrics Journal, Journal of Economic Theory.

This research entails that a given change is introduced into the ESM's assumption of "all firms in the economy are private, profit-maximisers, and produce private goods", and hence a certain change into the overall framework of the GE model itself. Another example in this respect from the referred sample:

> to assume 'an economy like that of the GE model, but– where (some economic) agents face ambiguity in the uncertainty about their economic decisions' (sic), which means that a slight modification is introduced into the standard assumption/ paradigm of the *homo economicus*; specifically, regarding its 'perfect-information' ingredient.

The usual scheme of this type of research papers (also in the sample) tends to be: i) a description of the specific aspect, situation, or particularity of a market economy to be dealt with, as well as the research objective in this regard; ii) the state of the art on the topic the particularity affects to (the so-far generally accepted model, within the literature of the GE paradigm); iii) the new or more specified proposed model, and its mathematical properties occasionally along with some quantitative data, for illustrative purposes; and iv) the conclusions or findings – about the novelty or advance in modelling the authors claim that their enhanced explanatory model brings about (the contribution). The above third step more than the first one-would actually contain the empirical part the authors could claim for their work: an abstract, mathematical, formulation (modelling) of the actually addressed *issue* regarding the specific economic *case, problem,* or *situation* referred to in the first step.

Alternatively, some modelling of such a specific issue has already been developed in the literature on the subject (e.g., a given element concerning a specific type of oligopoly situation); in which case the novelty of the new research consists of re-modelling it, by introducing some conceptual specificities or methodological variants as regards the pre-existing one in the literature. All of that – abstractions and modelling – entails introducing *instrumental* micro-suppositions, like some given mathematical conditions as for the *future-profit functions* and *reaction functions* of companies A, B, and C that define the referred oligopoly; the scope of the *asymmetry of information* for one or the other; the degree of *risk aversion* of this or that agent in the model, and/or the mathematical properties of A's utility function. That is, it entails introducing new specific variables, deductive micro-assumptions, and mathematical relationships.

As can be deduced from the examples, in most instances some variables in the micro-model would not be observable, or measurable; e.g., it is virtually impossible to know the *reaction function* of a given economic agent within an oligopoly, or to measure its degree of *risk aversion*. This remark is relevant, since any possible further attempt to empirically contrast the relevance of the resulting micro-model (the contribution of the research paper) would become unworkable.

In some other cases, the considered specificity has a purely instrumental character, in the sense that the work deals in fact with an analytical tool; for example (from the abovementioned sample): to develop and analyse a given figured games-theory exercise. Also, the paper's specificity and objectives may be basically methodological; thus, for example (also from the sample): the core of the paper consists of developing a new mathematical model to better theorise on the consequences on (the GE-model's concept of) social-welfare from assuming 'unequal income distribution' (so, in abstract terms) in the economy.

On balance, few of these standard economic theory works of mathematical-modelling (2 out of 11, in the arbitrarily-at-random sample mentioned above) actually consider empiric aspects, or stylised facets of economies' workings, or present some descriptive/quantitative data in this respect. In the rare cases they do, the data, however, are not used to contrast the specific model featured in the article (were such data actually the ones required for that) but rather as an illustration of its theoretical implications as well as the advantages the proposed/new model brings about as regards previous ones in the literature on the matter. By way of example (from the sample):

> A research paper that assumes an economy (such as that of the standard GE model, but) with inflation, where 'money is a medium of exchange and inflation is a tax on its usage' (sic). As can be seen, this means relaxing the standard model assumption of prices stability, plus introducing the ancillary hypothesis of 'inflation as a tax on the use of money'. The paper's stated objective is to mathematically derive the theoretical deviation, in terms of social-welfare, that such assumptions entail regarding the standard General Equilibrium formulation. As an illustration of this, statistical data on (US Treasury's) quarterly rate of Money Stock over GDP are managed. Finally, the paper's most substantial finding that is clearly presented as such is "(it has been argued here) how it can be desirable to have inflation above the Friedman rule ...".
>
> **Remark:** *We might well ask: why in this case taking indirect measures (Money Stock and GDP) when one might take the direct, and equally available, measure for the core variable in the paper the Inflation Rate? This is even more so when, as is the case, this strategy of 'indirect data' entails a given, if unknown, error element – as far as Inflation Rate also depends, besides on the above two variables, on other socio-economic variables (such as the state of the affairs, people's expectations, etc)–. To venture an answer to the question, it cannot be entirely dismissed that, were the direct measure to be used*

> *in the paper, some future referee might then deem that the paper was somehow simple, or that its authors did not master the standard theory on Inflation.*

As a result of this epistemology or 'mode of research production', the nature of the findings of these theoretical-mathematical-modelling works usually comes down to being internal to the theoretical standard model itself. Substantively, they consist of mathematically demonstrating whether the new modified or more precise model (of a slightly less-simplified assumed economy) will have, or tend to, an equilibrium, and what would (mathematically) characterise it. Or the core contribution consists of demonstrating what the complementary mathematical conditions would be for an equilibrium to exist. A consequence of the dominance of the mathematical modelling language is that in most instances the papers' findings are to a great deal hardly intelligible for economists working on topics different from that of the paper in question – mainly because the *dialect's* entry costs are a deterrent for them: The findings are phrased in a code that makes that even to ascertain which fragment or spot of the economic world they refer to becomes almost impossible for out-of-the-speciality readers. The extreme cases along these lines of *closed deductivism* are those research works whose findings just consist of a chain of mathematical proofs of formal *lemmas* and *theorems*. In this not-infrequent event (2 out of 9 in our sample), it is rather hard to deem whether the research paper in question can actually be considered to be about economics or rather about pure mathematics.

To sum up, for most of the research works on economic theory strictly speaking – also those in the sample, the specificity considered is not actually an empirical element or situation. They consist rather of a blend of over-simplification and micro stylised-facts. The would-be empiricist element considered is presented by referring to a (quite) specific economic reality, identifiable as such by the reader, and which in principle seems a more or less relevant issue to be addressed; for example, a certain situation in the oligopolistic telecommunications sector of country 'X'. This setting leads the readers of the paper or advanced textbook, most of whom are also economists, to the idea that, in this case, the work in question actually goes in the line of approaching a given part of the standard theoretical framework to the economic reality; what could at first be interpreted as part of a sort of 'micro-step-by-step' overall research programme. However, when the paper develops the formalisation of such specificity, within the standard model framework, the empiricist specificity tends to be reduced to a situation as highly of-detail as it is abstract, like, by way of example, the following mix of over-simplifications and micro-abstract scenario:

> Let us suppose an economy that .. [here the usual ESM over-simplifications], where, for a given product/sector, 'X', there are just two active companies, and there is no foreign trade. And let us also suppose that the exchange relationship between present and future profits for company XA comes defined by the following function of current values ... [here a mathematical expression], in which the interest rate is determined by .. [idem], and the borrowing level of the companies involved is not limited.

More in general, regarding this type of theoretical research works, a characteristic asymmetry is observed between, on the one hand, the over-simplification of the standard theoretical model used as a framework, and, on the other hand, the thoroughness as regards both the mathematical formalisation of the specific, though stylised (or just imagined), case chosen as well as the micro-assumptions embedded in such formalisation. That is, specific situations/cases are introduced into the standard theoretical framework and implicitly presented as attempts to bring this general model somehow closer to real market economies. The empiricist contents would thus consist of the manner the facet of the specific economic reality referred to in step *i)* is taken into account in theoretical terms. Nevertheless, in the best of cases the overall result tends to be a new theoretical modelling that is equally far from economic reality, albeit with an even somewhat more complex or sophisticated (mathematical) formulation. This makes such a model even less accessible for non-specialists in the corresponding specific field of (micro)economic theory – because of the high entry costs involved in reading it. At the time, for the same reason – the mathematical language effect, the contribution tends to be seen reverentially from the outside: as a scientific work that must be very rigorous, about a subject that must surely be extremely complicated.

Furthermore, in this type of 'mode of research production', it is usually the case that, as regards the mathematically deduced conditions for the assumed economy (for example, that the second derivative of the reaction function of the economic-agent 'x' is negative) it is not possible to verify whether or not such conditions occur in the real world. This impossibility, following the scientific method, somehow makes useless any conclusion derived from assuming that these deduced conditions are in place. However, surprisingly these questions do not seem to be of much concern among mainstream theorists.

A possible explanation for this is that theorists in the mainstream tradition could be implicitly assuming, 'why bother about verification or falsification when we are seeking the conditions that *should be met* in a supposed economy (of an abstract society) for it to reach a general equilibrium and therefore a social optimum of economic welfare?' Perhaps this stance might not be good scientific practice, but it could respond to a certain pressure, on the dedicated theorists in these fields, diffusely present within their academic environment (Lawson, 2017:32-33). This hovering pressure would convey the strong idea/premise: 'if *the stated math conditions* are fulfilled, equilibrium is automatically reached in the economy, and thus, the resulting economic situation is socially the best possible one. Therefore, the only thing public powers (of the assumed abstract society) should do is to promote and/or maintain *such conditions*, so that markets operate freely, without obstructions, etc.'.

(2) Basically econometric research works

As pointed out before, economic theory papers with econometric contents are usually also based upon a given theoretical model on the topic to be dealt with, as a framework for their specific research. It may simply consist of an adaptation of the mainstream state of the art on the topic, according to the specificity, case, or subject under consideration (re-modelling). Taking this fitted model as a basis then the paper develops the operative econometric model to be applied (multivariate regressions, mostly), which entails specifying functional forms and their variables. The quantitative application of such a model tends to make up the core of the concerned research piece: *a)* databases description and discussion, *b)* 'running' the model, and *c)* statistic and econometric analysis of the quantitative results: interpretation and discussion of the obtained parameters' estimates, and of their corresponding maximum-error-level tests. Therefore, these are a kind of research works from which 'a priori' an empirical approach and hypotheses' contrasting could be expected.

For these economics papers with basically econometric contents (9 out of 20 in the above for-illustrative-purpose sample), the degree of empiricism is rather the reverse than for the former basically-theoretical works: most of them do consider specific cases, situations, or causal relationships; albeit also quite specific, such as e.g. (from the abovementioned sample):

> '*Pricing in the US market for TV channel-packs*: its effects on *consumer* surplus'. Or also: '*contracts of firm-based vocational-training* (apprenticeship): *degree of actual delivery* by firms involved and *why it differs among countries* (comparison of two countries practices)'.

In general, since these are research works developed around econometrics tools, their usual orientation is to determine or explore causal relationships. To add to the former examples:

> '(assessing the quantitative effect of) *financial development*, at country or industry level, on the *degree of verticality in a specific industry*, and which other independent variables within such an industry could be relevant in this respect'.

As in the case of the previous group of economic-theory mathematical-modelling research works, a non-negligible fraction of those properly *econo*metrics' (3 out of 9 in our arbitrarily-at-random sample) is in fact of mainly methodological contents. In such cases, the quantitative data and the econometric development itself play basically the role of illustrating the differences brought about by the proposed new econometric model or methodology, as regards the pre-existing ones (methodology's state of the art). Terms such as *calibration* and *validation* are usually associated with this kind of research works. In these methodological works, the specific empirical situation taken as a base, as well as the related quantitative data employed to run the econometric model, is actually not the relevant element of the paper. By way of example (from the sample): a work that takes as an element of reality 'the causal relationship between *having attended a Catholic high school*, and *schooling results* (in the US)', but this just in order to discuss the technicalities around resorting to an *instrumental variable* (IV) in an econometric model.

Also, in some of these *econometrics* works in the sample the research topic or causal relationship considered does not properly concern economics but rather other disciplines; like *sociology*, as is precisely the case of the above example; and the same happens regarding another paper that develops a full econometric analysis on the relationship between the *degree of use of mobile phones*, and *political mobilisation* this, regarding street demonstrations, in several African countries. To which an additional paper concerning rather to *economic geography* must be added:

> '*geographical distribution of poverty* within a city, London, at present, as a consequence of *geographically concentrated income shocks in the past* (referring to a sudden downturn in housing prices in a neighbourhood, due to a cholera epidemic in the 19th. century)'.

Aside from the above econometric works that are simply methodological or refer to non-economic issues, the rest (5 out of the 9 in the sub-sample) are properly speaking research works on economics that use econometric tools. The nature of their empirical findings might illustrate on the possibilities of this kind of research works. A common feature of them is a blend of, on the one hand, considering very specific 'cases' or micro-aspects of an economy (e.g., 'ambiguity aversion of stock exchange's agents regarding assets-pricing and stocks returns variability') and, on the other hand, taking large generic databases as empirical data for running the econometric model (like the US Standard & Poor's index on returns on stocks, for years 1871-1993; sic). This feature leads in most cases, almost inevitably, to empirical findings which are close to trivial. Thus, in the case of the former paper, "The key intuition is that an ambiguity-averse agent behaves pessimistically by attaching more weight to the pricing kernel in bad times …". Alternatively, consider this other (also from the sample) research work's finding:

> The summary of the research question in the paper is about 'the behaviour of macroeconomic forecasters as such, regarding the occurrence of natural disasters across decades: did forecasters revise frequently, and how, their forecasts? What are, in this respect, the differences between attentive and inattentive agents? ...'. The paper's quantitative data are statistics of observed errors in forecasting macro variables (deviations forecast vs. real). And the most substantive finding in the paper seems to be '(forecasters) are persistently heterogeneous in how often they revise ...'.

Finally, the use of rigorous mathematics with 'approximate' data is also a feature to be remarked on. It is not easy, for certain topics, to obtain the required quantitative data for the variables in a refined, mathematically complex, econometric model; especially in the case of those economic-theory-tilted econometric works. The fact that these usually consider in their model a specific case/situation but in abstract terms (apparent empiricism) means that in many cases some variables in the model are not properly or directly observable. This situation leads authors to resort to proxy variables and/or estimates, or even to estimates of proxy variables. Consequently, the real meaning of the values obtained for the parameters from 'running' the regression model – as well as of the values of the corresponding confidence-degree tests – tends too often to remain in the realm of a numerical illustration of the theoretical/econometric model developed in the paper in question. Nevertheless, the simple fact of using quantitative data –as well as mathematically complex econometric models – tends to generate a sort of over-self-confidence in the quantitative results obtained. Or these results are so cautiously interpreted by the authors in the 'conclusions' – because of having got from indirect approximate data, that these may easily drift into almost trivial statements.

The 'Econometrics Illusion'

Widening the perspective regarding the above, it is worth underlining a consequence that is often left unattended: the fact of resorting to proxy variables and/or estimates in an econometric work, involves certain, unknown but inevitably significant, error levels for parameters' estimates and their confidence intervals. That clashes with the meticulous attention normally paid – and pages devoted to in the abovementioned step *c* of a paper – to applying and discussing mathematically sophisticated statistical tests intended to evaluate whether the *degree of error* for the estimates obtained for the parameters is acceptable; say, below 5% error. In this regard, it does not make much sense as a scientific practice to be extremely rigorous in the application of t-statistic and other more sophisticated statistical tests, while in previous step *a*, in order to build the database to be used, estimates have been made and/or *proxy* variables have been taken. For, in such a non-infrequent event, the degree of error derived from the quantitative database itself is inevitably high, although unknown; and therefore, so is the degree of error of the results of the econometric model. In these instances, with authors neglecting those error elements whose level we don't know or cannot quantify (related to resorting to proxy variables and estimates), a sort of self-deceit regarding the validity of the quantitative results obtained from running the model occurs; which is thus implicitly passed on to the readers.

By way of example: we may apply rigorous econometric processing to a set of databases that includes estimates and proxy variables more or less related to the causal relationships under consideration. And, as a result, to obtain that the sign and value found for the parameter of independent variable 'x' – regarding dependent variable 'Y' – have associated a Wilcoxson-z statistical index of, for example, 2.3; thereby inferring that the relationship found between the two variables has a possible degree of error not higher than 5%, and thus that such a relationship can be considered as significant. However, the initial error level introduced through estimates and proxies is unknown, not measurable, although in most of these cases there are enough indications to deem that the degree of error brought about by the use of a proxy may be such (say, 20%) that, if it were to appear in the paper's part devoted to econometric/statistic tests, it would lead the authors to dismiss the quantitative results as clearly non-significant.

This kind of methodological asymmetry within a research work – a sophisticated mathematical econometric model, together 'approximate' data to run it – may well encompass a waste of time, both for the researcher/s and their target audience. First, insofar the work's conclusions depend on subjective options taken along the quantification of the econometric model's variables; options whose accuracy is not usually verifiable afterward, for the same reason that proxies or estimates were initially taken (or, simply, because of the presence of non-observable variables in the econometric model). Second, because, due to the psychological effect the sophisticated mathematical part of the work induces on readers (since such a part of the work has comparatively required considerably more effort from them), these end up attributing to the work's conclusions a rigour that it cannot actually be claimed for.

Nonetheless, in the face of ones of these econometric papers, if it has been praised by the authors' peers i.e., a research work likely publishable in high impact-factor journals, one might confidently guess that it will, in any case, be a demonstration that its authors have not only a high level of training in mathematical modelling within mainstream economics – and specifically in the corresponding line of specialisation – but also have a complete command of the state of the art in complex econometric techniques and statistical tests.

A more general and serious remark on econometrics works has been developed by Peter Swann. The objection he raises concerns the use of the econometric core tool itself: the regression methodology. He warns that the degree of confidence of the obtained parameter-estimates, whose degree is signalled by their corresponding statistical tests, may frequently be misleading. This is nothing that experienced econometricians might not be aware of, though it is largely ignored in ordinary econometric practice. To argue his remark, Swann (2019: 12-27) builds a simulation of 400 pairs of 'observations' – for variables y and x – which, when plotted on a y L x diagram, give way to a rounded amorphous cloud of points, thereby showing that there does not appear to be any clear or substantive causal relationship of variable y regarding variable x. However, when an OLS regression is carried out with such data, the obtained estimate for parameter b, (in $\hat{y} = a + b \bullet x$), is associated with a t-statistic (for the null hypothesis) equal to 3, which means a 'degree of confidence' of 95 %; that is, that there is just 5% probability for the real value of 'b' being zero. In other words, that it is rather unlikely (5% chances) that the assertion 'a substantive relationship between y and x actually exists' is wrong. That is, an econometric result that is clearly at odds with the mentioned graphical reading of the data series in the scatter-plot. Swann develops an explanation for this paradox, starting by underlining "that with enough data, we can almost always obtain a reasonably high t-statistic even if the scatter-plot looks very amorphous ..." (p. 17).

To tackle this problem, he defends focusing on the sensitivity analysis, emphasising as more significant the use of *confidence intervals* for the parameter/s estimate/s; and also develops a complementary measure in this respect: a signal-to-noise ratio – where the *noise* would refer to the effect of other determining, independent, variables that are either identified but absent in the econometric model or simply unknown.

He completes his argument by warning against the *econometric illusion* generated by the fact that the standard regression tool may produce "reasonable precise parameter estimates from (... an) apparently amorphous scatter-plot, as if by a 'conjuring trick'. The trick is to make the *independence assumption*"; i.e., to assume that 'variable y only depends on the independent variables included in the regression model. (p. 26).

In this vein, the objection by Lawson to the 'econometrics project' within mainstream economics pointed to even more basics. It does not concern risks of 'false positives' from econometric tools (regression models) as illustrated by Swann, but rather the econometrics fundamentals: he questions the usefulness of Econometrics itself as epistemology/methodology, or mode of scientific production, in economics. Lawson (1997: 69-85) extends Lucas' critique in this respect, arguing that "(...) the econometric models actually constructed, the probabilistic relationships identified as connecting sets of measurable events or state of affaires, are unstable (along time and places). The theory upon which most econometric analyses are based presupposes the existence of stable parameter relations. But the observed practices of econometricians indicate that the models actually derived are not sufficiently stable to allow the successful forecasting of events occurring outside the period for which the models were initially constructed." (pp. 71-72).

That is, the research strategy of seeking to determine and quantify, in terms of probability, causal relationships regarding economic issues through the econometric research programme, would not be useful in economics as an explanatory, knowledge-providing discipline. This is not just because the variable to explain always depends on other socio-economic variables absent from the model – non-quantitative ones included, but also mainly because all causal effects among economic variables are subject to changes over time. This implies that in a set of time-series covering, say, twenty-five years – which might be taken for running an econometric model, the causal relationships among variables are probably different from one sub-set of years to others (think in this respect, for example, about the before-mentioned econometric paper using nothing less than 1871-1993 time series), while the assumption underpinning econometric regressions is that such relationships are constant. Perhaps this Lawson's epistemological overall amendment of econometrics is especially relevant in the case of causal relationships in macroeconomics; mainly regarding those more clearly related to the design of economic policies.

6.4 Economic theory works, and quantum of knowledge provided

Mathematical micro-modelling plus 'Abstract Empirism'

Summing up, the described mainstream strategy – of focusing on a rather specific economic issue, situation, or state of affairs, but in abstract terms – is a common feature of those papers in mainstream economic theory that 'a priori' suggest an empirical approach. This is an academic practice that could even become in a way self-deceiving for authors themselves: in this kind of research works the usual starting section presents the theoretical approach – framed within the GE model's abstractions – and states the research objective in terms of addressing a ground-level, real-world, economic issue. However, the subsequent treatment normally drifts toward micro-aspects of it, and in abstract terms, i.e., drifts toward micro-abstractions. And the mathematical modelling is then worked on by introducing a mix of deductivist assumptions and empiricist details (a stylised fact).

Such stylised fact is, at best, inspired by a more or less relevant specificity (e.g., 'the behaviour of unit-costs in the case of '*cleaning costs of offices*'). Some assumed specifications in this respect are introduced into the corresponding parcel of the standard model (e.g., the standard Cobb-Douglas function). The so developed new partial model using the standard GE's assumptions (e.g., a costs function built upon the C-D production function) is further narrowed down, introducing micro-assumptions concerning a particularity within the stylised fact (e.g., by focusing on generic technicalities of *cleaning costs* of *offices computers*). The final conclusion would then refer to the mathematical properties of the new partial model (about the parameters of the particular C-D costs function developed under the usual general equilibrium conditions).

This research strategy, moreover, entails a risk of circularity; i.e., of conclusions that are actually reflections of the very assumptions embedded into the base model, (in the above example: the oversimplifications and deductive assumptions of the standard C-D function itself). Thus, considering a given research work of this type, the above sequence, or research strategy, has formally allowed the authors to use and refine the state of the art of the GE theory as a framework (in the above example, about Costs Functions), at the time that the paper talks about having considered *empirical* facts – even if in abstract terms. That would illustrate the sense of the term empiricism used here: abstract empirism.

Obviously, the kind of results we may expect from such a type of research would be generic statements. The outcome tends to be a formal empiricist micro-model which, nevertheless, risks having scarce relevance regarding the specific part of the economic reality that the paper initially stated to be its 'realistic' research target. This is mainly because of the blend of over-simplifications (GE-theory framework) and deductive micro-assumptions upon which this kind of research work is actually built. "In fact, most mainstream economists (…) have never concerned themselves much with the workings of the economic system as a whole (whether via an equilibrium framework or otherwise). The dominant concern, rather, has been, and remains, with highly specific or partial analyses of some highly restricted sectors or forms of behaviour. Very often the focus is on 'micro' decision making or 'behaviour'. Even (or perhaps especially) here though the contributions have more or less always been unrealistic and have rarely if ever generated (as opposed to imported) insight" (Lawson, 2015, p.149). Consequently, due to the chosen procedure itself (epistemology), the outcome is just that the modelling developed and the mathematical conclusions of an apparently 'looking-at-reality' paper – which will eventually be published in a prestigious academic journal – remain to a large extent disconnected in fact from the economic reality the authors announced at the beginning of the paper they were going to analyse and/or formalise.

It could be concluded, therefore, that behind the empiricist paradox discussed in the previous section there is basically a sort of an *abstract empirism* – that is, *empiricism,* as a result of introducing some highly specific, minute, economic aspects, albeit in rather abstract terms, into the framework of the GE theory. The result is that marginal modifications are introduced into the standard-model's formulation by surgically relaxing this or that oversimplification or setting forth a nuance in this or that deductive assumption of the standard GE theory, by adding micro-assumptions.

Explanatory power of Conventional Economic Theory Research

Some theoretical models making part of the GE theory tradition, and that mainstream researchers take as a basis for their works, can indeed be a good academic tool for introducing a given economic reality to economics students: by describing it in a stylised way; for instance, the *state of the art* regarding theoretically explaining oligopoly situations. [Another equally good tool for this purpose could likely be to invite to the classroom a top manager from an oligopolistic enterprise (better then to avoid the qualifying adjective), to talk about their company's business model, its markets, competitors, top decision-making, etc.][7]. However, the explanatory model itself can hardly be useful to the advance of knowledge on the topic, or for economic policy decision-makers, for the same reasons argued before: the predictions resulting from the model are so generic about so-specific issues that boil down to equivalent to common knowledge in this respect within the economic and business world, if not to common sense. Alternatively, such predictions may simply be irrelevant regarding real oligopoly situations, mainly because such predictions are a mix of over-simplifications and deductive assumptions about the economic system (GE theory) together with unverifiable arbitrary micro-assumptions regarding specific imagined oligopoly situations (e.g., about 'the *reaction function* of economic agent X'; or 'the *degree of risk aversion* of agent Y').

There is, thus, in the mainstream, a contrast between, on the one hand, over-simplifications and (unnecessarily) unrealistic assumptions regarding the whole economic system (basic standard model), and, on the other hand, a formal fine-detailing as regards the stylised fact introduced or the 'specific' problem addressed; together with the introduction of micro-assumptions about it, which are generally not verifiable (reaction functions, ... etc.). This means that the connection between the explanatory contents of the results/conclusions of a theoretical work and the specific real-life situation, namely referred to by the authors at the beginning of the paper, does not go beyond the stage of good intentions.

---

[7] Following this example, if the invited manager had devoted time enough to read a typical paper on the topic and getting into the model in it, as well as into the mathematical results set forth, s/he likely did not learn anything new about the reality of the oligopolistic situations; anything useful. In any case, there is so far no evidence that, from mathematical modelling as those mentioned above, verifiable predictions had been deduced that turned out to be relevant for policy-makers or companies' decision makers. I would sincerely be glad if I were corrected in this respect.

Consequently, the conclusions/findings in published modern neoclassical papers have a high probability of being, at best, non-testable statements, which, thereby, have little chance of being useful as regards knowledge improvement on the specific aspect of the economic or business reality considered. Alternatively, the findings are almost trivial; either because they consist in fact of generic statements that add nothing new to what direct observation plus common sense already tell us (insofar as we all are subjects and 'patients' of the economy's workings, and that a large part of us are also economic agents as employees in business undertakings), or because such findings were in fact already implicit in the deductivist assumptions made throughout the mathematical model-building stage. In other words, the quantum of information or knowledge on the workings of the economic world brought about – by the work carried out taking the new, 'more precise', mathematical model as a basis – usually tends to be close to nil. There is also an aggravating factor: the approach, body, and conclusions of this kind of research papers in economic theory are expressed in a specialised mathematical terminology and language that have high entry costs; this even for other academic economists who are not specialists in the concerned field. It is a kind of inner language to the speciality which has, for outsiders, similar effects to the use of Latin in scholastic debates, or when it was used for communicating medical diagnoses in the Modern Age.

Mathematic language itself induces a perception of 'empiricism'

As reiterated, there is a dominance of *mathematical modelling* and of *mathematical language* in mainstream economics – if both expressions might be differentiated: the former as a theoretical project and, thus, a way of tackling and analysing the economic issues, and the latter as a preferential argumentation and communication tool in the field; a feature more apparent in those mainly-*methodological* economic-theory works.

Regarding the implications of the first (mathematical modelling), we might well consider it as "A *methodological* ideology (that) thus prevails in much of the modern economics academy whereupon a reliance upon mathematical methods is the proper way to proceed. In fact, some heterodox economists, just like their mainstream counterparts, have come to accept, as an unexamined presupposition, that contributions that are not mathematical are not serious, scientific, or other than woolly" (Lawson 2017, p. 38). The elements of mathematical modelling "(...) are tools. And like all tools they are appropriate for some tasks and conditions and not others. In certain contexts, tools used inappropriately can be positively harmful. This has been (and is usually) the case with the application of mathematical methods in economics. It has forced the discipline into irrelevancy at best, whilst diverting resources away from potentially insightful alternative projects and applications." (Lawson, 2015, p. 8).

As for the second dimension mentioned, mathematics as *the* language in economics, with *dialects* by specialities, the exemplified argument developed by Philip Klein (2006: 108-109) in this respect is a definite illustration:

> "(…) it is by no means uncommon nowadays for the math and the accoutrements of math to be presented more prominently than any underlying economic problems to which the material under review might pertain.

We present an example, selected more or less at random, from the *Journal of Economic Theory*, one of the newest (1969) of the highly prestigious journals (at least in the United States). The article is entitled 'Continuous approximations of stochastic evolutionary game dynamics'. The abstract of the article is as follows:" (below on the left)

'Continuous approximations that are ordinary differential equations (ODEs) or stochastic differential equations (SDEs) are often used to study the properties of discrete processes. We show that different ways of taking the continuous limit of the same model may result either an ODE or an SDE and study the manner in which each approximates the discrete model. We compare the asymptotic properties of the continuous equations with those of the discrete dynamics and show that they tend to provide a better approximation when a greater amount of variance of the discrete model is preserved in the continuous limit' (here, the authors and article reference)[8].	'Prose sentences in essays on economics might be declarative or exclamatory. Declarative or exclamatory sentences (DS or ES) are often used to describe the shocking properties of a given interrelationship. We show that the shocking aspects of a given interrelationship can be highlighted either by using ES or by using colourful adjectives in DS. We study the manner in which each highlights that which is shocking. We compare the flexibility that one acquires from the use of a variety of adjectives with the succinct properties which one finds are attached to a short ES. We consider whether succinctness or adjectival variety offers a better approximation of the reality which is inherent in the relationship under consideration'.

Klein continues:

> "We select this abstract (left hand side above), not because there is anything unusual about it, but on the contrary, because it seems quite typical (…). There does not appear to be one scintilla of a reference to any specific economic subject or problem in this article. It is all about econometric method. It is not unlike writing

[8] JET, N. 94:2, Oct 2000, 161-193

> a piece in the old days (when economists still fumbled with words) which might have read: .. (the text above on the right) ".

I have taken the liberty of putting here both Klein's texts in parallel (and underlining parallel expressions) to better highlight the informal comparison he is cleverly suggesting to the reader. He continues:

> "It can be left to the reader to consider whether or not the comparison is a fair one. (…). The comparison seems appropriate because just as rhetoric can improve writing on many subjects of which economics is but one, it seems clear that the subject of the abstract presented might be applied to many fields besides economics where differential equations can be appropriately employed." (Klein, 2006: 108-109).

Definitely, mainstream economics is mathematic/s/al, at the same time that as what the first adjective itself indicates: it has had, since the last 1940s, an overpowering position compared with others (and previous) ways of reasoning, thinking about, and explaining how economies function. This factual situation might, in a way, be considered as the outcome of a sort of *selection process* for economics approaches, driven across time by a given 'social-academic environment'. That is, as a result of a certain 'competitive pressure' favouring the mathematical approach, which, consequently, ousted incumbent and alternative approaches. This outlook concerning the issue has been argued, by an already quoted well-known analyst on the topic, as a driving idea to reflect on the 'environmental' elements of the overlying 'selective pressure':

> " (...) the rise to prominence of the mathematising project in economics conforms (or has aspects that conform) to a significant degree to the (Darwinian) evolutionary model, to the natural-selection metaphor. It is indeed a success story for the practices

concerned in terms of their eventual rise to dominance[9]. But it does not appear to be a success story by any wider or more laudatory criterion. In fact, if measured against the criterion of progress in knowledge and understanding of the social realm, modern economics is something of an unfortunate episode.". (Lawson, 2015: 247-248)

Summary: abstract-micro-empiricism in mainstream economics

Regarding the initially noted paradox about empiricism in mainstream economics' works, it can be concluded that the empirical element is more apparent than real. The 'pieces of the real economic world' formally addressed, in most cases boil down in fact to a sort of 'abstract micro-empiricism'. This basically consists of marginally relaxing some oversimplification of the GE model, or adding some detail to one of its core deductive assumptions (i.e., adding a micro-assumption). Thus, the academic paradigm of the General Equilibrium of Competitive Markets (perfect competition) has been employed over recent decades to introduce into it countless micro-situations and, therefore, additional micro-suppositions. This has mostly had a paradoxical result (insofar as being opposite to what is invoked by mainstream theorists): further distancing the so reformulated standard model from a reasonable representation and/or explanation of the functioning and overall outcomes of real market economies. These *ad hoc* micro models, resulting from that 'mode of production' of scientific contributions, end up drawing pictures that hardly tell us about real-world issues. Instead, they refer, by way of example, to 'an economy where one of its three

[9] In a subsequent work Lawson argues more explicitly about the social-economic and academic 'environmental' conditions and forces that, after World War II, would generate such a 'selection process'. In short: the decisive promotion of mathematical modern neoclassical economics by a conjunction of outside bodies (research's funding by public institutions and by private corporations) and the acquiescence in this respect of the top management of key academic institutions (in the US): Lawson, 2017, pp. 33-34.

production factors is available in variable quantities, there are two consumers, one of which has a quasi-concave utility function, and ...'. Always with the dominant, omnipresent, idea of whether or not such a modelled economy (i.e., its mathematical formulation) will tend to an equilibrium (i.e. the equations system to have a solution) or to more than one; or what will characterise (which mathematical conditions) this theoretical equilibrium; or what additional conditions (here, new deductive assumptions) would formally (mathematically) guarantee such equilibrium – also usually phrased as 'to reach a *Paretian* optimum of social economic welfare'.

The results from this kind of research strategy or theoretical approach tend to be a blend of over-simplifications about the overall economy (such as, e.g., 'let us suppose that there are two firms in the only non-perfect-competition sector, that there is no foreign trade, and that, ..') along with the formulation of some highly precise assumptions regarding certain elements of the sector/product taken as the 'empirical case' (e.g., costs function), or about the clients for it (e.g., utility functions), etc.

More precisely, as for those economics research works on economic theory itself, they mostly refer to a detailed case, problem or state of the affairs that could at first reasonably be associated with a particular aspect or detail of the workings of real economies, and that is presented as a way of bringing the standard GE model closer to the real world. However, these detailed cases are managed in abstract terms. This results in a sort of 'abstract empiricism' developed from micro assumptions inserted into the GE model's framework of assumptions. Thus, the contributions of most of the research works resulting from the mainstream approach consist of introducing a given modelled specificity within the overall GE model's presuppositions. There are also those of basically methodological content, in the sense of them being devoted to exploring mathematical properties of (a variant of) a model; (see the former example by Klein). To underline two basic features of this kind of modelling, and of the assumptions it leads us to make, one would be, of course, its overwhelming reliance on mathematical language. The other is its contributions consisting of micro-analysis, which are usually phrased as 'micro-foundations of ...', meaning what it would perhaps be more precise to express as a 'microscopic approach to a simplified outline of ...'.

Regarding basically econometrics' research works, the specific case, situation, or problem under analysis is equally micro-casuistic, though in these cases they are considered in empirical terms. Most of these papers are oriented to determine or deduce causal relationships (explanations), mainly through the development of regression and variance-analysis models. In this regard, there tends to also be a kind of imbalance; in this case between, on the one hand, the econometric apparatus, and, on the other hand, the nature of the quantitative, statistical, data used to run it (as concerns the degree of data aggregation, actual fitness of the database to this or that variable in the model, etc.). A consequence of this mismatch is that, when acknowledged by authors, their cautious interpretations of the quantitative results easily lead to conclusions or findings that may be close to trivial, or to a lack of relevance in terms of the quantum of knowledge provided.

Appendix G

A brief on the contents of the arbitrarily-at-random sample of research papers used in 6.3

Insofar as any kind of representativeness may be granted to the aforementioned for-illustrative-purpose sample of research papers in top economics journals, below follows descriptive notes resulting from dissecting papers' content:

- Approximately half of them are about *economic theory* strictly speaking (11 out of 20); the rest are basically of econometrics contents.

- Among the basically theoretical ones, (mathematical modelling), most of them (6 out of 11) do not actually consider a specific economic subject, situation etc. Their empirist specificity consists of introducing small modifications (micro-assumptions) within the standard GE model; e.g., a given partial modification of the *homo economicus* paradigm. As for the rest, in three of them the casuistic specificity considered is basically methodological (how to better measure income distribution, or the 'volatility of equity-market returns') or purely instrumental (e.g., an exercise on games theory). Thus, only a couple of them actually consider a specific real-world-identifiable situation or stylised fact – and even present some quantitative data in this respect, although just as an illustration of, both, the theoretical deductions from the mathematical model and the differences regarding previous models.

- As for the papers with basically econometric contents (9), most of them (6) do deal with specific real cases or situations; quite specific, micro-topics in fact, likewise that stated for the basically theoretical papers. The rest (3) are of mainly methodological contents: alternative techniques in econometric modelling, and options and properties regarding statistical tests; in these cases, the empirical data is used to illustrate or exemplify the respective methodological contribution.

Remark on statistical sources: Two of the papers (by different authors) use the same database: Standard & Poor's 500, 1871-199x, index of trading prices and returns, of US stock exchange; and 2 other papers work on the US 1802-20xx index of the same stock exchange market. That is, the databases in 4 out of the 9 econometric-type papers are of the same type, scope, and from the same country. This suggests that sometimes the availability of large databases is what ends up determining which research topics are chosen in economics. Moreover, 4 other papers also use (different) statistical data from the US. Adding these to the prior ones, it shows the weight of the particularities and available statistical data of a given country, US, in the type of econometric research published in leading *international* journals in economics.

This second bunch of research papers (econometric content's) also confirms a general remark regarding one of the features of the empirical research in economics (in social sciences, in fact), which merits to be underlined here: unlike what is the usual in experimental sciences, the quantitative results presented in a published paper are normally not verifiable, replicable, by readers; normally, other researchers.

> "If we focus on empirical contributions, specifically, it is clear that there are few attempts to repeat the results of others, progress the results of others, or even acknowledge the results of others. Even econometricians using identical, or almost identical, data sets are regularly found to produce quite contrasting conclusions, usually with little attempt at explanation. (Lawson, 2015, p. 149-50).

Indeed, it is not expected that you would put in your paper an appendix with the data series you gathered and used to run your econometric model; nor the equivalent: to describe the raw-data sources, the gathering processes and criteria, and the steps you covered to build your databases so that other researchers might exactly reproduce them. Therefore, it is between impossible and extremely difficult for other researchers to carry out a lab-replication to verify your econometric results and findings. Consequently, there is among us a professional custom of making an act of faith regarding the quantitative or qualitative results of published papers. There may be discussion or critiques on such results but limited to the interpretation of the econometric model's technicalities and alternatives, to the suitability of the applied statistic tests, etc.. This non-easy replicability would explain the almost absolute absence in economics research fields of reported cases of fraud (i.e., researchers that had manipulated their raw data or their results) in contrast with what we may sporadically read about concerning some cases in experimental sciences. The alternative explanatory hypothesis of a higher professional honesty level among social sciences authors is, in my opinion, quite unlikely.

Finally, another noteworthy frequent feature of the dominant research programme/epistemology in mainstream economics: after having introduced into the standard model certain hypotheses referring to a specific, though abstract, economic subject or situation (stylised facts), the formal conclusions that are drawn tend nevertheless to be sort of generalised, as if they were of general validity. That is, they are implicitly extended as applicable 'by approximation' to the real economies in which we interact. This tends especially to be the case when such conclusions contribute someway to reinforcing the standard paradigm: the image of a "virtuous automatism" theoretically resulting from the interplay of individual selfishness – mathematical version 2.0 of the popular (reductionist) version of Smith's "invisible hand" metaphor–; and, thereby, 'the no-need, or inconvenience, of public powers intervening in the economy, as a condition for 'optimising collective economic welfare'.

Chapter 7
Economics to explain the workings of our real economies

Modelling the functioning of a real market economy, not of an imagined one

In former section 6.2 an empirical-inductive explanatory model of the world of Production, Costs and Firms' behaviour in this respect has been summarised. Continuing this line, explanatory models showing the patterns empirically deduced regarding the rest of the rest of the economic topics dealt in the text are made precise below; mainly regarding Markets' Pricing and equilibria, Prices/Costs relationship (firms' profit rates), and markets structure (in the competition/monopoly axis).

The chapter closes with a final section that seeks to illustrate one of the most visible social repercussions of the standard model's core paradigm beyond economics: the case of the mythification of 'Competition' the term so used, in an abstract way and with a capital letter as if a meta-concept, an unquestionable, not-to-be discussed concept; as a driving-idea uncritically pervading the dominant political-economic discourse in our societies.

7.1 A realistic explanatory model of the supply side of the market for a given product or service

The aforementioned assertion/ conclusion on the absence of decreasing returns i.e., that the overall pattern observed for the average cost of a good (in the long-run; or, 'industry's average cost) is that it tends to be constant or decreasing, in relation to the volume of units produced – has moreover two relevant conceptual derivatives or consequences: 1) We can not actually talk about a *supply (price) function* for this or that good where the price required by supplier firms in the market is higher the higher be the total volume of quantities to supply in the long-run. In graphical language: we can not actually talk about a right-forward *growing* 'supply *price's* curve' for a good's *industry* or market, as the standard model's one, represented in figure 4. The pattern empirically observed in this regard would indeed come graphically expressed by a flat line parallel-above the long-run average cost (or industry average cost) of the good in question, as represented by the diagram in figure 7. And 2): without the standard assumption of 'decreasing returns', the 'theoretical corpus of the general *equilibrium of competitive markets*' cannot be sustained. Let us overview the scope, for economics as a discipline, of these two empirical-induced assertions.

The traditional '(growing) *supply price* curve', contrasted against empirical evidence

As we saw (3.4), the overall pattern observed for the average cost of a good in the long-run, *lrAC*, is that it tends to be non-increasing in relation to the size or productive dimension of a producer enterprise. Therefore, the *industry's* average cost, IC (the mean for all the producer firms in the *industry*) will tend to show the same overall pattern. That is, *lrAC* and *IC* are quantitatively equivalent concepts – whether the market for the good in question is covered by one, three, four, or 'many' producer firms with a size equal to or greater than the respective *minimal* optimal scale (*mos*), and that operate with similar efficiency. Therefore, the corresponding *industry's marginal cost* (IMC), would tend to be equally non-increasing (figure 6a). Therefore, the same applies to the respective *supply price* function since, as a theoretical concept, it is defined in the standard economic theory as 'equal to the *industry's marginal cost,* from the volume of units of the corresponding *mos* onward. Consequently, the standard model's postulate of the 'supply price's curve for any good [P_s=f(Q)] *as increasing* – which would mean: "the greater the sum of the quantities of product to be placed in the market by the sector's set of companies, the higher the price they are *forced* to ask" cannot be sustained. Nevertheless, this thesis of 'a growing supply price' (figure 4 in chapter 2) is another paradigm that occupies a central place in the ESM for postulating the automatism toward a *competitive equilibrium* in any *free* market industry.

Certainly, as we have seen (3.4, 3.5), when we move to contrast such standard theoretical reflection with empirical evidence, the fact is that in the reality of our economies we do not observe cases of sectors/ industries showing a supply price's function of the type: 'the greater the quantity to supply by all firms, the higher the selling price'. In the overwhelming majority of cases, the set of enterprises supplying a good ('the industry') tend, in the long-run, to increase their joint volume of production/sales *at the same or lower sale price* (supply price); without an apparent limit – as represented in figure 7, Ch. 3. This can easily be exemplified merely by reviewing the historic trend regarding goods such as televisions, clothing items, cars, or photovoltaic modules, for instance[1]. The same applies to agricultural products in general (milk, cereal 'x', ...). As well as to mining, against what is usually sustained (3.5.2): the possible exceptions sometimes suggested regarding the mining of rare earths or metals can actually be discarded. First, because of a lack of empirical data to ascertain whether they are indeed exceptions to the above-stated pattern; and second, because these commodities are dealt rather in a worldwide

[1] To take, as an example to the contrary, that of 'in days previous to Christmas, both the volumes and prices of select seafood are higher (or a similar popular phrasing)', entails a certain misunderstanding within economics. It would imply forgetting the concept of 'temporary shift (rightward) in the demand line', while supply is limited *in the short run.* Such a situation leads to (temporary) higher prices (and possibly to some, lesser, increase in average cost in the short-run, insofar as – to continue with the seafood example – fishery undertakings stress their capture capacity at the time), and ultimately to *higher margin rates* for suppliers. (See, on this, next entry on *short-run* market price).

market; which leaves them outside the theoretical framework and reasoning of 'the *supply (price) function vs. demand (price) function,* which refers to a given economy (a country, a State)', that is the conceptual framework of the ESM's paradigm.

Furthermore, within the ESM theoretical framework itself, to postulate that the overall pattern for the *supply price's function* (*supply price,* as a function of the *sum of the units* offered by every enterprise active in the market) for any good/industry responds to a *growing curve,* implies an internal formal contradiction or incoherence – as pointed out before (2.5.3, 6.2). An incoherence that affects the standard diagram-argument for the 'market equilibrium point' since the construct of an 'increasing *supply price*' is a key piece to build such standard concept (2.4).

Without the assumption of 'decreasing returns', the paradigm of the *general equilibrium of competitive markets* cannot be sustained

The above standard construct of 'the supply price in the market for any product or service grows with the total quantity to supply' (in diagram terms: 'the supply price function, P_s=f(Q), responds to a growing curve') relies, as we have seen, on the standard deductive assumption of 'decreasing returns to scale beyond the corresponding optimal scale for a good'. And, in turn, such a deductive assumption –it has been largely argued here: 3.4 to 3.7, 6.2..) is not at all supported by empirical evidence. A consequence of this is that the ESM, the 'theory of the General Equilibrium of competitive markets', losses its basis.

The fact is that extensive, mostly obvious, and historically reiterated, empirical evidence on *non-decreasing* returns to scale in the production/provision of goods in general has been put on the table of academic economists at least since the beginning of the

20th century. This, moreover, by renowned authors (like Sraffa, Lancaster, Cohen, Mansfield, Shepherd, ...); though this has been, however, without too much success. Their observations have been neglected, or simply ignored (3.7); at least by most of the authors of the reference economics/ microeconomics textbooks as well as university professors on these matters. More precisely, such observations have been mostly, although not totally ignored (2.5). Let us recap on this, given its implications.

The relevant issue in this regard is that, as a result of contrasting with empirical evidence, the ESM's deductive hypothesis of 'decreasing returns' should be rejected. And, without this hypothesis, its postulate of 'the spontaneous tendency, for any good, for there to be *many* modest producer enterprises, all operating with the same minimum average cost, and competing in the market on the basis of taking the price as given; i.e., without any of them having any influence on it (2.2)',[2] cannot be sustained. Nor can therefore be sustained its theoretical deduction: the paradigm of a generalised *perfect competition* in every market; i.e., the paradigm of the general equilibrium of competitive markets. It cannot be sustained because, in short, both, the deductive and empirical evidence show that there is nothing objective in the real economic world that prevents a given enterprise from growing well beyond the corresponding minimum-optimal-scale for its product or service and, thereby, achieving a significant market share, which may become a dominant, oligopolistic, or monopolistic, position.

What is surprising is that despite the reiteration of the overwhelming empirical evidence against this classical assumption of "decreasing

---

[2] To cite, as references for such assertion, two renowned exponents of the mathematical orthodox formulation of the general equilibrium model, we may see: Arrow, 1985: 112, and 2000: 172-4; and Mas-Colell, 1995: 336, 338.

returns to scale", it still is this 'U' *hypothesis* that remains dominant in academic texts and university syllabuses. A likely explanation in this respect may be that such a hypothesis of "decreasing returns" is precisely necessary to sustain the edifice of the standard model, as we have seen. To put it the other way round: if in mainstream economics the empirical evidence was assumed that, in general, the average cost of a good in the long-run tends to be constant (or even decreasing), the standard postulate of 'the free operation of the market generates a spontaneous tendency to perfectly competitive markets' couldn't be sustained. A similar, parallel, consequence would come out if the standard economic theory embraced the obvious fact that its assumption of 'equality in income distribution' does not hold in our societies/ market-economies, not even as a rough approximation. Were they taken into account in the standard approach, then it could not be postulated that the theoretical result associated with its mathematical model of Competitive General Equilibrium 'will be *an optimum of social (economic) welfare*'.

Last but not least, if the standard (micro) economic theory were to acknowledge the overall evidence of *non-decreasing returns* – which in diagram-mathematical terms means that the relationship *long-run average cost* regarding the *units of product* starts, graphically, as a decreasing curve and continues as a rather flat straight line, or something tilted downward, as in fig. 6a, then it would not be possible for such standard approach to use the elegant and relatively simple mathematical formulation that characterises – and conditions it. That is, to define and represent the unit costs of a good as continuous functions, perfect vertical parabolas; which means, for example, thee exists a single point of 'minimum' value for the corresponding unit cost. This standard graphical expression/definition presupposes (and obviously suggest to the readers of manuals or classroom attendants) that the world of production and firms' workings responds to – or may generally be described by – elegant second-order, perfectly differentiable, functions. Whose first and second derivatives are in turn used (albeit in an abstract, generic, way; e.g., $f''(q) = 0$, to say 'the independent variable has a minimum, at the considered q point') to build the system of simultaneous equations – also stated in abstract terms– whose conditioned optimisation defines the *general equilibrium* math model. This, to finally postulate that such system of equations will have a solution: a maximum of social-economic wellbeing (the 'general equilibrium' itself).

Of course, to mathematically formulate the pattern observed in the real world regarding the relationship between *average-cost* and *volume of production* of a producer enterprise (outlined in figures 5 and 6a in chapter 3) would obviously be considerably more complex than using simple parabolas.

> "To the extent that economist concern themselves with phenomena such as consumption, production, investment or human well-being, standard economic analyses involve the formulation of consumption, production, investment, and utility functions respectively. It is this emphasis upon functional relations that I shall argue is inappropriate to the analysis of most social phenomena"
> (Lawson, Tony, "Modern Economics: the Problem and a Solution", Fullbrook, 2004: 22)

I am sorry to repeat myself, but I must point out that highlighting the above assertions here does not constitute a very original work by me. Remarkable economists, such as those quoted above, have been pointing this out at least since the beginning of the 20th century. Some writers have even highlighted this with humour:

Figure 1: *The model is obstructing our clear view of the prevailing market, and the prevailing market is blinding us from other possible, equally "free" markets."*

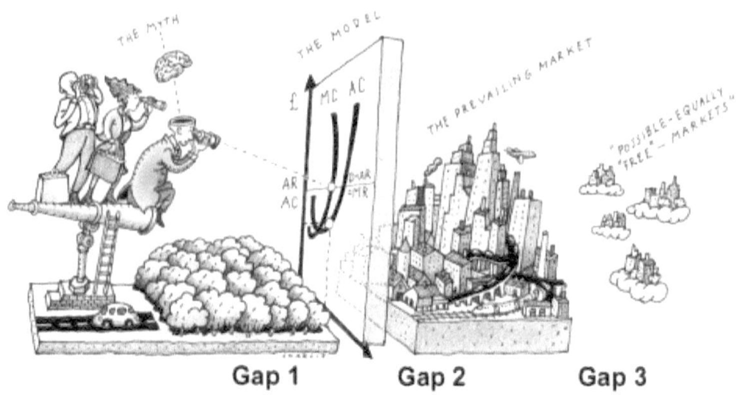

Tomas Bjorkman, "The Market Myth", *Cadmus Journal*, (2016), 2(6), p. 47.

Consequently, I must admit that the likelihood of my reiteration in this book having some echo in academia or in future authors of texts on economics/ economic theory – that will then be used for teaching economics – can be estimated as quite remote.

7.2 Empirically induced models of prices formation, enterprises' profits, and markets' structures

According to the empirical evidence on the general absence of decreasing returns, we may conclude that, a priori, there are no 'technological-economic' external impediments for a company that produce a given good to grow progressively in size to produce more and more units *at the same minimum-average-cost*; or even something lower. Thus, it can produce as many units as is able to place in the market maintaining or increasing its profits in the medium to long-run. Thereby, there is nothing of a technical-economic nature that prevents a company from ending up dominating to some extent the market for a given good; that is, achieving significant market power: power over the price.

That is indeed what is observed as a general pattern: companies tending to grow as much as their selling possibilities in the market allow – if this may increase to some degree their profits expectations, in the medium to long run. More generally, observational evidence points out that such an objective of growth, of reaching a greater size as a company, is mainly pursued because it provides certain economic advantages. This, logically, has consequences for the type of markets – in the competition/ monopoly axis – that tend to prevail in our market economies.

Overall pattern of enterprises' commercial behaviour: a realistic approach to prices determination – and, thus, profits

The ordinary mark-up pricing

Let us start this concluding remarks on these topics of market transactions by reiterating the obvious fact, widely argued in chapter 4, that firms, companies, do not sell generally at a price equal to their average cost, without obtaining profits, as the economics standard model, ESM, assumes as the default situation. The fact that, in this respect, we may find in some standard manuals that the term '*average cost*' is, more-or-less-implicitly, understood as 'the average cost properly said plus a certain value as '*normal-profit-per-unit*' does not substantially modify the oxymoron of 'in equilibrium (in a market/ capitalist economy) enterprises obtain zero profits'.

This mainstream theoretical concept of '*normal'-profit-per-unit,* ***npu,*** tends to be argued either in terms of certain remuneration on the financial capital invested by the company's owners, or of business-risks assumed. However, to use the concept of *average cost* in that way – with the underlying meaning of including a theoretical 'normal' unitary profit *as a cost* – is a semantic licence regarding the concepts of 'costs' and 'profits' that clashes considerably with reality: Neither in the field of National Accounting nor common language, nor of course in business accounting, nor legal-fiscal and regulatory language, are the profits (and costs) of companies understood in this way. Consequently, it can be said that such a 'semantic licence' has indeed an ideological effect on being used as a piece (terminology) of the ESM paradigm. Moreover, this effect – whether or not intended – transcends the framework of Economics as a discipline (see in this respect 'A biased definition, with ideological implications' in section 4.1).

In short, in the real business world selling prices are generally higher than the corresponding average cost. Enterprises, companies, normally operate at a profit. This is not because they behave in a fraudulent or irregular way, but because, obviously, it is something that is part of the system, consubstantial to a market economy, to a decentralised system of cost-minimising private undertakings in search of business opportunities (profits). This, within the limits of certain, established social norms and a given legal framework, of course. A legal framework in which, with a few exceptions (regulation of certain public services), prices are free, in the sense that are determined within a public relationship between offeror/supplier and buyer/customer.

The overall dynamism shown by market economies in general, would be another consubstantial element of the system. That dynamism in terms of, for example, generating innovations and offering goods that respond to the (changing) tastes and preferences of citizens; and which develops in a dialectical relationship with the former element, profits: in the business world of a market economy based on private enterprises, the expectations of (higher) profits are the main driver for companies getting engaged into activities aimed at innovating in products, services, technology, etc.

In any case, the overall pattern of direct observation shows that enterprises normally operate with a profit margin; and in the case of many large companies, with comparatively high or very high margin rates. More precisely, it is hardly controversial that in our market economies firms make their decisions regarding selling prices, and commercial strategies in general – marketing, advertising, market segmentation according to the type of customers/users, etc., trying to maximise their profit in the medium to long term; because, certainly, firms' profits also depend on these commercial policies. In other words, their profit is not mechanically pre-determined/limited by external parameters. 'Pricing policy' is an important part of business management.

The most commonly observed way in which enterprises determine/decide their *offering* prices is by applying a certain *surcharge percentage* on the corresponding average cost. This is traditionally known as *mark-up*; i.e., *price* = *average cost* x (1 + *margin rate/100*); $P = AC \cdot (1+m)$; (4.1). It is not precisely a discovery to acknowledge that such a net margin rate over cost, m, may be greater or lesser depending on the market power the concerned enterprise holds regarding the product/service considered. As well as it can also be observed that, considering all the enterprises supplying a specific product or service i.e., the industry or sector, when the market situation is one of reasonable or strong competition among them, their respective margin rates tend to converge around a certain limit/minimum value, *m*, below which the owners of those enterprises are not willing to continue to be so for a long.

More generally speaking, in these cases of 'reasonable competition' the empirical-induced overall pattern for the *supply price function* of the corresponding sector can be outlined as:

(offering/supply) *Price* = (*industry's average cost*) x $(1 + \overline{m})$; $P_s = IC\ (1+ \overline{m})$; where $\overline{m}$ stands for the average margin rate the enterprises offering the good in question apply. To put this in our traditional graphical language: the 'supply price curve' would basically be a horizontal line, at the level of the value *IC* $(1+\overline{m})$ monetary units, (taking, to simplify, the more usual case where IC is approximately constant – as discussed before), as represented in the diagram below.

Following at this sector or industry level, what is the order of magnitude of net margin rates in our economies? In general terms, this depends notably on the positions held by the sector's producer/supplier enterprises with regard to the *competition/market-power axis*, regarding the good in question. As well as also on the specific economic situation at the time – both the general one in the economy (country) and that of the sector considered, among other things.

> Publicly available empirical data on this subject are usually in terms of average values for sets of enterprises, m: those of a country, or more generally those of several specific sectors ('industries') of this or that country. This inevitably means that these data are average values for different companies, which may enjoy different degrees of market power and, therefore, quite different net margin rates. Summarising in this regard what has been developed in section 4.1, research on all US publicly-listed companies shows average values of: 1965, m = 15 %; 1980, m = 9%; 2012, m = 16%. As another example: using data from the 'Central de Balances' of the Spanish Central Bank, which gathers information on annual accounts for a wide sample of companies (over 480.000), it has been worked out that the average rate of net profits over total operating costs for 2017 was of the order of m = 9%.

Dynamics of markets' results

Simply de facto 'equilibria' …

Taking a specific product or service, for a given time period we can obviously observe – as a simplification – that a certain *quantity* has been traded at the sector level, at a specific (average) *price*. We may, following tradition, name such a pair of figures 'equilibrium point'; where the term *equilibrium* comes, in this context, associated with the long-run scenario. In this regard, a second element to stress on the topic of price-determination – at sector level – is that markets' results over time (i.e., transacted quantities and the respective prices) would qualify as a time succession of 'equilibria'.

Considering the market of a given good (sector), the combination of, on the one hand, its *industry average cost, IC(q)* – or its long-run average cost, *lrAC*; indistinctly, together with the *average net margin rate* of the enterprises active in the sector (*m*), and, on the other hand, the *demand function* for the good, $P_d(q)$, determines one 'market equilibrium point': a given *price,* and a given *quantity* (volume of units). This equilibrium point corresponds to the time for which the observation is made; i.e., a specific economic situation and a given state of the overall socio-legal-economic environment. The latter i.e., to also *consider the time dimension* – is fundamental to provide a minimally realistic schematic description of the subject. This is mainly because i) the *demand (function)* for a given good, $P_d(q)$, is subject to changes over time: buyers' tastes or preferences change; the level of real income changes; the prices of other related goods change; etc. In graphical terms, we tend to speak of 'demand function shifts (to the right/left)'. On the other hand, ii) the average mark-up, the *net margin rate* for the sector as a whole, m, also tends to oscillate over time. It may be greater or lesser, depending on the (better or worse) overall economic situation, and in some sectors it also shows seasonal variations, related to short-term, seasonal, demand shifts[3].

[3] The example commented before of "at Christmas time demand for selected seafood soars, as well as its prices" illustrates the case of a seasonal increase in the margin rate favoured by a temporary demand shift 'to-the-right' (much more quantities demanded at a given price). This is without ruling out that, in this short-term scenario, the also seasonal reactive scaling up in capturing activities by fishing undertakings may mean that their average costs increase somewhat.

Finally, iii) these two 'variables' together with the *industry's average cost, IC(q)*, which, as we have seen (figure 6a) in general tends to be constant or somewhat decreasing– determine that, *at a given time, one specific market equilibrium point (price- quantity)*, is *observed*. To express this graphically – as a version of figure 7 (the possibility of indefinite economies of scale is omitted here, to simplify):

Figure 9: *Market Equilibrium point, for a good/'industry' at a given time*

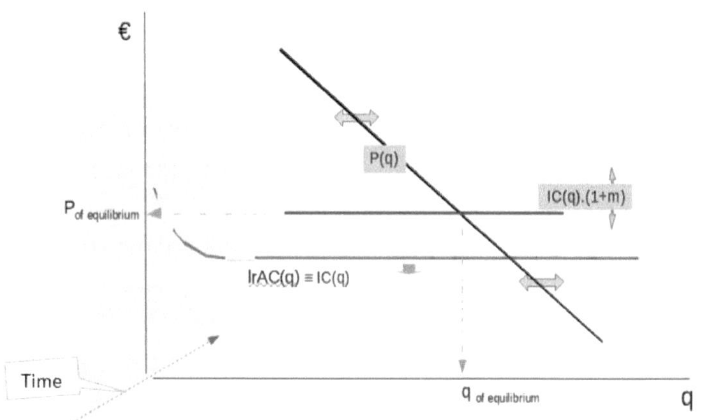

Where arrow, ▭, indicates that, for most goods, in the very-long-run, technological innovations may displace downward the full-efficiency, minimum, average cost, *IC*.

To put this in the compact expression by Steve Keen: "The majority of industries are instead likely to be better represented by (...) prices as being determined exclusively by costs, while demand set the quantity sold" (2011:136).

... in the long-run and in the short-run

The diagrammatical conceptual model of 'market equilibrium point', even in the closer-to-reality version (the above one; or the more detailed one in fig. 7, chapter 3) does not offer a properly useful formal explanation of how prices change and come determined in our market economies; mainly because it does not explain the fact of price oscillation for this or that product, sector, or industry. A reality usually phrased simply as *market price's time series*. The referred model-diagram tells us simply about which is the price –and quantity – that tends to prevail in the market for a given product, a certain demand's position given, *provided that* the conditions in the production sphere for the concerned good, (factors' prices, available technologies, etc.) keep steady. That is, if such conditions remain the same as those at a given (say, present) time; hence the third axis, time, in the diagram.

This traditional concept of market equilibrium responds, thus, to the long-run scenario, as we have seen before (3.4). But prices' oscillation occurs also and especially in the short-run when an unexpected change in the demand for a good is produced; for example, a jump upward. In such a case, market price increases, because of two main causes: 1) the fact that the industry's incumbent enterprises proceed to an immediate, improvised, increase in the volume of production – as an answer to the jump in demand – may entail a something higher average cost for them, because of forcing up their production capacity, say, in a weeks' time (3.3). The same may happen – something higher average cost – in the case firms from other industries may improvise to produce the good in question, temporarily adapting part of their production structure. In both cases, these firms' decisions respond to the fact of them being aware that a price substantially higher than the pre-existing one in the industry may now be charged to buyers. And 2) speculative or 'auction' pricing – what is rather business common knowledge: that part of the production volume that keeps being carried out by industry's firms as before – and therefore, at an average cost equal to before – is also sold at the new higher price. Which means a profit per unit higher than before for these incumbent enterprises; that is, the average mark-up rate becomes (temporarily) higher.

The production capacity of the whole of the industry/sector is a given one – which ideally has resulted from adapting to the average or steady demand. When this demand goes unexpectedly up, the sector/industry may have no capacity for immediately increasing the production volume significantly. Such an increase may require a given time for the incumbent enterprises; as well as a certain investment. In other words, in the face of a demand jump, in the short-run there is an *excess demand* regarding the installed production capacity of the whole industry's firms. This situation of excess demand allows these companies to (temporarily) apply a higher price, and thus get a higher unit profit – their average mark-up rate increases. At least, this is what we normally observe in such cases:

When a relative scarcity arises in a market in the short/mid-run, the corresponding price goes up immediately; *the price tends in some days, if not hours, to that the buyers are now 'prepared' to pay, i.e., to the maximum price the market 'accepts' at a given time* (see next below the illustrative example about oil prices). Not any discovery. This is indeed something of a millenary 'law' in trade; surprisingly skipped by standard economics when talking about prices if possible.

This market price situation endures until, in a given time: a) the market demand returns to the previous level, 0; or b) demand stabilises at some higher level than before, and the incumbent ones have accordingly expanded their production capacity, and/or new producer companies enter the industry. In both cases, once there is no excess demand (regarding the existing industry's production capacity), the market price goes down to the prior level, and so does the firms' average mark-up rate. Or the price may even be something lower in the case the industry's higher production volume had brought about some technological improvement associated with a lower long-run average cost.

The above sequence demand jump, market scarcity, the price gets multiplied, industry's capacity is adapted (or excess demand disappears), the price goes down– may be illustrated by, for example, what happened regarding the industry of surgical masks or medical ventilators during the first months of the 2020 Covid-19 pandemic.

Figure 10

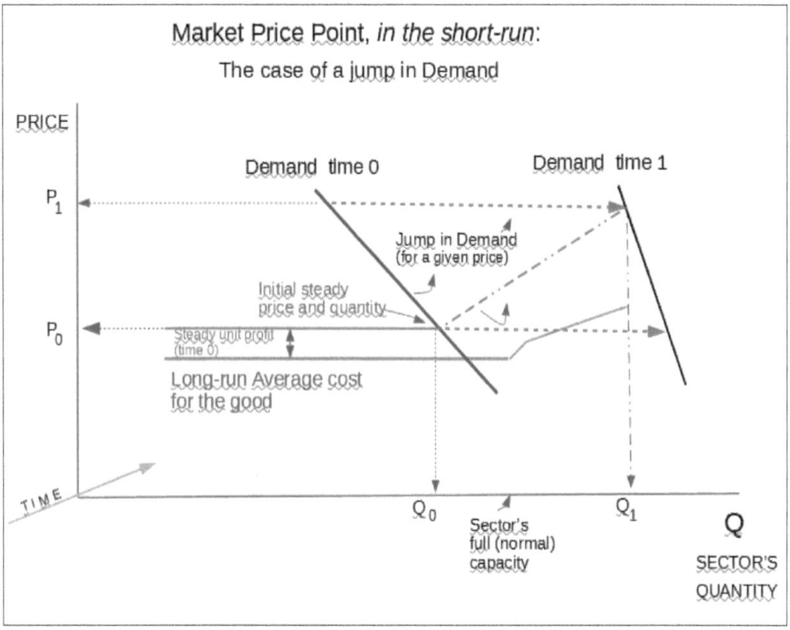

During the Covid-19 crisis, we might guess that those companies producing medical mechanical ventilators were operating at approximately their full occupancy level, covering an international volume of demand perhaps slightly growing. But demand got suddenly multiplied. Buyers of medical ventilators – public and private hospitals – shown then prepared to pay, say, whatever price to get more ventilators. And even some manufacturing firms of other sectors improvised production lines of ventilators.

In any case, the pre-existing producers sold their production (which they logically obtained at the same average cost as before or just marginally higher) at 'market price'; so getting extraordinary profits per unit. This is not because of a 'greedy' behaviour; it is just how markets work under such a supervening excess demand: the market price tends to that the buyers are prepared to accept at each time.

It could be argued that the above two examples would rather refer to the respective *international* market; but it seems reasonable to take them also as illustrative of other cases of temporary mismatch between demand and supply capacity regarding a domestic market; (think, for instance, of the before referred case of seafood in Christmas time). By way of a well-known example regarding auction-type price formation (in this case, also regarding an international market):

> Oil extraction costs are rather stable for the main producer companies; both in the short and medium-term. But when those companies publicly agree (OPEC cartel) on significantly reducing their whole production – and therefore the volumes they are going to offer next day, oil markets' price goes up in some hours' time. And the reverse when they decide to increase the millions-of-barrels per day to produce.

Firms' market power: completing the picture

The role of product differentiation and product innovation

The determining business reality of 'product differentiation & innovation' favours oligopolistic/ monopolistic situations, and therefore comparatively high profit margins, *m*.

Products/services differentiation is a defining feature in market economies, especially so since the mid 20th century: 1) different *variants* of one same good (regarding size and/or specific uses), 2) different *models* (of a good; or of this or that *variant* of it) in terms of quality or performance attributes, and 3) differences that affect to the *subjective perception/appraisal by potential customers* of this or that product of the provider company, or of the company itself, (5.1). In this context, *innovation* certainly plays a fundamental role. As one of the firms' key activities, it is in some cases associated precisely with differentiation practice types: defining new variants or different models, with different uses, characteristics, or quality/performance levels. Though, in most cases, the companies' innovation tasks tend to be aimed at the development of entirely new products/services. Regarding the third type of differentiation (that related to the subjective appreciation by buyers) this is largely a result of the enterprises' marketing and advertising policies, which are basically based on their use of *trade marks*, promoted and popularised through regular advertising campaigns; (whose costs – it worth underlining here obviously form part of the total costs of the enterprise concerned, which then are allocated among its different outputs).

In any case, product differentiation is a systemic, not anecdotal, practice in our economies; it is present in most enterprises. The main consequence of this is that this practice translates into a certain multiplicity of 'industries'; *industry* being understood here as a specific '*good*' and 'its *market*' in the sense, for both terms, assumed so far, and usual in economics. This means that each product's *variant* or *model* has its own average-cost, price, and market (and, therefore, say, its own 'equilibrium point' diagram like the one above!). In business language: *market segmentation*. This business reality entails, indeed, more possibilities of business situations of an oligopolistic/monopolistic type. In any case, the omnipresence of 'product differentiation' makes it quite usual that enterprises have a certain market power for this or that of their products/services (5.1). A reflection of this is that expressions such as '*gaining market share*', '*finding a niche market*' (i.e., a quasi-monopoly), 'marketing strategy', etc., are common and popular among professionals; a set of terms that relate to realities that long ago became key aim-ideas in the world of business management.

Implications from taking into account foreign trade

When we abandon the ESM's over-simplification that the economy is closed and so we move to *take into account the reality of foreign trade,* new elements are added to the former scheme, that help to explain the market structures regarding the axis competition/ monopoly–actually observed (following entry).

The standard concept of the market equilibrium point is developed under the simplifying assumption of among others a closed economy: This concept, in turn, is a required piece to formulate the General Equilibrium of competitive markets' theory, which also requires assuming full employment of labour and the rest of production factors: full employment of factors by domestic enterprises, which is also assumed pay to workers an equilibrium salary, etc. Therefore, when such simplifying assumption of no-foreign-trade is dropped, the explanatory value, regarding the workings of our market economies, of the concept/diagram of the market equilibrium point gets notably blurred.

This concept/diagram does not offer a useful explanation of the workings of firms, industries, and markets in our economies: when international trade is taken into account, foreign suppliers (may) add to the domestic ones, so giving way to a different meaning for the supply function. And the demand for the concerned product is then the sum of the domestic plus the foreign one; so, formally, the utility functions of people of other countries' (economies') come into play.

The fact of a given economy is significantly open to foreign trade no, or quite low, import tariffs makes that the way current diagram models describe prices formation, and, thereby, firms' profits, through the analytical tools of the *supply price* function and market equilibrium point, gets less useful: For some key products, services, and intermediate goods (raw materials, commodities, ..) the domestic market (prices, and availability) depends mainly or totally on foreign trade. For these cases, the usual standard diagrams that refer to a closed economy – are scarcely useful as explanatory models.

As for firms' market power, the fact that the possibility of exporting a certain good exists means that the effective market-demand can be greater than the domestic, internal demand. This opens the possibility to companies operating in such a sector to produce and sell on a larger scale, and so exploit possible indefinite increasing returns. Thus, in the specific case of a good whose technical-economic situation is, according to its internal demand, that of a *natural monopoly* – the volume of domestic demand is lower than de volume of units associated with the technically minimum-optimal-scale, if such a good is exportable the situation may cease to be that of a natural monopoly.

When we move to consider that the good under consideration may be imported, the consequence, in terms of the type of market that will tend to prevail is unpredictable: the entry of one (or more) foreign companies into the market can lead either to a greater degree of competition or the opposite. The latter is observed when, for example, one of the foreign newcomers is a large international company, with huge commercial power and financial capacity: such a company, by adopting a temporary downward pricing strategy (predatory policy), might achieve a high market-share, thus displacing incumbent companies.

As for foreign trade taken at the whole economy level, in the sense of its repercussions on key socio-economic variables (income level, employment, trade balance, salaries level, etc.), the overview about developed in 5.3.3 would be representative.

Enterprises' market power and markets structure

Summary on the empirical evidence regarding the degree of competition/monopoly

The ESM's premise that '*companies generally take the price as given, determined externally, in the market* (as if by an imaginary neutral auctioneer)', *is actually not borne out by empirical evidence.*

It is self-evident that most private companies tend in general to gain market power: growing in size as much as they can, thus trying to exploit remnant economies of scale and/or gain 'market share'. Or also by seeking (or generating) 'niche markets', that is, by coming across a product/service for which competition from other companies will not exist, or it will be minimal; in short, a certain monopoly situation; if even temporary. In business management, this is actually spoken of as a certain company's ideal objective, and also labelled in the professional jargon as 'the firm achieving a *competitive advantage*'. A policy that could also be described as 'competing (searching for a niche market) for having (almost) no competition'.

All of this is logically aimed at increasing the firm's margin rates. Consequently, the existence of companies that hold positions of certain dominance over their specific market/s (price is not taken as a given, but as a variable: 'pricing policy' is crucial to business management) is not exceptional but rather something that is indeed common, relatively usual, in our market economies. This is true whether we are talking about *unit cost-demand price* situations that would allow for several efficient producer firms (situations type IV, III, or II in Fig. 8, in chapter 4), as well as, of course, of those technological and demand's price situations that define a 'natural monopoly' (type I in Fig. 8).

The fact that for a certain good (product or service) the technical conditions for a competitive market exist (fig. 8, scenario IV), does not mean that the actual result ends up like that.

When, at a price somehow above the minimum average cost of the good in question, the volume of market demand, *Q units,* is 'many' times higher than the volume corresponding to the *minimal optimal scale* for that good (q^{mos} units), then the conditions for a competitive coexistence of 'many' (a maximum of Q/q^{mo}) enterprises in that market are present. That is, several undertakings of similar efficiency and size might operate at the same minimum average cost. Thus, the conditions exist for that market to be competitive. However, there is no guarantee that this will end being the case (4.2.1).

What is observed for such situations, which in principle would allow strong competition, is that the result is: sometimes a more or less competitive market, sometimes an oligopolistic one, and sometimes a de facto monopoly. And this is in similar proportions as the next circle diagram illustrates. What makes the situation lean toward one type of market or another is the interaction of the commercial strategies and policies of the companies operating in that market. In particular, it is a question of how specific would-be competing firms 'play' those practices aimed at gaining market share: offering certain product differentiation, exploiting synergies derived from producing other goods, carrying out merger operations, or buying out competing undertakings.

Empirical data show that the situations of companies with market power are not a minority. The three typical market structures – reasonably competitive market, oligopoly to varying degrees, and de facto monopoly– are observed with similar frequencies.

Market situations where a more or less strong market dominance/ control (high market share) by one or a few firms exists (i.e., a monopolistic or oligopolistic structure) are observed significantly quite more often than assumed in standard Economics/ Microeconomics texts. Generic evidence of this will be obvious, for example, to people with experience in business management or simply in carrying out activities within the business areas of *sales* and *purchasing*.

In more concrete terms, we have the direct empirical evidence provided by studies and research based on public statistics. These are studies that try to determine the *structure of specific markets* (sectors, 'industries', in this or that country) regarding the 'monopoly ↔ competition' axis. This structure has traditionally been measured by a *market concentration index* (4.2.2). Thus, for instance, an index C4 = 80 (%) means that the four companies with the highest turnover account for 80% of the total sales in the sector; which would mean a market structure of, at least, oligopoly.

Thus, for instance, such figure may result from a situation such as: four companies, each with a market share of 20%. But also from a market situation such as: one company holding a 40% market share, the second in the ranking, 20%, and the third and fourth, 10% each. As well as from a situation such as: a leading company with 65% of the sector's sales, and second, third and fourth companies with around 5% market share each. This latter one, thus, would correspond rather to an *oligopoly-monopoly* market situation.

In any case, market concentration indexes are measures that give us an idea of the degree of market power of the companies operating in specific sectors/industries, in this or that country. And such a measure, concentration degree, is obviously related to the profit rates of the companies concerned: the greater the market power of a company or a few companies in an 'industry'/sector, the greater the possibility of it/them applying a higher net margin rate, ***m***.

Historical data of these empirical measures have been surveyed in point 4.2.2. This is the case, for example, of Sutton's research on 197 industrial sectors in the USA, in which C4 indices in the order of 60%, 70%, and 90% appear with a clearly significant frequency in its tables. Or also, for the United Kingdom, the study, with similar results, for certain relevant sectors of its economy, published by its public statistics agency (ONS). Or, among others, the results published by another British public agency[4], applying, in this case, the other (also commonly used) market concentration index, the '***H***' index[5]. This latter report offers a study based on more recent data (corresponding to 2015), consisting of a statistical grouping of British companies in 380 sectors, the results of which can be summarised, by way of example, in the following diagram:

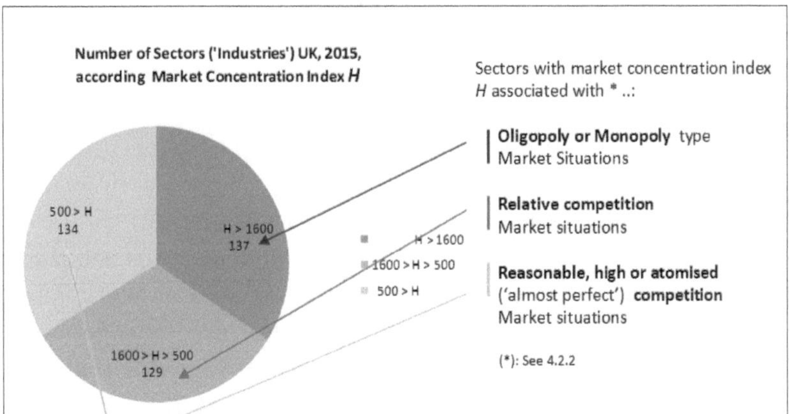

In short, the available measurements on market-share concentration in specific 'industries' of certain countries corroborate the generic evidence mentioned at the beginning: situations of greater or lesser dominance of specific markets by specific companies are not sporadic

[4] Department of Business, Innovation & Skills (see study's reference in 4.2.2)

[5] Herfindahl-Hirschman Index. This index results from adding –instead of the market shares of the leading 4 or 5 companies in a sector – *the squares of the market share of all the companies in the sector*. It is therefore a more exhaustive index – since it requires obtaining and working on much more data.

or exceptional in our market economies but rather, on the contrary, are characteristic, systemic. The concentration of market shares shown by the *C* or *H* indexes for this or that sector ('industry', a grouping of related products or services) is directly associated with positions of dominance in that market by one or a few companies. In particular, measures of $H > 1600$ or $C4 > 80$ for a given *industry* point to a 'strong' degree of market dominance, this meaning companies in an oligopolistic or monopolistic situation. These are, therefore, situations that allow the involved companies to apply comparatively higher net profit margins; in the sense of significantly higher than the average values for companies in sectors with lower market concentration, in the country concerned.

Reviewing standard conjectures on natural monopoly situations and marginal cost pricing

The 'technical' situation of natural monopoly *for a given good (the units demanded, whatever the selling price, are lower than the units associated to the minimum optimal scale for a producer firm,* q^{mos} *units; figure 8, situation I) is far more frequent in practice than what is assumed in the economics standard model. But the vast majority of these situations do not refer to socially sensitive or strategic goods regarding which we could expect that public authorities would regulate their market, as the ESM tacitly assumes* (4.3).

Most large elements of scientific and medical equipment (such as a nuclear magnetic resonance unit, or a scanning electron microscope) and industrial equipment (such as power generation turbines, or industrial robots), as well as commercial aircraft and most luxury products (such as yachts), fall under the technical concept of 'natural monopoly' summarised above: were they produced by the tens of thousands per year instead of by the hundreds, then their average cost would be quite lower. But, obviously, cases like these are not socially sensitive goods. It is merely that their parameters regarding unit-cost/ demanded-units make that the companies that produce/supply these goods are in a technical situation that in economics is defined as a 'natural monopoly'. In any case, they are in a kind of monopolistic situation; which means that they usually operate with a quite high profit margin. It also means that, if, for instance, the comparatively low demand for such goods were to double or triple, the average cost of production would certainly be notably lower for the producing companies, and the price would thus also probably be lower.

There also are, however, other, different, cases: certain socially sensitive and/or strategic products or services such as the distribution of electricity, gas, water, telecommunications, as well as urban transport, that also present technical features of natural monopoly; at least in part. The distinctive element here is that these are public services on which there is usually a political-social consensus regarding the need for them to be regulated by public authorities; especially regarding their prices, quality parameters, and access conditions for users. In some cases like urban transport, the consensus is not only on being regulated but also subsidised to some extent. However, this regulation (and subsidy) is not established precisely because such services may be qualified, on technical/economic grounds, as situations of 'natural monopoly' – as the theoretical paradigm of the 'marginalist criterion' postulates. Such a regulation and eventually subsidy relies, in these cases – and independently of technical/economic issues, precisely upon the fact that they are socially sensitive or strategic products/services. In the above example: in the sense that the acknowledged social costs from urban traffic pollution and congestion (negative externalities) can be reduced by promoting public transport. And one way to do this is by public authorities setting the regulated price (tariff), to be paid by public transport users, below the average cost, and subsidising accordingly to the operator enterprise.

Linked precisely to the above (price regulation, below unit cost), in mainstream texts we find an icon of ESM's *Marginalism*: the prior discussed *marginal cost pricing.*

Marginal Cost Pricing *is a traditional postulate of mainstream economic theory, derived from the concept of 'optimal price' (market equilibrium point) of the ESM's General Equilibrium model. It has been discussed to some extent in 4.3.1 due to its historical impact as an Economic Policy recommendation*. Given its role as a generally-accepted postulate – with fiscal consequences on public sector decisions it will be useful to summarise its implications as well as a rebuttal, in this final section.

In short, this theoretical proposition states according to the ESM's general equilibrium model that « an overall social-economic optimum is characterized for, and therefore requires that, the condition *Price* = *Marginal Cost* be met for each good in the economy (*allocative efficiency condition*). This condition is met (in the *general equilibrium* model) for all goods, except for those whose situation is that of a *natural monopoly*. In these exceptional cases, the long-run average cost of the single producing enterprise is always decreasing. Hereby, marginal cost is lower than average cost (*lrMC* < *lrAC*), for any demanded quantity. Consequently, to ensure that the said allocative condition – *Price* = *Marginal Cost* – is fully met in the whole economy, in these exceptional cases public powers must enforce it to be met, by ordering the producer company that the price be equal to the marginal cost. Since this entails a Price lower than the corresponding average cost, the producer enterprise will then come obliged to operate at a loss. Thereby, it *will have to be compensated for that, by a subsidy from public budgets* (allocative subsidy)'.

As the italics above underline, this is a *normative proposition*, an economic policy recommendation. It is the case, however, that this proposition can not actually be sustained, for two reasons, as developed in section 4.3. First, if we are consistent with the argument of the general equilibrium model, applying this normative proposition leads in fact to an absurd scenario. Second, the proposition is indeed an inconsistent deduction within the theoretical framework of the general equilibrium model itself. Let us review why:

Regarding the *absurd scenario*: To be consistent with the theoretical argument of the marginalist criterion, public authorities should in fact set a price below cost, and consequently subsidise, companies producing, for example, industrial and scientific heavy equipment, luxury goods such as yachts, etc., to mention former examples. This is because 'these are goods whose < unit-costs / demand volume > situation is that of a natural monopoly (*average cost* higher than *marginal cost*). This absurdity would be the formal consequence of the standard theoretical argument summarized above – on which the marginalist proposition is based. That is, on the grounds of assuring the theoretical *allocative efficiency* in the economy, the marginalist proposition would imply regarding the referred products whose technical cost/demand situation is that of natural monopoly– that public authorities set their prices below the respective average cost, and, consequently, subsidise to the producer firms; or more exactly, to the buyers of the concerned goods (4.3.1.b; 4.3.2).

As for the *theoretical inconsistency* (4.3.1.c), briefly outlined: In the context of the system of simultaneous equations of the *general equilibrium* model, the condition of 'price = marginal cost' for every good in the economy is a first-order mathematical condition for a conditioned optimization (maximization) of the *social utility function*. But one second-order condition for such maximization is that, for the point (unit cost, and quantity) for which the first condition is met, *the average cost of the good considered is not decreasing*; which means that the cost-and-demand situation for such a good is not that of (precisely) a natural monopoly.[6]

[6] It must be pointed out that to stress here this inconsistency is far from an original remark on my part. There is even a specific traditional field in economic theory in this respect: 'the problem of non-convexities'. This specialised literature mainly aims to formulate mathematical conditions – for abstract concepts such as *production functions* for specific goods of an economy – that define specific situations where the non-fulfilment of the referred second-order condition would be not a theoretical problem. These are complex mathematical conditions whose fulfilment, nevertheless, would not be objectively possible to verify in a real economy. (4.3.1.c; and Vergés, 2010, pp. 113-116). In any case, the existence of this, also modern-neoclassical, line of work ('non-convexities') has not meant that the 'standard' *marginal cost pricing* proposition has lost its old limelight within conventional economics.

7.3 Socio-political incidence of mainstream economics' standard model; 'competition' used as a myth

The standard economic theory of international trade conditions international trade policies

The standard neo-classical explanatory model, ESM, presupposes as a simplification that the economy whose workings it explains is a closed one, without foreign trade. When this oversimplification is dropped, the analytical picture changes substantially; a change in addition to what has been pointed out regarding market-price's point in the previous section. It is about the repercussions of foreign trade as a whole on the social-economic wellbeing in the concerned country. In classical economics, this issue early gave way to formal elaborations implicitly linked to the economic policy debate on protectionism vs. free foreign trade. An elaboration that led to the classical *theory* (or *doctrine*) *of international trade* of David Ricardo, or *theory/law of comparative advantages*. Though this is usually presented as a specific explanatory theory, it is clearly linked to the ESM's paradigm of the *general equilibrium of competitive markets*; and, more precisely, to the deductive assumptions that sustain it.

In a way, this theory of *comparative advantages* extends the orthodox idea of 'free market/competition' to the realm of international trade. Its most outstanding distillate – which (also) transcends the field of economics, is the widespread economic policy idea of promoting 'free international trade as a source of economic advantages for the (all) countries involved'. In other words, the *economic policy recipe* of 'promoting free international trade overall, because it benefits all participants' is based on the theory of comparative advantages. This is therefore a relevant topic, which has been discussed in some detail in section 5.3. Certain aspects of that discussion (5.3.5) do, however, deserve, to be distilled here.

A 'classical' theory with a high impact outside economic theory

As with the classical topic of *decreasing returns*, the standard theory of international trade is based on several theoretical assumptions, and on a key concept: the existence of productivity differences (comparative advantages) between countries, for the production of specific goods. In its basic formulation – where a situation of two countries and two goods is considered – this leads to a theoretical conclusion, regarding foreign trade, which, in fact, operates as a normative proposition: 'free bilateral trade between two countries, based on specialization – each country focuses on producing the good for which it has a comparative advantage, is beneficial for both countries. This, in the sense that, by opening up to free trade, each country, devoting the same workforce and other resources ('capital') it employs under autarky to produce both goods, will have, as a result of specialization & exchange, more units of one and the other good available for consumption (or investment).

Another parallelism with the ESM's topic of *decreasing returns* is that this theory or model of *comparative advantages* is essentially based on an argument by classical economists and, specifically, on a formulation by, also, David Ricardo. And the third parallelism is that the theory of comparative advantage has also widely transcended the field of economics. In the political arena, its proposition is used to defend free trade between countries, opening up to the outside world, tariff 'disarmament', etc., as an indisputable virtuous pattern in international trade relations, 'as economic theory has demonstrated'. In short, if the general model, ESM, is used in the economic policy arena often skipping on the premises and assumptions on which it is based to defend the primacy of free market rules in the domestic economy, the *theory of comparative advantage* is used often (also) neglecting the premises and assumptions on which it is based – to defend the idea that free foreign trade is an indisputable source of economic advantages for the countries involved. This academic topic makes part, indeed, of an old debate in economic policy and among economists -at least since the time of the last mercantilism.

Those elements of the debate with the most contemporary relevance are underlined below.

The explanatory goodness of a theory or model depends largely on the realism of its assumptions. These upon which the classical formulation of the theory of comparative advantage is based are mainly: « Mobility of financial Capital from one country to the other is not possible, nor it is for Labour. There is full employment in both countries. Wages are similar in both countries (applying the exchange rate) before engaging in trade, or they tend to equalise throughout free trade. The trade between the two countries is carried out between economic agents in a framework of free competition (import/export companies with similar bargaining power). As a result of free exchange, the *trade balance* between the two countries tends to *be balanced* ». In short, it is assumed that the two involved countries are quite similar socially and commercially, except that each has a certain comparative advantage regarding the other. Of course, it is also assumed that they do not apply import tariffs; besides of the obvious simplifications of 'two countries, two goods, and two factors'.

Certainly, in academic economics this basic theory or model of comparative advantage has oriented over time to become more general; mainly via mathematical language: generalizing the Ricardian model to more than two countries (multilateral trade), to more than two goods, relaxing some of the assumptions, etc. (references to this have been offered in Appendix D). These mathematical models inevitably incorporate new, more specific theoretical assumptions, more variables – not always easy to quantify, and logically reach rather complex theoretical conclusions. Hence, it is not an easy task for economists working on this topic to test such theoretical results empirically. Among other things, this is mainly because any of the variables that are usually taken to measure the effects on social welfare of a country that opened up to free foreign trade – say, employment, unemployment, average salaries, GDP per capita, etc. simultaneously depend on other variables alien to foreign trade; which, moreover, not always are quantitative but also consist of economic policy measures and regulations. Probably because of this complexity – that makes these less simplified, mathematical, models be rather confined to academic life, the basic Ricardian model (as presented in 5.3.2., a to c, and summarised above) is, in fact, the one that continues to dominate in the manuals; that is, its corresponding thesis/proposition. This is what graduates in economics will generally remember on the topic: 'free international trade between two countries (based on their respective comparative advantage) will benefit both'. Where, 'free trade' means eliminating tariffs and other forms of restrictions on imports; or, in a frequent equivalent expression, 'to dismantle tariff barriers' with the negative connotation the terms 'dismantle' and 'barriers' convey: tariffs on imports implicitly presented as something intrinsically negative and where the content of the parenthesis above (what the respective comparative advantage of each country would be) is often left as something rather indeterminate, fuzzy.

What empirical contrasting of the standard theory of international trade tells us

As abovementioned, contrasting the general proposition of the classical model or that resulting from neoclassical complex mathematical formulations derived from it– with empirical evidence on the matter, regarding this or that country, faces certainly serious difficulties. It is, nevertheless, more feasible to verify to what extent the basic assumptions of the theory are or are not reasonably fulfilled in reality overall – since the relevance of the theoretical reasoning and the validity of a model's proposition depend to a great extent on the degree of realism of the underpinning assumptions. As well as also to review what economic history and recent generic observational evidence show us so far about the socio-economic repercussions of the currently dominant 'international free trade' which led to globalization.

Following these guidelines, from the discussion at the end of the previous chapter 5, it merits to be underlined that,

- The assumption of 'non-mobility of Capital, from one country to another with a relatively higher productivity in some production (comparative advantage)', is not given overall. At least since the years of the turn of the century, from the 19th to the 20th, and, to a much greater extent, with the practical worldwide liberalisation of capital flows since the 1990s.

- The assumption of 'full employment in each country' does not generally hold, except in an approximate way for a few pairs of countries; nor is the approximation proposed in this respect 'constant employment', after vs. before liberalisation confirmed.

- Regarding the assumption of parity or of a trend towards equalisation of wages between countries, the fact is that wage differences between countries involved in a mutual trade are in practice more than significant and, in general, relatively stable. Moreover, these easily observed strong stable differences are precisely the basis of a significant part of international trade; which, therefore, would not respond to the theory of 'comparative advantage' itself; unless we shift the original reasoning by moving to consider the fact of persistently lower wages as a comparative advantage in itself (we will return to this below).

- The assumption of (a trend towards) equilibrium in the ex-post *trade balance* is also not generally met. The consequences of this for a particular country depend on the sign of the imbalance, its relative importance, and its historical trend. In this respect, observational evidence (like that in Appendix E) shows that many countries that followed the path or recommendation of opening to foreign trade have significant recurrent deficits in their trade balance, year after year; this is notably among less developed countries.

Taking the first three assumptions, their non-fulfilment means that the traditional model's argument cannot in fact be sustained. By way of example, let us consider the first one: with Capital mobility between countries, if the situation using the traditional Ricardian example is that country P has an absolute advantage (greater efficiency, productivity) in both productions, 'cloth' and 'wine', the result of free trade would be rather that Capital from country E would be invested in country P to produce both goods there, part of which would then be exported to country E by those investors.

As for the non-fulfilment of the fourth assumption, and specifically in the case of a country with recurrent and proportionally relevant deficits in its trade balance, socio-economic variables not considered in the standard model become relevant since these *recurrent* deficits have social costs for the country: First, annual *trade balance* deficits may have to be covered by external borrowing, with the consequent financial burden. Or the deficit comes covered by an inflow of foreign capital (a surplus in the country's *capital balance*); in which case, diverse economic consequences can be derived. One of them may be, for instance, that the inflow of foreign capital means that the decision power over part of the country's wealth (heritage, domestic companies' shares) moves to another country's residents. Secondly, scenarios of recurrent deficits in the *trade balance* are frequently associated with an *induced increase in unemployment*, due to a loss of domestic economic activity as a consequence of reiterated imports-exports disequilibria. Therefore, social costs derived from that increase in unemployment arise. The conjecture or recurrent argument in standard economics regarding that the people who become unemployed displaced by new imports or delocalisation/ offshoring will get employment in other/new economic activities within a reasonable time (here, sometimes it is added: 'if the labour market is flexible enough'), is also not met in quite many cases.

Economic history and current generic evidence teach us that the proposition of the standard theory that sustain the International Liberalisation's agenda ('under free foreign trade based on the respective comparative advantage, both (all) countries involved benefit economically') certainly clashes in many cases with generic observations on different countries (5.3.3a).

- Since historically 'free international trade' is, in economic policy, the opposite to *protectionism*, a traditional criticism of the theoretical model refers to a point widely debated in the economic literature on the subject: the fact that historically the traditionally more industrialized countries (England, USA, Germany, ...) did not manage to become so (19th century and first half of the 20th century) by precisely practicing a 'free foreign trade', without imports tariffs or restrictions. Rather, some kind of protectionism or international position of dominance (imperialism) was decisive for them in this regard. From this critical outlook, the fact that currently industrialized countries press, within international bodies, for less developed countries to agree to 'tariff dismantling' is in the words of a well-known academic economist (5.3.3a) like 'kicking away the ladder' (of industrial development) for these less industrialized countries.

- The very basic idea of the classical model that each country has one (at least) comparative advantage on which to base (and benefit from) its foreign trade – does not seem to be realistic, at least over the last decades. There do not seem to be as many comparative advantages as there are countries, worldwide (5.3.4). This is the case, unless we consider as a comparative advantage (contradicting one of the assumptions of the standard model) the fact that wages in a country are persistently remarkably low in comparison to those of its trading, more developed, partners; or the fact that a country 'achieves' the 'comparative advantage' of having specialised in producing a specific product or service on a very large scale: literally, to produce it "for the whole world". That is, the advantage of exploiting indefinite increasing returns of scale.

- With regard to the two above points, it should be stressed, however, that in many cases – imports from, or delocalisation to, countries with comparatively very low wages, as well as specialization of some of these countries in manufacturing a product in conditions of large mass production, to export it– this type of 'unequal trade' has, over the last two decades, certainly allowed millions of people to be lifted out of situations of extreme poverty in these (then) less developed countries. This is certainly socially invaluable. Though, of course, it has no relationship with the line of argument of the theory of international trade; that is, with the economic concept of *comparative advantage.*

To express the former in more general terms, the premise of the standard theory that foreign trade takes place between 'countries with similar conditions' does not hold in general. In addition to those mismatches mentioned above, differences regarding industrial/ technological development, and the presence, in this or that country, of large companies with multinational commercial power, are strongly determinant. And there are also substantial differences in the legal and regulatory framework. All of this makes it easy for analysts to find more or less stable or encrusted situations of what has been called an *unequal exchange.*

Social repercussions of International Liberalisation, apart from the theoretical model: Winners and losers

In the basic model of the *comparative advantages,* as well as in the specialised literature on the field (more complex models), there is a tendency to the reasoning in terms of 'countries', as if they were the economic agents that 'export' and 'import' specific goods at specific prices. This induces certain mystification, due to its excessive simplifying ellipsis. It is obviously *enterprises* from this or that country that mostly decide what to produce, export, import, or delocalise; to/from which foreign firms, at what prices, or under what conditions; not 'the countries'. *Countries,* i.e., the public authorities, decide whether or not to set, or not, tariffs or restrictions, and eventually have to cover the social costs derived, for example, from persistent trade deficits.

Following this line, if the aim is to ascertain whether or not free foreign trade benefits "all parties", or in which cases, or how, it is necessary to distinguish, at least, between *enterprises* as the 'economic agents' in the foreign trade as legal entities (with annual income statements, etc.), the *workers* they employ, and the *State.* Because ,in terms of *social welfare,* 'the parties' basically encompasses certain enterprises, their employees, and the Public Sector of each country. A specific but very relevant kind of foreign trade, *delocalisation,* illustrates this well. Summarising the discussion on this in 5.3.5: The *companies* of the 'host' country (with low salaries) win, in terms of their income statements. The workers they employ also obtain some gain; some of them because previously were virtually unemployed, and all of them because of a possible induced increase in their low salaries. And the country's *public treasury* probably gains too, in the way of a certain increase in tax collection. As for the developed, 'guest', country, a *company* that has delocalised benefits, or in any case does not lose (otherwise it would not have decided to delocalise). However, *the workers* that, as a consequence, have become, directly and indirectly, unemployed, experience a loss, not only because the unemployment benefit they may receive is below their lost salary, but also due to the non-monetary cost entailed by the unemployed situation itself. And *public powers* will also experience a loss: the increase in unemployment benefits to pay, as well as other related contingencies.

Furthermore, unemployment induced by international liberalisation also occurs 'on the other side': in less developed countries with comparatively low salaries. There are cases where everything seems to indicate that the country has a given properly comparative advantage, but where, nevertheless, this advantage does not become effective, even though the country has been open to free international trade for years. This, due to the fact that other also less-developed countries have the same comparative advantage, perhaps even to a greater extent; or because the advantage of another 'competing' country consists simply of it being home to a large firm with great international commercial power in terms of selling and purchasing; a case, the latter, where the standard model's tacit assumption of 'free competition among equals' would be not fulfilled. Whatever the case, the result for the first country is persistent commercial deficits, and a more o less endemic induced increase in unemployment (as in the real case-example developed in 5.3.5).

Specialisation, dependence, and vulnerability. Last but not least, the fact that a given country becomes specialised in something, in line with the theory of comparative advantages, inevitably entails stopping producing other products or services in the country. This leads to a certain situation of dependency on the outside world concerning those goods. Depending on its nature, this dependence may be rather anecdotal, in terms of socio-economic repercussions: pure international division of work. But, in the case of certain goods, such dependence may somehow condition the future of the country's citizens. Thus, if a country, as a consequence of free foreign trade dynamics, has stopped producing certain technological-content products, there is a high probability that it will become technologically dependent on abroad to some extent. Dependence can moreover lead to *vulnerability* (as a country, as a society) if it affects certain basic foods or key health products or also some information technology items. In these cases, if everything runs fine in the complex multilateral mechanism of international flows and relations, this dependence or vulnerability does not in principle translate into social dysfunctions and costs for the country. At least in the short run: the country even 'benefits' from importing these products at a 'very competitive' (cheaper) price. However, in the case of not so smooth course of international relations or of the world transport web, in the event of a disruption in international supply chains or the financial and trade sys tem, a country may become dramatically dependent on other countries for critical goods. Something that may have unpredictable social consequences for many countries, regardless of their level of development like the distortion and subsequent shortage of basic healthcare supplies unleashed by the 2020's Covid-19 pandemic revealed.

Incidence on economic policy measures of mainstream economics' driving *principles*

The mainstream economics' practice of continuing to maintain non-contrasted axioms, assumptions, and premises of conventional neoclassical theory condensed in the ESM, apart from not properly responding to the scientific method as regards a theoretical explanation of the real economic world, has significant ideological consequences in socio-economic life. This is mainly through two driving tenets: *Equilibrium* and *Competition*.

'Equilibrium'

The following remark on this topic is not regarding the concept in technical terms, as when referring to the market equilibrium point for a good, as usually represented by a Price/Quantity diagram as in figure 4a (in chapter 2), fig. 7 (in chapter 3), and fig. 9 and 10 (in this one). For a given product or service, over a given time period – weeks, months, we may observe that the customers as a whole buy each period a certain quantity at a certain average price. Thus, there is always a market equilibrium point, so to say; even if subject to changes over time: we may speak of dynamic equilibria. This is the case independently of the market structure for the specific product/ service. In this regard, as we saw, observational evidence shows that market situations of lesser or greater dominance by one or a few enterprises (monopoly or oligopoly structure) are considerably more frequent than is normally implied or assumed in mainstream economics/ microeconomics textbooks (4.2.2).

This *de-facto* dynamic equilibrium is not, however, the driving idea that pervades mainstream economics and beyond. It is that concept of equilibrium associated with the construct of *general competitive* equilibrium as a whole: In manuals and classrooms, the formal description of market economies consciously or unconsciously transmitted is dominated by the core idea more often than not, implicit that a market economy is *a system normally, 'by default', in an overall equilibrium*. This, moreover, would be a virtuous equilibrium since would be associated with an optimum economic social wellbeing. An equilibrium that, nevertheless, would risk being distorted, not only by a deficit of competition in this or that market/sector but also by governments' economic policy measures or interventions. Thus, the underlying message to readers or students is that free markets overall labour market included, as well as the markets for the rest of the production factors leads to a system of automatic equilibrium for each product, service, or commodity. That is, to a general equilibrium whose required conditions are supposed should constitute the target of any benevolent government. In short, 'Equilibrium' appears as the core concept in mainstream economics; both at introductory and upper academic levels.

This is striking if we take into account that the main recurrent issues raised by economic reality, the main socio-economic problems that challenge economists, have to do precisely with more o less permanent or recurrent economic *disequilibria*. To start with, that of *unemployment*; which, however, from the perspective of the standard model, it is a disequilibrium due to the fact that wages do not fall enough for the *demand* for labour to increase so as to come close to the labour *supply*. And similar considerations receive other disequilibria or they are considered either as imperfections, regarding the model, such as persistent and significant *inequality in income distribution* in our societies, *foreign trade unbalances, public budget's deficits* caused by economic downturns, etc.

These disequilibria are indeed dealt with in specialised fields of academic economics, although with no visible substantive incidence on the overall standard model's paradigms. Let us consider, by way of example, the first disequilibrium: *unemployment*. In this respect, we have on the one hand, the academic descriptive-analytical branch of 'labour economics'; and, on the other hand, the 'economic theory of labour market' usually in different university departments. Articles and advanced textbooks in the latter line tend generally to take a micro-approach, to focus on micro-topics; for example, the effects of a specific scheme of unemployment benefits on the unemployment level. These usually consist of academic works whose presentation suggests a plausible likelihood of being of interest to Labour relations' analysts and economic policy makers. However, and despite their tendency to use the mainstream economics' epistemological framework, starting by building their models with the usual ESM mathematical language, overall these works do not seem to reach up beyond their own specialists' field, as far as the mainstream academic economics corpus is concerned. That is, these contributions have not appreciably changed the dominance of the abstract and totemic idea of *equilibrium* in present mainstream textbooks and manuals.

Marginalism

Marginalism is an epistemological major feature of mainstream economics as we have seen through chapter 2 and discussed in section 3.3 ('A look to marginalism'). Were we asked to suggest a few terms to denote mainstream economics' basic defining elements, we could perhaps choose 'marginalism', 'mathematical discourse' and 'self-regulating (economic) system' (equilibrium). On the other hand, Marginalism is moreover one of the ESM's theoretical tenets that have implications beyond the economics discipline. It is present in socio-economic debates and economic policies' design, regarding significant social issues. One of these is the field of *wages' bargaining and policies*, as for the use, in this regard, of the theoretical construct of 'marginal physical productivity of Labour'; and another one, the *regulation of the electricity market* in a country, as for applying the rule of 'marginal cost pricing' we have seen in 4.3.1, (d) and (e), the core piece of the General Equilibrium model.

(a) 'Marginal physical productivity of labour', in *wages bargaining* arguments. The neoclassical standard topic of '(decreasing) Marginal Physical Productivity of Labour' (units of product obtained by a firm from increasing the hired workers by one the fixed Capital endowment remaining constant) stems from the classical Cobb-Douglas production function (as we have seen in section 2.4): namely, it is its first derivative regarding the variable *Labour*.

In modern neoclassical economics, this concept leads to talk about the 'salary-and-employment-of-equilibrium' for a given production or sector. This 'salary of equilibrium' with its implicit normative meaning of 'the fair salary to be paid' is defined as 'the market value of the marginal physical product of labour'. By way of example, if by hiring one more worker the volume of production of the firm increases in U units, the net[7] market value of these units of product would be according to the mainstream setting the 'salary of equilibrium' that

---

[7] 'Net' value, in the sense of deducing from sales' revenues the firm's costs for factors other than 'Labour'; the usually most relevant ones: costs of raw materials, intermediate goods, energy, etc.; (in the over-simplified scheme of the Cobb-Douglas production function, the only other factor is Capital, which is supposed to be constant when talking of 'marginal physical product of Labour').

will end by paying the firm to all its workers; (an illustrative critical example about this may be seen in Schlefer, 2012:104). This is, thus, a neoclassical *normative* postulate since it is telling us which the *fair salary* to be paid by firms should be in each case. Though, not always its formulation makes explicit such normative character. On the contrary, in most instances, its formulation, in teaching and textbooks, is in terms of: 'economic rationality in the world of production makes that, in the production of a given good, the involved producer enterprises end by paying the corresponding *salary of equilibrium*'.

In any case, curiously enough, such a postulate sound somehow as *materialist* as the also classical Karl Marx's theoretical description of the determination of salaries in the capitalist economy. In both cases, what is supposed to determine salaries would be not a human but a technical issue: in the case of orthodox neoclassical theory, the net market value of the increase in production resulting from hiring an additional worker over a month; that is, a technical value; instead of a value somehow associated with the cost-of-living for a person. In both theories, salary would thus be a value disconnected from what an ordinary person would need in order to lead a decent life whatever the latter might mean in each personal, historical and geographical context. Following with this admittedly arguablecomparison of both theoretical explanations, let us note that the mainstream economics *argument* (salary = market's net value of the marginal physical product of labour) would be rather the same if the question to formalise on was about another 'living non-human production factor'; as it could be the case of a producer firm that also hires non-human living beings; (you could imagine the owner of a vast grassland that rents dairy cows from nearby peasant families, on a monthly basis, to produce pasteurised packed milk: how much would it be the 'fair monthly-rent per cow' to be paid? Obviously: 'the net market value of the marginal product ...', etc.).

Coming back to the issue of salaries determination, let us underline an asymmetry when comparing both theories: Marx's materialist formal description of the determination of salaries in a capitalist economy tends to easily be deemed as *ideological* not only in orthodox-dominated ambiences. While, when the similarly-materialist neoclassical theoretical explanation regarding the 'salary of equilibrium' is read in a mainstream textbook, this description tends to be widely understood as *scientific*.

Anyway, this ESM theoretical concept of 'marginal physical *productivity* of labour' and its (also theoretical) use to define the 'salary of equilibrium', is, as noted above, an example of orthodox economics' concepts that reach beyond economics itself, playing a direct role in socio-economic life. In this case as for in-practice-assumed ideas regarding collective bargaining, wages negotiation, between workers (or union) and the corresponding company (or industry/sector's employers' association). The starting point of the latter in the bargaining uses to refer to the 'principle' that the percentage increase in salaries cannot be higher than the increase in productivity over, e.g., last year; regardless of which the consumers' prices inflation rate has been over the same period; even if this is twice the statistical increase in productivity. Moreover, was this just the case, expert economists around the collective bargaining would warn against salaries increasing higher than productivity, because that would even accelerate the inflation rate –"so making, in the short-middle term, such salary increases ineffective as for real purchasing power".

Let us note that such arguments and experts' warnings are mathematically equivalent to defending preserving the margin rates of the involved companies; at the same time that the collective utility of the involved workers reduces, proportionally to the difference between the increase in the cost of living and the increase in salaries.

(b) 'Marginal cost pricing', and the *design of the electricity market.* Another of these ideological consequences of the mainstream paradigm beyond economics itself, connected with the tenet of *equilibrium*, is the surprising direct impact of the standard model, or (micro) economic theory, ESM, on *government regulations* and public decisions regarding prices. This impact is basically through the soaring idea/dogma, discussed before, of 'marginal cost of a good, at the whole industry level, grows when total output grows'. In other words, the graphic image learned in classrooms and manuals regarding the 'supply price's curve' as increasing (fig. 4 and 4a, in chapter 3) is a deep-rooted academic belief among economist that advise or act in public regulatory bodies. This theoretical paradigm is accompanied by the standard *marginalist* postulate/prescription: 'the social optimum requires that the price of any good, *the equilibrium price, be equal to its marginal cost*'.

This ESM's binomial explains, for example, the peculiar design established for the regulated *electricity's market* in many countries. Broadly speaking, this consists of a mandatory market with daily auctions, managed by a regulatory body, in which the contracting price per kWh is officially set as *equal to the highest price* of the offers of the day, by the different power producer companies (suppliers), required to jointly meet the day's total demand. The origin of this counterintuitive system is that such a specific market is not a price-regulated market as usual, but, so to say, an artificial on-purpose *designed market*. Its design, moreover, responds implicitly to the above standard theoretical marginalist idea. This, in the sense that the designers considered that the suppliers' offer with the highest price that enters in the contracting pool of the day **is** '*the marginal cost for the day*' (sic)[8]; and that, thereby as standard economic theory taught the economists responsible for the design 'it is well known that the optimum requires the price to be equal to the marginal cost'.

---

[8] In fact, different contracting prices for different time bands along the day are worked out, applying the said pricing criteria, (!).

In other words, a kind of mandatory market has been designed based/ inspired on a mainstream textbooks' paradigm, to be run daily by a public auctioneer. This is a market to operate on the basis of a daily *trading/contracting* session, according to a reverse auction. Thus, the rule in this *designed market* is that the price to be set for the following day to be paid by all the buying companies (electricity distributors) that sit on one side of the table, and that will be perceived by all the suppliers (the power producer companies, sitting on the other side) will be a price equal to that of the most expensive offer (a given quantity at a given price) that the auctioneer has had to include in the contracting pool in order to meet the total demand for the day. One doesn't need to have a background in economics to guess the joy of those producer companies that had offered a given quantity of KWh at a lower price that day, and came out of the auction with a more advantageous contract under their arm: the specific KWh they offered, but at a higher price; nor to judge the peculiar logic of that *designed*-market; as well as to guess the 'perverse' behaviour to which it can easily give way as observational evidence regarding this or that country bring out.

This design and functioning of the electricity market leads frequently, as can be guessed, to absurd, illogic results. More even when other equally easy pricing options would be available: for example, simply the weighted average of offering prices for the basket of MWh contracted in the day. This absurdity is, nevertheless, denied or rather justified by most mainstream economists and countries' system administrators. Their argument is that according to the marginalist paradigm the producer that has offered some given MWh at the lowest supply price is, logically, operating at a lower average cost; which means that is using a more efficient, cheaper technology (say, wind or solar). From a social perspective, this technology should, consequently, be promoted. And the extraordinary profit margin this 'offeror' gets for its MWh is an incentive for it and/or other companies that get aware of that to invest in expanding the use of this technology.

In short, a distilled of the ESM: high extraordinary profits drive investment toward the activity in question; in this case, to cheaper technologies to produce electricity.

This mainstream argument clashes, however, against two realities. First, the fact that the future mix of technologies for electricity production in a country is normally the object of the energy policy of its public authorities, through their long-run strategic plans and laws on the matter. These programmes are what actually define the kind and timing of power plants that will have to be closed, and the type, scope, and timing of the new ones that will have to be set up. And second, (something that has been omitted above) the most usual in the electricity daily market (say, regarding OECD countries) is that the few big power corporations active in the country, explicit or implicitly, sit on both sides of the contracting table (as producer/sellers and as distributors/buyers), and tend to represent, in both sides, a dominant share of the MWh daily contracted. Hence, their incentive for changing the market system is rather scarce.

Along the same line regarding the impact of standard theory on regulatory practices, we find the persistent traditional postulate/prescription of '*marginal cost pricing/ allocative subsidy*' of the mainstream economics literature, already discussed before (4.3.1 and 7.2).

'Competition'

Another wide ideological consequence of the standard model beyond economics itself is that in recent decades *Competition* so understood, with a capital letter has implicitly become *sort of a myth* in economic policy and the political arena in general.

Competition is, of course, consubstantial to trade; and trade is certainly consubstantial to the division of labour and specialisation, and thereby to economic progress and development. Over centuries, people have gone to towns' 'market square', where vendors were *competing* showing their products and shouting out their qualities and prices to potential customers so that the latter could choose what to buy, and from who. The current equivalent is a dense, interlinked, multi-level network of "markets", both for citizens to buy final products and for enterprises to purchase intermediate goods. Certainly, competition fosters efficiency and improvements in products and services, including innovations that give way to new ones. It is thus a 'good practice', an essential *means* to facilitate the economic development of society. Excuse me for these truisms.

There are, certainly, some exceptions: products or services for which it is not easy, sometimes almost not possible, for citizens, individual buyers, users, or consumers to reasonably have elements, information, or knowledge to evaluate the actual utility, convenience, and implications of the good in question. The fact that would-be consumers/users of a given good have such possibility of knowing or estimating the outcome reasonably to expect from contracting it is a required technical condition for the abovementioned virtues of competition to be actually so. This is a technical condition that most professional economists, both orthodox and heterodox, will coincide in underlining.

However, what appears to have become a problem in this regard, in certain academic and political instances, is the mythification of Competition: to tacitly consider it as *an end in itself* instead of as a *means* to improve social wellbeing.

> "... competition is a business behaviour, not a market structure".
> (Blaug, 1998: 15).

Thus, the problem does not arise regarding *competition* in itself, as an observable entrepreneurial behaviour (product differentiation via innovation, cost minimising, dynamics of the struggle for customers' purchases, etc.) but regarding taking *Competition* as an abstract concept raised to the category of supreme-indisputable value in public decisions: i.e., Competition as something thaumaturgical, as an end in itself; as a mantra on what is 'socially optimum' whenever it is the case of prescribing a certain type of economic policies. Here are some examples in this regard.

- Public TVs in some OECD countries stopped broadcasting advertisements by the last decade of the 20th century, as a result of new laws passed in this regard. Consequently, they no longer had commercials as a source of funding. The main argument in the private companies' demands and political pressures for passing a legal regulation in this respect was that Public TV commercials constituted *unfair competition* concerning the brand-new private TV channels, newly established in the country (since the repeal of the public monopoly on TV broadcasting, some years before). The argument of unfair competition was accompanied by invoking the fact that public TV in some countries had not broadcast commercials since its very beginning. This 'unfair competition' would consist of the fact that, in so far as public TV channels were partially funded by state subsidies, this, it was argued, allowed them to contract commercials with advertising firms or agencies at a somewhat lower price than that applied by private TV channels, which meant that the latter lost advertising contracts.

  [This argument clashes, however, with the, then already customary, practice in the TV commercial spots market: the price per minute of broadcast tended (tends) to be established according to the audience rating of the specific (private or public) TV channel; and more specifically, to that of each time slot or particular programme].

  In any event, once the corresponding ban on broadcasting commercials on public TV in this or that country was decreed, such a political decision was inevitably followed by an increase in public subsidy, i.e., a certain increase in public expenditure.

To argue that the existing regulation of public TV (which allowed it to be partially funded by advertising) represents 'unfair competition' is tantamount to subverting the terms of the matter regarding the relationship between *politics* and the *economy,* in the sense of placing the latter before the former. Historically, in a market economy, private enterprise define their activity and market transactions by taking into account the laws and rules that the corresponding society has politically adopted, as well as some socially established customs (e.g., festivities). In short, there is a certain social-legal framework agreed upon through political institutions. And private enterprises take their decisions within it, trying to obtain profits. In contrast, the above argument on *unfair competition* is in some ways equivalent to reversing the terms: for private enterprises (TV channels) to have greater opportunities for turnover and profits, it was argued that the established legislation should be modified; a legal change that, moreover, will have a recurrent cost for public powers in terms of an increase in public expenditure. All this claimed in the name of 'Competition', taken it as an absolute principle in social life. This constitutes an example of mystification/ mythification of the concept, with the overall result of positioning *politics as dependent on the* (private enterprises) *economy.* Here follows another example in this regard.

- **New digital business.** (Extracted from a corporate statement): The firm is one of the *new economy's* multinational 'companies/ platforms' (the reader may think of Cabify, Uber, Deliveroo, Glovo, and the likes). A company that employs people under the formula that they register as 'independent contractors' (and other people call 'false self-employed'), and establish with them a relationship basically through a mobile application. The referred corporate statement was submitted by such a firm to the US's

SEC (in April 2019, with the occasion of the company asking to be admitted to public trade on the Stock Exchange[9]). Under the document's heading 'Legal and Regulatory Risks Related to Our Business' (p. 54) the company asserts its "... willingness to extend its activity to specific countries (Argentina, Germany, Italy, Japan, South Korea, and Spain) (where) our ... (xxx) ... business model has been blocked, capped, or suspended, (....), due primarily to laws and significant regulatory restrictions". In another point it specifies: "Our business would be adversely affected if (workers) were classified as employees instead of independent contractors".(p. 28). The firm underlines its intention to "face regulatory obstacles ...", and concludes with "We have incurred, and expect that we will continue to incur, significant costs in defending our right to operate in accordance with our business model ...".

In short, a 'new-economy', 'technological', multinational claims for itself the (universal?) right to operate 'its business model' in whatever country, on the grounds of an abstract 'free-market, free-competition' principle. This 'right', the firm claims, would currently be 'limited' by the existing regulations in certain countries as the ones detailed, specifically regarding the conditions of provision of the company's service and/or the labour relations to apply. Thus, key issues related to political options that have been formally decided by democratic states, regarding the type of market economy and employment relationships, are publicly presented by the multinational in question as 'obstacles' to 'its right' to a 'free market/competition', which is, thus, taken as a superior principle!

- In July 2015 the European Commission (EC) ruled that it was not justified that Spanish local *corner stores* were waived from

---

[9] https://www.sec.gov/Archives/edgar/data/1543151/000119312519103850/d647752ds1.htm#toc647752_2

> a specific tax to business-stores in general, as it had been established by three regional parliaments. Such a tax exemption responded to the regional governments' political objective of levying the tax mainly from large shopping centres, suburban and peripheral malls, so as to contain the expansion of these peripheral macro-centres, and thus favour small and medium-sized local neighbourhood stores, in municipalities' traditional quarters. Nevertheless, the EC decided that exempting those local commercial establishments from this tax constituted an 'unlawful aid'; and therefore a source of 'unfair competition' (i.e., unfair competition of small corner stores regarding large commercial chains, generally multinational companies).
>
> In short, an EU rule prevents a parliament of a member country from establishing a differentiated tax in its territory, aimed precisely at pursuing a certain policy with respect to the shopping sector; a policy which is related in turn to the desired urban model, to the very concept of a city and, in a certain way, of social life that is collectively preferred.

Let us follow with the latter example. The EU's tacit principle on which the mentioned ruling is based, and therefore the referred ban, is that of the absolute virtue of Competition; as a sort of implicitly assumed dogma of faith which is also perceived in many European Directives. According to that dogma, business stores in general like enterprises in any sector must be allowed to compete freely with each other, so that 'the best ones' (the most competitive) survive because this is to the benefit of users or customers. The paradox is that, in this case, the latter coincides with the citizens who have elected the Parliament itself that has legislated on the local policy regarding shopping-establishments in relation to the-model-of-city! Furthermore, free competition among business facilities (companies, chains) that are highly different-in-size is not or does not have the virtues attributed to the 'competition among equals' that the mainstream economics' approach presupposes: the theoretical idea of 'free competition' as an indisputable source of advantages for users/customers, and ultimately for the society.

The symmetric myth of '(public) unfair competition'

Taking these examples together shows us how the concept of competition somehow losses its original instrumental meaning of a technical question of business dynamics i.e., a means, regarding the type of economy/society that is collectively preferred and how, it distorted, becomes an end in itself, used dialectically as a totem.

It is easy to deduce what are or can be the logical consequences of an uncritical tacit acceptance of this argument, common to the previous examples. Thus, by way of example, according to such argument, it would result that public schools in countries like France or Spain, for example, would be 'unfairly competing' with private schools since these public schools are free, or almost free, and offer similar levels of quality. Or, to see it from another perspective, let us think of a certain less-developed country with insufficient provision of schools, in which all or most of the existing ones are private. And that the democratic-representative institutions of the country plan to take a strategic leap forward to solve the deficit of schools, by creating an important network of public schools looking itself for that at the mirror of, e.g., France. It would not be surprising that such a political project was strongly opposed by some local economic experts as well as some others in international organisations. They could allege that such a political initiative would represent 'unfair competition' regarding incumbent private schools in the country; and that, moreover, such a hindrance to competition would translate into inefficiency in the whole educational system, thereby diminishing the general welfare. This is indeed an argument-assertion frequently issued, under the background register of 'this-is-the-way-things-are', and from a conviction and professional security anchored on assuming the theoretical paradigm of the ESM and its *general equilibrium of competitive markets* as an indisputable reference framework.

Were this myth/argumentation taken to its logical extreme, we can not rule out hearing a similar assertion about something as normal as public authorities improving roads or building new free motorways. According to the argument derived from competition-as-a-myth, this would also be considered 'unfair competition'; in this case regarding private toll-road companies.

According to this particular logic or idea (more properly, ideology) of 'unfair competition (by public authorities)', it may occur that some day an expert economist advising, for instance, a consortium of private hospitals, defends the political argument that 'the Public Health System of this or that European country should no longer be free of charge because that represents 'unfair competition' (with the private sector). Furthermore, s/he could claim that 'it would be better (more efficient) for the management of the System to be privatised'. Or we could hear a similar political statement regarding another basic element of the welfare state.

This could, indeed, eve go further on: The argument of competition-as-myth could end up being applied to any economic activity/intervention by public authorities. What could, thus, lead to the absurdity that any (public) *economic policy* that is, any measure aimed at correcting or complementing certain market results could be considered as something negative because it distorts the functioning of markets; or it to be considered as 'unfair competition' regarding both, existing and future, private enterprises. In short, this type of supposedly-neutral economic reasoning illustrates in fact the ideology of *politics subordinated to the economy* (or to a certain conception of it).

The above may sound like an exaggerated extrapolation. Although, ... by way of example:

- In an interview with a senior executive officer of a top European bank, published in a well-known newspaper (2015), when asked about the measures taken at the time by the ECB and other central banks, the following judgment is significant in his response: "... What the ECB, and previously the Fed, is doing now is not harmless; that is, they are distorting the functioning of markets. Nevertheless, markets mean risk and our task is to manage it properly".

That is, in the face of the economic policy measures by central banks (*monetary easing*) designed precisely to modify/correct market results (lack of liquidity for governments and companies), the perception of a significant financial business manager which, openly and self-confidently, transmits is that these measures mean 'a (negative) distortion of *the* market'; of the financial market in the first place. This talk takes place at a time (May 2015) when the 'great recession/crisis', unleashed in 2008, precisely from the financial sector, had not yet been overcome in the EU countries where the referred bank mainly operates.

The myth also has a self-convincing function, or by-product. Competition authorities –such as the 'Competition and Markets Authority' (UK), 'Autorité de la Concurrence' (France), 'FTC-Bureau of Competition' (US), 'Comisión Nacional de Mercados y de la Competencia' (Spain), 'Autoritá Garante de la Concorrenza e del Mercato' (Italy), 'Bundeskartellamt' (Germany), etc. have proven to be effective in modern economies to regulate price and access conditions for basic or socially sensitive public services, such as the distribution (last mile) of electricity, gas, and water, as well as telecommunications or passenger transport. Nevertheless, when it is the case of other activities, decisions, and resolutions of such agencies, the matter is rather different: For example, about giving or not the green light to the merger of two large companies of the same sector or activity; or analysing whether to oblige a given big corporation to divided itself into two or more companies, 'to favour competition'. As for these kinds of tasks and decisions, it is difficult avoiding the feeling of witnessing micro-regulatory interventions that are more formal than effective. This, even though they are presented and probably 'experienced' by their protagonists within the regulatory bodies as fundamental corrections (of deviations) on a market economy, in order to increase (effective) competition in it. However, looking at the matter from the outlook of the actual workings of the business world, it seems quite obvious that the possibility that a substantive social benefit will be derived from these specific anti-monopolistic decisions (benefit, in terms of final prices? for which buyers? ...) are rather remote. Moreover, such a possible future beneficial effect can never be verified, because in practice it is something that will not be actually observable.

Nevertheless, such 'antitrust' activities and institutional efforts by national (and multinational) agencies contribute to generating a reassuring idea among the involved collectives: that a fundamental institutional lever is available to control 'those possible monopolistic situations that sometimes occur', and thus 'achieve in a capitalist economic system that situations of near-perfect competition predominate'. On the other hand, as an external effect of these institutional activities, a message would be collectively self-generated, and acknowledged by mainstream economists: that the referred activities and efforts of the *agencies for the defence of competition* allow 'bringing the economic reality of markets reasonably closer to what the model of the *general equilibrium* of competitive markets describes'. Regarding this, I refer the reader, by way of contrast, to the sections where the statistical landscape about actual market structures/concentration is reviewed (4.2.2 and 7.2).

Furthermore, this mythical character *de facto* assigned to the concept of *Competition* also emerges in the case of an easily observable inconsistency: when a good or service is provided by a foreign company under conditions of quasi-monopoly on an international scale, national – or multinational – competition enforcement agencies rarely act – or they act limitedly. Mainly because they have no proper authority to do so; or this is not clear since in this case 'we are talking about the worldwide market'. There may be, then, a paradox: a situation of dominance over a specific local market (product or service), that makes part of a market-dominance situation at an international level, may, in practice, not be considered a distortion of market competition worthy of attention in this or that country; while in a similar situation played out by a domestic company, attention would likely be paid to it.

References

Arrow, Kenneth J. (1985) "The Potentials and Limits of the Market in Resource Allocation", in Feiwel, G. (ed.): *Issues in Contemporary Microeconomics and Welfare*, Chapter 2; Macmillan, London., 1985.

Arrow, Kenneth J. (2000) "Increasing returns: historiographic issues and path dependence", *The European Journal of the History of Economic Thought*; 72:2, 171-180.

Arthur, Brian. (1996), "Increasing Returns and the New World of Business", *Harvard Business Review*, July-Aug, 1996, pp. 100-109.

Backhouse, Roger E. (2011), *The Puzzle of Modern Economics*, Cambridge University Press.

Beckenstein, A. R. (1975) "Scale Economies in the Multiplant Firm: Theory and Empirical Evidence", *The Bell Journal of Economics*, Vol. 6, No. 2, pp. 644-657.

Bergmann, Barbara R. (2007) "Needed: A New Empiricism", *Economists' Voice*, March 2007; Berkely Electronic Press.

Blaug, Mark (1957), *Ricardian Economics*, Yale University Press.

Blaug, Mark (1968), *Economic Theory in Retrospect*, (1st. ed., revised), and (1985, 4th ed.) Cambridge University Press.

Blaug, Mark (1998) "Disturbing Currents in Modern Economics", Challenge, 41:3, 11-34

Blinder, Aland. S., E. Canetti, D. Lebow and J. B. Rudd (1998) *Asking about Prices: A new approach to understanding price stickiness*, New York: Russell Sage Foundation.

Browning, Edgard. K. & Browning, J. M. (1989), *Microeconomic Theory and Applications*, Addison-Wesley.

Clarke, Roger (1989), *Industrial Economics*, Basil Blackwell

Cohen, Avi J. (1983) "The laws of returns under competitive conditions: progress in microeconomics since Sraffa (1926)?", *Eastern Economic Journal*, 9(3): 213–20.

Cohen, Avi J. (1996) 'Why haven't introductory textbooks resolved Sraffa's 1926 complaints? , in N. Aslanbeigui and M. I. Naples (eds), *Rethinking Economic Principles: Critical essays on introductory textbooks*, Chicago, IL: Irwin, pp. 81–91

Eaton, B. Curtis, and Eaton, D. F. (1996), *Microeconomics*, Prentice Hall.

Estrin, S., Laidler, D. and Dietrich, M. (2012), *Microeconomics*, Pearson

Frank, Robert H. (2007), *Microeconomics and Behaviour* (7th ed.), McGraw-Hill/Irwin

Fullbrook, Edward (2004), *A Guide to What's Wrong with Economics*, Anthem Press.

Gilpin, Robert (1987), *The Political Economy of International Relations*, Princeton University Press.

Gravelle, Hugh and Rees, Ray (2006) *Microeconomía* (3 Ed.), Pearson-Prentice Hall

Hague, D. C. (1974), *Economía de la Empresa*, Ed. Ariel

Jehle, Geoffrey A. & Reny, P. J. (2011), *Advanced Microeconomic Theory*, Prentice Hall

Jones, Trefor (2004), *Business Economics and Managerial Decision Making*, John Wiley & Sons, Ltd. West Sussex.

Keen, Steve (2011) *Debunking Economics, Revised Ed.*, Zed Books

Klein, Philip A. (2006), *Economics Confronts the Economy*, Edward Elgar

Komlos, John (2019) "Foundations of Real-World Economics", (2nd. Ed.), Routledge, New York – Abingdon (UK)

Koutsoyiannis, Anna (1977), *Modern Microeconomics,* The MacMillan Press

Krugman, Paul (1996), "Ricardo's Difficult Idea"; *http://web.mit.edu/krugman/www/ricardo.htm,* (Retrieved as of 17/05/2021)

Krugman, Paul & Wells, Robin (2013), *Microeconomía,* Ed. Reverté

Krugman, Paul R./ Obstfeld, Maurice, and Melitz, Marc J. (2017) *International Trade, Theory and Policy,* 10th. Pearson.

Lancaster, Kevin, (1974), *Introduction to Modern Microeconomics,* Rand McNally & Co, US.

Lancaster, Kevin., (1977), *Modern Economics: Principles and Policy,* (2nd. ed.), Rand McNally, Chicago

Lawson, Tony (1997), *Economics & reality,* Routledge.

Lawson, Tony (2003), *Reorienting Economics,* Routledge, London.

Lawson, Tony (2015), *The Nature and State of Modern Economics,* Routledge

Lawson, Tony (2017), "What is wrong with modern economics, and why does it stay wrong", *Journal of Australian Political Economy,* No. 80, pp. 26-42.

Leontief, Wassily (1982), "Academic Economics", *Science,* Vol. 217, Issue 4555, pp. 104-107.

Leontief, Wassily (1953), "Domestic Production and Foreign Trade; The American Capital Position Re-Examined", *Proceedings of the American Philosophical Society,* Sep. 28, 97(4), pp. 332-349.

Mankiw, N. G. (1998), *Principios de Microeconomía* , McGraw-Hill

Mankiw, N. G., McKenzie, K. J., and Rowe, N. (2006), *Principles of Microeconomics,* 3rd. ed. Toronto, Thomson Nelson

Mansfield, Edward (1994), *Microeconomics: theory & applications* (8th. edition), W. W. Norton

Marshall, Alfred (1898), *Elements of Economics: 1st Volume: Elements of Economics of Industry*; 2nd. Ed. Macmillan and Co., London

Mas-Colell, A., Whinston, M. D. and Green, J. R. (1995), *Microeconomic Theory*, Oxford University Press.

McCormick, R. E. (1993), *Managerial Economics*

Milgrom, Paul and Roberts, John (1992), *Economics, Organization & Management*, Prentice Hall, NJ

Milward, R., Parker, D. M., Rosenthal, L., Sumner, M. T., and Topham, N., (1983), (eds) *Public Sector Economics*, London Longman

Monchón, Francisco (2009) *Economía, Teoría y Política* (6th ed.) McGraw-Hill

Morgan, W., Katz, M., and Rosen, H. (2009), *Microeconomics*, London. McGraw-Hill Higher Education

Morgenstern, Oskar (1972) Thirteen Critical Points in Contemporary Economic Theory: An Interpretation Author(s), *Journal of Economic Literature*, 10(4) 1163-89.

Pindyck, R. S. (2013), *Microeconomia*, Pearson.

Quirck, James P. (1980), *Microeconomía*, Antoni Bosch Editor

Samuelson, Paul and Nordhaus, William D. (2010) *Economics*, 19th Ed. McGraw-Hill

Samuelson, William F. and Marks, Stephen G. (2012), *Managerial Economics*, 7th Ed., John Wiley & Sons, NJ.

Schlefer, Jonathan (2012), *The Assumptions Economists Make*, Harvard University Press

Schotter, A. (2009), *Microeconomics: A Modern Approach*, Cengage Learning

Schumacher, Reinhard (2013), "Deconstructing the Theory of Comparative Advantage", *World Economic Review*, no 2, Feb 2013; 83-105.

Sloman, John, (1996), *Introducción a la Microeconomía*, Pearson Educación

Shepherd, W. G., and J. M. Shepherd (2004), *The Economics of Industrial Organization*, 5th edn, Long Grove, IL: Waveland Press.

Skidelsky, Robert (2020), *What's wrong with economics? A primer for the perplexed*, Yale University Press. London.

Sraffa, P. (1926) 'The laws of returns under competitive conditions', *Economic Journal*, 36(4): 535–50.

Sutton, John (1998), *Technology and Market Structure*, The MIT Press

Swann, G. M. Peter (2019), *Economics as Anatomy; Radical Innovation in Empirical Economics*, Edward Elgar, Cheltenham (UK)

Varian, Hal R. , (2014), *Intermediate Microeconomics*, W. W. Norton & Company

Varian, Hal R., (1992), *Análisis Microeconómico*, Antoni Bosch editor.

Varian, Hal R. (1987), *Microeconomía intermedia*, Antoni Bosch editor.

Vegara, Josep. M. (2014), *La obra de Kenneth Arrow: Una selección*, IEF, Madrid

Vergés, Joaquim. (2010), *Economía política de la intervención sobre el mercado'*, Ed. Pirámide – Madrid

Vergés, J. (2020), "Economics as a Science –or viewed from the perspective of scientists in other fields", *Cadmus Journal*, Vol. 4, Issue 2 – May-July.

Zamagni, S. (1987) , *Microeconomic Theory: An introduction*, Oxford; New York, N.Y. : Basil Blackwell

https://scholar.google.com.hk/citations?user=6PbrMlIAAAAJ&hl=en (Marshall)

www.ingramcontent.com/pod-product-compliance
Ingram Content Group UK Ltd.
Pitfield, Milton Keynes, MK11 3LW, UK
UKHW041133071026
15587UKWH00009B/455

9 781804 410561